PHILOSOPHY AND RELIGION IN PLATO'S DIALOGUES

In ancient Greece, philosophers developed new and dazzling ideas about divinity, drawing on the deep well of poetry, myth, and religious practices even as they set out to construct new theological ideas. Andrea Nightingale argues that Plato shared in this culture and appropriated specific Greek religious discourses and practices to present his metaphysical philosophy. In particular, he used the Greek conception of divine epiphany—a god appearing to humans—to claim that the Forms and the cosmos manifested their divinity epiphanically to the philosopher. The human soul becomes wise and godlike by contemplating these divine beings. Nightingale also offers a detailed discussion of the Eleusinian Mysteries and the Orphic Mysteries and shows how these mystery religions influenced Plato's thinking. This book offers a robust challenge to the idea that Plato is a secular thinker.

ANDREA NIGHTINGALE is Professor of Classics at Stanford University. She has authored *Genres in Dialogue: Plato and the Construct of Philosophy* (Cambridge, 1995), *Spectacles of Truth in Classical Greek Philosophy: Theoria in Its Cultural Context* (Cambridge, 2004), and *Once out of Nature: Augustine on Time and the Body* (Chicago, 2011).

PHILOSOPHY AND RELIGION IN PLATO'S DIALOGUES

ANDREA NIGHTINGALE

Stanford University

CAMBRIDGE
UNIVERSITY PRESS

CAMBRIDGE
UNIVERSITY PRESS

University Printing House, Cambridge CB2 8BS, United Kingdom

One Liberty Plaza, 20th Floor, New York, NY 10006, USA

477 Williamstown Road, Port Melbourne, VIC 3207, Australia

314–321, 3rd Floor, Plot 3, Splendor Forum, Jasola District Centre,
New Delhi – 110025, India

79 Anson Road, #06–04/06, Singapore 079906

Cambridge University Press is part of the University of Cambridge.

It furthers the University's mission by disseminating knowledge in the pursuit of
education, learning, and research at the highest international levels of excellence.

www.cambridge.org
Information on this title: www.cambridge.org/9781108837309
DOI: 10.1017/9781108938815

First published 2021

Printed in the United Kingdom by TJ Books Limited, Padstow Cornwall

A catalogue record for this publication is available from the British Library.

ISBN 978-1-108-83730-9 Hardback

For my husband Mark
with all my love

Contents

List of Figures   page ix
Acknowledgements   x

Introduction   1
   0.1 Philosophy and Religion?   4
   0.2 Divinity-Markers for the Forms and the Soul   8
   0.3 Philosophic Eros as "Daimonic" or "Divine" Desire   23
   0.4 Divine Epiphanies of the Forms and the Cosmos   29

1: The Forms, the Good, and the Divine   45
   1.1 The Forms and Their Attributes   46
   1.2 The Divinity-Marker *Theios* for the Forms   49
   1.3 The Form of the Good   55

2: Eternal Longings   64
   2.1 Divine Epiphany in Ancient Greece   67
   2.2 The Mortal Soul in the *Symposium*   73
   2.3 Desiring Immortality with Power in Aristophanes' Speech   76
   2.4 Desiring Immortality with Goodness in Socrates' Speech   79
   2.5 Metaphysical Desire   85
   2.6 The Eleusinian Mysteries   88
   2.7 The Divine Epiphany of Beauty   96
   2.8 Metaphysical Desire and the Desire for Immortality
      in the Ladder of Love   102
   2.9 Daimonic Eros   104
   2.10 Alcibiades Profanes the "Mysteries" of Philosophy   107

3: Dialogue of Self and Soul   114
   3.1 The Double Narrative in the *Phaedo*   117
   3.2 Plato's Conception of the Soul   119
   3.3 Dwelling in Divine Regions in the Afterlife   130
   3.4 Pythagoreanism and Orphism in the *Phaedo*   135
   3.5 Orphism in the Classical Period   139
   3.6 Plato's Adaptation of the Orphic Mysteries   148

3.7 The Orphic Divinity-Markers for the Soul   151
3.8 The Matter of Vision in the Eschatology   155
3.9 Beauty and Vision   161

4: Wings of Desire   168
    4.1 The Soul   170
    4.2 Divine Encounters in the *Phaedrus*   175
    4.3 Naturalistic and Allegorical Interpretations of the Boreas
         and Oreithuia Myth   177
    4.4 Nympholepsy   181
    4.5 Pious Philosophical Discourse   184
    4.6 Souls, Gods, Forms   186
    4.7 Inspiration, Madness, and Enhanced Reason   189
    4.8 Two Epiphanies of the Form of Beauty   203

5: The Gods Made Visible   213
    5.1 Timaeus as a Religious Exegete   221
    5.2 Divinities in the Cosmos   224
         5.2.1 The Demiurge   224
         5.2.2 The Cosmic Soul and Body   227
         5.2.3 Star Gods   229
         5.2.4 Ancillary Gods   230
         5.2.5 Rational Human Souls   231
    5.3 Heavenly Bodies: Radiant and Shadowy   232
    5.4 The Cosmos Looks at Itself through Human Eyes   237
    5.5 Peregrinations of the Human Soul   244
    5.6 Becoming like God   250
    5.7 Earthly and Divine Time   253
    5.8 The Cosmos as a Beautiful Religious Artifact   255
         5.8.1 The Cosmos as a Divine Dance at a Religious Festival   255
         5.8.2 The Cosmos as an *Agalma* of the Forms   259

Conclusion   262

Bibliography   266
Index   292

Figures

0.1 Eros flying over an altar with a votive gift. Athenian Red–   *page* 23
     figure Pelike, 450–400 BCE. Vienna, Kunsthistorisches
     Museum Collection, 636

0.2 Eros flying with phiale and fillet, Red–figure Skyphos,   24
     475–425 BCE. Basel Antikenmuseum und Sammlung
     Ludwig KA426

0.3 Eros flying; two naked boys with strigils. Athenian   26
     Red–Figure Oinochoe. Vatican City, Museo Gregoriano
     Etrusco Vaticano Collection, 16524

0.4 Naked woman bringing votive box to Eros (domestic).   27
     Red–Figure Pelike, 450–400 BCE. University of Mississippi,
     University Museums, 73.3.196

Acknowledgements

I want to thank my wonderful mother, Diana de Armas Wilson, for her love, bravery, brilliance, and wit. With her usual grace and generosity, she read the manuscript of this book and offered incisive comments. I am grateful beyond words to my beloved father, Douglas Wilson, who died long ago but lives always in my heart. I thank my sister, Fiona Theodoredis, for her love, wisdom, and humor. And for being my rock. And thank you, Amal and Kai Theodoredis, for your lovely and luminous selves. I am deeply grateful to Rachel Jacoff for generously reading parts of the manuscript and helping me to dig more deeply into Plato. I can never thank her enough for her love and support. I am endlessly grateful to Tony Long for reading early drafts of the manuscript and for his staunch support over all these years. I count myself lucky to have this brilliant man as a teacher, interlocutor, and friend. I also want to thank Robert Harrison for reading early drafts of this book and for guiding me throughout its gestation. Robert has fed my mind with his dazzling ideas for so many decades – our conversations have been epiphanic. I give special thanks to Rush Rehm, brother of my heart. Rush read parts of this book and helped me to think more deeply about Greek culture. Our long friendship is one of the great gifts of my life.

I have many people to thank for helping me with this book. Natasha Peponi got me started on my ideas in a long lunch in my garden. I am grateful to have her as a friend and colleague. I want to thank Debbie Steiner for her generous support during this difficult patch in my life. And for introducing me to Greek art. I am grateful to my dear friend and colleague, John Tennant, for reading my work and offering so much intellectual and spiritual support. I would like to thank James Collins for his support and thoughtful comments on my work, and for our long friendship. Thank you, Julia Kindt, for answering my questions about Greek religion from across the ocean; Thomas Sheehan, for helping me to understand Heidegger's ideas on ontotheology; and Eric Csapo, for answering queries and offering support. I am honored to have worked with so many great scholars and students at Stanford. I give special thanks to my research assistants: Thomas Slabon, who read the book manuscript before submission and caught many of my errors; Alyson Melzer, who created the index; and Verity Walsh, who read the proofs. Thanks also to Sepp Gumbrecht and the members of the Philosophical Reading Group at Stanford for so many years of vital conversation. I am hugely thankful to the anonymous readers, who offered invaluable comments and criticisms on the manuscript. And I am, as always, deeply grateful to my editor, Michael Sharp. Michael moved the manuscript from submission to publication during the Covid-19 pandemic with enormous grace and expertise.

I give special thanks to the cloud forests in Mindo, Ecuador. Hiking your lush trails and seeing your wondrous beings – winged, footed, and rooted – showed me how gods manifest themselves on this earth. A thousand thanks to Jamalia Sweets, who sat in my lap and purred every single day that I wrote this manuscript. This book is dedicated to my beloved husband, the ever-fixed Mark Hollingsworth. You are my rara avis.

Introduction

The hardest thing of all is to see what is really there.
                                        –J. A. Baker, *The Peregrine*

In ancient Greece, philosophers developed new and dazzling ideas about divinity. These thinkers drew on a deep well of poetry, myth, and religious practices even as they set out to construct new theological ideas. Ancient Greek religion had a wondrous heterogeneity – rituals and cult practices varied dramatically in different geographical regions. Greek religion was far more open to diverse theological ideas than monotheistic religions. In contrast to the sacred scriptures of the monotheists, Greek religion relied on a vast array of myths handed down from one generation to another through poetry and song. These myths surrounded and sustained religious rituals and festivals. In Greek culture, there was no separation of religion and state – to live in a political community meant that one participated in religious rituals and festivals.[1] Indeed, Greek city-states organized almost all public religious events. The Greeks worshipped the gods daily and sought to get messages from the gods by way of oracles, divination, and omens. The gods could appear epiphanically to people in the form of humans, animals, and statues, or send angry messages through earthquakes and droughts. To alter Thales' famous saying, almost all things were full of gods.

   Modern scholars find ancient Greek religion baffling. As secular thinkers living in an age dominated by science, we approach Greek religion with great skepticism. This makes it difficult for us to comprehend Greek

---

[1] To be sure, some individuals articulated skeptical or atheistic views of the gods. In the late fifth century BCE, for example, Athens charged a number of men with impiety. In this period, Athens went through a religious crisis due, in part, to the plague that hit the city in 430 BCE (see especially Rubel 2000, who offers an excellent account of this crisis and the extreme Athenian reaction to "impious" men; see also Whitmarsh 2015: 71–137). Of course Socrates was put on trial for not acknowledging traditional gods and for introducing new gods. To "acknowledge the gods," one had to go to public festivals and rituals. Note that articulating skeptical or atheistic ideas did not necessarily mean that one opted out of rituals and festivals.

ideas about the gods and their divine manifestations. Although we cannot fully grasp the Greek phenomenon of divine epiphany, modern poets have offered serious meditations on the topic. Consider Robert Frost's "The Most of It," which features a skeptical man confronting a possible divine epiphany in the animal world:

> He thought he kept the universe alone;
> For all the voice in answer he could wake
> Was but the mocking echo of his own
> From some tree-hidden cliff across the lake.
> Some morning from the boulder-broken beach
> He would cry out on life, that what it wants
> Is not its own love back in copy speech,
> But counter-love, original response.
> And nothing ever came of what he cried
> Unless it was the embodiment that crashed
> In the cliff's talus on the other side,
> And then in the far distant water splashed,
> But after a time allowed for it to swim,
> Instead of proving human when it neared
> And someone else additional to him,
> As a great buck it powerfully appeared,
> Pushing the crumpled water up ahead,
> And landed pouring like a waterfall,
> And stumbled through the rocks with horny tread,
> And forced the underbrush – and that was all.

The man in this poem lives in a secular world in which humans "keep the universe alone." He goes to a lake near a cliff and cries out to the world to send him some sort of answer, a "counter-love" responding to his own. He seeks an "original response" from the world, not a mere "mocking echo" of his own voice. Since the man visits the lake alone, he seems to be looking for something more than human. When he cries out, he creates an echo on "the tree-hidden cliff across the lake." This echo takes the form of an "embodiment" that crashes from the cliff, splashes into the water, and swims towards the man. Strangely, the aerial body of the man's voice evokes a new body that comes directly back to him from the cliff, moving along the path of an echo. The embodiment is unidentifiable at first. The man thinks it might be human, someone "additional to him." But a very different being manifests itself: "as a great buck it powerfully appeared." This being appears *as* a buck. This wording makes the appearance of the buck seem mysterious and perhaps even divine. Indeed, the buck's arrival appears to be the "original response" that the man had longed for. We don't know who or what authors this response. Is it a god manifesting itself or just a buck arriving coincidentally after the man cries out? In the last line of the poem, the buck walks into the brush and "that was all." This line suggests that the man sees nothing but an animal. The poem, then, presents a possible divine epiphany but it rejects this idea at the end. The man lives in a secular universe that has conditioned him to see the world in a specific way.

The ancient Greeks did not consider themselves to "keep the universe alone." In this culture, the gods occupied the heavens, earth, and under-world. In addition to the Olympian gods, the Greeks had local and house-hold gods, not to mention river and tree gods. In the Athenian region of Attica in the classical period, for example, the Athenians had 200 distinct deities.[2] The Greeks had to worship and appease specific gods daily to gain favor and avert divine anger. This included prayers, sacrifices, offerings, rituals, dances, and religious festivals. They also sought to receive messages from the gods: they had a huge network of oracles, prophets, and diviners who could relay divine messages or read omens. Not surprisingly, a divine epiphany – the physical appearance of a god to humans – constituted a major religious event. Humans detected the god's presence by the radiance and miraculousness of its bodily form. The god effectively saturated a body with divinity. In poetic narratives of epiphany, for example, a god suddenly appears to humans in a bodily form that is awesome, utterly beautiful, and radiant with light. The people who see this epiphany react with fear, wonder, and awe. A divine epiphany, when accepted by a community, had a foundational aspect in Greek religion. As we see in inscriptions, divine epiphanies led the Greeks to create altars, shrines, and temples.

Plato, too, did not think that humans kept the universe alone. In his middle-period dialogues, the gods played important roles in human life and the afterlife. These gods had perfect reason, and they judged human lives with complete justice. In the late dialogues *Timaeus* and *Laws*, gods took on an even greater role: they moved the heavens and governed the entire cosmos. Philosophers could see the "visible gods" in the bodies of the star-gods. Plato also gave the soul divine capacities: living in a human body on earth, it could actualize its divinity by practicing philosophy. Finally, Plato identified the Forms as divine. When the philosopher contemplated the Forms, then, each with its own essence, he also encountered divinity.[3]

---

[2] Garland 1992: 14; Parker 2005: 397.
[3] I have chosen to use the masculine pronoun "he" for "the philosopher" because Plato regularly refers to the philosopher as male. To be sure, he allows Diotima and Aspasia to speak as wise women. But he

Plato drew on the Greek notion that gods appeared to humans in epiphanies, but he recast this idea in terms of intellectual vision. He reached for
the phenomenon of epiphany because it featured an immediate encounter
with the divine. In epiphanies, a god appeared in the human realm and
presented an immediate and visible presence. As I argue, Plato depicts the
philosopher as seeing a divine epiphany when he contemplates the Forms.

0.1   Philosophy and Religion?

In the Enlightenment, if not before, philosophy parted ways with religion.
Philosophers and scientific thinkers conceived of religion as antithetical to
reason. This enlightenment valorization of reason, aided by the rise of
modern science, ushered in the secular age in which we now dwell. Not
surprisingly, modern scholars in the discipline of philosophy interpret the
ancient philosophers in secular terms. Indeed, most ancient philosophy
scholars have analyzed Greek philosophical ideas completely outside of
their religious context. If we examine the ancient philosophers in the
cultural context of ancient Greece, however, we quickly discover the
affiliations between philosophy and religion. Most philosophers in archaic
and classical Greece presented ideas and discourses about the gods. These
thinkers engaged in *theologia*, articulating new ideas about the gods and
divine beings.[4]

Starting in the sixth century BCE, philosophers rejected the traditional
Greek conceptions of the gods and offered new ideas about divinity. To
cite one example, Xenophanes (sixth to fifth centuries BCE) identified
a god that was radically different from the anthropomorphic gods celebrated in poetry and the visual arts. As he claimed, "god is one, greatest
among gods and men, not at all like mortals in body or in thought" (εἷς
θεός, ἔν τε θεοῖσι καὶ ἀνθρώποισι μέγιστος, οὔ τι δέμας θνητοῖσιν ὁμοίιος
οὐδὲ νόημα; B23).[5] Unlike the traditional Greek gods, whose bodies,
emotions, and thoughts changed over time, Xenophanes' god "always
remains in the same state, moving not at all, and it is not fitting that he
comes and goes to different places at different times" (B26).[6] Still, this god

___

does not call them "philosophers." Only in the *Republic* does he refer to women as philosophers (the
philosopher queens).

[4] A recent volume on ancient Greek "theology" (E. Eidinow, J. Kindt, and R. Osborne, eds., *Theologies
of Ancient Greek Religion*) has offered an excellent corrective to the notion that the Greeks did not
have theologies.

[5] In this manuscript, all the translations are my own unless I identify another translator.

[6] B26: αἰεὶ δ᾽ ἐν ταὐτῷ μίμνει κινούμενος οὐδέν, οὐδὲ μετέρχεσθαί μιν ἐπιπρέπει ἄλλοτε ἄλλη.

has a mind with its own special motion: "but without effort he shakes all things by the thought of his mind."[7] Xenophanes' god could not be more different than the Greek gods portrayed in the dominant religious tradition. Other presocratic philosophers in the sixth and fifth centuries BCE also turned away from the traditional gods, but they looked to nature instead, identifying the cosmos, or elements in the cosmos, as divine. A few thinkers created cosmic systems that completely dispensed of the gods altogether. The exact nature of the gods was an open and vibrant field of inquiry in ancient Greece.

The presocratic philosophers' ideas about god and nature have generated a wide range of scholarly interpretations. Some have argued that these philosophers offered "rationalized" or "detheologized" accounts of the divine realm. Scholars who adopt this position argue that the ancient philosophers embraced (or moved towards) a secular view of the world. They identify a philosophic discourse as secular if it speaks of divine beings in "abstract," "demythologized," or "naturalized" terms. Rick Benitez offers a useful summary of this tradition of interpretation:

> We can observe two tendencies in this tradition. First, there is a tendency to regard ancient philosophical theology as reducing the gods from persons to abstract principles . . . . Second, there is a tendency to regard philosophical theology as reducing the gods from agents to a standard of teleological perfection.[8]

To make this tradition of interpretation clear, let us look at one example. Consider the following fragment from Diogenes of Apollonia: "In my view, that which possesses intelligence is what men call Air, and all things are governed by this and it rules everything, and this very thing I consider to be god, reaching everywhere and organizing things and existing in everything."[9] A secular reading of this fragment would identify Diogenes' "Air" as a cosmic first-principle rather than as a divine being. In this reading, Diogenes' god effectively disappears.

Other scholars take the opposite approach. They locate the presocratic philosophers squarely in the cultural context of the Greek wisdom

---

[7] B25: ἀλλ' ἀπάνευθε πόνοιο νόου φρενὶ πάντα κραδαίνει.

[8] Benitez 2016: 305–6. Benitez focuses in particular on Plato and Aristotle. As he rightly argues, we cannot detheologize Plato.

[9] καί μοι δοκεῖ τὸ τὴν νόησιν ἔχον εἶναι ὁ ἀὴρ καλούμενος ὑπὸ τῶν ἀνθρώπων, καὶ ὑπὸ τούτου πάντας καὶ κυβερνᾶσθαι καὶ πάντων κρατεῖν, αὐτὸ γάρ μοι τοῦτο θεὸς δοκεῖ εἶναι καὶ ἐπὶ πᾶν ἀφῖχθαι καὶ πάντα διατιθέναι καὶ ἐν παντὶ ἐνεῖναι (DK B64). See Mansfeld 1985 and 2013 for an argument in favor of secularity; cf. Graham 2013, who offers a persuasive rejection of arguments for detheologization (he focuses on the Ionian philosophers).

tradition, which included gurus, prophets, and miracle-workers. Far from being pure rationalists, they claim, thinkers like Parmenides and Empedocles were "religious mystics" or "wonder-workers."[10] These scholars focus on the "irrational" and overtly religious aspects of ancient philosophic discourses. Most scholars, however, have taken up a position in between these extreme ends of the spectrum: they examine these philosophers in both philosophical and theological terms.[11] As David Sedley observes: "That the world is governed by a divine power is a pervasive assumption of presocratic thought. This assumption does not always focus specifically on the world's origins, but where it does, it is a widespread view that the world's original creation exhibited divine causation."[12] Sedley uses the term "rational theology" to capture the complex nature of presocratic thinking.

When we come to Plato and Aristotle, we find a more monolithic scholarly approach: the vast majority of scholars simply ignore the theological elements in their writings. There are several reasons for this. First, Plato and Aristotle set forth detailed philosophical arguments, and they explicitly valorize this mode of discourse (even though they also use rhetoric, allegory, and myth).[13] For the most part, they use rhetorical and mythic discourse to articulate their theological ideas. Scholars in the discipline of philosophy tend to focus on their philosophical arguments alone, which present a set of doctrines and ideas that can be understood through rational analysis. Second, we have a large number of Plato's and Aristotle's writings and these deal with many different philosophic topics.[14] Due to the sheer abundance of these texts, scholars have to pick and choose what they want to study. This means that they can ignore material that falls outside of their scholarly purview. In the case of the presocratic philosophers, by contrast, the tiny number of extant fragments demands that we give every single word full attention. Finally, given our secular mode of thinking, we tend to pass over Plato's and Aristotle's theological ideas as mere "window dressing."

---

[10] The literature on this topic is vast. For useful recent discussions, see Mansfeld 2013; Kingsley 1995; Bremmer 1999; Broadie 1999; Long 1999b; Curd 2002 and 2013; Laks 2003; Lesher 2008; Sedley 2008: 1–8 and passim; Mikalson 2010; Graham 2013; Benitez 2016; Tor 2017: chapter 1.

[11] See, e.g., Long 1999b; Most 2003; Lesher 2008; Robinson 2008; Sedley 2008: 1–7; Curd 2013; Graham 2013; Sassi 2013; Tor 2017.

[12] Sedley 2008: 2.

[13] Aristotle's dialogues featured rhetorical arguments and short mythic narratives (alas, we only have these in fragments). He also uses rhetorical arguments in his ethical and political discourses.

[14] Since we have a tiny few fragments from the presocratic writers, we tend to give full weight to everything they say. For this reason, their references to god and the divine are rarely ignored.

Although it is difficult if not impossible to get outside of the Enlightenment opposition between reason and religion, we must remember that this is a relatively recent cultural construct. Certainly, the ancient Greeks did not conceive of philosophy as opposed to religion. Indeed, it took a long time for the ancient thinkers to create terminologies and distinctions that identified *"philosophia"* as a unique discipline and a special mode of wisdom. In early Greece, presocratic thinkers ranked themselves among "wise men" (*sophoi*).[15] In fact, Plato was the first to identify philosophy as a specific discipline and to oppose it to other kinds of wisdom.[16] He did not, however, set "reason" in opposition to "religion," and he most certainly did not create a detheologized philosophy.

In this book, I analyze the theological aspects of Plato's metaphysics, psychology, and cosmology. I examine the interpenetration of philosophy and theology in four dialogues – the *Symposium*, *Phaedo*, *Phaedrus*, and *Timaeus*. This includes an investigation of the religious language that Plato uses for the Forms, the soul, and the cosmos. Plato regularly calls the realm of the Forms "divine," and he sees in the cosmos a divine soul that moves the heavens. He also identifies the rational part of the human soul as "godlike" and capable of achieving divinity. Finally, he treats philosophic eros as a "daimonic" or "divine" desire that lifts the mind to the divine realm of the Forms.[17] The philosopher who apprehends the Forms or the cosmos engages in a sacred way of knowing and seeing.

Modern scholars have focused almost exclusively on the rationalist aspects of Plato's philosophy. Some have examined Plato as a theological philosopher, but they make up a small minority.[18] Philosophers tend to ignore Plato's references to Greek religious practices because these fall outside of the modern philosophical enterprise. If we elide the religious discourse in his dialogues, however, we see only one "rational" strand of

---

[15] Before Plato, these men did not call themselves *"philosophoi"* (see Nightingale 1995: 1–59). See Martin 1993 for an excellent account of the seven sages and the Greek wisdom culture.

[16] I discuss this claim in detail in Nightingale 1995: chapter 1.

[17] To be sure, the Greeks conceived of daimons as divinities. I separate "daimonic desire" and "divine desire" because Plato identifies Eros as a daimon (*daimon*) in the *Symposium* and as a god (*theos*) in the *Phaedrus*.

[18] See, e.g., Cornford 1912; Burnet 1916, 1928; Taylor 1926; Santayana 1927; Festugière 1932; Hackforth 1936, 1972; Solmsen 1942; Bluck 1949; Vlastos 1965; Karfík 2004; Bordt 2006; McPherran 2006a, 2006b. Morgan 1990 presents an excellent book-length study that focuses specifically on the Greek religious elements in Platonic thinking. More recently, scholars have offered detailed studies of Plato's use of the Orphic and Eleusinian Mysteries in his dialogue. See especially Riedweg 1987; Bernabé 1995, 1997, 2007b, 2011 (on Orphism); and Martín-Velasco/Blanco 2016. All scholars who have worked on the *Timaeus* fully acknowledge the theological aspects of the dialogue, though they tend not to link this up with Plato's earlier theological philosophy.

Plato's philosophy. This does not do justice to his philosophical program. Plato regularly refers to religious rituals, festivals, and mystery cults in his discussions of the soul and the Forms. To understand his philosophy, we need to locate his ideas in the context of Greek religious discourses and practices. In this book, I aim to challenge the secularizing approach to Platonic philosophy. Plato's theory of the Forms and the soul have distinct and quite prominent theological aspects. If we ignore this aspect of his philosophy, we lose an essential part of his thinking.

Plato lived and worked in a culture permeated with religious ideas and practices. The Greeks worshipped gods throughout the day and held public festivals for the gods that lasted for days or even weeks. In Athens, festivals for the gods took up a full third of the year. The Greeks prayed and offered sacrifices at daily meals, births, weddings, and funerals. All political gatherings, official events, and military expeditions included prayers and sacrifices to the gods. At religious festivals, singers and actors regularly performed poems that celebrated the gods. Men, women, girls, and boys danced in honor of the gods at these festivals. Statues of the gods stood all over the city, and vase painters created scenes of the gods acting in mythic or civic contexts. One cannot overemphasize the level of religious activity in ancient Greece. If we view Plato in this religious context, we can begin to see his philosophy in a new light.

In my investigation of Plato's theological philosophy, I draw on philosophy, literature, history, religious studies, and anthropology. I examine four Platonic dialogues in detail, analyzing the interaction of philosophical arguments and theological discourses. I also offer detailed discussions of the religious rituals, festivals, and mystery cults that informed Plato's thinking. In particular, I discuss the Orphic and Eleusinian Mysteries, the Greek conceptions of divine inspiration, and the Greek belief that gods appeared to humans in divine epiphanies. To fully understand Plato's theories of the soul and the Forms, I argue, we must locate them in their cultural and religious context.

0.2   Divinity-Markers for the Forms and the Soul

Theological readings of Plato go back to antiquity. Indeed, Plato's thinking had a massive impact on early religious thinkers and on philosophers whose work explored theological topics. In late antiquity, neoplatonic philosophers and commentators interpreted Plato's dialogues theologically as well as philosophically. One thinks in particular of Iamblichus, Proclus, Olympiodorus, and Damascius. Plato also influenced philosophers and theologians working in monotheistic religious cultures. Starting in late antiquity, Christian thinkers embraced Plato's soul-body dualism and his conception of the Good. The tradition of Christian Platonists began with Clement of Alexandria, Origen, and Augustine in late antiquity and continued on to renaissance thinkers such as Ficino, Pico de la Mirandola, Castiglione, and Tullia d'Aragona. Plato also had a major influence on Islamic thinkers. After the philosopher al-Kindi (801–873) wrote and supervised translations of Plato's dialogues into Arabic, thinkers such as al-Farabi, al-Ghazali, and ibn Sina (aka Avicenna) used Plato's philosophy to articulate ideas about god, the soul, and the cosmos.[19] In the Jewish tradition, thinkers like Philo and Abravanel (aka Leon Ebreo) borrowed Platonic ideas to develop their theological philosophies.[20]

Philosophic approaches to Plato changed dramatically in the Enlightenment. Many philosophers leveled trenchant attacks on Platonic metaphysics, focusing on his soul-body dualism and the theory of the Forms. I will not discuss these attacks, but I do want to mention two modern philosophers who showcased the theological aspects of Plato's thinking. First, Heidegger presented detailed discussions of the "ontotheological" structure of Greek metaphysics, especially that of Plato and Aristotle.[21] Heidegger uses the term "ontotheology" to capture the idea that Greek metaphysics featured an unholy alliance of ontology and theology. According to Heidegger, Plato and Aristotle identified "the Being of beings," i.e., the ontological foundation of all things, and then associated this with the "most high" or "supreme being" in the universe,

---

[19] Islamic thinkers received many of Plato's ideas indirectly, through neoplatonic and peripatetic sources. Note also that al-Farabi differs from the other Islamic thinkers because he saw religion as subordinate to philosophy – he viewed religious texts as offering symbolic representations of the first cause and the primary principles of reality (intelligence, soul, matter), which could only be grasped by philosophy.

[20] I discuss the reception of Plato in detail in Nightingale 2020.

[21] This is a horribly simplistic articulation of Heidegger's complex account of the ontotheological structure of Greek metaphysics (he starts with Thales and Anaximander and moves down to Aristotle, presenting careful readings of each philosopher). Heidegger saw all of Western metaphysics as having an ontotheological structure, but his discussion starts with the Greek metaphysical philosophers. Heidegger discussed ontotheology in many texts; see especially 1949/2008, 1961/1973, 1963/1973. As Heidegger claims, when metaphysics "thinks of the totality of beings as such . . . with regard to the supreme, all-founding being," it is engaging in theology (1957/2002: 139). In *Identity and Difference*, he states: "Metaphysics thinks of the Being of beings both [ontologically] in [terms of] the ground-giving unity of what is most general, that is, of what is uniformly valid everywhere, and also [theologically] in the founding unity of the all, that is, of the Most High above all others. The Being of beings is thus thought of in advance as the grounding ground" (1957/2002: 125). For an excellent study of Heidegger's conception of ontotheology, see Thomson 2005.

god or the divine.[22] Of course Heidegger radically opposed this theological approach to ontology. Paul Ricoeur offers a different and, to my mind, more incisive account of the ontotheological aspects of Plato. He locates divinity in the plurality of the Forms rather than in a "most supreme being." In his analysis of Plato's "rational religion," Ricoeur states: in Plato, "we have lost the unitary function of the Parmenidean being; the divine gets reconstituted in a philosophy of being that is no longer a philosophy of the one; this distributive structure, linked to the discontinuity of naming, implies a sort of distribution of the divine, a polytheism of Forms."[23] I find Ricoeur's investigation of Plato's ontology particularly suggestive, but I want to clarify his notion of the "polytheism of Forms." To address this issue, I will study Plato's philosophy in the context of the polytheistic religious discourses and practices of the Greeks. This provides us with the rich set of religious ideas that informed Plato's thinking.

Scholars of ancient philosophy have long noted the language of divinity that Plato uses in his discussions of the Forms. Though most scholars treat his theological discourses as mere window dressing, some take Plato at his word.[24] Gregory Vlastos, for example, claims that the Forms have a higher divine status than the gods:

> Not only does Plato call the Forms "divine," but he distinctly implies that they are more divine than the gods. If the latter seems preposterous, we need only recall those attributes of divinity – eternity, perfection not flawed by passion or risked in action – of which the gods of cult and myth were more caricatures than exemplars. It is, therefore, understandable that one who exalted these attributes above all others should have found in the Forms, and only there, entities fully worthy of his adoration and feel his vision of them as a communion. Thus, in one and the same experience Plato finds happiness, beauty, knowledge, moral sustenance and regeneration, and a mystical sense of kinship with eternal perfection.[25]

[22] As Heidegger puts it: "The question of Being, as the question of the Being of beings, is double in form. On the one hand, it asks: What is a being in general as a being? In the history of philosophy, reflections which fall within the domain of this question acquire the title ontology. The question 'What is a being?' [or 'What is that which is?'] simultaneously asks: Which being is the highest [or supreme] being, and in what sense is it the highest being? This is the question of God and of the divine. We call the domain of this question theology. This duality in the question of the Being of beings can be united under the title ontotheology."

[23] Ricoeur 2013: 132.

[24] For scholars who have treated Plato in theological as well as philosophical terms, see, e.g., Pater 1901; Cornford 1912; Burnet 1916, 1928; Taylor 1926; Santayana 1927; Festugière 1932; Hackforth 1936, 1972; Bluck 1949; Vlastos 1965; Morgan 1990; McPherran 2006a; Long 2020. The number of scholars who take this position has gone downhill since the 1960s (in part because, after World War 2, many humanists distanced themselves from Christianity).

[25] Vlastos 1965–1966: 15; Morgan 1990 and Long 2020 have also had a great deal of influence on my project.

Following Vlastos, I interpret the theory of the Forms in theological as well as philosophical terms. In Plato's middle-period dialogues, the philosopher achieves knowledge of the essence of the Forms, but he also encounters divinity. Plato presents these two aspects of his thinking in different literary styles – analytical arguments and rhetorical/mythic discourses. Plato reaches for nonanalytic discourses to conjure up the divine realm. This language gestures towards the ineffable divinity of the Forms. As I will suggest, the philosopher can achieve knowledge of the essence of a given Form, but he cannot fully take in its divinity. For this reason, Plato's discourse oscillates between the effable and ineffable.

To give a full exposition of these ideas, I will examine the divine aspects of the Forms, the soul, and philosophic eros, and discuss how these theological elements operate (and co-operate) in Plato's philosophy. I will begin by identifying the "divinity-markers" of the Forms in Plato's middle-period dialogues. Plato marks the Forms as divine in many different ways. We can better understand the complexity of Plato's theological philosophy by distinguishing the different ways in which he refers to the Forms as divine.

Before I list and examine the divinity-markers for the Forms, however, I want to briefly discuss Plato's views of the Greek gods (as they were traditionally understood), as well as his own conception of the gods. Once we understand Plato's ideas about god, we can see how the gods and the divine Forms operate together in his philosophical system. As we will see, Plato rejected traditional Greek conceptions of the gods and presented a new set of theological ideas.

For the ancient Greeks, the gods were immense and ever-present powers that acted in mysterious ways. These deities lived outside of human morality and could not be judged in human terms. Still, they kept a close eye on human actions and responded to good and bad behavior. Humans had to pay very careful attention to the gods and worship them in the right ways. The gods were whimsical and unreliable beings – if they took offense, they became violently angry and jealous of their prerogatives. The Greeks ascribed envy and anger to the gods as a way of accounting for natural events that brought harm to humans, especially those who had endeavored to live pious and good lives. However, as Esther Eidinow observes, divine envy could be seen in different ways: it could be "a blast of malice, likely to be wholly undeserved by its targets; a revelation of godly avarice; an instrument of divine justice, delivered as punishment for some impiety (be it action or character); a godly slapdown intended to keep mortals under control; and/or a mechanism for the maintenance of cosmic boundaries."[26] The actions of the gods could be quite confounding. In the Greek world, humans could not treat the gods as reliable, yet they had to offer reliable and regular worship. Finally, since the gods stood outside of human morality, they did not provide a model for ethical deliberation or action.

Plato viewed the gods in radically different terms. He repudiated the idea that the gods feel anger, spite, and envy. Rather, he claimed, they are perfectly good and provide the ethical paradigm for human behavior. They contemplate the Forms and also oversee the human realm in a just and wise manner. In short, Plato conceived of the gods as reliable. They judge humans justly and mete out the right rewards and punishments. In the *Republic*, Plato attacks the dominant Greek conceptions of the gods head-on. As Socrates asks, "What are the right ways to speak about the gods (*theologias*)? These should show what a god really is."[27] He then lists the attributes of the gods: they are absolutely good, unchanging, beneficent, beautiful, true, and simple (379b–380e).[28] Since the gods do not change in terms of their moods and behaviors, they lack the anthropomorphic qualities assigned to them in the traditional Greek religion.

In the middle-period dialogues, Plato completely reconceived of the gods.[29] In particular, he rejected the Greek belief that gods appeared in bodily forms to humans. As Socrates claims in the *Republic*, the gods do not change or appear in different forms: they are perfectly good and have a single, incorporeal form (378b–c). In short, the gods do not manifest themselves epiphanically in the physical world. In addition, these gods could not be swayed by prayers or sacrifices. Indeed, Plato utterly opposed the idea that one could gain divine aid by supplicating the gods or offering gifts and sacrifices. He saw this traditional mode of worship in terms of base economic exchange (i.e., bribery). In Plato, the gods did not operate in this economy of exchange. In his view, a human rightly serves the gods by practicing philosophy and becoming virtuous and wise. Indeed, the proper mode of worship is to imitate the gods' goodness and wisdom, and to pray to them for aid in one's philosophical practice. This activity is not transactional but aspirational.

---

[26] Eidinow 2016: 207.

[27] *Rep.* 379a: οἱ τύποι περὶ θεολογίας τίνες ἂν εἶεν; τοιοίδε πού τινες . . . οἷος τυγχάνει ὁ θεὸς ὤν.

[28] Good: ἀγαθός; beneficial: ὠφέλιμος; unchanging in form: ἕκαστος αὐτῶν μένει ἀεὶ ἁπλῶς ἐν τῇ αὑτοῦ μορφῇ; beautiful and virtuous: οὐ γάρ που ἐνδεᾶ γε φήσομεν τὸν θεὸν κάλλους ἢ ἀρετῆς εἶναι; true: πάντῃ ἄρα ἀψευδὲς τὸ δαιμόνιόν τε καὶ τὸ θεῖον; simple: ἁπλοῦν τε εἶναι καὶ πάντων ἥκιστα τῆς ἑαυτοῦ ἰδέας ἐκβαίνειν (380d–382e).

[29] The *Euthyphro*, an early dialogue, calls into question traditional ideas about the gods but does not present a clear account of the nature of god.

Let us turn now to the Forms. Plato applies many of the attributes of the (platonic) gods to the Forms: they are perfectly good, true, simple, and unchanging.[30] Of course the gods and the Forms differ in key ways: the gods have minds and govern the cosmos, while the Forms exist separately from the universe and lack personal agency. They do not have rational capacities or the power to oversee the earthly and psychic realm. For this reason, Plato's philosophers do not worship or pray to the Forms. The Forms are ontologically higher than the gods. Plato identifies them as having a unique kind of divinity.

To set up my discussion of the divine-markers of the Forms, I want to address two issues very briefly: (1) the range of the Forms, i.e., what properties or things in the world participated in the Forms, and (2) the varied terminology that Plato used to identify the Forms. In terms of the range of the Forms, scholars distinguish "value Forms" (e.g., Good, Just, Beautiful) and "logical/mathematical Forms" (e.g., Equal, Odd, Large, Dual).[31] In some dialogues, Plato focuses only on value Forms; in others, he discusses both value Forms and logical/mathematical Forms. He does not, however, explicitly discuss the range of the Forms in the middle-period dialogues, with the exception of the *Parmenides* (which comes at the end of the middle-period dialogues). In this dialogue, Plato criticizes certain aspects of the theory of the Forms and also raises questions about the scope of the Forms. In this text, Socrates affirms that there are logical/mathematical Forms (Likeness, One, Many) and value Forms (Justice, Beauty, Goodness), but he expresses uncertainty about Forms of humans, water, and fire, and actively rejects Forms of mud, hair, and dirt. However, he admits to feeling confusion about these latter categories (130b–d). We can infer that Plato himself had not fully resolved the question of the exact range of the Forms.

In terms of naming or identifying the Forms, Plato uses a number of different locutions. At times, he calls them *eidê* (the appearance or form of a thing) or *ideai* (the look or appearance of a thing). Both of these terms come from words for vision and reflect Plato's ocularcentrism. More often, he refers to Forms as "Being" or "that which is" (*ousia*, noun; *einai*, verb)

---

[30]   The Forms and the gods are perfect in different ways: the gods have perfect intellectual and ethical qualities, while the Forms are perfect in terms of their essence and being. In addition, the gods can move, while the Forms are immobile.

[31]   Scholars also note that, on rare occasions, Plato mentions Forms of artefacts (e.g., couch) and natural types (e.g., fire). To figure out the scope of the Forms, scholars have to examine each reference to an individual Form in the middle-period dialogues and, putting all these together, present a general hypothesis about the range of the Forms.

or, in the plural, "Beings" or "things that are" (*ta onta*).[32] Note also that Plato uses the terms *ousia, to on,* and *ta onta* to refer to the Forms as a group: they are "Being" or "Beings." Plato also identifies the Forms by mentioning some or all of their properties: eternal, unchanging, uniform, incorporeal, and intelligible. He can also refer to a Form as "itself by itself" (*auto kath' hauto*). In discussing an individual form, the Form of Beauty for example, Plato regularly uses the phrase "Beauty itself" (αὐτὸ τὸ καλόν). When he discusses the philosopher's contemplation of the Forms, Plato refers to him as knowing "Being(s)" or knowing, e.g., "what Beauty is" (ὃ ἔστι καλόν). Plato also represents the philosopher as "seeing" or "beholding" (*horan, theorein, theasthai*) the Forms. These ocular verbs, when they refer to an indefinite object ("them"; "these things"), can serve to identify the Forms. Finally, Plato tends to put the Forms in a "place" (*topos*) or "realm" separate and higher than the physical realm.

Plato presents different accounts of the divinity of the Forms in different dialogues. In some texts, he grants divinity to a single Form; in others, he refers to the entire group of the Forms as divine. For example, in the *Symposium,* he identifies the Form of Beauty as "divine" (*theios*) but does not mention any other Form. In the *Phaedo,* which deals with many value and logical/mathematical Forms, Plato identifies the group of the Forms as divine. In the *Republic,* he ranks the Form of the Good above the other Forms and identifies it as divine. And he also refers to the group of the Forms as divine. In the *Phaedrus,* he refers to Beauty as divine and also represents the group of the Forms as divine.

Plato refers to the Forms as divine in many different ways. To make this point clear, I have identified "divinity-markers" for the Forms and put these into six categories.

(1) **Theios Markers**: calling the Forms "divine" (*theios*).
(2) **Gods Markers**: comparing the Forms to the gods.
(3) **Poetic Narratives of Epiphany Markers**: using language from poetic narratives of divine epiphanies to describe the philosopher's vision of the Forms.
(4) **Eleusinian Mysteries Markers**: describing philosophic contemplation of the Forms in terms of the initiate's divine revelation at the Eleusinian Mysteries.

[32] Many scholars also translate *ta onta* as "realities." Throughout this book, I capitalize "Being" to make it clear that I am referring to the Forms and not to ordinary beings.

(5) **Orphic Markers**: comparison of the Forms to the salvific gods in the Orphic Mysteries.

(6) **Sacred Spectating (*theorein*) Markers**: using *theoria/theorein* ("sacred spectating" at temples and sanctuaries) to describe the philosophic contemplation of the Forms.

I will discuss these six divinity-markers in detail below. I separate these markers to show the complexity and richness of Plato's theological philosophy. As we will see, many religious ideas and rituals influenced Plato's thinking. But recognizing the religious aspects of Plato's thought poses challenges – a fact that has contributed to the scholarly tendency to ignore the religious aspects of Plato's philosophy. I want to note in advance that the last three divinity-markers (Eleusinian, Orphic, Sacred Spectating [*theoria*]) are almost impossible for the reader to spot in a text, let alone to understand. Consider a simple example found in the Orphic divinity-marker. Plato often uses the words "purification" (*katharsis*) and "release" (*lusis*), either separately or together. These common Greek words take on a specific meaning when they come up in passages where Plato refers to the Orphics. For example, throughout the *Phaedo* – which has many references to the Orphics – Plato uses "purification" and "release" in terms of the Orphic belief that the soul gets released from ancestral sin through purification and initiation. The reader will miss the religious resonance of these terms if he or she has not studied Orphism. The matter is made worse because Plato rarely mentions the Orphics explicitly; rather, he alludes to a ritual or doctrine without saying "these are Orphic." Since the Athenians had a fairly good grasp of Orphism, they could easily comprehend these references. To cite one more example, Plato often refers to the Orphic claim that the body is a "prison for the soul."[33] One can only understand this idea properly if one learns the rich Orphic myths about the human soul and its fall into the body.

We bump into the same problem when Plato uses the divinity-marker of the Eleusinian Mysteries. He refers to the Eleusinian initiation ceremonies in a number of dialogues, but those working with English translations of Plato's texts will simply read words like "initiation" or "initiate." Even if we read the dialogues in Greek, we may simply interpret "initiation" metaphorically. Once we understand the Eleusinian Mysteries and their strange rituals and ceremonies, these

---

[33] I will discuss this in detail in Chapter 2.

words take on a dense network of meanings. In addition, since the Eleusinian and Orphic Mysteries both featured initiation ceremonies, the reader needs to know which of the two Plato refers to when he uses words for "initiation." To clarify these ideas, I will discuss the Orphic and Eleusinian Mysteries in detail in Chapter 2 and Chapter 3. Finally, the divinity-marker of *theoria/theorein* tends to escape the reader: English translators use terms like "see" or "behold" for *theorein*, and "embassy" for *theoria*. These translations completely eclipse the religious meaning of these words. One can easily miss this divinity-marker if one is reading Plato in English.

Let me briefly describe the six divinity-markers that Plato gives to the Forms.

0.2.1 Theios *Divinity-Marker: Identification of the Forms as "Divine"* (Theios)

The Greeks used the word *theios* ("divine") for a wide range of entities. As A. A. Long observes:

> Many things besides Olympian divinities can have the *theios* attribute in Greek literature, including exceptional human beings and abstract entities such as nature or fortune; and *theios* admits of degrees, such that something may be more or be most divine. In using "divinity" instead of god I want to capture this breadth of reference, and I especially want to remove us from automatically thinking that anything divine in Greek must signify a being with the mind and intentions of a person.[34]

Plato calls individual Forms or the group of the Forms "divine" (*theios*). He often uses this adjective when he mentions the key attributes of the Forms (eternal, unchanging, eternal, incorporeal, uniform, separate from the physical world). Even though the Forms did not have minds or personal agency, Plato identified them as divine.

0.2.2 Gods *Divinity-Marker: Comparison of the Forms to the Gods and/or the Heavenly Realm of the Gods*

Plato links the Forms to the gods or to the realm of the gods in many passages. For example, in the *Republic*, he compares the Form of the Good to the sun god Helios: like the sun god in the physical realm, the

---

[34] Long 2020. On the word *theios* ("divine") in Plato, see Van Camp/Canart 1956.

Good illuminates the intelligible realm of the Forms and gives them both existence and intelligibility (more on this below). This comparison effectively marks the Form of the Good as divine. Plato also compares the Forms to the heavenly realm of the gods. As Socrates asks in the *Republic*: "Should we consider how [the city] will produce these philosophers and how one can lead them up into the light, just as some are said to have journeyed from Hades up to the gods (*ex Haidou ... eis theous anelthein*)?" (521c). By "up to the gods," Plato refers to the home of the gods on top of Mount Olympus, which stands in pure light above the clouds. Using the Gods divinity-marker, Plato compares the philosophic ascent to the Forms to a journey up to the gods on Mount Olympus. Of course the philosopher ascends up into the light-filled realm of the Forms rather than to the gods. Plato locates the divine realm of the Forms in a high and luminous region.

We also find the Gods divinity-marker in the eschatological narrative in the *Phaedo* and the Allegory of the Cave in the *Republic*. In these texts, Plato places ordinary humans in subterranean caves or hollows beneath the earth, that is, in realms that resemble Hades. The philosopher rationally "ascends" this dark human realm and reaches a higher divine realm.[35] Plato's metaphorics of light play an important role in the Gods divinity-marker. As Plato puts it in the *Sophist*: "but the philosopher, who is always attached to the Form of Being by way of reason, is hard to see because of the brilliant light of the place; for the eyes of the soul of the multitude are unable to endure seeing the divine." (254a–b).[36]

---

[35] Note also that, in the Allegory of the Cave, Plato represents the philosopher who has made it up to the realm of the Forms as quoting the ghost of Homer's Achilles when he is in Hades: the philosopher would rather live up above "as a landless man on earth, serving another" rather than dwell in the cave where men lord over others by spouting false opinions (*Rep.* 516d–e). Achilles utters these lines in Hades, claiming that he would rather toil on earth for another rather than have power in Hades (*Od.* 11.489). Plato's philosopher, by contrast, speaks this line after journeying up and out of the hellish cave. By coming up out of the cave, the philosopher makes it up from hell to the surface of "earth." He has left the cave for the realm of the Forms and wants to stay there. To be sure, the notion of the philosopher in the realm of the Forms being "a landless man on earth, serving another" may seem like a stretch. After all, he is contemplating the Forms. But we can see that the desire to be "up above on earth" works in the case of both Achilles and the philosopher. Plato changes the myth by allowing a person to leave Hades for the luminous, divine realm of the Forms.

[36] *Sophist* 254a–b: ὁ δέ γε φιλόσοφος, τῇ τοῦ ὄντος ἀεὶ διὰ λογισμῶν προσκείμενος ἰδέᾳ, διὰ τὸ λαμπρὸν αὖ τῆς χώρας οὐδαμῶς εὐπετὴς ὀφθῆναι· τὰ γὰρ τῆς τῶν πολλῶν ψυχῆς ὄμματα καρτερεῖν πρὸς τὸ θεῖον ἀφορῶντα ἀδύνατα. To be sure, the *Sophist* is a late dialogue that adopts a different conception of the Forms. But Plato still uses the metaphorics of light and calls the realm of the Forms "divine."

0.2.3 Poetic Narratives of Epiphany Divinity-Marker: Use of the Discourse from Poetic Narratives of Divine Epiphany to Describe the Appearance of the Divine Forms to the Philosopher

Plato marks the divinity of the Forms by using the language of poetic narratives of epiphany to represent the philosopher beholding a divine Form. In the *Phaedrus*, for example, the philosophic lover "sees the face of the beloved, which was flashing like lightning (ἀστράπτουσαν)." The lover instantly recollects the Form of Beauty, which shines in the face of the beloved boy and strikes him like lightning. As we will see, in poetic narratives of epiphany, a god appears to humans as a lightning bolt or some other dazzling celestial body (*HH* 2.281, *HH* 5.86–91, *HH* 3.442). In addition, in poetic epiphanic narratives, the human viewers respond to the god with fear, awe, and reverence (*HH* 2.188–90, *HH* 2.282–3, *HH* 5.182, *Iliad* 1.199–200). Plato uses the same language in his narratives of the philosopher seeing the Forms. In the *Phaedrus*, the philosopher who was looking at his beautiful beloved "was carried to the true nature of Beauty, and he saw it standing with Self-Control upon a holy pedestal. When he saw this, he felt terror and fell backward in reverence" (254b–c).[37] Here, the philosopher acts as if he has seen an epiphany of a god. The Form, then, has an epiphanic aspect: Beauty manifests its divine presence to the philosopher.

In the next three divinity-markers for the Forms, Plato uses language and ideas from Greek religious festivals and rituals. In these cases, Plato does not simply identify the Forms as divine. Rather, he describes the contemplation of the Forms in terms of specific religious practices. Since festivals and mystery rituals took place in the context of specific social and political practices, they require detailed examination. Understanding these divinity-markers allows us to give a thicker description of Plato's theological enterprise.

0.2.4 Eleusinian Mysteries Divinity-Marker: Comparison of the Philosopher Seeing the Forms to the Initiate's Divine Revelation in the Eleusinian Mysteries

To understand this divinity-marker, I need to offer a brief discussion of the Eleusinian Mysteries.[38] This was a hugely popular mystery cult: most Athenians got initiated, and people from all over the Greek world came to

---

[37] *Phaedrus* 254b–c: εἶδον τὴν ὄψιν τὴν τῶν παιδικῶν ἀστράπτουσαν. ἰδόντος δὲ τοῦ ἡνιόχου ἡ μνήμη πρὸς τὴν τοῦ κάλλους φύσιν ἠνέχθη, καὶ πάλιν εἶδεν αὐτὴν μετὰ σωφροσύνης ἐν ἁγνῷ βάθρῳ βεβῶσαν· ἰδοῦσα δὲ ἔδεισέ τε καὶ σεφθεῖσα ἀνέπεσεν ὑπτία.

[38] I will discuss the Eleusinian Mysteries in detail in Chapter 2.

undergo initiation as well. The initiation into the mysteries took place within an Athenian civic festival for Demeter and Persephone. This festival had events open to the public and "mystery" rituals open only to initiands and initiates. All initiates had to keep their experiences secret from non-initiates. That said, for the Athenians, this experience was an open secret because so many people in the city got initiated. Athenian readers of Plato, then, could easily understand his references to the final initiation ceremony (the *epopteia*, i.e., the "seeing"). The Eleusinian Mysteries featured two initiation cere-monies: the individual (male or female) went through the first initiation as a *mustês* at Agrai in Athens, and the second as an *epoptês* at Eleusis. In the first initiation, the *mustês* learns about the gods but remains blind to the divinities (*muein* means "to close" the eyes or lips); in the second initiation, the individual sees a divine revelation as an *epoptês* ("he who sees"). At the climax of the second initiation ceremony, the *epoptês* saw (or was supposed to see) an epiphany of the goddess.[39] As Kevin Clinton observes:

> The hierophant's task was ἱερὰ φαίνειν, which could mean "to show sacred objects" or "to make the sacred appear." In the latter case he did more than show sacred objects, i.e., he *made gods appear* in addition to the sacred objects, or perhaps was mainly associated with the appearance of the gods.[40]

In short, the Eleusinian Mysteries featured a ritually induced divine epiphany at the climax of the ceremonies. Plato uses language from the Eleusinian Mysteries to indicate that the philosopher sees the Forms in terms of a divine epiphany. In the *Symposium*, for example, Diotima says to Socrates: "Perhaps even you might be initiated as a *mustês* in these love matters. But as to the final rites and the visions of the *epoptês*, which is the goal for the person advancing rightly, I don't know if you can follow."[41] Here, Plato conceives of the ascent to the Form of Beauty in terms of the two initiations at the Eleusinian Mysteries. Socrates might be a *mustês*, a developing philosopher, but has not reached the level of the *epoptês*, the perfected philosopher. Only the philosopher who gets to the top of the Ladder of Love sees the epiphany of the divine Form of Beauty as an *epoptês*. When Plato represents the philosopher contemplating the Forms as an *epoptês*, then, he indicates that the philosopher sees a divine epiphany.

---

[39] In this ceremony, the hierophants performed a "sacred drama" representing Hades' abduction of Persephone (aka Kore), Demeter's misery over her lost child, and her recovery of Persephone for half of the year. As we will see in Chapter 1, this sacred drama functioned, in part, to evoke (or, as some claim, manipulate) a divine epiphany.

[40] Clinton 2004: 85, my italics.

[41] *Symp.* 209e–210a: ταῦτα μὲν οὖν τὰ ἐρωτικὰ ἴσως, ὦ Σώκρατες, κἄν σὺ μυηθείης· τὰ δὲ τέλεα καὶ ἐποπτικά, ὧν ἕνεκα καὶ ταῦτα ἔστιν, ἐάν τις ὀρθῶς μετίῃ, οὐκ οἶδ᾽ εἰ οἷός τ᾽ ἂν εἴης.

0.2.5   Orphic Divinity-Marker: Comparison of the Perfect Philosophic Soul Everlastingly "Dwelling with" the Forms to the Orphic Initiate's Eternal Life with the Salvific Gods after Death

Plato uses the myths and initiation ceremonies of the Orphic Mysteries to refer to the philosophic soul's everlasting life with the Forms. This divinity-marker is complex because it refers to the divinity of both the Forms and the soul. Let me briefly summarize the myths and rituals of the Orphics.[42] Orphism was a private religion run by freelance practitioners all over the Greek world. The Orphic practitioners used books of poems ascribed to Orpheus and Musaeus (legendary figures) in their teachings and rituals. The poems contained a cosmogony and an anthropology. In the Orphic theogony, Zeus and Demeter give birth to Persephone; Zeus then rapes Persephone, and she gives birth to Dionysus. The Titans kill and eat Dionysus, and Zeus destroys them with a thunderbolt. This event brings humans onto the scene: human souls were born from the soot of the burned Titans. The human soul is part Titanic and part Dionysian. Though it is divine and immortal, it carries the original sin of its Titanic forefathers. Because of this sin, the gods punished human souls by "imprisoning" them in a body and making them undergo reincarnation. In the Orphic soteriology, if the soul "purifies" itself and goes through initiation, the gods "release" it from the cycle of reincarnation and it lives an everlastingly blessed life with the gods in Hades.

Plato borrows a number of ideas and phrases from the Orphics. He uses Orphic phrases to describe (1) the immortal soul's imprisonment in the body; (2) the soul's purification by philosophy; and (3) the philosophic soul's final release from reincarnation after death and its everlasting life in the divine realm of the Forms. Let me cite a few examples of Plato's use of the Orphics. In the *Phaedo*, Socrates refers to philosophy as bringing "release and purification" to the "imprisoned" soul.[43] He also claims that the philosophic soul, which is akin to the Forms, goes to the divine realm of the Forms after death:

> The [philosopher's soul,] following reason and always being with it, *beholding what is divine*, true, and not the object of opinion [i.e., the Forms], and being nourished by this, thinks that it must live in this way as long as it is alive, *and when it dies, goes to what is akin to itself and gains release from human evils*. (*Phaedo* 84a–b, my italics)[44]

---

[42] I will discuss this in detail in Chapter 2.

[43] *Phaedo* 82d; see also 67a, 67d, 82d, 82e, 114b–c, and *Rep.* 364e–365a.

[44] *Phaedo* 84a–b: ἑπομένη τῷ λογισμῷ καὶ ἀεὶ ἐν τούτῳ οὖσα, τὸ ἀληθὲς καὶ τὸ θεῖον καὶ τὸ ἀδόξαστον θεωμένη καὶ ὑπ᾽ ἐκείνου τρεφομένη, ζῆν τε οἴεται οὕτω δεῖν ἕως ἂν ζῇ, καὶ ἐπειδὰν τελευτήσῃ, εἰς τὸ συγγενὲς καὶ εἰς τὸ τοιοῦτον ἀφικομένη ἀπηλλάχθαι τῶν ἀνθρωπίνων κακῶν.

As I argue, Plato uses these phrases to conjure up the entire Orphic myth of sin and salvation. Plato alters the myth, however, by suggesting that the disembodied philosophic soul dwells everlastingly in the divine realm of the Forms (rather than with the gods in Hades).

0.2.6   Sacred Spectating (Theorein) Divinity-Marker: Comparison of the Philosopher to the Religious Pilgrim Seeing Sacred Sights at a Sanctuary (Theoros/Theoria/Theorein)

Plato regularly claims that the philosopher "theorizes" the Forms. The word *theorein* means "to see or spectate." For the Greeks, *"theoria"* (noun) or *"theorein"* (verb) referred to a practice in which pilgrims (*theoroi*) made journeys to sanctuaries and religious festivals to see sacred objects and spectacles. When the Greeks attended these festivals, the objects and events they saw were sacralized by a series of rituals. This led them to engage in "ritualized visualization": they saw statues, temples, and events in the sanctuary as sacred and replete with divinity. In some cases, a god could manifest its divine presence in a statue.[45]

Plato often uses the verb *theorein* to describe the philosopher's contemplation of the Forms. His terminology of the philosopher "theorizing" the Forms is based on the Greek religious practice of *theoria*.[46] Plato uses the word *theoria* and its cognates to mark out the philosophic "vision" of the Forms. As I have argued elsewhere, Plato developed this ocularcentric vocabulary to identify philosophic contemplation as a sacred way of seeing.[47] We can quickly grasp this idea in a passage from the Allegory of the Cave: after the philosopher makes his way out of the cave, he beholds the Forms and, eventually, looks directly at the divine Form of the Good. The philosopher gains knowledge of the essence of each Form, but he also beholds the divine. As Socrates puts it, when the philosopher goes back down into the cave, "he returns from divine theorizings" (ἀπὸ θείων . . . θεωριῶν . . . ἐλθών; 517d).

In a more detailed passage in the *Republic*, Plato compares the philosophers to spectators at religious festivals. He likens "the lovers of sights and sounds" to the "lover of wisdom." Socrates describes the lovers of sights and sounds as people who "run around to all the Dionysian festivals, never leaving a single one out, either in the towns or in the cities" (475d). He identifies the lovers of sights and sounds, then, as pilgrims (*theoroi*) who journey to religious festivals of Dionysus to see (*theorein*) rituals and

---

[45] I discuss ritualized visualization and gods manifesting divinity in statues in Chapter 2.
[46] Nightingale 2004.   [47] Nightingale 2004.

spectacles. Through ritualized visualization, the *theoros* sensed the presence
of the god in his or her statue or in some other manifestation. In this
passage, Socrates likens the philosophers to the "lovers of sights" (now
leaving out the lovers of sounds): these individuals, he claims, are "lovers of
the sight of truth" (τοὺς τῆς ἀληθείας . . . φιλοθεάμονας; 475e). By comparing the philosopher to spectators at Dionysian festivals, then, Plato identifies philosophy as a mode of sacred spectating. I will not discuss the *theoria*
divinity-marker in this book, since I analyzed it in detail in *Spectacles of
Truth in Classical Greek Philosophy*.

In addition to marking the divinity of the Forms, Plato also grants
divinity to the soul. The soul has the rational capacity to achieve divinity
but can also live a lowly life in the earthly realm. The soul becomes divine
by practicing philosophy and apprehending the Forms. I will discuss these
divinity-markers of the soul in the chapters to come, but I will briefly
identify them here. First, Plato calls the soul *theios* or *theoeidês* ("godlike").
Second, he compares the soul to the gods by way of argument or myth.
Third, he affirms the likeness or kinship of the soul to the divine Forms. As
Socrates says in the *Phaedo*: "the soul is *most like* the divine (*theios*),
immortal, intelligible, uniform, indissoluble, and ever unchanging
[Forms]; but the body is most like the human, mortal, multiformed,
unintelligible, dissoluble, and ever unconstant to itself" (80b, my italics).[48]
Of course, the soul differs from the Forms in essential ways, but the
contemplation of the Forms allows it to actualize its divine capacities.
Indeed, the realm of the Forms is the proper place for the soul to dwell. As
we saw in the *Phaedo* passage above (84a–b), the philosophic soul will go to
the divine realm of the Forms, its "kin," after death. Finally, Plato gives the
immortal soul divinity-markers that come from Orphism. The Orphics
identified the soul as a fallen divinity. The soul could regain its original
status as a god by undergoing purification and initiation. In a fourth-
century BCE Orphic gold tablet, for example, a god in the underworld
speaks to the initiated soul as a divinity: "You have never endured this
before. You have become a god instead of a mortal."[49] Plato took seriously
the Orphic idea that the purified soul became divine when it left the body
in death. But he transferred this idea to the soul of the philosopher: when

[48] τῷ μὲν θείῳ καὶ ἀθανάτῳ καὶ νοητῷ καὶ μονοειδεῖ καὶ ἀδιαλύτῳ καὶ ἀεὶ ὡσαύτως κατὰ ταὐτὰ
ἔχοντι ἑαυτῷ ὁμοιότατον εἶναι ψυχή, τῷ δὲ ἀνθρωπίνῳ καὶ θνητῷ καὶ πολυειδεῖ καὶ ἀνοήτῳ καὶ
διαλυτῷ καὶ μηδέποτε κατὰ ταὐτὰ ἔχοντι ἑαυτῷ ὁμοιότατον αὖ εἶναι σῶμα.
[49] *OF* 487.3–4=fragment 3.3–4 in Graf/Johnston 2007 (*OF* 487). I use Graf/Johnston's translations,
with minor alterations, in this book.

the soul has contemplated the Forms and grasped the divine realm where they reside, it becomes divine upon leaving the body at death.

0.3   Philosophic Eros as "Daimonic" or "Divine" Desire

Figure 0.1 Eros flying over an altar with a votive gift. Athenian Red–figure Pelike, 450–400 BCE. Vienna, Kunsthistorisches Museum Collection, 636

Figure 0.2 Eros flying with phiale and fillet, Red–figure Skyphos, 475–425 BCE.
Basel Antikenmuseum und Sammlung Ludwig KA426

Scholars working on Plato's theories of philosophic desire have not taken into account the divine aspects of Platonic eros. This is strange, because the speakers in the *Symposium* give speeches on the god Eros and Socrates celebrates the god Eros in the *Phaedrus*. As I argue, in these two dialogues, Eros functions as a special divinity-marker for the soul. In his mythic accounts of Eros in the *Symposium* and *Phaedrus*, Plato calls Eros a daimon and a god (respectively). He does this to mark a divine aspect of the soul: the mind's erotic desire for the divine realm of the Forms. Plato adopts the Greek conception of Eros as a god but locates this divinity within the soul (Eros does not act externally on the soul). He presents mythic accounts of the *daimôn* and *theos* Eros to foreground the divine aspects of philosophical desire. As I argue, he places "daimonic" or "divine" desire in the rational part of the soul.

Let us look briefly at the god himself. In terms of cult, the Athenians worshipped Eros at an altar in the grove of the Academy, and also in the sanctuary of Aphrodite on the north slope of the Acropolis (see Figure 0.1, Eros flying over an altar with a votive gift).[50] We have many statues and vase

[50] We do not know what altar Eros flies to in this image. See Stafford 2013 for a detailed discussion of Eros in art and in cult. See also Pirenne-Delforge 1994; Graf 1995; Calame 1996; Rosensweig 2004 on

paintings of Eros from the classical period that represent this god. First, Greek artists generally represented Eros as a naked young male who had wings (see Figures 0.1–0.4). In terms of his sphere of influence, the Greeks conceived of Eros as presiding over both homosexual and heterosexual love affairs. For example, the Athenians erected an altar to Eros in the sixth century BCE in the Academy, an area that included a large public gymnasium where males of different ages gathered to exercise, socialize, and pursue erotic relationships. In this and other gymnasia, the Greeks worshipped Eros alongside Hermes and Heracles. Pausanias claims that the Athenians put the altar of Eros "in the front of the entrance to the Academy" (1.30.1), a placement marking its importance.[51] We have a large number of vase paintings that feature Eros in gymnastic settings: in this arena, Eros presided over homoerotic relationships (see Figure 0.3, Eros flying; two naked boys with strigils).[52] At the sanctuary of Aphrodite on the Acropolis, by contrast, the Athenians worshipped Eros and Aphrodite as gods of heterosexual relationships, marriage, and fertility. We find images on vase paintings and votive gifts that foreground this aspect of Eros (see Figure 0.4, woman giving Eros a votive gift in a domestic context). Finally, Eros takes his place among the pantheon of gods on the east frieze on the Parthenon.[53]

Plato understood these different roles of Eros, and even borrowed the image of winged Eros from artistic representations. However, he completely transformed the notion of erotic desire: Eros aims at the Forms, not a human body. In the *Symposium*, Plato represents Eros as a *daimôn* rather than a god (*theos*). What does he mean by a *daimôn*? Speaking very generally, the Greeks treated daimons as a lower order of divinities: they did not give them names but believed that they had power over human life.[54] As Diotima claims, the entire daimonic realm brings humans into contact with the

---

the cult of Eros and Aphrodite. There are several literary passages that seem to deny that Eros was worshipped in cult: Euripides' *Hippolytus* 538–40, where the chorus says "we do not worship Eros"; and Plato's *Symposium* (189c), where Aristophanes says that they do not have temples, altars, and sacrifices for Eros. As Stafford rightly notes (2013: 177), "this is not incompatible with cult activity on a modest scale"; cf. Breitenberger 2007.

[51] Hermeias in his commentary on Plato's *Phaedrus* 231 claims that the great torch race at the Panathenaia started at the Altar of Eros. If this claim is accurate, it links the altar of Eros at the Academy with the worship of Athena.

[52] We know that these males are boys because they have no beards; the strigils indicate that they are in a gymnastic or athletic context. Shapiro 1992 offers a useful discussion of the visual and textual evidence for Eros' role in homoerotic relationships.

[53] On the Parthenon frieze, the figure of Eros, seated on Aphrodite's lap, is smaller than the other gods. But he is clearly worshipped by the people in the procession. As Neils observes (1999: 13), Aphrodite acknowledges the procession of worshippers coming towards them by pointing this out to Eros.

[54] Gasparro 2015. I will discuss this in detail in Chapter 2.

Figure 0.3 Eros flying; two naked boys with strigils. Athenian Red–Figure
Oinochoe. Vatican City, Museo Gregoriano Etrusco Vaticano Collection, 16524

gods – daimons serve as mediators between these two realms.[55] In her
account, one particular daimon, Eros, has a unique role as intermediary:
he drives the philosophic soul into contact with the divine Form of Beauty
(rather than with the gods). Eros is a go-between. In the *Symposium*, which
identifies the soul as mortal, Plato gives the soul a "daimonic desire" that
enables it to ascend to the divine realm of the Forms.

---

[55] This is Plato's conception of daimons, which he reconceives in later texts. The Greeks in general did
not share this view about daimons as intermediaries.

Figure 0.4 Naked woman bringing votive box to Eros (domestic). Red–Figure
Pelike, 450–400 BCE. University of Mississippi, University Museums, 73.3.196

In his mythic discourse on philosophic desire in the *Phaedrus*, by contrast,
Plato conceives of Eros as a god (*theos*). In his famous charioteer image, he
portrays the soul as a charioteer (reason) driving two horses (spirit and
appetite) and having wings. Plato takes the wings of Eros found in artistic
representations of the god and transfers these to the soul. The wings
symbolize the soul's eros for the Forms.[56] In his mythic representation of
the human soul in its preincarnate state, Plato portrays the soul as flying in
the heavens with the gods, who also have wings. In Plato's myth, these souls
fly up to the edge of the universe and contemplate the Forms. The gods too
are souls, and the fact that they have wings indicates that they also experience

---

[56] I capitalize "Eros" in passages where Plato refers to the god Eros; I use "eros" for all other passages.

eros. Since the gods themselves desire the Forms, I identify Eros as "divine desire." Both divine and human souls have a divine desire for the Forms.[57]

Plato's dialogues on eros focus in particular on the Form of Beauty. Since philosophic desire aims at the Forms in general, we must ask why Plato placed such great emphasis on beauty. As I argue, beauty has a unique "presence-effect" in human life (I borrow this term from Sepp Gumbrecht).[58] When we perceive beauty, we know this immediately. By contrast, when we identify justice, courage, and other virtues in the actions of an individual, we do not grasp this right away. In these cases, we take time to judge a person's actions. We identify a person or action as just, courageous, etc., only in retrospect. Of course, in some cases, we can identify someone as just or courageous relatively quickly, but we still must make this judgment in reference to our social and political values. In the case of beauty, we see it right away without consulting our values. To be sure, we may interrogate the ethical aspects of our experience of beauty retrospectively – "should I really have enjoyed seeing that beautiful object"? – but beauty always reveals itself in the present. As I suggest, Plato reached for the presence-effect of beauty to represent the "presentness" of the Forms. For Plato, a Form always exists, and it is disclosed to the philosophic mind as a presence. To conjure up the presentness of the Forms, Plato turned to the Form of Beauty. Just as beauty has a presence-effect in human life on earth, the Form of Beauty manifests itself in its full presence to the philosophic contemplator. All the Forms have this presentness, but Plato chose to portray the philosophic vision of the Form of Beauty to capture this idea. Indeed, he uses the metaphor of "seeing" precisely to emphasize the immediate presence of the Form to the eye of the mind.[59]

---

[57] As I argue, Plato does not conceive of *daimôn* or *theos* Eros as a god acting from outside the human soul. Erotic desire resides in the soul itself. Plato represents *daimôn* and *theos* Eros in mythic terms to present his new theological conception of eros.

[58] Gumbrecht 2004. Gumbrecht focuses on presence-effects in terms of phenomenology (not in terms of Plato's metaphysics). He distinguishes between "presence-effects" and "meaning-effects" – a person takes in the presence-effect of an event without imposing any sense of meaning. Gumbrecht gives examples of watching the performance of a Noh drama or a football game. As he claims, in cases like these, the presence and meaning-effects oscillate.

[59] This does not mean that every philosopher sees the Forms all at once. Rather, more or less mature philosophers will grasp the Forms at different levels: the perfected philosopher will contemplate the Forms in their fullness, while the developing philosopher will see and know one and another Form over a period of time. But the fact that philosophers dwell in time (and change over time) does not affect the being and presentness of the Forms.

Finally, in the dialogues on eros, Plato identifies this desire as lifting the philosophic mind *upwards* to the Forms. We see this rational ascent in the Ladder of Love in the *Symposium* and in "winged eros" in the *Phaedrus*. Although the Forms exist in an incorporeal realm outside of time and space, Plato depicts the soul's movement to the Forms in spatial terms: the soul ascends to higher beings. In the Greek imaginary, the gods lived up on Mount Olympus in the "aethereal" realm. Although gods could manifest themselves anywhere on earth, the poets represented the Olympian gods as living up above the clouds. Plato's notion of the Forms existing in a higher realm is based on the Greek idea that the gods live up above in a heavenly region. In his dialogues on eros, Plato represents the philosopher as ascending to the divine Forms.

0.4 Divine Epiphanies of the Forms and the Cosmos

Let me turn now to the philosopher's encounter with divinity when he contemplates the Forms or the divine cosmos. Plato presents two ways in which philosophers can see the divine: the rational contemplation of the Forms, and the astronomical study of the motions of the star-gods in the heavens. As I argue, when the philosophic soul grasps a Form, it also encounters the divine. To convey this idea, Plato uses poetic narratives of epiphany and refers to the initiate's divine revelation at the Eleusinian Mysteries. In addition, he represents divine epiphanies in the cosmology in the *Timaeus*: there, the cosmic soul shows its divinity to the philosopher by the orderly rotations of the "visible gods" in the heavens (*horatoi theoi*, 40d). In this late text, Plato reaches for the traditional Greek belief that gods appear to humans in material bodies.

To clarify these ideas, I will examine the phenomenon of divine epiphany in Greek culture in detail in Chapter 2. For now, I want to emphasize that the Greeks accepted divine epiphanies as real events. They believed that the gods revealed themselves in bodily forms to humans, and they actually perceived this phenomenon. As Georgia Petridou observes in her book on divine epiphany:

> It is important to recognize how culturally bound religious and perceptual experience really is. They are, in fact, as culturally specific as they are embedded in narratives. It is therefore essential to recognize that there is no such thing as a universal perceptual experience. Studies in socio-anthropology have emphasized the arbitrary and conventional character of representational systems; that is, the arbitrary and culturally conditioned

way we interpret, construct, and reconstruct reality in narratives and material objects.[60]

As Petridou rightly reminds us, we must examine the phenomenon of
epiphany in ancient Greece in its cultural context. The religious and
representational systems in ancient Greece provided them with a specific
sense of reality: the Greeks actually perceived their gods in bodily forms.

Of course the Greeks themselves had different beliefs about the gods and
their activities, and this ran along a spectrum. On the one end, we can place
the rationalist Thucydides, who did not give the gods any causal role in the
historical events he recounts in the *Histories*. Although he did represent the
Greeks as worshipping and consulting the gods regularly, Thucydides
himself only granted agency to human actions and natural events in his
historical account.[61] On the other end of the spectrum, we can put
Theophrastus' "Superstitious Man," who reacts to everything he sees as
manifesting a divine sign that calls for some sort of sacrifice, purification, or
ritual. For example, if he sees a reddish-brown snake in his house, he
invokes Sabazios, and if he encounters a "sacred snake," he immediately
sets up a hero shrine for it on that spot; and if he has a vivid dream, he goes
to dream-interpreters, prophets, and bird-augurers to find out what god to
pray to (*Characters* 16). Given this spectrum of beliefs, we must keep in
mind that not all Greeks shared the same ideas about the gods. Still, we
have a great deal of material and textual evidence for divine epiphanies.[62]
Indeed, starting in the third century BCE, the Greeks began to write texts
that recorded epiphanies that occured in different city-states at different
times in history.[63] In ancient Greece, divine epiphanies constituted a major
religious event. Indeed, they grounded religious cults and rituals. As Verity
Platt observes:

> Epiphany holds a special place within the category of divine signs as a form
> of unmediated encounter which, unlike oracular pronouncements or
> omens, can be experienced independently of preordained systems of spe-
> cialized interpretation. Indeed, *epiphany functions as the cognitive device by
> which such systems can be proven valid.* That the potential of the immediate
> visionary perception of a deity's *eidos* was an important element of Greek

---

[60] Petridou 2015: 12. See also Anderson 2018: chapter 10.
[61] This does not mean that Thucydides was an atheist. It simply means that he had a specific view of
the causality of events in the human world that did not include divine agency.
[62] I will discuss this in detail in Chapter 2.
[63] Istros *FGrH* 334 F 50–52, *Epiphanies of Apollo*; *FGrH* 53, *Epiphanies of Heracles*; Syriskos *FGrH* 801
F 1, *Epiphanies of the Maiden of the Chersonesos*. In the Lindian Chronicle, one section has the
heading "epiphanies" (*FGrH* 532 D).

thought is suggested by the frequency with which epiphanies occur within poetic and historiographical narratives, where they are closely related to both the establishment of cults and festivals and moments of crisis or change.[64]

As I argue, just as divine epiphanies provided the cognitive device that validated the Greek religious system, the philosopher's epiphanic vision of the Forms and the cosmos validates Plato's philosophical system.[65] Religion in general and divine epiphany in particular served as the matrix for Plato's thinking about the divine. As we will see, Plato presented a whole new conception of human beings and their relation to divine beings.[66]

The divine aspect of the Forms has important ontological and epistemological ramifications. During contemplation, the philosophic soul confronts a Being that is ontologically much higher than itself. The philosopher can know and define the essence of Beauty (for example), but he cannot fully comprehend its divinity. His epistemic and linguistic powers have their limits. He cannot grasp the divinity of a Form or the divine realm of the Forms in thought or in language.

While one can readily understand Plato's claim in the *Timaeus* that the star-gods manifest divinity to the philosophic viewer, one may find it difficult to grasp how the Forms disclose divinity to the philosopher. Let me offer a brief preview of a Form appearing as a divine being to the philosopher. Consider Diotima's description of the philosophic lover's ascent to the Form of Beauty in the Ladder of Love in the *Symposium*. After describing the beauties on each rung on the ladder, she turns to the Form of Beauty at the top rung. She first prepares Socrates for her unveiling of this Form by referring to two levels of initiation at the Eleusinian Mysteries: she distinguishes between the first initiation of the *mustês* and the higher initiation of the *epoptês* (209e–210a; quoted above). She compares the philosophic lover who ascends the ladder to the *epoptês*, the highest initiate at the mysteries. At the Eleusinian Mysteries, this initiate sees a divine epiphany at the climax of the ceremonies.[67] In referring to the Eleusinian Mysteries, then, Diotima suggests that the philosopher who sees

---

[64] Platt 2011: 55 (my italics).

[65] To be sure, the reader can only accept Plato's claims by seeing the Forms him or herself – he/she must see them in an "autopsy" ("seeing for oneself"). Plato cannot show the Forms to the reader, but he sets forth narratives of an ideal philosopher ascending to the Forms and seeing them in their fullness.

[66] Of course Plato had read presocratic thinkers and studied their different conceptions of god. Still, he did not develop his theological philosophy simply in reference to philosophic thinkers.

[67] I will discuss this in detail in Chapter 2.

the Form of Beauty will see the divine. In short, Plato uses the divinity-marker of the Eleusinian Mysteries to indicate that the Form of Beauty appears as a divine epiphany.

In this passage in the *Symposium*, Plato also marks the divinity of the Form by using the language of poetic narratives of epiphany. Let me give one example of this kind of narrative from the Homeric *Hymn to Apollo*, which shows the god manifesting himself in anthropomorphic, therio-morphic, and material forms. In this poem, Apollo takes over a ship of unwitting Cretans and leads them to Delphi, where they will serve as his priests. Apollo manifests himself to the Cretans in three different forms. First, he "suddenly" leaps on their ship in the form of a "monstrous dolphin" (401–4). The sailors feel wonder and fear. Apollo stays on-board as a dolphin and moves the ship to Delphi. There, he "leaps off" the ship in the form (*eidomenos*) of a star shining in the middle of the day, "flashing with sparks" and making the entire region "radiant" (440–2). After going into his temple and lighting a fire there, Apollo leaps "swift as thought" back onto the ship, now in the form (*eidomenos*) of a "beautiful and powerful" man (450–1). Apollo then identifies himself by name to the sailors and proclaims that they will serve at his temple in Delphi. This poetic scene features key elements from poetic narratives of epiphany: the wondrousness of the appearance of the dolphin, star, and man; the suddenness of these events; and the beauty and radiance of the god. In each case, Apollo appears in a form that is saturated with divine and numinous elements. The Greeks identified a divine manifestation of a god by way of its radiance, beauty, or wondrousness. The god appeared as a "saturated phenomenon" (to borrow Jean-Luc Marion's term).[68]

In his discourse on the Form of Beauty, Plato draws on poetic narratives of epiphany. For example, as Diotima states in the *Symposium*: "he who has been educated in erotic matters up to this point, and has seen beauties in the right order, reaches the goal of his erotic pursuits: *suddenly* he will see a *beauty wondrous* in nature" (ἐξαίφνης κατόψεταί τι θαυμαστὸν τὴν φύσιν καλόν; 210e, my italics). In referring to this sudden and wondrous beauty, she indicates that the philosopher will have an epiphanic encounter with a divine being.

Plato uses both the Eleusinian Mysteries and Poetic Narratives of Epiphany divinity-markers to present a new kind of divine epiphany:

[68] I borrow this term from Jean-Luc Marion because it has great descriptive power. However, I do not use his phenomenological model (or the Kantian discourse that subtends it).

Beauty will not show itself (*phantasthêsetai*) to him [the philosopher] *as a face or hands or any other thing that partakes of the body*, or as some language or knowledge; it does not exist anywhere *in some other thing, such as in an animal or on earth or in the heavens*, but itself in itself with itself it is always singular in form, and all other beautiful things partake in it in such a way that, while these other things come into being and pass away, it doesn't become greater or smaller, nor does it suffer any change. (211a–b)[69]

This passage presents many important ideas about the Forms that require careful investigation (see Chapter 2). Here, I simply want to focus on one aspect of Beauty's "showing itself" to the philosophic viewer.

By referring to the *epoptês* at the Eleusinian Mysteries and using language from poetic narratives of epiphany, Plato signals to the reader that Beauty appears to the philosopher as a divine epiphany. In the passage above, he first presents this idea in negative terms, stating that Beauty does not appear in a *human form* (with face and hands), in an *animal form*, or in a form seen *on earth or in the heavens*. Here, Plato refers to the traditional Greek belief that gods could appear to humans in the forms of humans, animals, or natural and heavenly bodies. He thus brings up the traditional idea that a divine being could appear in human, animal, and natural forms only to reject it. Beauty does not appear *in* anything on earth but rather "itself by itself." In short, Plato walks the reader through three possible kinds of divine epiphanies – gods appearing in anthropomorphic, theriomorphic and elemental forms – but then introduces a new kind of divine epiphany: the philosopher sees the divine Form itself, face to face (as it were).

******

Let me say a few words about the organization of this book. I devote a single chapter to four dialogues: the *Symposium*, *Phaedo*, *Phaedrus*, and *Timaeus*. I find it impossible to interpret Plato's ideas without examining them in the context of the dialogue as a whole. I decided not to write on the *Republic* or the *Laws* because I could not investigate Plato's theological thinking without offering a full account of each dialogue. This would have required a second volume. I do examine important passages from the *Republic* throughout the book and discuss *Laws* 10 in the chapter on the *Timaeus*. I should admit that investigating the theological aspects of Plato's

---

[69] οὐδ᾽ αὖ φαντασθήσεται αὐτῷ τὸ καλὸν οἷον πρόσωπόν τι οὐδὲ χεῖρες οὐδὲ ἄλλο οὐδὲν ὧν σῶμα μετέχει, οὐδέ τις λόγος οὐδέ τις ἐπιστήμη, οὐδέ που ὂν ἐν ἑτέρῳ τινι, οἷον ἐν ζῴῳ ἢ ἐν γῇ ἢ ἐν οὐρανῷ ἢ ἔν τῳ ἄλλῳ, ἀλλ᾽ αὐτὸ καθ᾽ αὑτὸ μεθ᾽ αὑτοῦ μονοειδὲς ἀεὶ ὄν, τὰ δὲ ἄλλα πάντα καλὰ ἐκείνου μετέχοντα τρόπον τινὰ τοιοῦτον, οἷον γιγνομένων τε τῶν ἄλλων καὶ ἀπολλυμένων μηδὲν ἐκεῖνο μήτε τι πλέον μήτε ἔλαττον γίγνεσθαι μηδὲ πάσχειν μηδέν. (211a–b).

philosophy goes entirely against my training. This book charts a new path for myself and, I hope, for other scholars.

In Chapter 1, "The Forms, the Good, and the Divine," I begin by offering a brief account of the theory of Forms. Plato presented the Forms in terms of the dichotomies of Being/becoming and the intelligible/sensible. The former focuses on ontology, the latter on epistemology. I examine Plato's claim that the Forms are "Beings" (*ta onta*) or Being (*ousia*). I then discuss the "ideal attributes" of the Forms, i.e., the attributes that mark out the Forms qua Forms.[70] As Plato suggests, the Forms exist everlastingly and are changeless, eternal, uniform, and separate from the physical realm. Every single Form has these ideal attributes in addition to its own proper essence. When Plato refers to the Forms by way of some group of attributes, he often puts *theios* in this list. Can we identify "divine" as an ideal attribute of the Forms?

To address this issue, I analyze the passages in the middle-period dialogues that have the divinity-marker "divine" (*theios*). As we will see, Plato sometimes indicates that an individual Form (the Good, the Beautiful) is divine. More often, he calls the group of the Forms divine. As I argue, we should accept "divine" as an ideal attribute of the Forms even though this attribute cannot be fully analyzed by reason. In my view, we need to examine the Forms in theological as well as philosophical terms.

I close the chapter by discussing the highest divinity in Plato's philosophy, the Form of the Good. Plato presents this in a single dialogue, the *Republic*. He showcases the Good in the Analogy of the Sun-god (as I call it),[71] the Analogy of the Line, and the Allegory of the Cave. In these imagistic accounts, he represents the philosophic soul as apprehending the divine Good. If we follow the Analogy of the Sun-god, just as the Sun-god bathes the physical realm in its light, the divine Good bathes the realm of the Forms in its light. Indeed, as Plato indicates, the philosopher cannot know a Form (or anything else) without understanding its relation to the Good. He must relate everything in the realm of Being to the divine Good. If he does this properly, the philosopher glimpses the divinity of the Good whenever he engages in contemplation. The Good thus makes an epiphanic appearance to the philosophic contemplator.

---

[70] See Keyt 1969 for the terminology of "ideal" and "proper" attributes. He takes this idea from Aristotle's argument in *Topics* 137b3–13 (cf. 113a24–32, 144a4–22, 154a18–20), where Aristotle distinguishes between ideal and proper attributes.

[71] Plato uses the word *theos* twice when he introduces the Sun: *theôn, theon* (508a). I will discuss this in detail in Chapter 1.

In Chapter 2, "Eternal Longings," I discuss Plato's account of the soul, eros, and the philosophic ascent to the Form of Beauty in the *Symposium*.[72] Plato's ideas about the soul vary in the middle-period dialogues. In the *Symposium*, Plato conceives of the soul as mortal. In this text, a mortal philosopher contemplates a divine and eternal Form. As I argue, "daimonic eros" allows the mortal human to grasp the divine Forms.

Socrates' speech on eros features two kinds of desire: the desire for immortality and the metaphysical desire for the Forms. I discuss these desires separately even though Socrates weaves these together in his speech. Let us look briefly at the first kind of eros. As Socrates claims, all humans naturally desire immortality. Since they are mortal, however, they can only gain a partial immortality by giving birth to offspring that keep them alive in the minds of men after they die. Socrates valorizes the birthgiving of the soul over that of the body: the soul gives birth to offspring such as lawcodes, poems, inventions, and philosophic discourses. If these procreations are good, people in future generations will keep the person who created them alive for long periods of time. As Socrates indicates, psychic birthgiving provides the best way of achieving a partial immortality.

In desiring immortality, the individual wants an everlasting self. This desire has an internal object, as it were: one wants an immortal "me." Let us contrast this to the philosophic eros for the Forms, which I call "metaphysical desire." In contrast to the desire for immortality, which everyone feels, only the philosopher fully experiences metaphysical desire. This kind of desire directs him to an external and divine being that is ontologically higher than himself. Indeed, when the philosopher contemplates the Forms, he transcends himself for a period of time. While the desire for immortality aims for "more me," metaphysical desire drives the philosopher to transcend his human self while he contemplates the Forms.

In the *Symposium*, Socrates differs from the other speakers by insisting that Eros is a *daimôn*, not a god.[73] I will examine the *daimôn* Eros in the context of Greek views about *daimones* as well as in relation to Socrates' *daimonion* ("divine voice"). As Socrates claims, daimons function as intermediaries between humans and the gods; indeed, daimons bring humans

---

[72] Scholars generally place the *Phaedo* before the *Symposium* in terms of its date (although this has been debated). I do not want to wade into scholarly debates about dating. I have chosen to analyze the *Symposium* first because it focuses only on one Form and presents a brief representation of the soul's contemplation of the Forms. I begin with the simplest model and then move towards more complex accounts of the soul and Forms.

[73] Socrates presents Diotima's ideas in his speech. In my view, Diotima speaks for Plato. We should not identify Socrates with Plato.

into contact with the gods. Eros is a special kind of daimon, however, because he brings the philosopher into contact with the divine Forms rather than with the gods. Plato presents this idea about the *daimôn* Eros in mythic and rhetorical terms. For this reason, I do not identify eros as an actual divine being that acts from outside the soul. Rather, I claim that the soul itself has a "daimonic desire" that allows it to ascend to a divine realm.

Finally, Plato compares the philosopher ascending the Ladder of Love to the highest initiate (the *epoptês*) in the Eleusinian Mysteries. I present a detailed account of this mystery cult and the divine revelation that the initiate had at the climax of the initiation ceremony. As I argue, Plato refers to the Eleusinian *epoptês'* epiphanic vision of the goddess for a specific reason: to portray the philosopher as having an epiphany of the Form of Beauty. The philosophic soul sees the divine when it contemplates the Form of Beauty.

In Chapter 3, "Dialogue of Self and Soul," I discuss the philosophical and theological aspects of the soul and the Forms in the *Phaedo*. This dialogue features two dramas: that of Socrates as a human individual and that of the immortal soul. Since this is his last day on earth, Socrates stands at the threshold between his human life and the life of the soul that presently dwells in him. Indeed, Socrates speaks in the first person both as an individual on earth and as an everlasting soul heading for the next place on its journey. His "I" oscillates between the mortal individual to the immortal soul. Plato creates a threshold narrative that brings together the human individual and the immortal soul to explore ideas about the soul, the body, and immortality. In his view, the soul does not belong in a body, which is "alien" (*allotrion*) to it. Indeed, while living on earth, the soul should separate itself from the body and contemplate the Forms. In this way, the philosopher "practices death." This activity prepares his soul for a final release from the body and an everlasting life with the Forms. As I suggest, we cannot disentangle Plato's philosophic conception of the soul from his views about the salvation of the soul.

In the *Phaedo*, Plato sets forth the first full account of the immortal soul. He offers four arguments for the immortality of the soul, and presents a number of important ideas about the soul, especially its incarnation in bodies and its capacity to contemplate the incorporeal Forms. As he indicates, each soul retains its own identity as it lives in one body after another. Indeed, it can recollect its preincarnate vision of the Forms. Plato also introduces key ideas about the Forms in this text. He identifies the Forms as existing, invisible, changeless, eternal, and separate from the physical world. In this dialogue, Plato puts great emphasis on the realm of Forms – the incorporeal "place" where the philosophic soul goes when it separates from the body. This idea plays a key role in his narrative of salvation: after death, the perfect philosophical soul departs for the divine realm of the Forms and lives there everlastingly without a body.

Plato presents a number of new ideas about the soul in this text, parceling them out in different sections of the dialogue. To gain a full conception of the soul, I examine three arguments for the immortality of the soul – the Cyclical Argument, the Recollection Argument, and the Affinity Argument. These arguments deal with the "where," "when," and "what" of the soul. That is, they focus on (1) the places where the soul can dwell; (2) the time when the soul lived with the Forms and the temporal expanse of its life; and (3) what the soul is in terms of its substance. In particular, Plato conceives of the soul as immortal, everlasting, intelligent, capable of animating and moving bodies, and subject to reincarnation. I discuss his claim that the soul is "like" and "akin to" the Forms, and show the likenesses and the differences between these two beings. The soul has a kinship with the Forms insofar as it is invisible, godlike, and ontologically separate from the bodily realm. This kinship makes it gravitate to the Forms when it separates itself from the body. I also examine the soul's *nous* in the immortality arguments and in Socrates' discussion of Anaxagoras' cosmic *nous*.

In the *Phaedo*, Plato uses the Orphic divinity-marker for the soul and the Forms quite extensively. First, he borrows the Orphic language of "purification" (*katharsis*) and "release" (*lusis*). The Orphics used these terms in a religious sense: a soul living in a human body had to "purify" itself through rituals and undergo initiation so that it could be "released" at death and live with the gods in Hades. In Plato's reconception of these Orphic ideas, the philosophic soul "purifies" itself by separating itself from the body and contemplating the Forms. In doing this, it actualizes its divine capacities and becomes godlike. When its human body dies, the philosophic soul will be "released" from the body so that it can dwell in the divine realm of the Forms. Indeed, Plato uses the Orphic notion that the initiated soul "will dwell forever with the gods," but he applies this to the divine realm of the Forms. Finally, the Orphics very likely enacted a ritual of death in the initiation ceremony. As Alberto Bernabé suggests, for those celebrating the Orphic Mysteries, there "was indeed a sort of *imitatio mortis* in which they 'rehearsed' the transit to the netherworld so as to overcome their fear of death by hoping for their transition to the next life, as a kind of preparatory treatment against the real experience of death."[74]

[74] Bernabé 2016: 28.

As I argue, Plato borrowed this Orphic idea to claim that the philosophers had to "practice death."

Once Plato envisioned the soul as immortal, he had to give it a storyline. Otherwise, it would just be one damned life after another. Plato sets forth a "story of the soul" in the *Phaedo*, which he develops further in later dialogues. In this text, he works with Orphic ideas about the fall of the soul into bodies and its final salvation. The Orphic myths presented a cosmogony and an anthropology that effectively gives the immortal soul a plotline. For the Orphics, the human soul has divine origins but ends up in a mortal body as a punishment for an original crime against Dionysus. The soul falls into the body as a "prison," and it longs to escape from this misery. The soul will reincarnate endlessly unless it purifies itself and undergoes initiation. When an individual gets initiated, his or her soul is forgiven by the gods for its original crime and escapes from the cycle of reincarnation. Indeed, after the initiated person dies, its soul will go to live happily and everlastingly with the gods. It thus returns to its divine origins.

Plato based his story of the soul on Orphic myths and rituals. Plato's soul has a blessed preincarnate beginning, a period of incarnation and reincarnation in the prison of the body, and a possible return to its blessed state by the practice of philosophy. Although Plato used many sources to portray the life and journey of the soul, he borrowed heavily from the Orphics. In the *Phaedo*, Plato not only used the Orphics to mark the divinity of the Forms and the soul, but adopted elements of the Orphic anthropology to create a narrative of salvation. In short, the Orphic divinity-marker plays a complex role in the *Phaedo*. I discuss the Orphics in detail to show how this mystery religion influenced Plato's philosophy.

In Chapter 4, "Wings of Desire," I discuss Plato's conception of the soul, eros, and the Forms in the *Phaedrus*. By the time he wrote this dialogue, Plato had identified the soul as immortal, tripartite, and subject to reincarnation. In this text, he presents a new and important idea: the soul is the "first principle of motion" in the universe. All bodily motion ultimately derives from the soul. In addition to this new conception of the soul, Plato portrays Eros as a god, not a daimon. He identifies eros as a divine aspect of the human soul and the souls of the gods. In the *Phaedrus*, Plato moves beyond his conception of the "daimonic desire" of the mortal soul in the *Symposium*: here, the immortal soul has a "divine desire."

Plato gives the Forms a number of divinity-markers in this text. He also creates a mythic narrative that brings human souls, gods, and the Forms together in a sort of proto-cosmology. Plato portrays the gods as divine souls that move the heavenly bodies. They also contemplate the Forms with their perfect minds. Plato locates the Forms outside the edge of the heavens in a *hyperouranios topos*. Within this cosmological context, he depicts the gods and human souls as flying up to the edge of the physical universe and looking beyond that to see the Forms. Indeed, he indicates that the gods possess divinity by apprehending the divine realm of the Forms. Likewise, human souls can become godlike by contemplating the Forms. Plato thus brings the gods, the cosmos, and the Forms together into a single system. He places a salvational narrative of the human soul in this cosmic context.

The soul plays the starring role in this dialogue. This tripartite soul has a rational part, a spirited part, and an appetitive part. Plato portrays these three parts of the soul in a powerful image: a charioteer driving two horses, one white and one black (reason, spirit, and appetite). In addition – and this is key – all souls are winged. The wings signify erotic desire. The human soul, before incarnation, had wings, as do all the gods, but it loses most of its wings when it incarnates in a body. The wings, a "fourth" element in the tripartite soul, move the soul upwards to the Forms.[75] Plato's conception of the soul in this dialogue goes beyond the tripartite theory of the soul in the *Republic*. Although that dialogue featured philosophic eros, it did not identify this as a divine desire.[76]

The *Phaedrus* features many divine elements. At the opening of the dialogue, Socrates and Phaedrus sit down in a "sacred place" with a shrine of the nymphs and an altar of Boreas nearby. They proceed to discuss an Athenian myth that generated the erection of the altar to Boreas. The myth features a god "possessing" a human: the wind-god Boreas snatches Oreithuia, the daughter of the Athenian king Erechtheus, so that he can impregnate her and beget the wind-gods Calais and Zetes (the "Boreads"). Socrates raises a key theological question about this story: how should one interpret this and other myths about the gods? Should they accept the literal meaning of the myth or read it in naturalistic terms? I discuss this topic in terms of Plato's conception of myth and its theological capacities.

Divine inspiration and madness (*mania*) come up repeatedly in this dialogue. In Socrates' second speech, he identifies four kinds of inspiration: priests or priestesses inspired at oracular centers; poets inspired by the

---

[75] I am not suggesting that the soul has four parts. Rather, Plato depicts the three parts of the soul as the charioteer and two horses, and then he adds the wings so that he can represent a distinct and divine aspect of the soul: the eros of the rational part of the soul.

[76] On philosophic eros in the *Republic*, see especially 490a–b. For a good discussion of eros in the *Republic*, see Ludwig 2007.

Muses; initiates inspired by Dionysus in mystery rites; and the philosopher inspired by Eros. The Greeks accepted divine possession and understood it within the framework of religious rites and institutions. They identified certain individuals as divinely inspired by way of the roles they played in specific cultural contexts. Indeed, in many cases, a possessed individual entered an altered state of consciousness that gave him or her a heightened level of discourse. Although the Greeks did recognize mental illness as a disease, they did not identify divinely inspired individuals as mentally ill. The inspired person's altered state of consciousness featured a different kind of *mania*. For the Greeks, *mania* had a much wider range of meaning than "madness" in the modern sense. To make this clear, I will discuss Greek conceptions of divine inspiration and madness in detail.

How should we interpret Plato's conception of *theos* Eros in this dialogue? In his second speech, Socrates states that Eros inspires the philosopher with divine "madness" (*mania*) that allows him to contemplate the Forms.[77] Since he presents this idea in mythic terms, however, we cannot interpret this claim literally. As I argue, the god Eros does not act on the philosopher externally. Rather, Plato puts eros inside the rational part of the soul: reason has a divine desire for the Forms. In this dialogue, Plato presents the paradox that philosophic wisdom takes the form of divine madness. This raises questions about what he means by "reason" or the "rational part of the soul." Plato had already conceived of the soul's reason as having eros in the *Republic* (490a–b), but he now conceives of eros as bringing on *mania*. The philosopher now has a "manic mind," as it were, that enables him to ascend to the Forms. The love-mad philosopher achieves an enhanced state of mind, "manic reason."

To articulate these theological ideas, Plato uses discourses from the Eleusinian Mysteries and poetic narratives of divine epiphanies. Indeed, in Socrates' second speech, he presents two epiphanic narratives that represent the soul contemplating the Forms. In the first epiphanic narrative, the soul saw the Forms before it was incarnated; in the second, a philosophic lover sees the Form of Beauty as he beholds the beauty of his beloved boyfriend. In both of these narratives, Plato uses Eleusinian and Poetic Narratives of Epiphany divinity-markers in his descriptions of the soul's vision of the Forms. These indicate that the philosopher sees a divine epiphany of Beauty during contemplation.

In Chapter 5, "The Gods Made Visible," I examine the soul, the gods, and the cosmos in the *Timaeus*. In this late dialogue, Plato presents his

---

[77] I capitalize "Eros" in passages where Plato refers to the god Eros; I use "eros" for other passages.

fullest theological philosophy. He uses many of his middle-period theories about the Forms and the soul, but he brings them together in a new context. In particular, he retains his views on the ontological hierarchy of the Forms over the soul and body; the tripartite soul; the soul "becoming like god" by contemplating the Forms; and the salvational story of the soul. But Plato now puts the souls, bodies, gods, and Forms into a grand cosmic scheme. He thus introduces new ideas about the soul, the Forms, and the gods.

At the opening of his speech, Timaeus divides Being (*ousia*), i.e., the Forms, from "becoming" (*gignomenon*). He also introduces the Form of Animal (the "Intelligible Animal," *noêton zôon*), which serves as the paradigm for the animate cosmos. For the rest of the dialogue, Timaeus discusses the creation of the cosmos, including the cosmic soul and body and the human soul and body. This includes a discourse on the atomic triangles that make up the four elements and bodies, and the receptacle that gives bodily particulars a place to appear as they become something and then pass away. Finally, Timaeus presents a teleological system that grants human souls the possibility of leaving mortal bodies on earth and returning to their native stars.

To understand this complex theological cosmology, one has to examine the specific capacities and activities of the soul, including the divine cosmic soul, the star-gods, and the human soul. I place special emphasis on the human soul, which has the unique capacity to occupy multiple bodies. The Demiurge creates the human soul as divine, immortal, incorporeal, and rational. I call this the "rational human soul" to emphasize that this soul is reason through and through; only when incarnated in mortal bodies does it take on the two irrational parts of the soul (spirit and appetite). The Demiurge creates the rational human soul out of the same materials and in the same structure as the divine cosmic soul (though the materials are less pure). The rational human soul, then, is divine (though it has a lesser level of divinity). The soul starts out its life in a star-body and sees "the nature of the all," i.e., the universe. What does it actually grasp at this point in its life? Since the human soul has no sensory organs at this time, it cannot see the physical phenomena of the cosmos. It apprehends the nature of the universe purely at the intelligible level. I will examine the knowledge that the human soul gained at its first beginning.[78]

---

[78] Plato does not refer to the doctrine of recollection in this dialogue. Still, we must address the question of the rational human soul's knowledge when it lived in a star.

When incarnated in a body on earth, the rational human soul has one mission: to return to its native star. It can do this by practicing philosophy. This includes mastering astronomy. By studying the stars, the philosopher sees that they move in perfect circular motions in the heavens – motions that manifest the activity of a divine cosmic soul. Indeed, the incorporeal reason of the cosmic soul moves in circles. The philosopher must imitate the cosmic soul's rational motions and thereby perfect the circles in his own mind. In this way, his soul "becomes like god." If the soul lives a successful philosophical life, it leaves the mortal realm and returns to its native star.

In addition to having this individual mission, the rational human soul plays a key role in the cosmos. As Timaeus states, the Form of Animal included mortal beings, and thus the perfected cosmos must have mortal creatures. In addition, I argue, human souls help to perfect the cosmos by perceiving the universe at the phenomenal level. The cosmos has no eyes or sensory organs: it apprehends its own body rationally. Only humans can see and understand the cosmos at the phenomenal level. The Demiurge created the cosmos to be seen as well as understood. Indeed, the cosmos would be less perfect if it were not seen as a physical phenomenon. Only philosophers see the divinity, goodness, and beauty of the cosmos on both the intellectual and visual level. The cosmos can see itself, as it were, through the eyes of the philosopher.

In the *Timaeus*, Plato places special emphasis on human vision. As he indicates, the gods give humans the gift of vision so that they can under-stand number, study the cosmos, and practice philosophy. Indeed, Plato presents a complex theory of physical vision in this text: he shows how the eye, the object of vision, and light work together in visual perception. I examine Plato's theory of vision and show how the human capacity to see operates in the cosmic scheme.

As Plato indicates, humans have eyes so that they can study the heavens and see the "visible gods" (*horatoi theoi*). Seeing the perfect rotations of the star-gods allows the philosopher to see the divine workings of the cosmic soul. In this dialogue, Plato offers a different conception of the philosopher seeing a divine epiphany. He focuses on the physical vision of the stars rather than the intellectual vision of the divine realm of the Forms. Here, Plato uses traditional Greek ideas about divine epiphany: for the Greeks, the gods appeared in various bodily forms, including in heavenly bodies.

Beauty shines brightly in this dialogue. Plato calls the cosmos, the triangular atoms, and the four elements "beautiful," and describes the cosmos as a divine artwork or "*agalma*" that is a wonder to behold (37c). Indeed, the heavenly bodies in the cosmos perform a beautiful "choric dance" (*choreia*; 40c). Here, Plato refers to a cultural practice that was central to religious life in ancient Greece: circular dances performed for the gods at religious festivals. As Leslie Kurke observes, "a beautiful choral performance was thought to conjure divine presence at a festival, while for the space of the song and dance, the chorus and human audience fused or merged, and both were briefly assimilated to the divine."[79] Like ordinary spectators of choric dances, the philosophic viewers "fuse" with god – i.e., the cosmic god – when they behold the dance of the stars. In contrast to ordinary Greek spectators, however, the philosophers can actually "become like god" in a full way.

Finally, I discuss Plato's notion of time. As I suggest, the *Timaeus* features two kinds of time: divine time and earthly time. Plato famously presents the idea that time is the "moving image of eternity" (37d; *eikô. . .kineton tina aiônos*). In the passing of time, the cosmic soul moves its heavenly bodies in perfect rotations to enact a mobile "image" (*eikôn*) of the eternal and unchanging Form of Animal. The cosmos everlastingly, beautifully, and harmoniously imitates an incorporeal, eternal, and changeless Being in the medium of time, body, and space. Although the cosmos moves in time, it does not age or deteriorate or suffer the ill effects of time's forward arrow. The cosmic soul, with its perfect circular rotations and its ongoing contemplation of the Forms, dwells in "divine time." Humans, by contrast, age and deteriorate in time's forward arrow. They suffer diseases and bodily changes, and eventually die. Humans live in a different time zone, as it were, than the cosmic soul and the star gods. I call this "earthly time." The task of the philosopher is to learn how to dwell in divine time. This means that he must identify himself with his rational soul, not his mortal body. As Plato claims, the philosopher must correct the rational "circles" in his mind by studying the cosmic soul: in doing this, he attunes himself to divine time.

In the Conclusion, I bring together the different philosophical and theological ideas that have emerged in the dialogues. I examine the dramatic contexts of the *Symposium*, *Phaedo*, *Phaedrus*, and *Timaeus* – a symposium, a prison, a pastoral setting outside the city walls, and a private home – and show how this affects the mood of each text. I also investigate the mix of discourses that Plato uses in each dialogue. The topic, context, and discourses of each dialogue bring out different aspects of Plato's theological philosophy.

---

[79] Kurke 2012: 222.

Plato's theological philosophy has some clear and coherent strands, but it does not take on a systematic form. Rather, his thinking features the creative and magmatic interplay of analytic argument and theological discourse. To be sure, Plato regularly claimed that the philosopher must engage in dialogue and argumentation. This individual must give an account of his views and present arguments for his ideas. And Plato himself put a good deal of argumentation in his dialogues. To articulate the nature and manifestation of the divine, however, he reached for other kinds of discourse – myth, poetry, rhetoric, and allegory. Indeed, in Plato's texts, we confront an oscillation between the effable and the ineffable: the philosopher knows and gives an account of the essence of a Form, but he cannot put his encounter with divinity into language.

CHAPTER I

The Forms, the Good, and the Divine

When you consider the radiance, that it
does not withhold
itself but pours its abundance without
selection into every
nook and cranny not overhung or
hidden.   —Ammons, *The City Limits*

I shall speak in a clearer voice
fish will become fish
sea-weed will be sea-weed
and sea-monsters will remain as such
I shall no longer abuse words
turn fish into larks
sea-weed into rose-bushes and sea-monsters
into typewriters
All that will remain will be the mermaids
stripped clean of brine
by the distance of time   —Queneau, *Project*

The ancient Greeks conceived of the gods as having knowledge of the past
and the future. Humans, mere "creatures of a day," had finite and limited
minds. Some early Greek philosophers, however, claimed to have gained
the wisdom of the gods, having received this in a divine revelation or by
aligning their thoughts with the divine mind. Indeed, thinkers such as
Xenophanes, Parmenides, Heraclitus, Empedocles, and Diogenes of
Apollonia presented rich and varied ideas about god and the human
grasp of the divine.[1] Plato follows in this tradition by granting the
human soul the divine capacity to apprehend the divine realm of the
Forms.

---

[1] To be sure, Parmenides does not identify "what is" as divine. However, he does get access to "what is"
by way of a revelation from the goddess. To this extent, he comes to know divine truths.

In this chapter, I will present a brief outline of the theory of the Forms. This will provide the backdrop for later discussions of the Forms. I analyze the Forms in Plato's ontology and epistemology. I also discuss the "ideal attributes" of the Forms, that is, the attributes of the Forms qua Forms. Since Plato sometimes includes "divine" (*theios*) in lists of the Forms' attributes, I ask whether "divine" counts as an ideal attribute of the Forms. To offer evidence that "divine" is an ideal attribute of the Forms, I examine passages that feature the first of the six divinity-markers that Plato gives to the Forms, the adjective *theios*. I choose to focus on the *theios* divinity-marker because it explicitly marks the Forms as divine.

I close by discussing one exceptional Form, the Good. Plato discusses this in a single dialogue, the *Republic*. As I will argue, the Good has a unique divine status in Plato's metaphysics. Plato showcases the Good in the Analogy of the Sun-god (as I call it), the Analogy of the Line, and the Allegory of the Cave. After analyzing the causal and divine aspects of the Form of the Good, I claim that the Forms derive their being, essence, and divinity from the Good. The philosopher who apprehends an individual Form, then, will glimpse the divine Good illuminating the realm of the Forms. If this is on target, then, the Form of the Good has an epiphanic aspect. This discussion of the Good will set up my analysis of the soul, the Forms, and divine disclosure in later chapters.

1.1   The Forms and Their Attributes

Plato never presented a systematic account of the Forms. Scholars have to piece this together by examining passages on the Forms in different dialogues. It is beyond the scope of this book to analyze Plato's theory of Forms. Rather, I will outline the basic ideas in Plato's epistemology and ontology.

Plato's theory of Forms has its roots in Socrates' "what is it" questions. In Plato's early dialogues, Socrates asks, "what is courage?" or "what is piety?", and then attempts to find a definition that successfully answers this question. The "what is it" question focuses on the essence of a virtue. The early texts end aporetically – Socrates never provides a clear definition of the virtue in question. Plato's theory of Forms, which he lays out in the middle-period dialogues, offers a solution to Socrates' "what is it" question: for each property found in souls and in bodies, there is a distinct essence that exists in the intelligible realm. The Forms exist separately from all sensible instances. Plato identifies the Forms as "Being" (*ousia, to on*) and places these over and against the particulars, or "becoming" (*gignomenon*).

The latter term refers to the fact that things in the physical realm continuously change. The Forms are not immanent in the things of this world; rather, particulars in the physical realm "participate" or "have a share in" them. At times, however, Plato indicates that particulars "resemble," "imitate," or are an "image" of the Forms. In short, he presents several different conceptions of the relation of the particular to the Form. Plato never fully explains what he means by "participation" or "imitation," but he examines this topic in a late middle-period dialogue, the *Parmenides.* In that text, Socrates identifies participation in terms of resemblance (132d).

Plato regularly conceived of the Forms as "Being" (*ousia*) or "Beings" (*ta onta*). Indeed, in referring to the Forms, Plato can use the participle *on* (the Form "being" [something]), the substantive participle *to on* or *ta onta* ("that which exists," "those which exist"[2]), and the noun *ousia* ("being"). In addition, he identifies each Form as having its own essence. Thus, when Plato refers to a single Form and asks, for example, "what is Beauty?", he examines the essence of beauty. In addition, Plato conceives of the Form of Beauty as itself beautiful. This last claim has raised many scholarly questions about the self-predication of the Forms.[3]

Considered epistemologically, the Forms are objects of knowledge *par excellence.* In Plato's view, we cannot gain knowledge through our sensory apprehension of the world. Particulars in the physical world constantly change and can never provide a solid or stable object of knowledge. The Forms have properties that distinguish them from entities in the physical realm: they "exist," are "changeless," "eternal," "singular in form," and "separate" from the physical realm. Each Form has an essence that can be grasped by the mind trained in dialectic. The philosopher who apprehends a Form attains knowledge and truth.

To discuss Plato's epistemology, one has to address the three meanings of the verb *einai* ("to be"):

(1) Existential: the knowledge that something exists, or the knowledge of the existence of F
(2) Predicative: the knowledge of what it is to be F
(3) Veridical: the knowledge of the truth of F

Platonic scholars have offered detailed discussions of Plato's use of *einai* and its cognates in the passages on the Forms. They identify the meaning of *einai* by examining each passage in its context. In some cases, all three

---

[2] Scholars also translate this as "that which is real," "the realities."
[3] I will not discuss the scholarly controversy on this subject, which is beyond the scope of this study.

senses of this word are in play; in other cases, only one sense of the verb makes sense in the context. When we investigate a single Form, we do not simply look at its existential aspect (1). We want to understand not just *that it is* but also *what it is* (2). In short, we want to understand the essence of this individual Form. In addition, we want to know that the Form we conceive of actually exists, and that the definition of the essence we come up with matches the Form's essence. The philosopher who grasps a Form must provide a definition of its essence that is incontrovertibly true (3).

In Plato's epistemology, one has to both know and define the Form. Plato sometimes presents these as two distinct activities: one articulates a definition after one has grasped a Form. Of course, the philosopher examining the Forms will present an argument. However, Plato tends to depict the philosopher who contemplates a Form as "seeing" or "behold-ing" it (rather than discussing it during the time of contemplation). For example, he represents the philosopher at the top of the Ladder of Love or outside of the cave as looking at a Form all by himself. He does not engage in discussion during this time, though he may be debating ideas within his own mind. Of course Plato constructs an idealized picture of the philoso-pher ascending to the Forms. He wants to capture the idea of the mind transcending the social and physical realm to grasp the Forms. To be sure, there may be a guide in the early parts of the philosopher's intellectual journey to the Forms, but this individual sees the Forms entirely on his own. This experience is autoptic. Plato could have represented a collective philosophical ascent (cf. Augustine in *Confessions* 9, where he and Monica collectively and interactively ascend to God), but he resisted this idea.

Considered ontologically, the Forms are Beings (*to on, ta onta*) that stand in opposition to becoming (*to gignomenon, ta gignomena*).[4] They exist separately in an incorporeal, changeless, atemporal realm. Scholars refer to this division as the Two-World Theory. Indeed, Plato sometimes speaks of the "place" (*topos*) where the Forms exist, which he conceives of in opposition to the physical world qua place (*Rep.* 508c). Particulars in the realm of becoming are ontologically dependent on the Forms (but not vice versa). Note that the division between Being and becoming operates even in the absence of the human knower.

Particulars only take on their characteristics by "participating in" or "being an image of" the Forms. As I have mentioned, Plato does not fully

---

[4] Note that some scholars have claimed that Plato did not understand "to be" as a complete existential as well as an incomplete predicate (Michael Frede [1967, 1992], and G. E. L. Owen [1971]). I disagree with this position.

explain how participation or imitation works. He uses this terminology to indicate the ontological superiority of the Forms over the particulars. To cite one example from the *Phaedo*, Socrates says that when someone looks at two equal pieces of wood, he thinks: "the thing that I am seeing wants to be of such a kind as those things that exist [the Forms], but it falls short and is not able to be equal like that [the Form of Equal], and it is baser" (βούλεται μὲν τοῦτο ὃ νῦν ἐγὼ ὁρῶ εἶναι οἷον ἄλλο τι τῶν ὄντων, ἐνδεῖ δὲ καὶ οὐ δύναται τοιοῦτον εἶναι [ἴσον] οἷον ἐκεῖνο, ἀλλ᾽ ἔστιν φαυλότερον; 74d–e). The particular "falls short" of or is ontologically "deficient" in relation to the Forms. It takes on the property of a Form for a time by way of participating in it. Consider another example from the *Timaeus*, a late dialogue. Using the image model for the relation of the particular to the Form, Timaeus states: "The image, since that very thing [i.e. the Form] on account of which it comes into being does not belong to it, always moves around as a phantasm of something else – it is fitting that the image comes into being in something else, somehow clinging to Being or in itself is nothing at all" (ὡς εἰκόνι μέν, ἐπείπερ οὐδ᾽ αὐτὸ τοῦτο ἐφ᾽ ᾧ γέγονεν ἑαυτῆς ἐστιν, ἑτέρου δέ τινος ἀεὶ φέρεται φάντασμα, διὰ ταῦτα ἐν ἑτέρῳ προσήκει τινὶ γίγνεσθαι, οὐσίας ἁμωσγέπως ἀντεχομένην, ἢ μηδὲν τὸ παράπαν αὐτὴν εἶναι; 52c). This reference to the particular as an "image" or "phantasm of something else," i.e., a Form, and as "clinging" to the Being of the Forms showcases the low ontological status of the particulars. To be sure, the *Timaeus* features a complex cosmology that goes well beyond the Form-particular ontology in the middle dialogues. But, even without this cosmological architecture, we find the same ontology of the Forms and particulars in the middle-period dialogues.

Let us turn now to the ideal attributes of the Forms. Scholars have identified the ideal attributes of the Forms as follows: they exist and are eternal, unchanging, intelligible, singular in form, imperishable, and separate from the physical realm. Plato often refers to the Forms by listing some or all of their ideal attributes. In a number of passages, he adds "divine" (*theios*) to a list of the Forms' attributes. This raises the question of whether "divine" is an ideal attribute of the Forms.

1.2 The Divinity-Marker *Theios* for the Forms

As I suggested in the Introduction, Plato identifies the Forms as divine by way of a number of different divinity-markers. Here, I will discuss the first divinity-marker for the Forms: the identification of an individual Form or the Forms taken as a group as "divine" (*theios*). Plato uses many different locutions for the Forms. We need to be alert to this as we examine the passages that have the *theios* divinity-marker. When Plato refers to the Forms by listing some of their properties, I put these properties in italics.

I want to look first at a key passage in the *Phaedo*. In an argument that the soul is "akin" to the Forms, Socrates states: "the soul is most like the *divine, immortal, intelligible, singular in form, imperishable,* and *always unchanging*" (τῷ μὲν θείῳ καὶ ἀθανάτῳ καὶ νοητῷ καὶ μονοειδεῖ καὶ ἀδιαλύτῳ καὶ ἀεὶ ὡσαύτως κατὰ ταὐτὰ ἔχοντι ἑαυτῷ ὁμοιότατον εἶναι ψυχή; 80b). Here, Plato refers to the Forms by giving a full list of their attributes: divine, eternal (immortal), intelligible, singular in form, imperishable, and unchanging. Scholars have identified "eternal, intelligible, singular in form, imperishable, and unchanging" as ideal attributes of the Forms (they would identify "immortal" as signifying "eternal"). Yet we also find "divine" in this list of the ideal attributes of the Forms. Indeed, as we will see, Plato regularly identifies the Forms as divine.

Let us turn now to other passages in the *Phaedo* that feature the *theios* divinity-marker. Consider Socrates' statement about the soul and the Forms: "[the philosopher's soul,] following reason and always being with it, beholding what is *true, divine,* and *not the object of opinion*, and being nourished by this, thinks that it must live in this way as long as it is alive, and when it dies, goes to what is akin to it and like itself and gains release from human evils" (ἑπομένη τῷ λογισμῷ καὶ ἀεὶ ἐν τούτῳ οὖσα, τὸ ἀληθὲς καὶ τὸ θεῖον καὶ τὸ ἀδόξαστον θεωμένη καὶ ὑπ᾽ ἐκείνου τρεφομένη, ζῆν τε οἴεται οὕτω δεῖν ἕως ἂν ζῇ, καὶ ἐπειδὰν τελευτήσῃ, εἰς τὸ συγγενὲς καὶ εἰς τὸ τοιοῦτον ἀφικομένη; 84a–b). Plato refers to the Forms as "true," "divine," and "not grasped by opinion" (*adoxaston*). We know that the latter locution refers to the Forms because Plato regularly says that the philosopher attains "knowledge" of the Forms and does not simply "opine" about them. In addition, the Forms "nourish" the soul (Plato often uses this metaphor in passages referring to the soul's contemplation of the Forms). Here again, Plato identifies the Forms as a group as "divine."

In the following passage, Plato refers to the Forms in slightly different terms. As Socrates states:

> Then if it [the soul] is in such a condition, it goes away to that which is like itself, to the *invisible, divine, immortal,* and *wise,* and when it arrives there it is happy, freed from error and folly and fear and fierce loves and all the other human ills and, as is said by the initated, truly lives with the gods for the rest of time. (οὐκοῦν οὕτω μὲν ἔχουσα εἰς τὸ ὅμοιον αὐτῇ τὸ ἀιδὲς ἀπέρχεται, τὸ θεῖόν τε καὶ ἀθάνατον καὶ φρόνιμον, οἷ ἀφικομένη

ὑπάρχει αὐτῇ εὐδαίμονι εἶναι, πλάνης καὶ ἀνοίας καὶ φόβων καὶ ἀγρίων ἐρώτων καὶ τῶν ἄλλων κακῶν τῶν ἀνθρωπείων ἀπηλλαγμένῃ, ὥσπερ δὲ λέγεται κατὰ τῶν μεμυημένων, ὡς ἀληθῶς τὸν λοιπὸν χρόνον μετὰ θεῶν διάγουσα; 81a)

While Plato regularly uses "invisible," "immortal," and "divine" to refer to the Forms, he does not generally identify them as "wise" (*phronimon*). Indeed, "wise" seems to conjure up conscious beings such as the gods. One could argue that Plato refers to the gods rather than the Forms here. However, he does not refer to the gods using substantive adjectives (*to aides, to theion*): this locution refers to the Forms. In addition, in the *Phaedo*, Plato explicitly associates "the invisible" with the Forms (not the gods). He makes this point by first positing two kinds of beings in the universe (*eidē tôn ontôn*), the "visible and the invisible" (*to men horaton, te de aidês*). He then defines this division as follows: "the invisible is always the same and the visible is never the same" (τὸ μὲν ἀιδὲς ἀεὶ κατὰ ταὐτὰ ἔχον, τὸ δὲ ὁρατὸν μηδέποτε κατὰ ταὐτά; 79a). Plato thus separates the realm of the Forms, "the invisible," which never changes and is always the same, from the physical and visible realm, where things endlessly change. This Form-particular dualism does not include the gods, which are incorporeal but can move and change in terms of location. Thus, this passage refers to the Forms, not the gods. Here again, Plato identifies the Forms as a group as divine.

Let us look at one final passage in the *Phaedo* that refers to the divinity of the Forms. Socrates asserts this negatively, in terms of the non-philosopher's failure to grasp the Forms: the non-philosophical soul "has no portion in the being-together-with (*sunousia*) the *divine* and *pure* and *singular in form*" (ἄμοιρος εἶναι τῆς τοῦ θείου τε καὶ καθαροῦ καὶ μονοειδοῦς συνουσίας; 83e). We find one instance of an ideal attribute of the Form in this passage, "singular in form" (*tou ... monoeidous*). As scholars have observed, Plato regularly uses the definite article *to* with an adjective or participle to refer to the Forms as a group: the most common example of this is *to on*. In this passage, then, "the singular in form" (*to monoeidês*) refers not to one Form but to all of them. Plato once again identifies the group of Forms as divine. We may wonder what he means by speaking of the soul's "being-together-with" (*sunousia*) the Forms. This *sunousia* cannot involve the interaction of two living, conscious beings, for the Forms are not personal agents (indeed, they do not change at all). Rather, in contemplation, one kind of being, the soul, has a "being-together-with" a different kind of being, i.e., the Being of the Forms.

We turn now to Plato's use of the divinity-marker *theios* in the *Symposium*. In this dialogue, which only focuses on one Form, we find one use of *theios* for the Form of Beauty. As Diotima asks: "what if he [the lover] could look upon divine beauty itself, unique in its form?" (ἀλλ᾽ αὐτὸ τὸ θεῖον καλὸν δύναιτο μονοειδὲς κατιδεῖν; 211e). Here, Plato clearly identifies Beauty as divine. As we will see in the next chapter, Plato gives other divinity-markers to the Form of Beauty in this dialogue.

In Socrates' second speech in the *Phaedrus*, Plato uses *theios* for the Forms twice. First, he identifies "the divine" (*to theion*) with the Forms: "the divine is beautiful, wise, good, and all things of this kind: by these the wings of the soul are most of all nourished and grow" (τὸ δὲ θεῖον καλόν, σοφόν, ἀγαθόν, καὶ πᾶν ὅτι τοιοῦτον: τούτοις δὴ τρέφεταί τε καὶ αὔξεται μάλιστά γε τὸ τῆς ψυχῆς πτέρωμα; 246d–e). To be sure, Plato does not directly identify beauty, wisdom, or goodness as Forms in this passage, but the metaphor of nourishment makes this point clear. For Plato uses this metaphor several times in Socrates' speech specifically to refer to the soul contemplating the Forms. For example, as Socrates states: "the fitting pasture for the best part of the soul is in the meadow there [the realm of the Forms], and the nature of the wing, by which the soul is lifted up, is nourished by this" (οὗ δ᾽ ἕνεχ᾽ ἡ πολλὴ σπουδὴ τὸ ἀληθείας ἰδεῖν πεδίον οὗ ἐστιν, ἥ τε δὴ προσήκουσα ψυχῆς τῷ ἀρίστῳ νομὴ ἐκ τοῦ ἐκεῖ λειμῶνος τυγχάνει οὖσα, ἥ τε τοῦ πτεροῦ φύσις, ᾧ ψυχὴ κουφίζεται, τούτῳ τρέφεται; 248b–c). He also says that the divine souls who ascend to the edge of the heavens to contemplate the Forms go to a "meal and a feast" (*daita, thoinên*; 247a). Based on these verbal parallels, we can identify "the divine" that "nourishes" the wings of the soul in the passage above (246e) as the Forms of the Good, Beauty, and Wisdom and "all things of this kind." If this is on target, then Plato is once again suggesting that the group of Forms is divine, though he gives Goodness, Beauty, and Wisdom pride of place in this group.

Let us look at another example of the *theios* divinity-marker in the *Phaedrus*. As Socrates states, the philosopher gets "as close as possible, by way of recollection, to those things [the Forms] by *being close to which god is divine*" (πρὸς γὰρ ἐκείνοις ἀεί ἐστιν μνήμη κατὰ δύναμιν, πρὸς οἷσπερ θεὸς ὢν θεῖός ἐστιν; 249c, my italics). The gods are divine because they continually contemplate the Forms.[5] This indicates that the Forms themselves must have divinity. To be sure, Plato makes this point indirectly: we infer

---

[5] One also finds this idea in the *Timaeus*, a late-period dialogue, where the cosmic soul maintains perfect goodness and wisdom by contemplating the Forms.

the divinity of the Forms by way of the gods. Still, the logic of the sentence makes this clear. Since Plato refers to the Forms in the plural in this passage, he grants divinity to the Forms as a group.

Plato also uses the *theios* divinity-marker for the Forms in the *Republic.* For example, using the analogy of the soul's kinship with the Forms, Socrates states: "[the philosophic rulers] should examine the soul's love of wisdom and consider the things that it grasps and the sort of things it desires and associates with, since it is *akin* to that which is *divine, immortal,* and *always existing*" (εἰς τὴν φιλοσοφίαν αὐτῆς, καὶ ἐννοεῖν ὧν ἅπτεται καὶ οἵων ἐφίεται ὁμιλιῶν, ὡς συγγενὴς οὖσα τῷ τε θείῳ καὶ ἀθανάτῳ καὶ ἀεὶ ὄντι; 611e). Plato clearly refers to the Forms here ("always existing"). In addition, he regularly speaks of the philosophic soul as "desiring" the Forms and having a "kinship" with them. Here again, Plato identifies the group of the Forms as divine.

In *Republic* 6, Plato indicates that the soul becomes divine by contemplating the Forms. As Socrates observes:

> When the philosopher observes and sees things *that are ordered and always the same* [i.e. the Forms], and sees that they do not wrong one another or suffer wrong, but are all in harmony and in accordance with reason, he imitates them and likens himself to them as much as possible. Or do you think that there is any way for someone to associate with something he admires and not to imitate it? . . . The philosopher, associating himself with *what is harmonious and divine* (*theiôi*), becomes harmonious and divine (*theios*) as much as is possible for humans. (500c–d)[6]

Plato suggests that the philosopher achieves a divine state by contemplating the "divine" Forms. Once again, he refers to the group of Forms as "divine."

Plato also identifies the philosopher as engaging in a "divine" contemplative activity in the Allegory of the Cave: when the philosopher comes back down into the cave after contemplating the Forms, "he returns from divine theorizings" (ἀπὸ θείων . . . θεωριῶν . . . ἐλθών; 521d). In addition, he calls the intellectual virtue of the philosopher contemplating the Forms "divine." As Socrates states in a discussion of intellectual and moral virtue: "the virtue of thought (*phronêsai*), as it seems, is a more divine (*theioterou*) thing [than moral virtue], and never loses its power" (ἡ δὲ τοῦ φρονῆσαι

---

[6] *Rep.* 6.500c–d: ἀλλ᾽ εἰς τεταγμένα ἄττα καὶ κατὰ ταὐτὰ ἀεὶ ἔχοντα ὁρῶντας καὶ θεωμένους οὔτ᾽ ἀδικοῦντα οὔτ᾽ ἀδικούμενα ὑπ᾽ ἀλλήλων, κόσμῳ δὲ πάντα καὶ κατὰ λόγον ἔχοντα, ταῦτα μιμεῖσθαί τε καὶ ὅτι μάλιστα ἀφομοιοῦσθαι. ἢ οἴει τινὰ μηχανὴν εἶναι, ὅτῳ τις ὁμιλεῖ ἀγάμενος, μὴ μιμεῖσθαι ἐκεῖνο; . . . θείῳ δὴ καὶ κοσμίῳ ὅ γε φιλόσοφος ὁμιλῶν κόσμιός τε καὶ θεῖος εἰς τὸ δυνατὸν ἀνθρώπῳ γίγνεται.

παντὸς μᾶλλον θειοτέρου τινὸς τυγχάνει, ὡς ἔοικεν, οὖσα, ὃ τὴν μὲν δύναμιν οὐδέποτε ἀπόλλυσιν; 518e).

I want to consider, finally, the following passage in Book 6, which is a bit more complex. Here, Socrates says that the philosophic rulers, acting like painters or sculptors, should shape the human soul so that it reflects the Forms:

> As they [the rulers] work, I think, they would look frequently in both directions, towards Justice, Goodness, Temperance and all such things, and then to that in which [i.e. the soul] they would implant these [virtues] in men, mingling and mixing the human image from these pursuits, and deriving from this what Homer called, when it appeared in men, a "god in form" and an "image of the god." (Ἔπειτα, οἶμαι, ἀπεργαζόμενοι πυκνὰ ἂν ἑκατέρωσ᾿ ἀποβλέποιεν, πρός τε τὸ φύσει δίκαιον καὶ καλὸν καὶ σῶφρον καὶ πάντα τὰ τοιαῦτα, καὶ πρὸς ἐκεῖνο αὖ τὸ ἐν τοῖς ἀνθρώποις ἐμποιοῖεν, συμμειγνύντες τε καὶ κεραννύντες ἐκ τῶν ἐπιτηδευμάτων τὸ ἀνδρείκελον, ἀπ᾿ ἐκείνου τεκμαιρόμενοι, ὃ δὴ καὶ Ὅμηρος ἐκάλεσεν ἐν τοῖς ἀνθρώποις ἐγγιγνόμενον θεοειδές τε καὶ θεοείκελον; 501b)

As Socrates states, the rulers who educate the young philosophers must look at the Forms and then at the souls that they are educating. After mentioning the Forms by name – Justice, Goodness, and Temperance – he says that the rulers must "implant" these virtues in the souls of men by way of education. Of course the rulers do not simply sculpt virtuous people – they train the young philosophers to develop their own virtues over a long period of time. Note that Socrates describes the philosophically educated soul in Homeric language: this soul is a "god in form" (theoeides) and an "image of god" (theoeikelon). Homer uses these words to describe beautiful and virile bodies. But Plato applies them to the soul: the soul becomes a "god in form" and an "image of the god" because it develops its virtue in reference to the divine realm of the Forms.[7] In short, the "divine" Forms taken as a group make the soul godlike.

As this examination of the *theios* divinity-marker indicates, Plato refers to the group of the Forms as divine, and he also explicitly identifies Beauty, the Good, and Wisdom as divine. To be sure, he does not identify other individual Forms as divine. He discusses many individual Forms in the *Phaedo* and the *Republic*, but he never speaks of any individual Form as "divine." Still, he regularly uses *theios* when speaking of the Forms as a group. In addition, he puts "divine" in various lists of ideal attributes.

---

[7] Socrates makes a similar point when he refers to the philosophical soul as "in reality a divine thing" (*tôi onti theion*, 497c).

Why, then, do scholars refuse to include this in the ideal attributes of the Forms? No doubt this has to do with their belief that the philosopher must, by definition, focus on rational rather than theological ideas. These scholars would argue that we can understand "existing, unchanging, eternal, incorporeal, singular in form, and separate from the physical realm" by way of reason, but we cannot comprehend the "divine" by way of rational analysis. I agree that the divinity of the Forms resists rational and linguistic analysis. But I do not agree that, qua philosopher, Plato deals only with rational ideas: he is a theological philosopher. In my view, we should accept "divine" as an ideal attribute of the Forms, but we must treat this as a special kind of attribute.

1.3 The Form of the Good

Before I analyze the Form of the Good, I want to briefly discuss the Form of Beauty. Since Plato regularly links the Forms of Beauty and the Good, we must ask why he brings these two Forms together. Let me give a few examples of the intertwining of Beauty and the Good. In the *Republic*, Plato gives the Form of the Good an "inconceivable beauty" (*amêchanon kallon*); indeed, the Good "surpasses knowledge and truth in its beauty" (509a). The Good is not only good but beautiful. Plato also links these two Forms together in the following statement: "do you think that there is anything useful in the possession of everything but not the Good, or in knowing all other things without knowing Beauty and the Good?" (505a–b). Plato introduces Beauty into his discussion of the Form of the Good, but never explains this move.

Plato provides a metaphorical account of the link between these Forms in the *Philebus*, where he identifies beauty as the portal to goodness: "If we should say that we are standing at the doorway of the Good and its dwelling, would we in some way be speaking rightly? ... So now the power of the Good has taken residence in the nature of beauty" (ἆρ᾽ οὖν ἐπὶ μὲν τοῖς τοῦ ἀγαθοῦ νῦν ἤδη προθύροις (καὶ) τῆς οἰκήσεως ἐφεστάναι (τῆς τοῦ τοιούτου) λέγοντες ἴσως ὀρθῶς ἄν τινα τρόπον φαῖμεν; ... νῦν δὴ καταπέφευγεν ἡμῖν ἡ τοῦ ἀγαθοῦ δύναμις εἰς τὴν τοῦ καλοῦ φύσιν; 64c–e). Plato uses the metaphor of a house with a doorway or porch to indicate that Beauty serves as the portal to the Good.[8] When one encounters beautiful things in the world and sees their relation to Beauty, one stands at the entrance of the house of the Good.

---

[8] See O'Meara 2017: 68–9 for an excellent account of this passage.

Given that Plato regularly links Beauty to the Good, it comes as no surprise that he wrote two dialogues on Beauty. In the *Phaedrus*, he indicates that Beauty stands out among the Forms. As Socrates states: "the Form of Beauty shone radiantly (ἔλαμπεν) in its being among the Forms there; and coming here we have grasped it as it shines (στίλβον) most clearly (ἐναργέστατα) through the clearest (ἐναργεστάτης) of our senses" (250d). Beauty radiates a special aura. We can infer that it not only manifests its own essence but gestures towards the Good. While Plato never fully explains the link between Beauty and the Good, he clearly gives Beauty a special status among the Forms.

I turn now to the Form of the Good, which plays the leading role in Plato's metaphysics.[9] Put simply, the Good is the highest divinity in Plato's ontology. To be sure, Plato only treats the Good in one dialogue, the *Republic*. But he refers to the Good in passing in all the middle dialogues.[10] In the *Republic*, Plato describes this Form by way of metaphor, analogy, and allegory. This kind of language presents problems for the interpreter: metaphorical and imagistic language inevitably generates a surplus of meaning. Indeed, Socrates says that he will describe the Form of the Good only by way of its "offspring" (*ekgonon*, 508b–c), i.e., by an analogy to the Sun-god. Still, a close reading of Plato's discourse on the Form of the Good in this dialogue helps us to understand the Good and its unique role in Plato's middle-period metaphysics.

Let me first examine the Analogy of the Sun. First, I want to rename this as the "Analogy of the Sun-god." For, in this analogy, Socrates specifically refers to the sun as a god. Socrates introduces this analogy by asking about physical vision: "which of the gods in heaven (*tôn en ouranôi theôn*) do you identify as the lord and author (*kurion*) of this, whose light makes us able to see to the extent that we can and makes those things visible?."[11] Here, he refers to the sun god Helios. Socrates makes the same point in his next question: "is vision, then, dependent by nature on this god?" (ἆρ' οὖν ὧδε πέφυκεν ὄψις πρὸς τοῦτον τὸν θεόν; 508a). In these passages, Plato uses the Gods divinity-marker to convey the idea that the Form of Good is divine.

---

[9] There is a vast amount of literature on this topic. For recent discussions of the Form of the Good, Baltes 1997; Santas 1999; Ferber 2005; Rowe 2007; Shields 2008; Long forthcoming.

[10] Plato does not identify the Good as ontologically higher than the other Forms outside of the *Republic*. Still, out of all his middle-period dialogues, he offers the most detailed account of the Forms (and of the philosopher's grasp of the Forms) in the *Republic*. For this reason, scholars (including myself) accept that the Good plays a key role in other middle-period dialogues as well.

[11] I translate *kurios* as "lord and author" because there is no single English word that captures its meaning.

How does the Sun-god Analogy work? First, the Sun-god serves to "yoke" the seeing eye to the object of vision (*suzeuxis; zeugnumi*, 508a). The eye only gains the power to see by way of this divine light. As Socrates puts it, "does it [the eye] not get that power that it has as an overflow, as it were, dispensed by the sun?" (οὐκοῦν καὶ τὴν δύναμιν ἣν ἔχει ἐκ τούτου ταμιευομένην ὥσπερ ἐπίρρυτον κέκτηται; 508b). Translated more literally, the sun "dispenses its light from its treasury" (*tamieuomenên*). In addition, the Sun-god is not just a light unto itself, but it produces an "overflow" (*epirrhuton*) of its light into the realm around it. This overflow of light that allows the eye to see will play a key role in this passage. By identifying the Good as the light that yokes together the knower and the object of knowledge, the Forms, Plato ushers in the metaphorics of light. By this, I refer to Plato's regular use of metaphors that identify Goodness with light.

Plato offers an interesting explanation of the analogy between the Sun-god in the physical realm and the Form of the Good in the intelligible realm. Like the Sun-god, whose light generates "birth, growth, and nurture" in the physical realm, Goodness gives the Forms existence and intelligibility:

> You must say not only that the objects of knowledge are known by way of the being-present (*pareinai*) of the Good, but also that their existence and essence belongs to (*proseinai*) the Good, though the good is not being but is beyond being in dignity and power. (καὶ τοῖς γιγνωσκομένοις τοίνυν μὴ μόνον τὸ γιγνώσκεσθαι φάναι ὑπὸ τοῦ ἀγαθοῦ παρεῖναι, ἀλλὰ καὶ τὸ εἶναί τε καὶ τὴν οὐσίαν ὑπ᾽ ἐκείνου αὐτοῖς προσεῖναι, οὐκ οὐσίας ὄντος τοῦ ἀγαθοῦ, ἀλλ᾽ ἔτι ἐπέκεινα τῆς οὐσίας πρεσβείᾳ καὶ δυνάμει ὑπερέχοντος; 509b)

This passage has puzzled scholars. What does Plato mean by saying that the Good is "beyond being" (*epekeina tês ousias*)? And how exactly does the Good grant existence and essence to the Forms? It is impossible to offer a satisfactory answer to these questions. We must note, however, that the *pareinai* ("being-present") of the Good seems to contradict the claim that the Good is beyond being: *einai* in *pareinai* modifies the Good and thus implies that this Form has some sort of being. Or, alternatively, the Good manifests itself in the realm of the Forms as being (but is not, in itself, being). Indeed, in this passage, Plato uses two compound *einai* ("being") verbs: *pareinai* means "to be present (as a help)" or "to arrive at," and *proseinai* "to belong to" or "to be added to." Somehow the Good has a "being present" (*pareinai*) that allows the Forms to take on existence by way of "belonging to" (*proseinai*) the Good. If one uses the cognate noun for *pareinai*, then one can say that the *parousia* of the Good gives the Forms "existence and essence" (*to einai te kai tên ousian*).

The Form of the Good also makes the Forms intelligible to the mind:

> You must call this the Form of the Good, that which furnishes truth to those things that are known and dispenses the power of knowledge to the knower. Conceive of this as the cause of knowledge and of truth insofar as this is known. While both of these things, knowledge and truth, are beautiful, if you understand that this [the Good] is even more beautiful than they are, you would understand rightly. (Τοῦτο τοίνυν τὸ τὴν ἀλήθειαν παρέχον τοῖς γιγνωσκομένοις καὶ τῷ γιγνώσκοντι τὴν δύναμιν ἀποδιδὸν τὴν τοῦ ἀγαθοῦ ἰδέαν φάθι εἶναι: αἰτίαν δ᾽ ἐπιστήμης οὖσαν καὶ ἀληθείας, ὡς γιγνωσκομένης μὲν διανοοῦ, οὕτω δὲ καλῶν ἀμφοτέρων ὄντων, γνώσεώς τε καὶ ἀληθείας, ἄλλο καὶ κάλλιον ἔτι τούτων ἡγούμενος αὐτὸ ὀρθῶς ἡγήσῃ; 508d–e)

Without the Good, the Forms would not be intelligible to the mind. The Forms, then, derive their existence, essence, and intelligibility from the Good.

Since the Forms gain their existence and essence from the Good, they must get all of their ideal attributes from the Good. The ideal attributes traditionally identified by scholars – "eternal, unchanging, intelligible, singular in form, imperishable, and separate from the physical realm" – derive from the Good. If, as I have argued, "divine" is an ideal attribute of the Forms, then the Forms also derive their divinity from the Good.

Let me turn now to the passages in the *Republic* that mark the Good as the highest divinity in Plato's system. First, Plato treats the Good as a first cause. As Socrates states:

> This is how it seems to me: the Form of the Good is the last thing to be seen and scarcely seen in the realm of the known, but when it is seen one must conclude that this is the cause (*aitia*) of all that is right and beautiful, both begetting (*tekousa*) light and its lordly author in the visible realm and, being itself the lord and author in the intelligible realm, furnishing truth and reason (*alêtheian kai noun*) (517b–c)[12]

The Good *qua* "cause" (*aitia*) "begat" all things that are right and beautiful, including the Sun-god, with its light and lordly authorship in the visible realm. Indeed, as the "lord and author" of everything in the realm of the

---

[12] τὰ δ᾽ οὖν ἐμοὶ φαινόμενα οὕτω φαίνεται, ἐν τῷ γνωστῷ τελευταία ἡ τοῦ ἀγαθοῦ ἰδέα καὶ μόγις ὁρᾶσθαι, ὀφθεῖσα δὲ συλλογιστέα εἶναι ὡς ἄρα πᾶσι πάντων αὕτη ὀρθῶν τε καὶ καλῶν αἰτία, ἔν τε ὁρατῷ φῶς καὶ τὸν τούτου κύριον τεκοῦσα, ἔν τε νοητῷ αὐτὴ κυρία ἀλήθειαν καὶ νοῦν παρασχομένη.

Forms, the Good effectively causes all things.[13] Plato also gives the Good
a causal power in the following passage:

> Understand this as what I mean in speaking of the offspring of the Good,
> which the Good begat as an analogue of itself: as this [the Good] is in the
> intelligible region in relation to reason and the objects of reason, so is this
> [the Sun-god] in the visible realm in relation to sight and the object of sight.
> (τοῦτον τοίνυν ... φάναι με λέγειν τὸν τοῦ ἀγαθοῦ ἔκγονον, ὃν τἀγαθὸν
> ἐγέννησεν ἀνάλογον ἑαυτῷ, ὅτιπερ αὐτὸ ἐν τῷ νοητῷ τόπῳ πρός τε νοῦν
> καὶ τὰ νοούμενα, τοῦτο τοῦτον ἐν τῷ ὁρατῷ πρός τε ὄψιν καὶ τὰ ὁρώμενα;
> 508b–c)

The Good "begat" (*egennêsen*) the Sun-god, which allows for life in the
earthly world. To be sure, we cannot read Plato's metaphors literally, but
we can accept the idea that the Good is the first cause of all things.[14] This
suggests that the Good is the highest divinity in Plato's metaphysics.

The Analogy of the Line, which follows directly after the Analogy of the
Sun-god, identifies the Good as the "first principle (*archê*) of all things":

> Understand, then, the other section of the intelligible – I mean that which
> reason itself grasps by the power of dialectic, not treating the hypotheses as
> first principles but truly as hypotheses, using them as stepping stones and
> springboards, so that, going all the way to the first principle of all things, the
> unhypothetical, and grasping this, he then goes back down, holding onto
> those things that depend on this, and in this way comes to the conclusion,
> not using the senses at all but the Forms themselves, moving through Forms
> to Forms and ending with Forms. (τὸ τοίνυν ἕτερον μάνθανε τμῆμα τοῦ
> νοητοῦ λέγοντά με τοῦτο, οὗ αὐτὸς ὁ λόγος ἅπτεται τῇ τοῦ διαλέγεσθαι
> δυνάμει, τὰς ὑποθέσεις ποιούμενος οὐκ ἀρχὰς ἀλλὰ τῷ ὄντι ὑποθέσεις, οἷον
> ἐπιβάσεις τε καὶ ὁρμάς, ἵνα μέχρι τοῦ ἀνυποθέτου ἐπὶ τὴν τοῦ παντὸς
> ἀρχὴν ἰών, ἁψάμενος αὐτῆς, πάλιν αὖ ἐχόμενος τῶν ἐκείνης ἐχομένων,
> οὕτως ἐπὶ τελευτὴν καταβαίνῃ, αἰσθητῷ παντάπασιν οὐδενὶ
> προσχρώμενος, ἀλλ' εἴδεσιν αὐτοῖς δι' αὐτῶν εἰς αὐτά, καὶ τελευτᾷ εἰς
> εἴδη; 511b–c)

Although this passage does not mention the "Good" explicitly, the
references to "the first principle of things" and "the unhypothetical"
can only refer to the Good. As Plato suggests, the philosopher must go
beyond hypotheses to find the first principle, the Good. The philosopher

---

[13] Scholars have asked whether the Good is a formal or final cause. Given the metaphorical discourse in
this passage, however, any claim about the Good as a formal or final cause involves a good deal of
speculation. See Long's excellent comments on this passage (forthcoming).

[14] See Santas 1999 and Shields 2008 for examinations of this topic; they also offer useful discussions of
earlier scholarly literature.

does this by working with the Forms alone. Once he grasps the first principle, he can finally attain knowledge of the things that he had understood earlier by way of hypotheses. In addition, the philosopher must apprehend all things in relation to the Good. As Plato puts it (rather abstractly), he must grasp the hypothesized truths by way of the Forms alone which, in turn, "hold onto it" (*tôn ekeinês echomenôn*), i.e., the first principle. Since the Forms "hold onto" the Good, the philosopher's examination by way of the Forms leads him to their source, the Good. In short, the philosopher only achieves full knowledge when he finally grasps the Good. Plato presents this same idea imagistically in the Allegory of the Cave: when the philosophic soul leaves the cave, it first examines the entire realm of the Forms and then, finally, looks at the Form of the Good. Once it sees the Good, it understands the other Forms in reference to that.

By using the divinity-marker of the Sun-god and identifying the Good as the first cause of being and becoming, Plato identifies the Good as divine. Indeed, Plato treats the Good as the "most blessed" of all beings. As Socrates states: "we must examine whether the greater and more advanced part of this discipline extends towards this – to make one see the Form of the Good more easily; as we say, all things extend in that direction which compel the soul to turn towards that region in which the most blessed of being exists" (*esti to eudaimonestaton tou ontos*; 526d–e).[15] Ontologically, the Good stands over all the other Forms, and also the gods, souls, and bodily realm. As A. A. Long observes:

> Just as the sun causes genesis, but is not itself genesis, so the Form of the Good causes the existence and being of the Forms, but is not itself *being* but surpasses their being in dignity/seniority and power. Since the divine excellence of the Forms (especially justice and beauty) has already been assumed in their role as models for the philosopher to imitate, we must infer that the Form of the Good, a fortiori, is divinity par excellence (a super form, according to Proclus), as the words "far surpassing" the other Forms in dignity (*presbeia*) and power (*dunamis*) convey just by themselves.

Following Long and other scholars, I identify the Form of the Good as the highest divinity in Plato's metaphysics.[16]

---

[15] *Republic* 526d–e: τὸ δὲ πολὺ αὐτῆς καὶ πορρωτέρω προϊὸν σκοπεῖσθαι δεῖ εἴ τι πρὸς ἐκεῖνο τείνει, πρὸς τὸ ποιεῖν κατιδεῖν ῥᾷον τὴν τοῦ ἀγαθοῦ ἰδέαν. τείνει δέ, φαμέν, πάντα αὐτόσε, ὅσα ἀναγκάζει ψυχὴν εἰς ἐκεῖνον τὸν τόπον μεταστρέφεσθαι ἐν ᾧ ἐστι τὸ εὐδαιμονέστατον τοῦ ὄντος.

[16] For scholars who have identified the Form of the Good as a divinity, see Zeller 1889; Adam 1921: vol. 2, 51; Gerson 1990: 62 (with qualifications); Neschker-Henschke 1995; Bordt 2006. For arguments

Since Plato posits many Forms (rather than a Parmenidean "one"), the philosopher must investigate the Forms in relation to one another and, in particular, to the Good. Indeed, Plato emphasizes the harmonious relationship of the Forms. As Socrates states in Book 6:

> When the philosopher sees and beholds things that are ordered and always the same [i.e. the Forms], and sees that they do not wrong one another or suffer wrong, but are all in harmony (*kosmôi*) and in accordance with reason, he imitates them and likens himself to them as much as possible. Or do you think that there is any way for someone to associate with something he admires and not to imitate it? ... The philosopher, associating himself with what is harmonious and divine (*theôi dê kai kosmôi*), becomes harmonious and divine (*kosmios te kai theios*) as much as is possible for humans.[17] (500c–d)

Plato's repetition of *kosmos/kosmios* foregrounds the "harmony" of the Forms in their relation to one another. Of course, the philosopher's grasp of the interrelation of the Forms must include apprehending them in relation to the Good. Thus, in the Allegory of the Cave, Plato portrays the philosopher as examining the Forms as they appear in the light of the sun (i.e., the Good) and moving in advancing degrees towards the Good. Here again, Plato suggests that the philosopher apprehends the Forms in relation to each other and to the Good.

Plato also indicates that the philosopher cannot gain anything useful from his learning without knowing the Good:

> You have often heard that the Form of the Good is the greatest object of learning, and it is in relation to this that just things and the others become useful and beneficial. And you pretty much know that this is what I am going to speak about and to say: that we have no sufficient knowledge of this. But if we do not know this, even if we most of all understand other things in the absence of this [knowledge of the Good], you must understand that there is no benefit to us at all, just as there is no benefit if we possess something without the Good. Or do you think that there is anything useful in the possession of everything but not the Good, or in knowing all other things without knowing Beauty and the Good?[18] (505a–b).

---

against this position, see Hackforth 1936; Cherniss 1944: 605–6; Gerson 1990; McPherran 1991: 252–3 and 2006b; Benitez 1995; Santas 1999; Rowe 2007.

[17] 500c–d: ἀλλ' εἰς τεταγμένα ἄττα καὶ κατὰ ταὐτὰ ἀεὶ ἔχοντα ὁρῶντας καὶ θεωμένους οὔτ' ἀδικοῦντα οὔτ' ἀδικούμενα ὑπ' ἀλλήλων, κόσμῳ δὲ πάντα καὶ κατὰ λόγον ἔχοντα, ταῦτα μιμεῖσθαί τε καὶ ὅτι μάλιστα ἀφομοιοῦσθαι. ἢ οἴει τινὰ μηχανὴν εἶναι, ὅτῳ τις ὁμιλεῖ ἀγάμενος, μὴ μιμεῖσθαι ἐκεῖνο; ... θείῳ δὴ καὶ κοσμίῳ ὅ γε φιλόσοφος ὁμιλῶν κόσμιός τε καὶ θεῖος εἰς τὸ δυνατὸν ἀνθρώπῳ γίγνεται.

[18] *Rep.* 505a–b: ἐπεὶ ὅτι γε ἡ τοῦ ἀγαθοῦ ἰδέα μέγιστον μάθημα, πολλάκις ἀκήκοας, ᾗ καὶ δίκαια καὶ τἆλλα προσχρησάμενα χρήσιμα καὶ ὠφέλιμα γίγνεται. καὶ νῦν σχεδὸν οἶσθ' ὅτι μέλλω τοῦτο λέγειν, καὶ πρὸς τούτῳ ὅτι αὐτὴν οὐχ ἱκανῶς ἴσμεν· εἰ δὲ μὴ ἴσμεν, ἄνευ δὲ ταύτης εἰ ὅτι μάλιστα τἆλλα ἐπισταίμεθα, οἶσθ' ὅτι οὐδὲν ἡμῖν ὄφελος, ὥσπερ οὐδ' εἰ κεκτήμεθά τι ἄνευ τοῦ ἀγαθοῦ. ἢ οἴει

The Good makes the knowledge of any discipline, including mathematics, beneficial. Without this, a thinker gets no benefit at all. Even logic and mathematics, which one can understand outside of their relation to the Good, have no usefulness without being examined in relation to this Form.

Plato presents the Good as the ultimate object of knowledge, though he indicates that one cannot know this in any full way. As Socrates states: "For you have often heard that the Form of the Good is the greatest object of learning, and it is in relation to this [the Good] that just things and all the rest become useful and beneficial ... and I will say further that we do not have any adequate knowledge of this" (ἐπεὶ ὅτι γε ἡ τοῦ ἀγαθοῦ ἰδέα μέγιστον μάθημα, πολλάκις ἀκήκοας, ᾗ δὴ καὶ δίκαια καὶ τἆλλα προσχρησάμενα χρήσιμα καὶ ὠφέλιμα γίγνεται ... μέλλω τοῦτο λέγειν, καὶ πρὸς τούτῳ ὅτι αὐτὴν οὐχ ἱκανῶς ἴσμεν; 505a). Yet the philosopher cannot in fact know things rightly and act well in the world unless he grasps the Good: "If the just and the beautiful are not known in relation to the Good, we would possess worthless guardians because they are ignorant of this. And I divine that no-one will know these things sufficiently until he knows this [the Good]" (οἶμαι γοῦν, εἶπον, δίκαιά τε καὶ καλὰ ἀγνοούμενα ὅπῃ ποτὲ ἀγαθά ἐστιν, οὐ πολλοῦ τινος ἄξιον φύλακα κεκτῆσθαι ἂν ἑαυτῶν τὸν τοῦτο ἀγνοοῦντα· μαντεύομαι δὲ μηδένα αὐτὰ πρότερον γνώσεσθαι ἱκανῶς; 506a).

Plato may seem to contradict himself by saying that (1) one cannot know the Good fully, and (2) the philosopher will achieve this knowledge. On the one hand, he suggests that we have no adequate knowledge of the Good, yet the philosopher outside the cave looks directly at the Good and achieves complete knowledge. We can explain this seeming contradiction as follows: since Plato presents the philosopher-guardians in the context of an ideal city, the claim that the philosopher attains perfect knowledge is only valid in the case of this utopia; the actual, non-ideal philosopher, by contrast, will not achieve this level of knowledge. Thus, both of the claims above are true. Still, the non-ideal philosopher will gain at least some apprehension of the Good. For, when this philosopher grasps a Form, he will see it in the illumination of the Good. In doing so, he develops a specific way of seeing and knowing: he must see everything, both physical and intelligible, in the light of the Good.

τι πλέον εἶναι πᾶσαν κτῆσιν ἐκτῆσθαι, μὴ μέντοι ἀγαθήν; ἢ πάντα τἆλλα φρονεῖν ἄνευ τοῦ ἀγαθοῦ, καλὸν δὲ καὶ ἀγαθὸν μηδὲν φρονεῖν;

We have made four key statements about the Good:

1) The Good is the highest divinity in Plato's theological metaphysics.
2) The Good confers being, essence, intelligibility, and divinity on the Forms.
3) The Good yokes the Forms and the mind together so that the philosopher attains knowledge.
4) The philosopher only achieves knowledge of the essence of each individual Form by understanding this in relation to the Good.

I want to return to the Analogy of the Sun-god, where Plato indicates that the Good dispenses its light to the intelligible realm. If we follow the logic of this metaphor, then the philosopher who grasps a single Form will see it bathed in the light of the Good. Indeed, Plato suggests that "truth and Being" themselves shine when the philosophic soul contemplates the Forms. As Socrates states: "when [the soul] fixes itself on that region where truth and Being shine, it apprehends and knows this" (ὅταν μὲν οὗ καταλάμπει ἀλήθειά τε καὶ τὸ ὄν, εἰς τοῦτο ἀπερείσηται, ἐνόησέν τε καὶ ἔγνω αὐτό; 508d). Here, *to on* –"Being"– refers to the Forms. Thus, following the metaphor, we can say that the Forms shine with the reflective light of the Good, and that the mind grasps a "truth" that also reflects this light. The entire realm of the Forms, as it seems, shines with the ambient light of the divine Good. During contemplation, then, the philosopher's mind takes in a single Form (e.g., Justice or Equality) as well as the light of the Good that surrounds it. The light manifests the Good that causes and rules over this system.

The Good shows its power and divinity in the realm of the Forms in its "being present" (*pareinai*) in the intelligible region. The philosopher contemplating the Forms encounters the divine Good even if only by way of the Forms reflecting its light. Whenever he grasps the essence of a Form, then, he also encounters divinity. This gives the Good an epiphanic aspect. The Good always shows its divinity in the realm of the Forms. Any philosopher who contemplates one or more Forms will experience a divine epiphany of the Good.

CHAPTER 2

Eternal Longings

This lonely hill was always dear to me,
And this hedgerow, which cuts off the view
Of so much of the last horizon.
But sitting here and gazing, I can see
Beyond, in my mind's eye, unending spaces,
And superhuman silences, and depthless calm,
Till what I feel
Is almost fear. And when I hear
The wind stir in these branches, I begin
Comparing that endless stillness with this noise:
And the eternal comes to mind,
And the dead seasons, and the present
Living one, and how it sounds.
So my mind sinks in this immensity:
And foundering is sweet in such a sea.
                              –Leopardi, *The Infinite*

In Plato's *Symposium*, a group of intellectuals and artists give speeches in praise of the god Eros. The speakers engage in a playful competition with one another, showing off their wit, cultivation, and eloquence. Each articulates a different conception of Eros and his role in the human, divine, and cosmic realms. In Socrates' speech, philosophic desire takes center stage. Socrates focuses on two key desires: the desire for immortality and the metaphysical desire for the Forms. Both aim at something beyond the human, but they differ in key ways. I will examine both of these desires and show how they work together in the life of the philosopher.

In its most basic sense, the desire for immortality is a desire for an everlasting self. The Greeks understood immortality in terms of living like the gods. If attaining immortality means living like a god, it matters enormously how one conceives of the gods. For example, the Greeks and the Christians had/have very different conceptions of god, and this

64

determines their notions of immortality. The Greeks traditionally conceived of their gods as living forever, having perfect bodies, and possessing immense power over nature and human life. They did not, however, think of the gods as ethical beings – gods dwelled beyond human mortality. If one became immortal, then, a Greek person would live everlastingly in ageless and perfect bodies and also have great power.

As Plato indicates, all humans long for immortality, but very few experience the philosophical desire for the Forms. I call this "metaphysical desire." How do these two desires differ? The desire for immortality is self-oriented: one wants an immortal "me." With metaphysical desire, one wants to see and know external beings that are separate from – and ontologically higher than – oneself. Metaphysical desire aims at external objects – eternal, changeless Beings that exist in a divine realm. This kind of desire moves outwards, beyond the self. Metaphysical desire drives the soul to rationally grasp one kind of object, the Forms. Here, rather paradoxically, reason has its own desire. In some strange way, platonic "reason" is not purely rational. Or, to put it better, the mind has an intellectual and an erotic aspect. Note, finally, that Plato uses the word "eros" both for the longing for immortality and for metaphysical desire. In Socrates' speech, these desires are not explicitly separated. Indeed, Socrates weaves them together in his discourse. We need to prise these desires apart in order to fully understand Plato's theory of philosophical eros.

In this chapter, I will first present a detailed account of the phenomenon of divine epiphany in archaic and classical Greece. In a divine epiphany, a god manifested him or herself to humans in a bodily form. I examine the poetry, prose, and inscriptions in classical Greece that give evidence for this religious phenomenon. This discussion of divine epiphany provides the historical and religious basis for my argument that the Form of Beauty manifests itself to the philosopher's "eye of the mind" as a new kind of epiphany.

I then examine Plato's treatment of the soul in the *Symposium*. As I argue, Plato conceives of the soul as mortal in this text. This is the only middle-period dialogue that treats the soul as mortal. This examination sets up my discussion of Plato's meditation on the desire for immortality in the speeches of Aristophanes and Socrates. In Aristophanes' speech, the original humans ("o-humans," as I call them) did not have erotic desire. However, since they were mortal, they did desire immortality. They attacked the gods in an attempt to become gods themselves. The gods won this battle and punished the o-humans by cutting them in half and creating humans. In Aristophanes' myth, the o-humans wanted *immortality with godly power*, and humans also have this desire (on top of having erotic desire). In Socrates' speech, by contrast, humans desire *immortality with goodness*. As Socrates indicates, since the soul is mortal, it gains a partial immortality by way of giving birth to offspring, both at the level of the body and the soul. In the latter case, people give birth to psychic offspring in the form of lawcodes, poems, inventions, and philosophic discourses. Later generations keep that person alive by celebrating his or her creations. To be sure, the human longing for immortality does not get fully satisfied: the individual does not gain an everlasting self. Still, as Socrates claims, this person can live on in later generations if he or she gives birth to good psychic offspring.[1] In this way, he/she gains a *partial immortality with goodness*.

After discussing the desire for immortality in Socrates' speech, I turn to metaphysical desire, which comes to the fore in the Ladder of Love. I offer a detailed examination of the Ladder of Love in both philosophical and theological terms. As I argue, Plato portrays the philosopher's vision of the Form of Beauty in terms of a divine epiphany. The philosopher who grasps the essence of beauty also encounters divinity. Plato signals that the philosopher's contemplation of Beauty is epiphanic in two ways. First, he identifies this vision with the revelation of the goddess at the climax of the Eleusinian Mysteries. There, the initiate (*epoptês*) saw some sort of epiphany of Demeter. Second, Plato uses marked language from poetic narratives of epiphany to represent the philosopher's contemplation of Beauty. To clarify these ideas, I will offer a detailed discussion of the Eleusinian Mysteries and look at the language in poetic narratives of epiphany.

I also examine Plato's conception of eros as a *daimôn* in the *Symposium*. I discuss different ideas about daimons in Greek culture, and compare daimonic eros to Socrates' *daimonion* or "divine voice." I then analyze Plato's mythic discourse on the "daimon Eros" in Socrates' speech. As I argue, Plato does not conceive of eros as an actual daimon acting from outside the soul. Rather, he uses mythic language to convey the notion that the human soul possesses a "daimonic desire" for the Forms. Although scholars have written extensively on platonic desire, they rarely attend to the divine status of philosophic eros. I want to place eros in the context of Plato's theological thinking. In this chapter, I will capitalize "Eros" when

---

[1] Socrates focuses on men in his discussion of "great offspring," i.e., the lawcodes, inventions, and the philosophic discourses. But the character of Diotima, even if fictional, indicates that women can gain a partial immortality.

Socrates specifically refers to him as a god or daimon; I use the smaller-case "eros" when Socrates speaks about philosophic desire simply as a desire of the soul (this includes the desire for immortality and the metaphysical desire for the Forms).

Finally, I examine Alcibiades' speech in the *Symposium*, focusing in particular on his claim that he saw gods within Socrates' soul. To provide the historical background for my argument, I discuss Alcibiades' actions as an Athenian politician and, in particular, his profanation of the Eleusinian Mysteries in 415 BCE. In the *Symposium*, Alcibiades acts as a hierophant at the Eleusinian Mysteries when he gives his account of Socrates. In this role, he claims that he will "reveal" the gods that he once saw in Socrates. But he profanes the mysteries of philosophy (as it were) by misidentifying the divinity in question. The proper object of Alcibiades *qua* budding philosopher should be the divine Form of Beauty, not the mortal soul of Socrates.[2] I juxtapose Alcibiades' idolatrous claims about Socrates' divinity with Socrates' suggestion that the philosopher, like the *epoptês* in the mysteries, sees a divine revelation of the Form of Beauty. The divine epiphany that Alcibiades claims to have seen in the person of Socrates turns out to be a false idol.

2.1 Divine Epiphany in Ancient Greece

The Greeks accepted divine epiphanies as a real phenomenon. This was the way that the world revealed itself to them. As Greg Anderson observes: "the gods and other superhuman agencies were just as real, just as immediately present, and just as materially efficacious to the Athenians as all of our states, structures, systems, and sundry other man-made, world-ordering phenomena are to us today."[3] To be sure, the Greeks themselves had different beliefs about divine activity, and this ran along a spectrum: not all Greeks shared the same ideas about the gods. Still, we have a great deal of material and textual evidence for divine epiphanies in ancient Greece.

Though invisible to humans in ordinary life, the gods could manifest themselves in the phenomenal realm at any given time. They could reveal themselves to an individual or a group of people. The gods showed themselves in anthropomorphic, theriomorphic, or natural forms. The god "appeared" (*phainesthai*) in his or her "clear" (*enargês*) presence.[4]

---

[2] Obviously, in spite of spending time with Socrates and finding philosophy an attractive way of life, Alcibiades opted for politics over philosophy.
[3] Anderson 2018: 132. [4] Platt 2011: 56–7; Petridou 2016: 3–4.

The Greeks used the words *eidos/eidomai* to describe the "form" in which the gods appeared.[5] They identified a given phenomenon as a divine epiphany by way of its sudden, wondrous, radiant, and beautiful appearance.[6]

Consider the Homeric *Hymn to Dionysus*, which features some of the traditional language used for divine epiphanies. In this hymn, Dionysus "appears" (*ephanê*) to a group of Tyrsenian sailors first in the form of a handsome young man. They seize him and put him on their ship. He escapes their bonds and the sailors think that he "resembles no mortal man but the gods dwelling on Olympus" (*HH* 7.20–21). The master of the ship rejects the sailors' claims, but "suddenly there appeared wondrous events" (τάχα δέ σφιν ἐφαίνετο θαυματὰ ἔργα): immediately (*autika*), wine streams on the ship and a vine of grapes climbs up the mast. Fear (*tarbos*) takes hold of the sailors and they want to release him from the ship. But Dionysus, "revealing signs" (*phainôn sêmata*) of his divinity, turns into a lion and then a bear. The sailors rush away in "terror" (*ephobêthen*) and are struck with amazement (*ekplêgentes*). They jump into the sea and Dionysus turns them into dolphins (*HH* 7.33–50). In this hymn, the god "suddenly" takes on "wondrous" forms – human, animal, and plant. And the humans respond with "fear" and "amazement." We find these same words and ideas in other poetic narratives of epiphany.

Poetic narratives of divine epiphany often feature radiant and super-natural light. To take but one example, in Aristophanes' *Birds* (1709–14), the messenger describes the epiphany of Pisthetairus as follows: "More brilliant than the brightest star that illumines the earth, he is approaching his glittering golden palace; the sun itself does not shine with more dazzling glory" (trans. Geldart; προσέρχεται γὰρ οἷος οὔτε παμφαὴς ἀστὴρ ἰδεῖν ἔλαμψε χρυσαυγεῖ δρόμῳ, οὔθ᾽ ἡλίου τηλαυγὲς ἀκτίνων σέλας τοιοῦτον ἐξέλαμψεν). To be sure, Aristophanes presents a comic portrayal of a man becoming a god who manifests his divinity to humans, but he uses traditional vocabulary to describe this epiphany. As we can see from these examples, the gods saturate their various bodies and the area around with divinity.

For the Greeks, the gods could manifest themselves in visible forms at any time. As Fritz Graf observes: "To the Greek and Roman mind,

---

[5] Platt 2011: 51–5.

[6] For excellent accounts of poetic narratives of epiphany, see Platt 2011: 60–72, 170–212; Petridou 2015: 1–5, 31–44 et passim. Both of these scholars emphasize that the poets describe the epiphanic appearance of a god in terms of radiant light, beauty, magnitude, wondrousness, and clear presence (*enargeia*).

epiphanies were real, and they were vital. Gods were irrelevant if they could not manifest themselves to humans . . . . When they appeared in their bodily form, the gods were *enargeia* (i.e., clearly visible, manifest)."[7] We have abundant material and textual evidence for divine epiphanies in ancient Greece. To be sure, as religious outsiders, we cannot understand the Greeks' phenomenological experience of the epiphanies. Still, we must take seriously these ancient accounts.

The evidence for divine epiphanies comes from poetry, prose, and epigraphic texts, and also from the visual arts. As scholars have observed, the gods manifested themselves in humans, in statues, in animals, in natural elements, and in dreams.[8] They appeared either at random places or in the context of a religious sanctuary or festival. Indeed, in religious festivals, the Greeks engaged in rituals designed to invoke the presence of the god. The sacred space of the sanctuary and the rituals at the festival effectively sacralized the events and objects. As we will see, the Greeks engaged in "ritualized visualization" when they viewed objects and events at a festival or in a sanctuary. In these contexts, a number of rituals – including the invocations of a god (in prayer and in song) – prepared the worshippers to "see the god" or to engage in other modes of sacred spectating.

In epic poetry, the gods regularly appear to humans in anthropomorphic or animal forms. For example, consider the scene in Homer's *Odyssey* where Athena disguises herself as the old man Mentor and gives Nestor advice for aiding Telemachus (3.371–3): "when she had spoken, green-eyed Athena departed, taking on the form of a vulture, and wonder took hold of all those who were looking, and the old man was amazed when he saw this with his eyes" (ὣς ἄρα φωνήσασ' ἀπέβη γλαυκῶπις Ἀθήνη φήνῃ εἰδομένη· θάμβος δ' ἕλε πάντας Ἀχαιούς. θαύμαζεν δ' ὁ γεραιός, ὅπως ἴδεν ὀφθαλμοῖσι). The humans respond to Athena's sudden transformation from man to vulture with "wonder" and "amazement." Homer mentions the viewers' amazed response twice, and also emphasizes that Nestor "saw" this "with his eyes." As this scene reminds us, a god could hide his or her divinity from humans but also manifest this in a sudden epiphany.

In addition to poetic narratives of epiphany, we have a good deal of epigraphic evidence for historical individuals seeing divine epiphanies. To take a simple example, consider the fourth-century BCE inscription from

---

[7] Graf 2004: 113.
[8] See especially Versnel (1987), who notes the ambiguous aspects of divine epiphanies. For book-length studies of epiphanies, see Platt 2011; Petridou 2015.

the Athenian acropolis, which commemorates a vision of Athena seen by a woman named Meneia: "Meneia set this up to Athena, having seen a vision (ὄψιν ἰδοῦσα) of the goddess' *aretê*."[9] In this vision, Meneia sees the "miraculous presence or power" (*aretê*) of the goddess.[10] Of course we do not know what exactly Meneia saw, but it is noteworthy that she records her experience on a votive tablet. As Platt observes:

> As the Acropolis Meneia inscription confirms, it is precisely in this period that epiphanic experience began to be explicitly recorded and displayed in epigraphic media as well as votive reliefs. While the accessibility of civic deities such as Athena and the rise of private cults such as those of Asclepius, Pan, and the Nymphs influenced the increased prominence of epiphany within the material record, the visual language of naturalism and the "epigraphic habit" of the democratic polis provided the visual and verbal devices by which encounters with the divine could be commemorated by ordinary individuals.[11]

The Athenians started using the technology of writing in a full way in political, legal, and religious contexts in the fourth century BCE.[12] For this reason, we have a lot of inscriptional evidence from this period. The Meneia inscription shows us that ordinary people, including women (who had no legal or political power in Athens), had their experiences of divine epiphany inscribed on votive tablets. Based on the number of inscriptions we have found, we can conclude that divine epiphany was not a particularly rare event in classical Greece.

Let us turn to an epiphanic narrative found in a more detailed inscription. In a fourth-century BCE inscription in the sanctuary of Asclepius in Epidauros, Isyllos of Epidauros records a long account of his vision of a god.[13] As he says, he went to the sanctuary of Asclepius to seek healing for some sort of malady. While he was walking to the sanctuary, Isyllos saw the god Asclepius in the light of day wearing flashing gold armor. The god told Isyllos that he was on his way to Sparta, where he would help the Greeks in their battle with the Macedonians. Asclepius advised Isyllos to wait for him in the sanctuary – he would come back after the battle and heal him. At this point, Isyllos decides to rush to Sparta and tell the Greeks that Asclepius would support them and give them victory. After the Spartans won, they attributed their victory to the god's epiphany to Isyllos and instituted

---

[9] *IG* II/III² 4.326.
[10] This is generally agreed to be a dream vision: see Henrichs 2010a: 34–5, Keesling 2012: 476.
[11] Platt 2011: 43.   [12] See especially Thomas 1989, 1992, 1996.   [13] *IG* IV² 1, 128.

the festival of Asclepius Soter.[14] Obviously, the Spartans had accepted his report of this divine encounter.

Ancient historians also present narratives of epiphany. As Herodotus says in his account of the Persian Wars, the god Pan suddenly "came upon" (*metapiptei*) an Athenian long-distance runner named Philippides in the mountains above Tegea. Pan asks why the Athenians do not pay attention to him, especially when he has given them so many good things in the past and would do so in the future. Returning to Athens, Philippides tells the Athenians that "Pan had appeared (*phanênai*) to him." When the Athenians heard the report of Pan's message, they accepted it as valid. After this, they set up a sanctuary to the god on the Acropolis and worshipped him with yearly sacrifices and a torch race (6.105.1–106.1). As scholars have noted, whether Pan "appears" visually or audibly is not fully clear.[15] If this was an audible event, then the god "appeared" in a voice that had some sort of numinous aspect.

I find this account of Pan's epiphany useful because it shows the *do ut des* aspect of Greek religion. Pan effectively demands to be worshipped in response to the gifts he has given. Though he does not claim that he will turn against the Athenians if they fail to do this, he strongly implies this. Indeed Pan himself speaks in the language of exchange: as he says, he has already given the Athenians favors and expects to get things in return. This passage reminds us that the Greeks approached religion in terms of giving gifts and worship to the gods to get them to give good things in return. This kind of religious exchange may seem to have a transactional feel – in fact, Plato attacked traditional religion on precisely these terms. As he suggests, this is a base economic exchange (*emporian*).[16] The Greeks, however, believed that the gods strongly desired recognition and worship, and that they would convey benefits if worshipped properly.

In the examples discussed above, a Greek community accepted an individual's account of seeing an epiphany of a god.[17] Of course the Greeks did not automatically accept every epiphanic experience: they understood that an individual could fake this experience for private

---

[14] Strabo 8.6.15–84 gives a full account of the inscription with Isyllos' account of Asclepius appearing to him in an epiphany and of the Spartans' reaction to the news of the epiphany.

[15] See, e.g., Versnel 1987: 49, who leaves this question open though he leans towards a vocal epiphany; cf. Graf 2004: 115–16, who states that Pan's "appearance" was purely vocal.

[16] *Euthyphro* 15a; see also *Republic* 364c–e.

[17] This does not mean that every single member of a community or city-state accepted an individual's claim that he/she saw a divine epiphany. Still, we would not have these inscriptions and literary accounts if a community did not accept these views.

reasons.[18] For example, as Herodotus reports (1.60.3–5), Megacles contrived to put Peisistratus back on the throne in Athens by making a tall woman appear as Athena (wearing armor and driving a chariot) and having heralds in Athens proclaim that "Athena was bringing Peisistratus back to her acropolis." Herodotus finds this whole scene perfectly silly, though the event may have helped Peisistratus regain the throne.

Epiphanies were a central element of Greek religion: the human perception of the gods and their miraculous powers grounded religious worship. Indeed, divine epiphanies effectively validated religious cults and festivals. As Verity Platt observes in her discussion of miracles, omens, and oracles:

> Epiphany holds a special place within this category of divine signs as a form of unmediated encounter which, unlike oracular pronouncements or omens, can be experienced independently of preordained systems of specialized interpretation. Indeed, *epiphany functions as the cognitive device by which such systems can be proven valid.* That the potential of the immediate visionary perception of a deity's *eidos* was an important element of Greek thought is suggested by the frequency with which epiphanies occur within poetic and historiographical narratives, where they are closely related to both the establishment of cults and festivals and moments of crisis or change.[19]

Epiphanies served as the primary "cognitive device" by which the religious system could be validated. As I will argue, just as divine epiphanies provided the cognitive device that validated the Greek religious system, the philosopher's epiphanic vision of the Forms validates Plato's philosophical system.

In an epiphany, a god could manifest him or herself to a single person or to a group. If an individual saw an epiphany, the members of his/her community had to decide on its validity. When a community accepted an epiphany, it would set up a shrine or temple to the god and worship him/her in this sanctuary. We may ask how the Greeks experienced a divine epiphany. As Platt claims, "in the vocabulary of archaic Greek experience, an epiphany functions as the ultimate form of *thauma*, a 'wonder,' in which divine presence, or *eidos*, is asserted in profoundly physical terms and experienced phenomenologically as a sensory extravaganza ... and it has a powerful, often transformative affect upon its witnesses and their surroundings."[20] In poetic narratives of epiphany, the gods appear as huge,

---

[18] Platt 2011: 15–17.   [19] Platt 2011: 54–5 (my italics).

[20] Platt 2011: 36–7. For useful discussions of divine epiphanies in ancient Greece, see also Versnel 1987: 42–55; Cancik 1990: 290–6; Graf 2004; Petridou 2015.

beautiful, and radiant with light. The human viewers respond with fear, awe, and wonder.

2.2   The Mortal Soul in the *Symposium*

Plato's theory of metaphysical desire and the contemplation of the Forms cannot be understood unless we grasp his conception of the soul. As I argue, in the *Symposium*, Plato conceives of the soul as mortal. Most scholars have treated the soul in this dialogue as immortal, though there have been outliers. For example, in an article written in 1950, "Immortality in the *Symposium*," Reginald Hackforth argued that Plato had deliberately eliminated the immortal soul from Socrates' speech. Plato made this move, he claimed, because he had grown skeptical about his proofs for the immortality of the soul in the *Phaedo*. As Hackforth observed, previous scholars had simply assumed that the soul is immortal in Socrates' speech in spite of the fact that there is no textual evidence for this claim. These scholars took it for granted that the claims in the *Phaedo* about the immortal soul had to be valid in the *Symposium* as well.[21] After Hackforth's article, other scholars weighed in. For example, J. V. Luce attacked Hackforth's view, arguing that "the relation of the two doctrines [the immortal soul and the Forms] is one of logical entailment. If the Ideas exist, it can be deduced that the soul is immortal."[22] I do not agree that there is a logical entailment of these two platonic doctrines. Here, I will argue in favor of Hackforth's claim that the human soul is mortal.

In the *Symposium*, Socrates claims to have received his ideas about the soul and the Forms from Diotima, a priestess from Mantinea.[23] I will quote her discourse even though Socrates reports this in his own voice. First, Diotima conceives of the soul as mortal:

---

[21] Hackforth 1950.

[22] Luce 1952: 140; cf. Sedley 1995: 10, who argues that Plato did not conceive of the soul as immortal in his early dialogues, including the *Symposium*. Sedley (2009: 161), in his discussion of the philosopher seeing the Form of Beauty, thinks that there may be a possibility of the mortal soul becoming immortal (though he does not fully affirm this idea): "the riddling climax of her [Diotima's] speech has opened up an altogether new prospect: at the very pinnacle of intellectual progress, she hints, we can aspire to leave our mortal nature behind, acquiring in its place an immortal one. This parting shot, with its subtlest of hints that self-immortalization by procreation might culminate in a human being's personal apotheosis, suggests a way of closing the remaining gap between Platonic theory and the religious tradition. But could any such transition from a mortal to an immortal nature be accommodated to Plato's notion of either essential or conferred immortality? That is a question on which we are left to ponder."

[23] I take Diotima to be a fictional character created by Plato.

For here, according to the same logic, mortal nature seeks as much as possible to exist forever and to be immortal. In one way only can it succeed [in achieving immortality], and that is by generation, because it can always leave behind a new thing in place of the old. Since, in the time in which each living being can be said to be alive and the same – just as a person is said to be the same from childhood until he is an old man – nevertheless he does not possess the same properties within him even though he is called the same. He always becomes a new person, since he is losing things, such as his hair, his flesh, his bones, and his blood and his entire body. And this is not only true with respect to his body but also with respect to his soul (*kata tēn psuchēn*), for none of his customs, habits, opinions, desires, pleasures, pains, or fears ever stay the same in him; some of these come to being (*gignetai*) in him, while others perish (*apollutai*). And here is a yet stranger fact: not only do some aspects of knowledge (*epistēmai*) come to being (*gignontai*) in us and others perish (*apolluntai*), but we ourselves are never the same in regard to these possessions of knowledge, and each individual piece of knowledge suffers the same fate. That which we refer to as "practicing" (*meletan*) exists because our knowledge (*epistēmē*) is always departing. Forgetfulness is a departure (*exodos*) of knowledge while practicing once again implants a new memory (*kainēn ... mnēmēn*) in place of the memory that has departed, and so preserves our knowledge (*epistēmēn*) enough to make it seem (*dokein*) the same. Every mortal thing is preserved in this way; not by being exactly the same forever, like the divine, but because that which departs and gets old (*palaioumenon*) leaves behind another new thing that is similar to the original. Through this device, Socrates, a mortal thing partakes in immortality, both in its body and in all other respects. (207c–208b)

The soul ages and changes continually. Indeed, the mortal soul has to create some "new" idea in place of the "exodus" of the one that has perished. Like the body, the soul ages and loses things – its ideas and thoughts are forgotten and must be replaced with new ones once these have passed away. Diotima repeatedly uses *gignomai* and *apollumai* (coming-into-being and perishing) to describe different aspects of the soul, including its knowledge (*epistēmē*).

In Diotima's discourse, Plato sets the finite and changing soul in stark opposition to the eternal, changeless Forms.[24] Consider the language that she uses in discussing the soul and the Form of Beauty. First, as Diotima

---

[24] To be sure, the soul can contemplate the Forms by way of its reason. As Diotima notes, the philosopher "looks at Beauty with that by which beauty can be seen" (ᾧ ὁρατὸν τὸ καλόν; 212a). Here, she refers to the mind of the philosopher. This phrase, however, does not indicate that the soul's mind is immortal. See also her claim that the philosopher "beholds that [Beauty] *by that which it is right for him*" (ἐκεῖνο ᾧ δεῖ θεωμένου) to see the Forms (212a). Here again, she refers to reason, but not to immortality.

states, the soul preserves itself "not by being exactly the same, like the divine" (οὐ τῷ παντάπασιν τὸ αὐτὸ ἀεὶ εἶναι ὥσπερ τὸ θεῖον; 208a–b) but rather by studying and practicing so that its memory can hold onto what is lost. The Form, by contrast, "always exists, and does not come to be or pass away, grow or perish" (ἀεὶ ὂν καὶ οὔτε γιγνόμενον οὔτε ἀπολλύμενον, οὔτε αὐξανόμενον οὔτε φθίνον; 211a). This language of "coming to be and passing away" echoes Diotima's earlier claim that the soul's desires, passions, opinions, and knowledge "come to be and pass away" (207e–208b). The eternal and "divine" Forms thus stand in stark contrast to the soul, which ages, changes, and dies. It may seem that, during the time in which the philosopher contemplates the Form, his soul has escaped from the world of change, but this is a short-lived experience. In fact the philosopher's mind beholds Beauty even as his soul changes and ages in time.

This notion of a mortal and aging soul differs from Plato's conception of the soul in the *Phaedo, Meno, Republic, Phaedrus, Timaeus*, and *Laws*. In these dialogues, Plato identifies the soul as "immortal," "indestructible," and "akin to the divine." Thus, in the *Phaedo*, Plato places the soul in opposition to the body and aligns it with the Forms. Indeed, the soul is "akin" to the Forms. As Socrates states in the *Phaedo*: "but when [the soul] investigates by itself alone, it goes yonder to that which is pure, ever-existent, immortal and changeless; and, being akin (*suggenês*) to this [Being], the soul dwells with this always (*aei*), whenever it is by itself and allowed to do so, and it ceases from its wanderings and is always the same and unchanging (*aei kata tauta hôsautôs echei*) among the changeless [Forms], inasmuch as it lays hold of things of this kind" (79d). Consider also Socrates' statement in the *Republic*: "since the soul is not destroyed (*apollutai*) by any evil – either its own or that of another – it must necessarily exist always and if it exists always it is immortal" (610e–611a). Socrates also asserts the kinship between the soul and the divine realm of the Forms in book 10. As he says, rather than seeing the soul when it is marred by evil, the philosopher must "look at the soul's love of wisdom (*philosophian*) and at its knowledge of the beings that it touches, and at the sort of things it yearns for and associates with, since it is akin to that which is divine, immortal, and always existent" (συγγενὴς οὖσα τῷ τε θείῳ καὶ ἀθανάτῳ καὶ ἀεὶ ὄντι; 611e). In these dialogues, the immortal soul does not perish and has a kinship with the Forms. Diotima's discussion of the soul in the *Symposium* stands in stark contrast to the accounts in the other middle-period dialogues.

Plato's conception of the soul as mortal in the *Symposium* affects his discourse on immortality. In this text, he offers a complex meditation on the human desire for immortality. What kind of desire is this? The mortal person wants, first and foremost, to avoid death. The human awareness of death creates immense anxiety in the psyche. Temporally and existentially, we run ahead of ourselves and see that death awaits us in the future. Since the desire for immortality is rooted in the human sense of finitude and loss, we could call it a negative drive. This desire differs from others in that it derives from the angst of facing the abyss.

2.3   Desiring Immortality with Power in Aristophanes' Speech

Plato brings the desire for immortality to the fore in the very first speech in the dialogue. The speaker Phaedrus focuses on love and the longing for immortality. As he states, lovers (and even beloveds) willingly die noble deaths on behalf of their beloved partner so that they can have immortal glory. He cites the examples of Alcestis, who died in place of her husband Admetus, and Achilles, who chose death to avenge the slaying of his beloved Patroclus (Achilles knew that if he killed Hector he himself would die). These noble deaths brought Alcestis and Achilles great and lasting honor (180a–b). Phaedrus also says that the god Eros has "the greatest power in regard to the acquisition of virtue and happiness (*aretês kai eudaimonias ktêsin*) for men, whether they are alive or have passed away" (180b). As he states, a person "acquires" virtue and happiness by gaining everlasting fame. Here, Phaedrus articulates the common Greek notion that everlasting fame and glory makes a person happy and blessed in the eyes of later generations. Of course one cannot be happy individually after one dies, but one still has a share in blessedness.

Plato offers a deeper and more interesting exploration of the desire for immortality in Aristophanes' speech. Aristophanes' mythic discourse contains a brilliant meditation on the human sense of partiality and the longing for immortality. In this myth, Aristophanes claims that "original humans" (hereafter, "o-humans") were round and whole beings who did not experience eros. They produced offspring, but they did this by laying eggs in the earth, like cicadas. The o-humans had great power and chose to fight the gods. Indeed, by attacking the gods, they aimed to set themselves up as divinities. In short, although they did not have erotic desire, the o-humans longed to become gods. As mortal beings, they desired immortality.

Aristophanes compares the o-humans' assault on the gods to that of Ephialtes and Otus. In Greek myth, Ephialtes and Otus – "giants" conceived by Poseidon and a mortal mother – had immense power. For example, they imprisoned Ares for a year and later attacked the gods by piling Mount Ossa on Mount Olympus, and Mount Pelion on Mount Ossa. Ephialtes and Otus lost this battle, and Zeus punished them by chaining them forever in Hades. In Aristophanes' myth, the o-humans resemble Ephialtes and Otus in that they aimed to conquer the Olympians and become gods themselves. The o-humans want the everlasting power of the gods. Like the two giants, they lose this battle. In Aristophanes' myth, when the Olympians beat down the o-humans, Zeus says that he does not want to destroy them in the way that he had punished Ephialtes and Otus. He wants the o-humans to go on worshipping the gods on earth. He comes up with a new kind of punishment for their "outrageous" acts: he cuts the o-humans in half (190c–d).

What does this myth tell us about the o-humans and their desire for immortality? First, the o-humans wanted to have the life of the gods – an everlasting life full of ease and pleasure. But they seem most of all to want divine power (rather than mere ease). After all, they engage in a power struggle with the gods. Of course Aristophanes works with the traditional Greek gods in this myth. The Greek gods lived outside of human morality – they were not good or just in human terms but supremely powerful. These divinities could help or harm humans, depending on their moods and whims. They were moody and mysterious – for this reason, people had to worship and appease them regularly. It was this amoral divine power that the o-humans wanted. Indeed, the o-humans had "great ambitions" (*ta phronêmata megala eichon*; 190b), and this led to their violent attack on the gods. Not surprisingly, in Aristophanes' myth, the gods respond with anger and violence. Indeed, the story focuses on a power struggle. The o-humans did not aim to be good gods but rather powerful beings who could do whatever they wanted without suffering punishment. In this wonderfully funny myth, Plato presents an important meditation on the human desire for immortality.

As I have suggested, the o-humans desired *immortality with godly power*. As the offspring of o-humans, present-day humans (we infer) can still feel this desire for immortality with godly power. In Aristophanes' view, the desire for godly power is part of our human nature. In Socrates' speech, as we will see, Plato offers a different way of thinking about the desire for immortality. There, he will present the idea that humans long for *immortality with goodness*.

We are not yet finished with Aristophanes' speech. In this myth, Plato also explores the human sense of partiality. In the second half of the myth, the gods cut the o-humans in half. The half o-humans became actual humans, each being part of a larger whole. The humans immediately felt so much longing for their other half that they could not function at all and started to die. To avoid having humans die away as a race, the gods moved their genitals from the side to the front so that they could enjoy the pleasures of sex. They gave humans sexual eros. This did not provide a full union between the human halves, but it did allow people to temporarily unite with each other so that they could carry on living. Once they experienced eros, the humans groped to understand the intense desire that they felt: "There are people who live their entire lives together and still cannot say what it is that they want from each other. No one thinks that sexual intercourse is the reason why each lover feels so much joy in being with the other. Clearly, the soul of each lover longs for something else. But he cannot state what this is, but he only divines what he wants and guesses at it in riddles" (192c–d). In Aristophanes' view, humans most of all desire to be fused with their other halves and to become whole again.

In Aristophanes' myth, Hephaestus comes upon two lovers and asks them a key question: "what is it that you really desire?" This is the core question that Plato poses in the entire dialogue. In this comic myth, he explores an important aspect of the human condition: we continually feel longings that never get satisfied, but we nonetheless try to find an object that will offer fulfilment. Aristophanes offers a diagnosis of this problem: each human has lost its other half and wants to unite and become whole. Humans literally want "more me." In this case, "more me" means recovering one's original state. In this scene in the *Symposium*, Hephaestus offers to weld the two lovers back together and make them one being again. We should note, however, that if these humans returned to the wholeness of the o-humans, this would not in fact fulfil their core desire for immortality. For the o-humans will still have to die. Thus, after promising that he will weld these two lovers back together, Hephaestus says: "as long as you live, the pair of you, being one, can live your lives in common as one; and, when you die, in Hades you will be one instead of two, having shared a single death" (192e). Here, Plato reminds the reader that the o-humans were mortal. It was precisely their mortality that filled them with a desire to become gods. If Hephaistos did weld the humans back together and make them o-humans, he would not take away their longing for immortality. For, if the humans became o-humans, they would no longer feel sexual desire but would still desire the immortal life of the gods.

Aristophanes closes his myth with an optimistic message: "For not only does he [Eros] benefit us greatly in the present by leading us to that which is ours, but he also furnishes great hopes for the future: if we treat the god piously, he will bring us back to our primal nature and, by healing us, make us *blessed and happy*" (*makarious kai eudaimonas*; 193d, my italics). But, as we have seen, the o-humans in their "primal nature" were not "blessed" in the sense of being immortal. Indeed, if they were restored to their original nature, they would be back at square one: their eros would disappear but they would still desire immortality. In short, they would gain a better life, but their original longing for immortality remains.

In this humorous myth, Plato offers a poignant philosophical meditation. He addresses the human sense of longing and partiality. Why do we feel these longings? How can we address this painful predicament? As I have suggested, in Aristophanes' myth, the humans want "more-me," i.e., a "whole me," while the o-humans want "more-me" in terms of an everlasting self. They want the life of the gods, which includes having divine power. As this myth shows, the o-humans (and also present humans) long for "immortality with godly power." Socrates will reject this idea and offer a different account of the desire for immortality.

2.4 Desiring Immortality with Goodness in Socrates' Speech

Socrates prefaces his speech by saying that he will "tell the truth" about Eros. Indeed, he criticizes the other speakers for not giving a truthful account of the god. As he claims: "it was agreed, it seems, that each of you would seem to praise Eros but not really praise him. Thus, stirring up all kinds of words, you ascribe them to Love, and you say that he is of such a kind and the cause of so many great things, so that he seems to be the best and most beautiful, clearly for those who do not possess knowledge but not in fact for those who do" (198e–199a). Clearly, Socrates does not accept these conditions. Among other things, he objects to the other speakers' conception of "the best and most beautiful" (*kallistos kai aristos*) – whether this applies to gods or men – and thinks that this needs to be reconceived.

Socrates presents a dense and complicated account of Eros that needs careful examination. In the earlier part of the speech, he focuses on Eros as the desire for "immortality with goodness." In the last section of the speech, he identifies Eros as metaphysical desire, i.e., the desire for the Form of Beauty. In his discourse, these two desires are, to some extent, entangled with each other. But the desire for immortality differs from metaphysical desire. We need to prise these two desires apart to fully understand Plato's theory of love.

Let me look first at Diotima's discussion on the desire for immortality. She begins by convincing Socrates that Eros does not possess goodness, beauty, or wisdom but is endlessly pursuing these things. Indeed, Eros is not a god at all, since "all gods are happy and beautiful" and "those are happy who possess the good and beautiful" (εὐδαίμονας . . . τοὺς τἀγαθὰ καὶ τὰ καλὰ κεκτημένους; 202c). After positing the idea that the gods are fully good, beautiful, and happy, she says that Eros does not possess these things and therefore cannot be a god.[25] Diotima concludes that Eros is not a god but rather a *daimôn*, a being that is divine but does not have the full status of a god (more on this below).

As Diotima states, Eros lacks and "desires" (*erâ*) beauty (204d). This leads to an important exchange with Socrates, which runs as follows. Diotima: "what does the lover of beauty actually desire?" Socrates: the lover "wants beauty to be his." Diotima: "if the lover possesses beautiful things, what exactly will come to him?" Socrates responds with great bafflement. Due to his confusion, Diotima shifts the direction of the conversation. She restates her earlier question by substituting goodness for beauty: "what does the lover of goodness want?" Socrates answers, "he wants goodness to be his." "And what exactly will come to him if he possesses beauty?" "Happiness" (204e). Diotima accepts this answer and then concludes: "the happy (*eudaimones*) are happy by the possession of good things, and there is no need to ask why men wish to be happy. The answer you give has its telos" (205a). At this key moment, Diotima turns the discussion from beauty to goodness.

In this passage, Diotima sets forth the basic eudaimonist axiom: all people want to be happy and they achieve happiness by possessing good things. In terms of the "good things" in question, she first mentions a wide range of human activities: sports, money-making, and philosophy (205d). At this point, she offers a very general idea of the "good things" that people love and pursue. But she moves beyond this idea when she makes the following claim: "my account states that the lover does not seek a half or a whole unless that thing is good" (ὁ δ' ἐμὸς λόγος οὔτε ἡμίσεός φησιν εἶναι τὸν ἔρωτα οὔτε ὅλου, ἐὰν μὴ τυγχάνῃ γέ που . . . ἀγαθὸν ὄν; 205e). The lover only desires good things. This statement clearly refers to the ideas set

---

[25] Diotima does not explain what it means "to possess the good and the beautiful." She does address the philosopher's grasp of the Form of Beauty at the end of the speech, but she never discusses the Form of the Good (or the link between Beauty and the Good).

forth in Aristophanes' speech (though Diotima has not even heard that discourse!). Here, Plato invites the reader to compare Aristophanes' theory of love to the one that Diotima sets forth.

Two key ideas come up in this passage: (1) that the gods are happy because they are good and beautiful, and (2) that humans could become happy if they could possess these same qualities. Although humans cannot achieve the happiness of the gods, they can still move towards it by practicing philosophy and apprehending the Forms.

Diotima now introduces the topic of immortality. After claiming that all people desire the good, she states: everyone wants "the good to be theirs *forever (aei)*" (206a, my italics). Humans want to be *everlastingly* good and happy. However, since humans are mortal, they can only gain a partial form of immortality by producing good offspring through reproduction.[26] As Diotima states:

> Why reproduction? Because this is the ever-existing and immortal element for the mortal. A lover must desire *immortality together with goodness* (*athanasias ... meta agathou*) if what we agreed on earlier was right, that love desires the good to be one's own forever. It follows from our argument that love must desire immortality. (τί δὴ οὖν τῆς γεννήσεως; ὅτι ἀειγενές ἐστι καὶ ἀθάνατον ὡς θνητῷ ἡ γέννησις. ἀθανασίας δὲ ἀναγκαῖον ἐπιθυμεῖν μετὰ ἀγαθοῦ ἐκ τῶν ὡμολογημένων, εἴπερ τοῦ ἀγαθοῦ ἑαυτῷ εἶναι ἀεὶ ἔρως ἐστίν. ἀναγκαῖον δὴ ἐκ τούτου τοῦ λόγου καὶ τῆς ἀθανασίας τὸν ἔρωτα εἶναι; 206e–207a, my italics)

Here, Diotima yokes the desire for goodness with the desire for immortality. One wants immortality "with goodness" so that one's immortal self will be everlastingly good and happy. We can infer that gaining "immortality with goodness" entails a search for true goodness.

Diotima examines the human desire for immortality in some detail.[27] She first identifies this as a natural desire shared by animals and humans. Indeed, as she claims, animals' eagerness to mate and procreate gives evidence of their desire for immortality: "Do you not perceive how all animals – both footed and winged – are in a terrible state (δεινῶς διατίθεται) when they want to reproduce, being sick and in a lustful state, first to have sexual intercourse with each another, and then to nurture

---

[26] To be sure, if a person produces excellent offspring, he/she will not be around to enjoy this. Of course Diotima says that the individual "partakes in" immortality and happiness – he/she gets an everlasting life by way of his/her offspring.

[27] Note that she explicitly refers to the "love of immortality": τοῦ γὰρ ἀθανάτου ἐρῶσιν (208e; see also 208b).

the newborn? They are ready to fight on behalf of them, the weakest against the strongest, and to die on behalf of them" (207a–b).[28] As Diotima states, the animals' evident zeal to procreate indicates that they all desire immortality: "Mortal nature seeks as much as possible to exist forever and to be immortal" (207c–d).[29] This identifies the desire for immortality as an innate natural drive.[30]

To explain these ideas, Diotima asserts that the human body and mind continually change in the passing of time (207c–208b; quoted above). The soul and body of humans alter as one ages, and this brings deterioration and, eventually, death. For this reason, humans can only achieve a partial immortality. They do this by giving birth to offspring: "in one way only can mortal nature succeed [in achieving immortality], and that is by generation, because it can always leave behind a new thing in place of the old" (207c–d). Humans cannot achieve the immortality of the gods, who have the same body and individual identity forever. As Diotima claims:

> Every mortal thing is preserved in this way; not by being exactly the same forever, like the divine, but because that which departs and gets old (*palaioumenon*) leaves behind another new thing that is similar to the original. (208a–b)

Diotima first bolsters this idea by pointing to the irrational human ambition for lasting glory (φιλοτιμίαν): humans "are in a terrible state due to their desire to become famous and lay up immortal glory forever" (δεινῶς διάκεινται ἔρωτι τοῦ ὀνομαστοὶ γενέσθαι καὶ κλέος ἐς τὸν ἀεὶ χρόνον ἀθάνατον καταθέσθαι; 208c). The ambition for lasting glory, though irrational and obsessive, in fact manifests the desire for immortality.[31] In

---

[28] ἢ οὐκ αἰσθάνῃ ὡς δεινῶς διατίθεται πάντα τὰ θηρία ἐπειδὰν γεννᾶν ἐπιθυμήσῃ, καὶ τὰ πεζὰ καὶ τὰ πτηνά, νοσοῦντά τε πάντα καὶ ἐρωτικῶς διατιθέμενα, πρῶτον μὲν περὶ τὸ συμμιγῆναι ἀλλήλοις, ἔπειτα περὶ τὴν τροφὴν τοῦ γενομένου, καὶ ἕτοιμά ἐστιν ὑπὲρ τούτων καὶ διαμάχεσθαι τὰ ἀσθενέστατα τοῖς ἰσχυροτάτοις καὶ ὑπεραποθνήσκειν. Here, Plato uses *erotikôs* in terms of lust.

[29] ἐνταῦθα γὰρ τὸν αὐτὸν ἐκείνῳ λόγον ἡ θνητὴ φύσις ζητεῖ κατὰ τὸ δυνατὸν ἀεί τε εἶναι καὶ ἀθάνατος. δύναται δὲ ταύτῃ μόνον, τῇ γενέσει, ὅτι ἀεὶ καταλείπει ἕτερον νέον ἀντὶ τοῦ παλαιοῦ.

[30] Note that animals do not desire immortality per se: they have no concept of immortality (or any concepts at all), and thus have no idea that their children allow them to achieve a partial immortality. Rather, animals biologically feel sexual attraction for their mates and this leads to reproduction. Humans have this same natural drive to procreate, but they differ from animals in that they have reason and memory – this gives them a concept of immortality. Thus, Diotima's argument that the animal desire for procreation provides evidence for the *desire for immortality* does not fully hold up. She seems to conflate the animal desire for sex, a biological drive, with the desire for immortality, which is a human drive.

[31] Note that Diotima uses the exact phrase for human ambition that she did in her earlier discussion of animals: they are "in a terrible state" (δεινῶς διατίθεται; 207a, 208c) because of their desire to procreate. Like this animal desire, humans feel an irrational desire for fame. Of course Plato locates

the case of ambition for fame, Diotima articulates a very traditional Greek idea: that one can achieve undying fame by living or dying in some glorious way. This fame gives one a partial immortality.

Diotima claims that humans "give birth" to offspring in both body and soul. These two modes of birthgiving give people different kinds of partial immortality. I want to look carefully at the "birthgiving" of the soul. As Diotima suggests, while some people (women) have bodily pregnancies, there are some people who are "pregnant in soul" (οἱ ἐν ταῖς ψυχαῖς κυοῦσιν; 208e–209a). In this latter model, beauty functions as a midwife: the soul gives birth to offspring "in the presence of beauty." Diotima presents two models of psychic reproduction that confer partial immortality on an individual: (1) that of a poet or lawgiver who gives birth to a glorious poem or lawcode and gains everlasting fame, and (2) that of a philosophic lover who gives birth to and "rears up" his discursive children by engaging in dialogues with his beautiful beloved. Let me analyze these two models of psychic reproduction and explain how they operate in the desire for immortality.

In the first model of psychic reproduction, humans give birth to "intelligence and other virtues" (φρόνησίν τε καὶ τὴν ἄλλην ἀρετήν). Diotima puts two kinds of people in this category: "all poets" (οἱ ποιηταὶ πάντες) and "those craftsmen who are known as inventors" (τῶν δημιουργῶν ὅσοι λέγονται εὑρετικοὶ εἶναι; 209a).[32] Later, she expands this group, adding lawgivers (such as Solon and Lycurgus) to the mix (209d). The virtues of these people are embodied in poems, lawcodes, and lasting inventions. We must note, however, that poets, inventors, and lawgivers give birth to traditional forms of *phronêsis* and *aretê* rather than to philosophic virtue.

In the second model of psychic reproduction, Diotima refers to people who desire the greatest kind of *phronêsis*: "the ordering of cities and households is the greatest and most beautiful aspect of wisdom, which we call moderation and justice" (πολὺ δὲ μεγίστη . . . καὶ καλλίστη τῆς

---

the desire for fame and glory in the "spirited" (*thumoeidic*) part of the soul in the *Republic* (581a) and *Phaedrus* (253b). The spirited part of the soul is irrational, and thus its desire for glory can be seen as a drive that needs to be guided by reason (see Nehamas 2007: 116). These later texts on the tripartite soul and its *thumoeidic* part are in accord with Diotima's claim that humans are "disposed in a terrible way by their desire to become famous."

[32] One is struck by her claim that poets and craftsmen bring about intelligence and virtue: this conflicts with Plato's demotion of these putatively wise men in the early and middle dialogues. But in this dialogue, he indicates (via Diotima) that poets and inventors have created glorious things that rightly gave them immortal fame. Referring to Homer, Hesiod, and lawgivers like Solon and Lycurgus, Diotima says that "many shrines" have been set up for these men on account of their immortal children (209e).

φρονήσεως ἡ περὶ τὰ τῶν πόλεών τε καὶ οἰκήσεων διακόσμησις, ἧ δὴ ὄνομά ἐστι σωφροσύνη τε καὶ δικαιοσύνη; 209a). Diotima identifies these men as philosophic lovers. These individuals love beautiful boys but also, and more importantly, wisdom. As she claims, the lover must first find a beloved whose soul is "beautiful, noble, and well formed" (209b). In particular, he must see the beauty of the beloved's soul – this enables him to give birth to discourses about virtue: "straightaway toward such a boy [the beloved], the lover is resourceful in speaking about virtue, what makes a man good, and what he should pursue (εὐπορεῖ λόγων περὶ ἀρετῆς καὶ περὶ οἷον χρὴ εἶναι τὸν ἄνδρα τὸν ἀγαθὸν καὶ ἃ ἐπιτηδεύειν), and he attempts to educate him (παιδεύειν)" (209b–c). The lover, who is pregnant with the virtues of justice and moderation, gives birth to *logoi* that educate his beloved. Indeed, Diotima focuses on the lover's discursive offspring (*logoi*), which must be reared up together with the beloved. She does not explain how this enables the lover to develop his own virtues. We can infer that the lover grows in virtue by way of examining ideas in dialogues with his beloved. In short, the lover gives birth to discourses when he is in the presence of his beloved: the beauty of the boy serves as the midwife that enables him to give birth. The lover then rears his discursive offspring through philosophical investigation.

Since the philosophic lover does not give birth to a fixed text or object (like a poet, inventor, or lawgiver), he achieves a different kind of partial immortality. He gains this by educating a young man (or men), who will keep his ideas and discourses alive in later generations. This is why he must keep working on his ideas (his offspring) with his beloved. As Diotima states, the lover and beloved collectively raise his psychic "children": "When he [the philosophic lover] lays hold of that beautiful person and associates with him, he gives birth to and begets those things that he was pregnant with long ago . . . . And, together with him, he shares the nurturing of the newborn (τὸ γεννηθὲν συνεκτρέφει κοινῇ μετ' ἐκείνου), so that men of this kind have a much greater partnership with each other than do parents of [physical] children, and a firmer friendship, since they have shared in common more beautiful and immortal children (καλλιόνων καὶ ἀθανατωτέρων παίδων κεκοινωνηκότες; 209c).[33] The couple "collect-ively raise" (*sunektrephei*) the offspring and have a "partnership" in which they "share in common" the psychic children. This partnership supports the discursive "children" by presenting arguments and counterarguments

[33] Diotima refers to "children" in the plural; we can infer that the lover gives birth to many ideas and discourses when he is with his beloved.

about the philosopher's claims.[34] This means that the beloved must develop philosophical abilities himself. Only as a philosopher can he carry on his lover's line after he dies.

I want to conclude this section by returning to Diotima's claim that people become virtuous by possessing goodness, and that possessing goodness makes one happy. In Socrates' speech, Plato repeatedly emphasizes the notion of "possessing" goodness." For example, when Diotima asks what the lover of goodness wants," Socrates says that "he wants goodness to be his" (γενέσθαι αὐτῷ). As Diotima observes, "the happy are happy by the possession (*ktesei*) of good things" (204d–205a). Indeed, if one possesses good things forever (*aei*), one attains "immortality with goodness." But exactly how does one come into possession of goodness? Plato does not answer this question in the *Symposium*. Rather, he focuses on the "possession" or epistemic grasp of the Form of Beauty.

2.5 Metaphysical Desire

In the Ladder of Love, Diotima's speech takes a different turn. She introduces a new desire, the metaphysical desire for the Forms. As I have suggested, the human desire for immortality is self-oriented: one wants an everlasting self with goodness. Even the philosopher who gives birth to discourses that his beloved (and perhaps students) will carry on after he dies has a self-oriented desire: his *logoi* will live on. Metaphysical desire, by contrast, aims at an external object – a divine, ever-existing, incorporeal, unchanging, and unitary Form. As we will see, in the case of the Form of Beauty, the philosopher knows what beauty is and also understands that this is the object of his deepest desire. In addition, I will argue, the philosopher encounters divinity when he contemplates Beauty.

In the *Symposium*, metaphysical desire aims specifically at the Form of Beauty. In this part of Diotima's speech, eros takes on a new role: it desires the Forms. To understand this idea, we must go back to Diotima's discussion of Eros. As she says to Socrates (and as Socrates says to Agathon), he wrongly conceived of Eros as "beautiful in every way, as though Eros is the beautiful beloved boy sought by the lover" (204c). She identifies Eros as the lover, not the beautiful beloved. Eros is the love for beautiful objects. Diotima now introduces a new claim: Eros is not in fact a god. The gods are good, beautiful, and happy, but Eros lacks these things

---

[34] One could imagine that the beloved would have some of his own ideas to give birth to as he encounters beautiful things himself (though Diotima does not make this explicit).

(202c). Rather, Eros is a daimon who dwells in the in-between (*metaxu*): he lives in a realm between gods and mortals, between wisdom and ignorance, and between beauty and ugliness. Eros is not himself beautiful but actively desires beauty.

In this early part of her discourse, Diotima focuses exclusively on beauty.[35] As we have seen, she treats beauty as the object of love. She changes course, however, when she moves from the desire for beauty to the desire for goodness and immortality (see above). She discusses this new topic at some length: humans long for immortality with goodness, and beauty plays the role of the midwife. She will come back to the notion of beauty as an object of love in the Ladder of Love.

As scholars have noted, Beauty plays a dual role in the speech: it functions both as a midwife and as the object of desire. This makes it hard to understand Plato's theory of philosophic eros. Many scholars claim that the true object of this desire is "immortality with goodness" (beauty merely serves as an "occasion" that allows one to satisfy the desire for goodness and immortality).[36] They admit that the lover desires beauty as an object, but argue that this is not the final goal of desire.[37] In my view, Plato presents two different kinds of desire in this speech: the desire for immortality with goodness, and the metaphysical desire for the Form of Beauty. These can interlap with each other, but they are very different desires. While all humans share the longing for immortality, only a few people feel metaphysical desire for the Forms. Philosophers alone experience this desire, which aims at the Forms.

In Plato's middle-period dialogues, the philosopher desires all the Forms. But when Plato first offers an account of philosophic eros, he focuses on the Form of Beauty. Why this emphasis on beauty? Beauty has a special status in human life: it takes instant hold of the viewer and fills him or her with wonder and pleasure. The experience of beauty is immediate and undeniable, regardless of the object of beauty. To be sure, we may judge that we have enjoyed a beautiful object that we later think of as minor or even base. But the fact remains that we have an immediate and undeniable response to beauty. We know it when (and as) we see it. In the

---

[35] Socrates does say at the beginning that Love is not a god because gods are "good and beautiful" (202c–d). But this passing reference to the "good" does not override the fact that Diotima focuses on beauty before she turns to the desire for the good (cf. G. Lear 2007).

[36] See, e.g., Price 1990: 17; White 2004: 366–78; Ferrari 1992: 260; G. Lear 2007. Cf. Nehamas 2007, who argues that beauty is the final goal of the philosopher.

[37] Nehamas 2007 is a major exception. Cf. Sheffield 2006: 125–41, who claims that beauty is the primary "object" of love, while the "aim" of desire is happiness.

case of virtues like justice or courage, by contrast, it takes time to determine if a person or action was just or courageous. We decide this retrospectively, by consulting our own values. Beauty, however, is experienced in the present. It is precisely this "presence-effect" of beauty in the earthly realm that allows Plato to represent the philosopher as seeing the ever-existing Form of Beauty appearing in its divine presence.[38] Plato uses the presence-effect of beauty to showcase the presence of the Forms to the philosopher's mind. Indeed, the Forms appear to the philosopher as divine presences.

Let us consider the "presence-effect" of the Form of Beauty in the passage where Diotima discusses the philosophic lover giving birth in the presence of the beauty of his beloved. She uses a strange phrase to articulate this idea: "giving birth in the beautiful" (τόκος ἐν καλῷ; 206b). Or, as she puts it in a more highfalutin statement: people desire "the engendering and giving birth in the beautiful" (τῆς γεννήσεως καὶ τοῦ τόκου ἐν τῷ καλῷ; 206e). What does Diotima mean by giving birth "in" (en) the beautiful? She clarifies this point by saying that the pregnant person gives birth when he is *near* the beautiful: "when that which is pregnant *gets near* the beautiful, it becomes gracious and, being gladdened, it flows over and gives birth and begets" (ὅταν μὲν καλῷ προσπελάζῃ τὸ κυοῦν, ἵλεών τε γίγνεται καὶ εὐφραινόμενον διαχεῖται καὶ τίκτει τε καὶ γεννᾷ; 206d).

The philosophic lover sees the beauty of the beloved when he comes near him and is in his presence. In short, the lover does not want to get "in" or "inside" (en) the boy's beauty (whatever that would mean) but rather to get near it so as to behold its presence. Giving birth "in the beautiful," then, means birthgiving "in the presence of the beautiful." The lover "associates with" (homilôn) the beautiful boy by being near him and in his presence (209c). This allows him to behold beauty in its immediacy.[39]

In the Ladder of Love, Diotima uses the discourse of "being near to" and "associating with" in reference to the philosopher's contemplation of the Form of Beauty. As she states: "But what if he could see divine beauty itself, singular in form? Do you think that the life of this man is trifling – looking there and seeing this [Beauty] by the proper means, and *being together* with it?" (ἀλλ' αὐτὸ τὸ θεῖον καλὸν δύναιτο μονοειδὲς κατιδεῖν; ἆρ' οἴει ... φαῦλον βίον γίγνεσθαι ἐκεῖσε βλέποντος ἀνθρώπου καὶ ἐκεῖνο ᾧ δεῖ θεωμένου καὶ συνόντος αὐτῷ; 211e–212a, my italics). The philosopher

---

[38] I borrow this term from Sepp Gumbrecht. Gumbrecht 2004 focuses on presence-effects in terms of phenomenology.
[39] Of course the lover may lust to penetrate the boy, but we must separate this bodily desire from the eros for beauty (though the two are connected).

"sees" and enjoys a *sunousia*, a "being-together-with" the Form. Of course the Form is not a living, conscious being: it does not react to the philosopher in the sense of two agents "being together." Still, as these passages suggest, the philosopher comes into the presence of the Form and beholds Beauty.

In my view, Plato reached for the presence-effect of beauty to represent the "presentness" of Forms to the philosophic viewer. When the philosopher sees a Form, its eternal existence is manifested to him as a presence. The Form manifests itself during the period when the philosopher engages in contemplation. Since the philosopher dwells in time, the Form becomes present to the human in the "now" when he beholds the Forms. To conjure up the presentness of the Forms, Plato turned to the Form of Beauty. Just as beauty has a presence-effect in human life on earth, the Form of Beauty manifests itself in its full presence to the philosophic contemplator. Of course all the Forms have this presentness, but Plato focused on the Form of Beauty to capture this idea. Indeed, he uses the metaphor of "seeing" precisely to emphasize the immediate presence of the Form to the eye of the mind. As I will argue, the Form of Beauty manifests its divine presence epiphanically to the philosophic soul.

2.6 The Eleusinian Mysteries

Plato represents the Form of Beauty as appearing to the philosopher in terms of a divine epiphany. In the prelude to the Ladder of Love, he uses the discourse of poetic narratives of epiphany to alert the reader that the philosopher will encounter divinity when he contemplates Beauty. As Diotima states, the philosopher will "suddenly" behold a "wondrous and divine (*theion*)" beauty. Plato also uses the terminology of the final initiation rite in the Eleusinian Mysteries to conjure up the epiphany of divine Beauty. As Diotima says to Socrates: "Perhaps even you, Socrates, could be initiated as a *mustês* in these love matters. But as to the final rites and the visions of the *epoptês*, which is the goal of these things if a man advances rightly, I don't know if you are capable of this" (ταῦτα μὲν οὖν τὰ ἐρωτικὰ ἴσως, ὦ Σώκρατες, κἂν σὺ μυηθείης· τὰ δὲ τέλεα καὶ ἐποπτικά, ὧν ἕνεκα καὶ ταῦτα ἔστιν, ἐάν τις ὀρθῶς μετίῃ, οὐκ οἶδ᾽ εἰ οἷός τ᾽ ἂν εἴης; 209e–210a). Plato portrays the philosophic ascent to the Forms in terms of the lower and higher initiations in the Eleusinian Mysteries. By identifying the advanced philosopher as an *epoptês* of the Form, he indicates that the philosopher sees the Form as a new kind of divine epiphany.

We can only understand Plato's references to the mysteries by grasping the basic rituals and events in the Eleusinian Mysteries. For this reason, I will present a detailed account of this mystery religion. The Eleusinian Mysteries featured two initiation ceremonies: first, that of the *mustês*, who undergoes a preparatory initiation; second, that of the *epoptês*, who sees some sort of epiphany of Demeter in the final revelation.[40] In this and other Greek festivals, the celebrants experienced the presence of a god or goddess by way of "ritualized visualization." The elaborate rituals at festivals sacralized the events and objects that the celebrants witnessed. The sacred space of the sanctuary also played a key role in ritualized visualization. As Jaś Elsner observes, the sanctuary was a "liminal site in which the viewer enters the god's world and likewise the deity intrudes directly into the viewer's world in a highly ritualized context."[41] The ritualized mode of seeing "denies the appropriateness ... of interpreting images through the rules and desires of everyday life. It constructs a ritual barrier to the identifications and objectifications of the screen of [social] discourse and posits a sacred possibility for vision ...."[42] This "ritualized visuality" effectively screened out secular modes of viewing and allowed the celebrant to experience the presence of the god. In the case of the Eleusinian Mysteries, the initiands went through many days of preparatory rituals. The final initiation, the climax of the mysteries, took place at night in a building lit up by a blaze of torches. This allowed them to see some sort of divine revelation (more on this below).

The Eleusinian Mysteries took place in a festival for Demeter and Kore (aka Persephone).[43] Although this was an Athenian festival, it attracted people from all over Greece. It was hugely popular. This festival was open to the public, but the initiation ceremonies, which took place within this larger festival, were open only to initiands. All Greek-speaking people (men and women, free or enslaved) could undergo initiation, but non-Greek speakers (*barbaroi*) could not. The goal of initiation was to encounter the goddess and gain a happy afterlife. All initiates had to maintain full secrecy

---

[40] Note that Plato puts Socrates at the level of the *mustês*, probably because Plato had moved beyond him to develop his own metaphysics (though he leaves open the possibility that Socrates saw these higher realities).

[41] Elsner 2000: 61.   [42] Elsner 2000: 62; see also Rutherford 1998: 135.

[43] On the Eleusinian Mysteries, see Burkert 1985: 285–90; Clinton 1993: 110–24 and 2003: 50–78; Dillon 1997: 60–72; Sourvinou-Inwood 2003: 25–49; Parker 2005: 327–55; Bowden 2010: 26–48. The Eleusinian Mysteries have presented serious interpretive problems for scholars. First, those initiated in the mysteries were obliged to stay silent about the event. Second, some of the details of the ceremony were provided by sources from late antiquity. This means that scholars have to reconstruct the event to the extent that this is possible.

about the event, though some did break this rule and faced punishment.[44] That said, the rituals in the mysteries were an open secret in Athens because so many people got initiated and experienced this unique religious experience. Athenian readers of Plato, then, could easily understand his references to the final initiation ceremony (the *epopteia*).

The public religious festival for Demeter and Kore lasted for over a week. The day before the festival (the fourteenth day of the month of Boedromion), priestesses brought baskets of "holy objects" in wagons from Athens to the sanctuary at Eleusis along the Sacred Road. On the fifth or sixth day of the festival, a huge ritual procession (*pompê*) of Athenians and foreigners started out from the Temple of Demeter in Athens and journeyed to Eleusis. A huge mass of Athenians and foreigners made this fourteen-mile trip by foot or donkey. Along the way, the worshippers engaged in ritual washings, libations, sacrifices, sacred dances, singing (accompanied by the *auloi* or "pipes"), and loud chantings to the god Iakchos (whom scholars have identified as Dionysus). By the end of the day, the worshippers arrived at the sanctuary in Eleusis "together with the god Iakchos" in a state of exhilaration. As I mentioned above, the initiation ceremonies were only open to initiands. As Bremmer observes, when the initiands arrived at the sanctuary, "the night fell early, and the flickering of the thousands of torches must have produced a near psychedelic effect among the weary travellers."[45] Initiation took place in a building called the Telesterion. This unique architectural structure took the form of a walled and windowless building crisscrossed with columns on the inside. It had eight rows of raised steps along the walls so that a great number of people could participate in the ceremony. The initiates experienced the final revelation in this building. In short, this long festival led the initiates to have an extraordinary religious experience. As Robert Parker puts it: "there were prolonged preparations leading up both to initiation and final revelation – a build-up, an extension in time, a concentration of attention, quite unlike anything in normal Greek religious experience."[46]

An individual had to go to three events to have a full initiation in the mysteries. First, one had to attend the Lesser Mysteries, held in the sanctuary of the "Mother at Agrai" in February. After one had gone to this festival and partaken of the rituals, one became a *mustês*. The person is

---

[44] Alcibiades, who appears in this dialogue, was accused of the "profanation of the mysteries," i.e., revealing its secrets, in 415 BCE. The Athenians also accused Andocides of playing a role in this event (as Andocides' *de Mysteries* and Plutarch's *Alcibiades* attest). I will discuss Alcibiades further below.
[45] Bremmer 2014: 7.   [46] Parker 2011: 253.

now ready for initiation. At the Greater Mysteries, held in the sanctuary of Demeter at Eleusis in September–October, the individual would go through the first initiation. In this initiation, the *mustês* did not see the final revelation. He or she had to go back to the Greater Mysteries a year later to go through the final initiation as an *epoptês*. The word μύστης comes from the verb μύω, which means "to close" one's eyes or lips. The *mustês* is blind to the final revelations (because he or she does not attend the final initiation ceremony). The ἐπόπτης, by contrast, is "the person who sees." Of course the *mustês* does learn some key things during initiation. As Clement of Alexandria (circa 200 CE) states: "In the mysteries of the Greeks, the beginning involves purifications, just as among the barbarians it involves bathing. After this there are the Lesser Mysteries, which have the goal of teaching and preparing for the things to come, but the Greater [Mysteries] concern everything, where it is no longer a matter of learning but seeing and pondering nature and realities."[47] Though Clement was a Christian – as were so many sources for the Eleusinian Mysteries – he was born a pagan and had some understanding of the mystery rites. In this passage, he offers an interesting distinction between the *mustês'* "learning" and the *epoptês'* vision of "nature and realities."[48] To be sure, we cannot accept that Clement offered an objective account of the mysteries, but he does provide evidence that the initiands in the two initiations in the mystery rites had different experiences.

As Christiane Sourvinou-Inwood has shown, the Greater Eleusinian Mysteries was an "advent festival." She explains this kind of festival as follows:

> Advent festivals (and what we may call advent segments in more complex festivals) were focused on a deity's arrival and presence. Demeter, Persephone, Dionysos, and Apollo are the main deities involved in such rituals. There was a general perception that deities were present in their festivals, but in advent festivals the arrival and presence of the deity was focused on, and ritually enacted, in different ways.[49]

---

[47] *Stromata* 5.70.7–71.1: τῶν μυστηρίων τῶν παρ' "Ελλησιν ἄρχει μὲν τὰ καθάρσια, καθάπερ καὶ τοῖς βαρβάροις τὸ λουτρόν. μετὰ ταῦτα δ' ἐστὶ τὰ μικρὰ μυστήρια διδασκαλίας τινὰ ὑπόθεσιν ἔχοντα καὶ προπαρασκευῆς τῶν μελλόντων, τὰ δὲ μεγάλα περὶ τῶν συμπάντων, οὗ μανθάνειν οὐκέτι ὑπολείπεται, ἐποπτεύειν δὲ καὶ περινοεῖν τήν τε φύσιν καὶ τὰ πράγματα.

[48] Riedweg 1987: 2–29 uses Clement's scheme to identify three events in the Eleusinian Mysteries: preliminary purification rites, a teaching of the mysteries, and the final revelation. I do not think that one can make this large claim based only on Clement. Riedweg's views have heavily influenced scholars working on the Ladder of Love in Plato's *Symposium* and its relation to the Eleusinian Mysteries. See Edmonds 2017 for an excellent analysis of this issue.

[49] Sourvinou-Inwood 2003: 32.

In the advent festival of the Eleusinian Mysteries, a number of rituals took place. In particular, during the night-time rituals, the initiands watched three costumed hierophants mimetically performing the "sacred drama" of Demeter and Kore.[50] The drama featured Hades' abduction of Kore, Demeter's search for Kore, and Kore's return to earth. This drama served to ritually evoke the final epiphany of the goddess. In the "search" for Kore, the hierophants and initiates (*epoptai*) carried torches outside the Telesterion, looking for Kore in various places.[51] Finally, the hierophant sounded a gong to call Kore up from the underworld.[52] Once Kore had "arrived," the initiands went into the Telesterion and waited for the final revelation of Demeter (the *epopteia*).

All these rituals – the sacrifices, prayers, singing, chanting, dancing, watching/participating in the sacred drama – raised the initiands to a high level of excitement. This prepared them for the epiphany of the goddess, which was revealed in part by the hierophants at the climax of the ritual. As Clinton claims:

> The hierophant's task was of course ἱερὰ φαίνειν, which could mean "to show sacred objects" or "to make the sacred appear." In the latter case, he did more than show sacred objects, i.e., he made gods appear in addition to the sacred objects.[53]

In Clinton's reconstruction of the events, the priests showed images of Demeter or Kore in the midst of a blaze of torches.[54] Indeed, by way of a "ritually manipulated miracle," as Sourvinou-Inwood puts it, the goddess would appear epiphanically to the initiands at the climax of the ceremonies.[55] As she observes, "the re-enactment of Demeter's arrival, epiphany and withdrawal, Kore's return and the cult's foundation … gave a concrete expression of the goddesses' presence in the festival."[56] As we saw above, the Greek gods could manifest their divine presence in different forms – a human, an animal, or an inanimate body. We do not know the form in which Demeter appeared to the initiates. Indeed, as

---

[50] I follow Bremmer 2014: 11, who argues that the sacred drama took place on two nights (on the first night, Kore is "found" and "raised" from Hades; on the second, Demeter reveals herself). Cf. Clinton 1993: 118–19, who claims that the events took place in one night.

[51] Bremmer 2014: 11, following Clinton 1993, says that the search for Kore took place outside the Telesterion (because it had so many inner columns and was too small for this event); cf. Parker 2005: 355–6.

[52] Bremmer 2014: 11.   [53] Clinton 2004: 85.

[54] On this ritual, see Graf 1974: 134.n34); Burkert 1983: 288; Riedweg 1987: 52, 61–3; Clinton 1992: 89–90. Clinton 2004 explains how the Telesterion could be lit up from above and along the sides with torches. He also argues that this showing included "images" of the goddesses.

[55] Sourvinou-Inwood 2003: 32.   [56] Sourvinou-Inwood 2003: 39–40.

Petridou rightly reminds us, epiphanies happened in the eyes of the beholder, and each beholder was different.[57] Presumably, the initiands had different experiences during the initiation ceremony. Still, some must have seen the presence of the goddess.

Stobaeus presents a detailed account of the initiand's experience at the initiation ceremonies in the mysteries:

> At first there was wandering, and wearisome roaming, and some fearful and fruitless journeys through darkness and, just before the end (*telos*), every sort of terror, shuddering, trembling, sweat, and amazement. Out of these places some marvellous light (*phôs ti thaumasion*) came upon them, and pure places and meadows received them, containing voices, dances, and solemnities of sacred utterances and holy visions. Among these the completely initiated person [*memuêmenos*], being free and let loose, walks around crowned and celebrates mystic rites, and joins together with pure and pious people.[58]

To be sure, Stobaeus may have been referring to mystery cults in general in this passage, but his reference to wandering, darkness, dances, marvelous light, holy visions and pure meadows seems to conjure up the Eleusinian Mysteries.[59] As we have seen, in the sacred drama, the hierophants act out Demeter's wandering and search for Kore. In addition, the Eleusinian Mysteries featured a sudden blaze of light and the manipulation of images of the goddesses. This could well have created the "holy visions."

Blindness and vision play a huge role in the Eleusinian Mysteries. We see this theme playing out in the Homeric *Hymn to Demeter*. This poem offers important evidence for the ritual events in the Eleusinian Mysteries, and it also shows how humans could see, or fail to see, a god. We must remember that, in the Greek imaginary, the gods could be present among mortals but not recognized. They manifested their divinity to humans only when they chose to do so, and they could appear either partially or fully. Consider Demeter's different levels of appearance among humans in this hymn. She

---

[57] Petridou 2015: 50. As she notes, a god appeared epiphanically to a person (or group) depending on the "viewers' intentions, expectations, cultural references and psychological preconditioning."

[58] Stobaeus *Anth.* 4.52.49; Fr. 6 Dübner = fr. 178 Sandbach: πλάναι τὰ πρῶτα καὶ περιδρομαὶ κοπώδεις καὶ διὰ σκότους τινὲς ὕποπτοι πορεῖαι καὶ ἀτέλεστοι, εἶτα πρὸ τοῦ τέλους αὐτοῦ τὰ δεινὰ πάντα, φρίκη καὶ τρόμος καὶ ἱδρὼς καὶ θάμβος· ἐκ δὲ τούτου φῶς τι θαυμάσιον ἀπήντησεν καὶ τόποι καθαροὶ καὶ λειμῶνες ἐδέξαντο, φωνὰς καὶ χορείας καὶ σεμνότητας ἀκουσμάτων ἱερῶν καὶ φασμάτων ἁγίων ἔχοντες· ἐν αἷς ὁ παντελὴς ἤδη καὶ μεμυημένος ἐλεύθερος γεγονὼς καὶ ἄφετος περιιὼν ἐστεφανωμένος ὀργιάζει καὶ σύνεστιν ὁσίοις καὶ καθαροῖς ἀνδράσι.

[59] Some scholars argue that this passage refers to mysteries in general. See especially Burkert 1987: 91; Riedweg 1998: 367; and Bernabé 2009: 106. Others claim that this refers to the Eleusinian Mysteries: Meyer 1987: 8; Sourvinou-Inwood 2003: 33. Still others suggest that this refers to Orphic initiation (see Mylonas 1961: 265).

first arrives at Eleusis in disguise and no-one sees her divinity: "none of the men or deep-girdled women who saw her recognized her" (οὐδέ τις ἀνδρῶν εἰσορόων γίγνωσκε βαθυζώνων τε γυναικῶν; *HH* 2.94–7). Later, Demeter shows herself to Metaneira in a partial revelation: Metaneira senses that this is a god, but is not sure (188–90). Finally, Demeter manifests herself in a full epiphany to Metaneira and then to the royal women in Eleusis (268–76). She takes a human form, though her appearance is supernatural: "from afar, a light shone from the immortal body of the goddess, and her golden hair spread down over her shoulders, and the firm house was filled with brightness like a bolt of lightning" (τῆλε δὲ φέγγος ἀπὸ χροὸς ἀθανάτοιο / λάμπε θεᾶς, ξάνθαὶ δὲ κόμαι κατενήνοθεν ὤμους, / αὐγῆς δ' ἐπλήσθη πυκινὸς δόμος ἀστεροπῆς ὥς; *HH* 2.278–81). Here, the women see the full presence of the goddess.

The Homeric *Hymn to Demeter* presents the myths that took center stage in the Eleusinian Mysteries. As Petridou argues, the events in the hymn determined the specific rituals in the mysteries. In particular, the goddess shows her appearance to the initiands at different levels of clarity. Petridou breaks this down into three stages: the goddess manifests herself (A) in disguise, (B) in a partial revelation, and (C) in a full epiphany:

> This escalation of intensity in both the epiphanic *sēmeia* and the reactions of the human perceiver from stage B to stage C may allude to the two different degrees of initiation into the mysteries, that of the *myēsis* and that of the *epopteia*. It should not be surprising if a hymn, which accounts for the secret rites ordained by Demeter in Eleusis, actually reflects these very rites in its narrative structure. Stage A of the divine revelation could correspond to the preliminary and preparatory stage of the initiatory process (known also as *proteleia*) while stages B and C could allude to *myēsis* and the further advanced stage of *epopteia*.

In Petridou's view, the events narrated in the Homeric hymn correspond to the different levels of initiation at the Eleusinian Mysteries. Whether or not one accepts this claim, she is certainly right to suggest that, in the different initiation rituals, the initiand moves from blindness to partial vision to complete vision.[60]

For the Greeks, seeing a god and recognizing him or her are two quite different activities. As Petridou states: "the Homeric antithesis ἰδεῖν γιγνώσκειν [to see; to recognize], which is of cardinal importance to 'the epistemological aspect' of an epiphany, is heavily emphasized throughout

---

[60] Edmonds 2017 discusses this question and (rightly, in my view) states that we do not have enough evidence for Petridou's claim. I find Petridou's triadic scheme useful for heuristic reasons.

the whole text of the hymn. Vision (*idein*) cannot guarantee cognitive perception and analysis (*gignōskein*)."[61] We see this idea play out in the *Hymn to Demeter*, where the goddess first arrives among the Eleusinians but no one recognizes her. In principle, the individuals going through the first and the second initiation ceremonies at the mysteries experienced the presence of divinity in stages. In a full epiphany, one both sees and knows the god.

Let me conclude this discussion by noting two key elements in the rituals at the Eleusinian Mysteries: purification and radiant light. First, the initiands had to purify themselves repeatedly before the final initiation.[62] Of course purification was part of every Greek religious ritual. To take one simple example, a person had to sprinkle him or herself with pure water at the water basin (*perirrhanterion*) when entering a temple.[63] However, in the Eleusinian Mysteries, much more was required: all initiands had to take a "mystic piglet" from Athens to the sea to wash and kill it as a way of purifying themselves (the Greeks commonly used the blood of a piglet for purification). The initiands also had to observe a fast and refrain from sexual intercourse.[64] They could not undergo the initiation unless they were fully purified. Second, the night-time initiation ceremony for the *epoptai* in the mysteries featured a superabundance of light – hundreds of people held torches and fires burned in various places. As Robert Parker observes: "Above all there were light effects. Plutarch speaks of a great light at a climactic moment, Dio of 'the alternation of darkness and light' in the mystic experience, and the attestations, in literature and in art, of torches, light and 'mystic fire' are numerous indeed."[65] The rituals and events in the Eleusinian Mysteries that I have discussed in this section provide the religious context for Plato's depictions of the philosopher contemplating the Forms. This includes the philosopher who sees the Form of Beauty in the *Symposium*.

---

[61] Petridou 2015: 267.

[62] Clinton 2003 offers a detailed discussion of the purification rites in the Eleusinian Mysteries.

[63] Cole 2004: 43–7.   [64] Clinton 2003: 50–60; Parker 2005: 347; Bowden 2010: 33–5.

[65] Parker 2005: 353; see also Bérard 1985: 17–33. As we will see in the chapter on the *Phaedrus*, poetic narratives of epiphany feature a god or goddess who appears radiant with light. Of course Plato famously presented a "metaphysics of light": in the *Republic*, he compares the Form of the Good to the Sun-god (508a–509c); and in the *Phaedrus* he says that "the Form of Beauty shone radiantly (ἔλαμπεν) in its being among the Forms there; and coming here we have grasped it as it shines (στίλβον) most clearly through the clearest of our senses" (250d). Given that Plato refers to the Eleusinian Mysteries in his representations of the philosopher contemplating the Form(s), one could argue that he developed the metaphysics of light at least in part from the light-filled ceremonies at the Eleusinian Mysteries.

2.7 The Divine Epiphany of Beauty

In the Ladder of Love, Diotima speaks of the vision of Beauty as someone who has achieved this herself. She does not, however, describe her own vision of the Form in the first person. Socrates does not get an account of her "autopsy" of the Form. He hears about this ascent as an outside observer, as a mere *mustês* (210a). The readers of Plato's dialogue stand in a similar position: they read this account as outsiders and have to discover the truth themselves. To some extent, the Ladder of Love has a protreptic aim. Plato offers the reader a representation of an idealized philosopher pursuing and contemplating the Form. Here, he creates a sort of mini-drama that invites the readers to take up philosophy and ascend to the Form themselves.

I want to examine the philosopher's ascent up the Ladder of Love and his epiphanic vision of the Form of Beauty. Consider first Diotima's prefatory remarks about the philosophic ascent:

> He who has been educated in erotic matters (*ta erôtika*) up to this point, and has seen beauties properly and in order, reaches the goal (*telos*) of his erotic pursuits: suddenly he will see a beauty wondrous in nature, and this is the reason for all the earlier toils. (ὃς γὰρ ἂν μέχρι ἐνταῦθα πρὸς τὰ ἐρωτικὰ παιδαγωγηθῇ, θεώμενος ἐφεξῆς τε καὶ ὀρθῶς τὰ καλά, πρὸς τέλος ἤδη ἰὼν τῶν ἐρωτικῶν ἐξαίφνης κατόψεταί τι θαυμαστὸν τὴν φύσιν καλόν, τοῦτο ἐκεῖνο . . . οὗ δὴ ἕνεκεν καὶ οἱ ἔμπροσθεν πάντες πόνοι ἦσαν; 210e)

In Diotima's teleological account, the philosopher advances towards the "goal" (*telos*) of his pursuits in a specific order. He does everything "for the sake of" (*heneken*) seeing a "wondrous" vision of Beauty. Diotima treats this vision as an extraordinary experience.

Diotima describes the account of the philosopher's ascent of the ladder as follows:

> So when a man ascends from these things here, through loving boys correctly, and begins to see that Beauty, he has almost laid hold of the goal (*telos*). This is what it is for a man to advance correctly, or be led by another, in the matters of love (*ta erôtika*). He continually goes upwards, beginning from these beauties here and using them like upward stairs, from one beautiful body to two, and from two to all beautiful bodies, and from beautiful bodies to beautiful pursuits, and from pursuits to beautiful learnings (*mathêmata*), and from learnings, he comes at the end (*teleutêsai*) to that learning, which is the learning of nothing other than this very Beauty, so that in the end (*teleutôn*) he knows (*gnôi*) what beauty is. And there in life if anywhere, my dear

Socrates, . . . a person finds life worth living, seeing (*theômenôi*) Beauty itself.[66] (211b–d)

This passage presents several important ideas. First, Plato spatializes the philosopher's quest: he ascends up a series of rungs or stairs.[67] Plato uses the rhetoric of "always going upwards" (ἀεὶ ἐπανιέναι) on "upward stairs" (ἐπαναβασμοῖς) to convey the notion of upward movement. Second, his teleological language captures the erotic propulsion that drives the philosopher to his ultimate goal.

As the philosopher ascends the ladder, he achieves a new understanding at each rung. Every time he climbs a rung, he grasps that "this" beauty is "akin" to the beauties he has already perceived. Eventually, he sees that the beauties of the body, the soul, institutions, lawcodes, and disciplines of knowledge belong to a single kinship group. One could argue that he identifies each beautiful object subjectively (this particular body or soul is beautiful to him) but overcomes this subjective reaction by reasoning that the beauty of one given object is "akin" to the beauty of other objects. How, then, does his grasp of the kinship of these beauties lead him to apprehend the Form? Plato does not answer this question. Rather, he portrays the philosopher as moving from these individual beauties to seeing the "great sea of beauty" (*to polu pelagos . . . tou kalou*, 210d). The image of the sea evokes an immense container: a great sea that contains all the particular beauties in the world. It holds all the particular beauties together in a kinship group. This image of a sea of beauty sets up Plato's non-imagistic description of the Form of Beauty.

Diotima describes the Form of Beauty as follows:

> First, it always exists, and neither comes to be or passes away, nor does it grow or perish; next, it is not beautiful in this way and ugly in that way; nor beautiful at one time and ugly at another; it is not beautiful in relation to one thing and ugly in relation to another; it is not beautiful here but ugly there, as though it were beautiful to some and ugly to others. Nor will the beautiful appear (*phantasthêsetai*) to him as a face or hands or any other

---

[66] ὅταν δή τις ἀπὸ τῶνδε διὰ τὸ ὀρθῶς παιδεραστεῖν ἐπανιὼν ἐκεῖνο τὸ καλὸν ἄρχηται καθορᾶν, σχεδὸν ἄν τι ἅπτοιτο τοῦ τέλους. τοῦτο γὰρ δή ἐστι τὸ ὀρθῶς ἐπὶ τὰ ἐρωτικὰ ἰέναι ἢ ὑπ' ἄλλου ἄγεσθαι, ἀρχόμενον ἀπὸ τῶνδε τῶν καλῶν ἐκείνου ἕνεκα τοῦ καλοῦ ἀεὶ ἐπανιέναι, ὥσπερ ἐπαναβασμοῖς χρώμενον, ἀπὸ ἑνὸς ἐπὶ δύο καὶ ἀπὸ δυοῖν ἐπὶ πάντα τὰ καλὰ σώματα, καὶ ἀπὸ τῶν καλῶν σωμάτων ἐπὶ τὰ καλὰ ἐπιτηδεύματα, καὶ ἀπὸ τῶν ἐπιτηδευμάτων ἐπὶ τὰ καλὰ μαθήματα, καὶ ἀπὸ τῶν μαθημάτων ἐπ' ἐκεῖνο τὸ μάθημα τελευτῆσαι, ὅ ἐστιν οὐκ ἄλλου ἢ αὐτοῦ ἐκείνου τοῦ καλοῦ μάθημα, καὶ γνῷ αὐτὸ τελευτῶν ὅ ἐστι καλόν. ἐνταῦθα τοῦ βίου, ὦ φίλε Σώκρατες . . . εἴπερ που ἄλλοθι, βιωτὸν ἀνθρώπῳ, θεωμένῳ αὐτὸ τὸ καλόν.

[67] Plato uses "stairs" (211b, *epanibasmoi*), but I use "ladder" because this is the common way to identify this passage.

thing that partakes of the body, or as some specific discourse or knowledge; it does not exist anywhere in some other thing, such as in an animal or earth or heaven or in anything else, but itself by itself with itself. it is always one in form, and all other beautiful things partake in it in such a way that while these other things come into being and pass away, it does not become greater or smaller or suffer any change. (210e–211b)[68]

Using Beauty as a case in point, Plato sets forth the key attributes of the Forms: they are incorporeal, unchanging, and separate from particulars ("itself by itself with itself"), and exist everlastingly. He also presents the idea that particulars "participate" in the Forms: all beautiful particulars are beautiful because they "have a share in" Beauty.[69] Clearly, Plato has moved beyond the simple idea that all particular beauties are "akin" to one another. Rather, they have this kinship because they participate in the Form of Beauty. While we can easily grasp the notion of kinship, we may find it hard to understand how the particulars in the kinship group participate in the Form. As we saw in Chapter 1, Plato never fully explains the notion of participation in his dialogues. Leaving this aside, I want to focus on Plato's move from imagistic to non-imagistic language when he gets to the top of the ladder.

Consider the discursive leap that Plato makes when he moves from the "great sea" of beauty to the Form of Beauty. The sea of beauty presents the image of a container of the beauty-kinship group. The Form of Beauty is a separate, incorporeal being that does not "contain" anything. Thus, Plato starts with an image of something that has a shape and boundaries and then removes this bounded container. He then identifies Beauty as a being that has no shape or boundary: it does not contain anything at all. The Form of Beauty exists by itself as a unitary, everlasting, and incorporeal being. The beautiful particulars are not inside of the Form, as in a container; rather, they participate in it. Here, Plato makes a powerful rhetorical move: he starts with an image of a vast container and then conjures up a realm beyond images. At the "top" of the ladder, then, the rung itself disappears.

---

[68] πρῶτον μὲν ἀεὶ ὂν καὶ οὔτε γιγνόμενον οὔτε ἀπολλύμενον, οὔτε αὐξανόμενον οὔτε φθίνον, ἔπειτα οὐ τῇ μὲν καλόν, τῇ δ᾽ αἰσχρόν, οὐδὲ τοτὲ μέν, τοτὲ δὲ οὔ, οὐδὲ πρὸς μὲν τὸ καλόν, πρὸς δὲ τὸ αἰσχρόν, οὐδ᾽ ἔνθα μὲν καλόν, ἔνθα δὲ αἰσχρόν, ὡς τισὶ μὲν ὂν καλόν, τισὶ δὲ αἰσχρόν· οὐδ᾽ αὖ φαντασθήσεται αὐτῷ τὸ καλὸν οἷον πρόσωπόν τι οὐδὲ χεῖρες οὐδὲ ἄλλο οὐδὲν ὧν σῶμα μετέχει, οὐδέ τις λόγος οὐδέ τις ἐπιστήμη, οὐδέ που ὂν ἐν ἑτέρῳ τινι, οἷον ἐν ζῴῳ ἢ ἐν γῇ ἢ ἐν οὐρανῷ ἢ ἔν τῳ ἄλλῳ, ἀλλ᾽ αὐτὸ καθ᾽ αὑτὸ μεθ᾽ αὑτοῦ μονοειδὲς ἀεὶ ὄν, τὰ δὲ ἄλλα πάντα καλὰ ἐκείνου μετέχοντα τρόπον τινὰ τοιοῦτον, οἷον γιγνομένων τε τῶν ἄλλων καὶ ἀπολλυμένων μηδὲν ἐκεῖνο μήτε τι πλέον μήτε ἔλαττον γίγνεσθαι μηδὲ πάσχειν μηδέν.

[69] I will not discuss the long scholarly debate (still ongoing) about "participation," which is beyond the scope of this investigation.

This move allows the reader to sense the vast ontological gap between particular beauties in the human world on earth and the Form of Beauty. The philosophic soul that beholds the Form sees an eternal, incorporeal, and divine Being.

The Form of Beauty exists in a realm beyond that of humans. As Diotima states:

> What do we think would happen to someone if he sees Beauty itself, absolute, pure, unmixed, and not infected with the flesh and colors of the human world and so much other mortal nonsense, but could look at divine beauty itself in its singular form? (τί δῆτα, ἔφη, οἰόμεθα, εἴ τῳ γένοιτο αὐτὸ τὸ καλὸν ἰδεῖν εἰλικρινές, καθαρόν, ἄμεικτον, ἀλλὰ μὴ ἀνάπλεων σαρκῶν τε ἀνθρωπίνων καὶ χρωμάτων καὶ ἄλλης πολλῆς φλυαρίας θνητῆς, ἀλλ' αὐτὸ τὸ θεῖον καλὸν δύναιτο μονοειδὲς κατιδεῖν; 211d–e)

In emphasizing the superhuman separateness of Beauty, Diotima once again emphasizes the ontological difference between the particular beauties in the mortal realm and the Form of Beauty. Only by transcending the human realm can the philosopher grasp the essence of beauty – he will know what beauty is (211c–d). And, in addition to achieving this knowledge, the philosopher will encounter a divine being.

Plato represents the philosopher's vision of the Form of Beauty in terms of a divine epiphany. Indeed, he identifies the philosopher with the *epoptês* in the Eleusinian Mysteries, thus conjuring up the initiate's vision of the goddess at the climax of the initiation ceremony. Radcliffe Edmonds sets forth a similar idea.[70] He compares the philosopher's vision of Beauty in the *Symposium* to the initiate's affective and emotional response at the final initation ceremony in the Eleusinian Mysteries. He begins by emphasizing that the initiate at the mysteries did not learn something but rather went through an experience. He bases this on Aristotle's claim that "it is necessary for those initiated not to learn but to experience something (*ti ... pathein*) and to be put in a certain state" (τοὺς τελουμένους οὐ μαθεῖν τι δεῖν ἀλλὰ παθεῖν καὶ διατεθῆναι; Fr. 15 Ross). As Edmonds suggests, "the 'something' that is understood [in Aristotle's fragment] is a contact with the divine, perhaps even, as in Euripides' *Bacchae*, a face-to-face encounter with the deity."[71] As he claims:

> The close encounter with the divine in the Mysteries is a powerful affective experience that can be repeated, just like erotic encounters with beauty in its various manifestations, but the revelation of the Beautiful itself, like the

[70] Edmonds 2017: 199–215.   [71] Edmonds 2017: 199.

epopteia in the Mysteries, is a profound experience which alters the way one understands, not just future encounters with the beautiful but past ones as well.[72]

Edmonds emphasizes the emotional and experiential aspects of the philosophic lover's vision of Beauty.[73] I agree with his interpretation but want to take this further. As I argue, Plato's identification of the philosopher as an Eleusinian *epoptês* indicates that the philosopher will see a divine epiphany of Beauty.

Let me offer further evidence for this claim. In addition to referring to the *epoptês'* vision of the goddess in the Eleusinian Mysteries, Plato uses language from poetic narratives of epiphany to describe the philosopher's vision of the Form of Beauty.[74] As we have seen, the Homeric *Hymn to Apollo* and *Hymn to Dionysus* show the god manifesting himself in anthropomorphic, theoriomorphic, and material forms. Apollo appears as a dolphin, star, and man; Dionysus takes the form of a man, wine, grapevines, a lion, and a bear. Their appearances are wondrous, sudden, and feature an abundance of radiant light. Plato uses this same marked language in his description of the philosopher contemplating the Form of Beauty. As Diotima states: "he who has been educated in erotic matters up to this point, and has seen beauties in the right order, reaches the goal of his erotic pursuits: *suddenly* he will see a beauty *wondrous* in nature" (ἐξαίφνης κατόψεταί τι θαυμαστὸν τὴν φύσιν καλόν; 210e).[75] Although he borrows language from poetic narratives of epiphanies, Plato moves beyond the physical epiphanies of the gods. His philosopher sees true, incorporeal Beauty. Consider again Diotima's description of Beauty's appearance to the philosopher:

> Beauty will not show itself (*phantasthêsetai*) to him [the philosopher] *as a face or hands or any other thing that partakes of the body*, or as some language

---

[72] Edmonds 2017: 214–15.

[73] See also Porter's account of the affective aspects of the philosopher's vision of Beauty (2016: 563–8).

[74] Plato thus uses both the Eleusinian Mysteries divinity-marker and the Divine Epiphany divinity-marker (see my discussion of these in the Introduction).

[75] My italics. Plato also speaks of the sudden vision of truth in the Seventh Letter (I take this letter to be genuine). In this text, he adds that his philosophic vision cannot be put into language: "It [my philosophic knowledge] cannot be articulated in speech like other studies, but after one spends a great deal of time with and communes with these ideas, it is suddenly born in the soul like a light kindled from a leaping spark of fire, and then nourishes itself on that" (ῥητὸν γὰρ οὐδαμῶς ἐστιν ὡς ἄλλα μαθήματα, ἀλλ᾽ ἐκ πολλῆς συνουσίας γιγνομένης περὶ τὸ πρᾶγμα αὐτὸ καὶ τοῦ συζῆν ἐξαίφνης, οἷον ἀπὸ πυρὸς πηδήσαντος ἐξαφθὲν φῶς, ἐν τῇ ψυχῇ γενόμενον αὐτὸ ἑαυτὸ ἤδη τρέφει; 341c–d). This is part of a longer passage in which Plato sets forth the attributes of the Form (always existing, unchanging, singular in form, itself in itself with itself, i.e., separate) and refers to the particulars' participation in the Forms.

or knowledge; it does not exist anywhere *in some other thing, such as in an animal or in earth or in heaven,* but itself in itself with itself, it is always singular in form, and all other beautiful things partake in it in such a way that while these other things come into being and pass away, it doesn't become greater or smaller or suffer any change.[76] (210e–211b, my italics)

Plato first presents the revelation of the Form negatively: Beauty does not appear in a human form (with face and hands), in an animal form, or in a form on earth or in the heavens. The Form of Beauty does not appear *in* anything but rather "itself in itself with itself." In referring to the bodily forms in which Beauty does *not* appear, Plato points to the traditional Greek belief that gods could appear to humans in the form of humans, animals, and in natural and heavenly bodies. He brings up this traditional idea only to reject it. The Form of Beauty manifests itself as a new kind of divinity. This eternal and divine Being appears only to the mind. Plato thus stages a new kind of divine epiphany: the philosopher sees the divine Form itself, face to face (as it were).

What does it mean to know the essence of Beauty and to encounter the divine? Plato does not mention other Forms in this text, so we cannot offer a robust answer to this question. I will venture a few basic ideas here (in later chapters I will present a fuller analysis of this topic). Since the soul in this dialogue is mortal, it sees the Form as something that is vastly superior to itself ontologically. It achieves knowledge of the essence of beauty, but cannot fully grasp the divine. In other words, the philosopher can understand the nature of Beauty but not fully take in its divinity (or the divine realm that it occupies). The person who grasps Beauty, then, engages in a sacred way of seeing and knowing. The epiphanic appearance of Beauty gives the philosopher an entirely new sense of reality. He sees that divinity comes from a different and higher source, the Form of Beauty. On the one hand, the philosopher knows and can give an account of the essence of Beauty. But he also encounters something that goes beyond language. In this scenario, the philosopher experiences both knowledge and wonder. As we will see in the chapters to come, Plato presents the idea that the philosopher attains knowledge of the Form and reacts to it with religious wonder and awe.

---

[76] 211a–b: οὐδ᾽ αὖ φαντασθήσεται αὐτῷ τὸ καλὸν οἷον πρόσωπόν τι οὐδὲ χεῖρες οὐδὲ ἄλλο οὐδὲν ὧν σῶμα μετέχει, οὐδέ τις λόγος οὐδέ τις ἐπιστήμη, οὐδέ που ὂν ἐν ἑτέρῳ τινι, οἷον ἐν ζώῳ ἢ ἐν γῇ ἢ ἐν οὐρανῷ ἢ ἔν τῳ ἄλλῳ, ἀλλ᾽ αὐτὸ καθ᾽ αὑτὸ μεθ᾽ αὑτοῦ μονοειδὲς ἀεὶ ὄν, τὰ δὲ ἄλλα πάντα καλὰ ἐκείνου μετέχοντα τρόπον τινὰ τοιοῦτον, οἷον γιγνομένων τε τῶν ἄλλων καὶ ἀπολλυμένων μηδὲν ἐκεῖνο μήτε τι πλέον μήτε ἔλαττον γίγνεσθαι μηδὲ πάσχειν μηδέν.

2.8 Metaphysical Desire and the Desire for Immortality in the Ladder of Love

When the philosopher's metaphysical desire drives him to see the Form, he transcends his individual self for a period of time. This kind of desire has a different goal than the desire for immortality. Rather than gaining "more me" – an everlasting, immortal self – the philosopher gets "less me." His soul desires and, for a time, attains a rational state that transcends the human self. It apprehends Beauty as an essence and also encounters a divine being. The philosophic soul also gains a new understanding of how it should act and live a human life.

As I have suggested, in the case of metaphysical desire, one wants to grasp an eternal object; in the case of the desire for immortality, one aims for an everlasting self. Thus far, I have discussed the Ladder of Love in terms of metaphysical desire. However, the philosopher on the ladder also desires immortality, as we can see by his generation of psychic offspring. As Diotima stated earlier, humans naturally desire immortality and, insofar as they are mortal, they can achieve a partial immortality by producing offspring. In the case of the philosophic lover, she claimed, he gives birth to *logoi* that deal with virtue and education (209b–c).[77] We see the philosophic lover giving birth to educational discourses in the Ladder of Love. For example, when he moves up the ladder from loving bodies to loving a beautiful soul, he enters into a pedagogical relationship with the beloved[78]: "it shall suffice for the lover to love and care for [his beloved] and to beget and search for discourses (*logous*) which will make young men better" (ἐξαρκεῖν αὐτῷ καὶ ἐρᾶν καὶ κήδεσθαι καὶ τίκτειν λόγους τοιούτους καὶ ζητεῖν, οἵτινες ποιήσουσι βελτίους τοὺς νέους; 210c). Indeed, the lover who falls for a young man with a beautiful soul engages in a "search" (*zêtein*) that takes place *after* he has given birth to psychic children in the presence of his beloved. The philosopher's search specifically focuses on virtue and the right education for young men (209b–c). In

[77] Note that the lover described in the earlier passage (209c) and the philosopher ascending the ladder in this passage both give birth to *logoi* that deal with educating the young: this forges a clear link between the lover in 209b–c and the lover on the ladder of love.

[78] Since the beloved has a beautiful soul, we may infer that the lover must get to know this person well enough to determine that he has a beautiful soul. Of course, as scholars have observed, the lover on the upper rungs of the ladder seems to have little or no relationship with his beloved. For Diotima does not mention the beloved again, and this indicates that the lover may have left the beloved behind as he ascends the ladder. I do not want to enter into this debate – here, I focus on the lover–beloved relationship. Diotima does say that the philosophic lover engages in "unstinting philosophy" at the upper rungs of the ladder: this implies that he is engaging in philosophic dialogue (he is not doing philosophy simply on his own).

addition, at the end of Diotima's exposition on the Ladder of Love, she refers to the philosopher nurturing and "rearing" his offspring: "to that man begetting true virtue and rearing it up (*threpsamenôi*), he comes to be loved by the gods and, if any human is immortal, it is he" (212a). Even after he sees the Form of Beauty, then, the philosopher must rear up his children – his own virtues and the *logoi* that focus on virtue – by way of ongoing investigation.[79] This birthgiving allows him to achieve a partial immortality.

The philosophic lover's offspring do not add up to a fixed and final product. Indeed, the lover and his beloved (and other philosophic companions) work on ideas that are tested and revised again and again. There is no final end to this project – no "last word" or argument on the topic. Even if the philosopher reaches the point of contemplating the Form of Beauty and gives birth to "true virtue" ("because he has grasped true Beauty"), he still has to rear up his discursive offspring (212a).

How, then, do the desire for immortality and metaphysical desire cooperate in the Ladder of Love? The philosopher's metaphysical desire leads him to transcend himself and contemplate the Form, but this vision enables him to give birth to virtue and truly good discourses on earth. We must note, however, that the desire for immortality, portrayed in the birthgiving metaphor, and metaphysical desire, portrayed in the ascent metaphor, operate in different realms. The birthgiving metaphor functions in the human realm, where the philosopher's discourses can "live on" in the youths whom he has educated. This takes place on the horizontal plane of human history on earth: one gains partial immortality by giving birth to psychic offspring that "keeps one alive" in later generations. The ascent metaphor operates on a vertical plane: the soul's metaphysical desire moves it up to an incorporeal and timeless divine reality. Indeed, the human philosopher transcends himself and moves beyond the desire for immortality ("more me").

In the Ladder of Love, Plato presents his first account of metaphysical desire. This desire drives the soul to transcend the physical realm by way of reason. Metaphysical desire mobilizes the mind and directs it to the Forms. In this "forward movement of love" (as Alexander Nehamas so nicely puts it), the mortal and temporalized soul aspires to something that is beyond the human and earthly realm.[80] Although Plato initially identifies love as

---

[79] Earlier in her speech, Diotima had suggested that the philosopher gave birth to discourses (*logoi*); here, she claims that he gives birth to virtue (*aretê*). Presumably, the discourses and dialogues that he has about the virtues allow him to become more virtuous himself.

[80] Nehamas 2013: 124–5.

a lack (*endeia*), he turns this into a thrilling desire to know more and to move to a full understanding of the divine Form of Beauty.

2.9   Daimonic Eros

Plato treats Eros as a daimon in this dialogue. To understand this claim, we need to look at the Greek conception of daimons (*daimones*). As Gasparro observes:

> The word *daimon* retains, throughout Greek tradition from the Homeric poems to the very end, its meaning as a synonym of *theos* . . . . It embodies a supernatural presence and power, difficult for humans to identify, and it often intervenes unexpectedly, bringing with it risks for people . . . .The *daimon* appears as a divine agent intervening at will in human affairs, positively or negatively, for good or ill.[81]

Although daimons did not have individual names, the Greeks treated them as external powers that could affect human life in bad or good ways. We find references to daimons in the earliest Greek poems (Homer and Hesiod) and also in a wide range of later texts.[82] In some texts, we find a simple identification between daimons and gods; in other texts, they are separated in terms of their level of divinity. Indeed, the exact divine status of daimons remains quite vague.[83] We have no extant material evidence that people worshipped daimons in civic cults; but the Greeks may have honored them as household and/or personal gods. Plato took daimons seriously, perhaps because the historical Socrates regularly referred to his *daimonion*.[84] Indeed, in the *Laws*, Plato elevated daimons to the status of civic cult in the public feasts in the city of Magnesia. As the Athenian states:

---

[81] Gasparro 2015: 416–17.
[82] For references to the *daimones* in Greek texts through the fifth century BCE, see, e.g., Homer *Il.* 17.89–104; Hesiod *WD* 121–6; Parmenides B1.2–3, B12.3; Empedocles B 115, 117, 121, 124, 147; Heraclitus B 119; Pindar *Pyth.* 3.34; Aesch. *Pers.* 641, *Agam.* 1468, 1476–7, 1486–8; Euripides *Alc.* 1003; Hippocrates *Peri Partheneion* 8.466; Derveni Papyrus col. 3.4–6, 8.8, 9.4 (assuming this is a late fifth-century text). Of course these texts give daimons different levels of power.
[83] Hesiod, however, claims that the golden race of men became *daimones* after they died (*WD* 121–6).
[84] As we see in Plato and Xenophon's *Apologies*, the Athenians knew about Socrates' *daimonion*. What is Socrates' *daimonion*? In the *Apology* 31c, 40b, Socrates refers to his *daimonion* as a "voice" (*phêmê*). In the *Republic* 496c and *Phaedrus* 242b–d, he refers to it as a "divine sign" (*daimonion sêmeion*). In the *Theaetetus* 151a, he says that the *daimonion* is "something that comes to him." See also *Alcibiades* 103a–b, 105e–106a, 124c, 127e, where Socrates says that the *daimonion* provides "the god's" instructions to him (this dialogue may or may not be authentic). See also Xenophon *Mem* 1.1.4, which identifies Socrates' *daimonion* as a deity. For a good discussion of this topic, see Mikalson 2010b: 112–21.

"there shall be no fewer than 365 feasts established, so that one official must always be sacrificing to one of the gods or *daimones* on behalf of the city, its people, and their possessions" (ἔστωσαν γὰρ τῶν μὲν πέντε καὶ ἑξήκοντα καὶ τριακοσίων μηδὲν ἀπολείπουσαι, ὅπως ἂν μία γέ τις ἀρχὴ θύῃ θεῶν ἢ δαιμόνων τινὶ ἀεὶ ὑπὲρ πόλεώς τε καὶ αὐτῶν καὶ κτημάτων; *Laws* 828a–b). The lawgivers must also lay down rules for "hymns to the gods to be sung rightly, together with prayers and, after the gods, prayers along with encomiums should be addressed to the *daimones* and heroes" (801e).[85]

We must emphasize, however, that when Plato treats Eros as a daimon in the *Symposium*, he does this to mark a specific aspect of the soul as "daimonic." He does not identify Eros as an external deity but rather as a special element in the soul. In considering Plato's conception of daimonic Eros, I will stick to Diotima's account, which sometimes treats eros as a daimon and sometimes as mere desire. Diotima sets forth a triadic cosmic scheme, with daimons occupying the middle realm between gods and humans. She places the daimon Eros among other daimons who dwell "in between" (*metaxu*) gods and mortals:

> [The realm of daimons] – interpreting and carrying things over from humans to the gods and from the gods to humans (the former by way of prayers and sacrifices, and the latter by commands and requitals for the sacrifices) – is in the middle of these two realms and fills up the whole so that the universe is bound to itself. Through this [daimonic] realm all divination passes, and the skill of the priests in terms of sacrifices and rites, and incantations, and all prophecy and sorcery. God does not mingle with humans, but through this [the daimonic] all association and converse from gods comes to men, whether they are awake or asleep. The man who is wise in regard to such things is daimonic, but he who is wise in any other thing, either in the arts or crafts, is banausic. (202e–203a)[86]

---

[85] As Mikalson 2010b: 119 claims, it was Plato who first created "a distinct class of deities known as *daimones*." Although earlier poets and thinkers referred to daimons, Plato seems to be the first to see them as a class of beings that was ontologically lower than the gods. Plato's treatment of daimons gave rise to the tradition of "demonology," beginning with Philip of Opus' *Epinomis*.

[86] 202e–203a: ἑρμηνεῦον καὶ διαπορθμεῦον θεοῖς τὰ παρ᾽ ἀνθρώπων καὶ ἀνθρώποις τὰ παρὰ θεῶν, τῶν μὲν τὰς δεήσεις καὶ θυσίας, τῶν δὲ τὰς ἐπιτάξεις τε καὶ ἀμοιβὰς τῶν θυσιῶν, ἐν μέσῳ δὲ ὂν ἀμφοτέρων συμπληροῖ, ὥστε τὸ πᾶν αὐτὸ αὑτῷ συνδεδέσθαι. διὰ τούτου καὶ ἡ μαντικὴ πᾶσα χωρεῖ καὶ ἡ τῶν ἱερέων τέχνη τῶν τε περὶ τὰς θυσίας καὶ τελετὰς καὶ τὰς ἐπῳδὰς καὶ τὴν μαντείαν πᾶσαν καὶ γοητείαν. θεὸς δὲ ἀνθρώπῳ οὐ μείγνυται, ἀλλὰ διὰ τούτου πᾶσά ἐστιν ἡ ὁμιλία καὶ ἡ διάλεκτος θεοῖς πρὸς ἀνθρώπους, καὶ ἐγρηγορόσι καὶ καθεύδουσι· καὶ ὁ μὲν περὶ τὰ τοιαῦτα σοφὸς δαιμόνιος ἀνήρ, ὁ δὲ ἄλλο τι σοφὸς ὢν ἢ περὶ τέχνας ἢ χειρουργίας τινὰς βάναυσος.

Diotima presents a key claim here: all daimons transport human matters to the gods and vice versa. At a very general level, then, Eros connects the human to the divine realm.

Diotima rejects the notion of a god "possessing" a human: the gods do not themselves "mingle" with humans (203a). Rather, the gods "converse" with humans through the mediation of daimons. In her discussion of daimons, Diotima specifically mentions the daimons that assist prophets and priests in the realm of divination, whether they get divine messages in language (as at the Delphic oracle and other oracular centers), in omens, or in dreams. Of course the daimons involved in divination differ from Eros in their sphere of influence. The daimon Eros works in the sphere of desire. Eros is a special kind of daimon because it brings the philosopher into contact with divinities, but not with the gods. Rather, Eros leads the philosopher to the divine realm of the Forms. In short, Eros serves to connect the philosopher to divine Beauty (and, we infer, all the other Forms).

Diotima offers important information about the daimon Eros in her mythical personification of this deity. As she claims, the gods *Poros* (Resource) and *Penia* (Poverty) gave birth to Eros.[87] Given this parentage, Eros lacks wisdom but everlastingly moves towards it. As Diotima states: "Eros philosophizes (*philosophôn*) through his whole life ... he is neither poor nor rich but is in the middle between wisdom and ignorance" (φιλοσοφῶν διὰ παντὸς τοῦ βίου ... οὔτε ἀπορεῖ Ἔρως ποτὲ οὔτε πλουτεῖ, σοφίας τε αὖ καὶ ἀμαθίας ἐν μέσῳ ἐστίν; 203d–e). Here, she explicitly identifies Eros as a philosopher. Strangely, after presenting Eros *as a desire* that human beings feel, Diotima mythically represents him as a daimon who *feels desire*. And Eros not only feels desire, but he has a mind: he can understand gods and humans, and aims directly at the true objects of his desire (beauty, goodness, knowledge, truth). As we can see, Plato uses mythic language in this personification of Eros; for this reason, we cannot interpret this passage literally. Still, we can see that Plato directly links Eros with philosophy.

As I have suggested, eros is a daimonic aspect of the soul, not a separate divine being. In this dialogue, Plato does not conceive of the soul as "godlike" or "divine." Rather, the soul is mortal. But he does give the soul a daimonic element. At the same time, he gives the mind the capacity to contemplate the Forms: the philosopher "looks at Beauty with that by which beauty can be seen" (*hôi horaton to kalon*; 212a). But the

---

[87] Note that Penia effectively rapes Poros while he is in a drunken sleep (203b–c).

philosopher's mind needs daimonic desire to reach the Forms. In my view, Plato added this theological element to the soul to connect the mortal human mind to the divine realm of the Forms. Indeed, he makes this clear by creating a triadic cosmic structure that places daimons in between humans and the gods. Daimonic eros functions to move the mind above its mortal status so that it can apprehend the divine Forms. In short, the soul is mortal in the *Symposium*, but it has a daimonic element.

We may wonder how the daimon Eros fits with Socrates' *daimonion*, i.e., the daimonic sign or voice that stopped Socrates from doing or saying something.[88] As scholars have noted, the daimon Eros shares some qualities with Socrates: both Eros and Socrates are philosophers who pursue beauty, goodness, and wisdom, and they both go without shoes (Eros, 203d; Socrates, 220b). However, Socrates' *daimonion* differs substantially from the daimon Eros. The *daimonion* holds Socrates' back from doing something wrong, while the daimon Eros drives the philosopher forwards and upwards towards truth.

2.10   Alcibiades Profanes the "Mysteries" of Philosophy

In a great dramatic moment in the *Symposium*, the drunken Alcibiades crashes the drinking party. He arrives just after Socrates has finished his speech. Rather than giving a speech on Eros, Alcibiades chooses to give a eulogy of Socrates.

By putting Alcibiades in the dialogue and setting the party in 415 BCE, Plato foregrounds several important historical events in Athens that play a key role in this dialogue. To make this point clear, I will give a brief account of Alcibiades' personal and political activities in late fifth-century Athens. As a politician and general, Alcibiades played a pivotal role in the Peloponnesian war against Sparta and her allies (431–404 BCE). In particular, when the Athenians were debating whether to fight a war in Sicily in 415 BCE, Alcibiades argued vehemently in the assembly in favor of the Sicilian expedition. The Athenians voted for the expedition and chose Alcibiades as the general of the naval fleet. Right before the fleet left Athens, however, Alcibiades was accused of mutilating the Herms statues and of profaning the Eleusinian Mysteries at a private gathering. In the eyes of the Athenians, both of these actions were profoundly impious. In the

---

[88] There is a great deal of scholarship on Socrates' *daimonion*: see, e.g., Frank 1955; Vlastos 1989; Reeve 1989, 2014; Brickhouse and Smith 1990, 2014; McPherran 1991; Mikalson 2010b: 113–19. Note that Xenophon also referred quite regularly to Socrates' *daimonion*.

case of profaning the mysteries, Alcibiades was thought to have put on the costume of the hierophant at the Eleusinian Mysteries and acted out the religious rituals that took place at the initiation in a private gathering.[89] The Athenians chose to put Alcibiades on trial for this impious act, but they allowed him to set sail for Sicily with the understanding that he would stand trial when he returned. While he was sailing with the fleet, however, he received news that his enemies in Athens were plotting against him. He promptly jumped ship and fled to Sparta, where he lived for three years as a traitor to Athens. During this period, the fortunes of the Athenians spiralled downwards: their huge navy was utterly devastated in Sicily, and they eventually lost the war against Sparta in 404 BCE. The Spartans tore down the walls in Athens and ruled, for a time, oligarchically. Many Athenians held Alcibiades responsible for this terrible loss, and some claimed that Socrates' "teaching" had corrupted his character. Indeed, the relationship between Socrates and Alcibiades contributed to Socrates' trial for impiety in 399 BCE.

Plato foregrounds these political events by setting the drinking party in the *Symposium* right before Alcibiades profaned the mysteries and left on the Sicilian Expedition (415 BCE).[90] Indeed, he composed Alcibiades' speech in order to defend Socrates against the charge that he had harmed the city by teaching Alcibiades and other young men false and evil ideas. As I will argue, in his speech in the *Symposium*, Alcibiades re-enacts (or, rather, pre-enacts) his profanation of the Eleusinian Mysteries when he reveals the "divine" Socrates to the men at the drinking party. I want to examine Alcibiades' revelation of the "mysteries" of Socrates.

In describing his vision of the divinity he sees in Socrates' soul, Alcibiades takes recourse in images. He compares Socrates to a votary object found in the shops of Herms-makers: a box that has the image of an ugly satyr on the outside but contains little statues of the gods (*agalmata*) on the inside. This image allows Alcibiades to portray Socrates in terms of his outer appearance and his inner core. When he turns to reveal this inner core, Alcibiades speaks as a hierophant at the Eleusinian Mysteries: he tells his companions to "shut great doors over your ears, you who are uninitiated and boorish" (218b). This phrase refers to the religious rules at the Eleusinian Mysteries that prevented people at the public Athenian festival for Demeter and Kore who had not been initiated

---

[89] As Plutarch *Alcibiades* 22.3–4 indicates. There is a great deal of scholarship on this issue. See especially Graf 2000: 114–27; Rubel 2000: 220–9; Parker 2005: 353–5; Nails 2006; Sheffield 2006: 183–206, especially 204; Rijksbaron 2011; Todd 2014: 89–93; Edmonds 2017: 204–15.

[90] We can identify this dramatic date based on the tragic poet Agathon's victory at the Lenaia.

as *musteis* from participating in the mystery ceremonies. Alcibiades says that he will reveal the true Socrates to the initiated: "Believe me, not one of you knows him, but *I will reveal* (*dêlôsô*) him" (216c–d, my italics). Using the image of the votary box, Alcibiades says that Socrates' ugly outer appearance disguises the divinity within him:

> When he is serious and opened up, I don't know if anyone has seen the statues of the gods within him, but I myself saw them once, and they appeared so divine, golden and utterly beautiful and wondrous that, in brief, I had to do whatever he bid me. (σπουδάσαντος δὲ αὐτοῦ καὶ ἀνοιχθέντος οὐκ οἶδα εἴ τις ἑώρακεν τὰ ἐντὸς ἀγάλματα· ἀλλ' ἐγὼ ἤδη ποτ' εἶδον, καί μοι ἔδοξεν οὕτω θεῖα καὶ χρυσᾶ εἶναι καὶ πάγκαλα καὶ θαυμαστά, ὥστε ποιητέον εἶναι ἔμβραχυ ὅτι κελεύοι Σωκράτης; 216e–217a)

Using the language of vision, Alcibiades says that he saw statues of the gods (*agalmata … theia*) in Socrates' soul. Indeed, he treats Socrates as some sort of divine being.[91] He sees the divinity of Socrates and feels that he must obey him just as one obeys a god. To be sure, Alcibiades is using an image to explain the powerful experience that he had in his encounters with Socrates. But this image gives us a sense of how Alcibiades came to see and understand Socrates.[92]

As I have suggested, Alcibiades claims to have seen something divine in Socrates. One may object that Alcibiades sees statues (*agalmata*) of the gods, rather than an actual god, in Socrates. We must note, however, that in ancient Greece a god could manifest him or herself epiphanically in a statue. As Platt observes: statues of the gods "have the potential to be viewed as epiphanic embodiments of the deities they represent. They can simultaneously symbolize and constitute divine presence."[93] In certain ritualized ceremonies, the Greeks could see an epiphany of a god in his or her statue. Petridou identifies three contexts in which a god could appear in his or her statue:

> The cult statue of a deity was perceived as a form of epiphany: a) when it was thought to be animated by the gods and thus endowed with the power of speech, movement, and emotional expression … ; b) when animated by the expectations of its beholders in the appropriate ritual or crisis context … ; and finally, c) when the imagistic representation of the deity posed the same

---

[91] In the classical period, the Greeks used the word *agalma* primarily for statues of gods (see Gernet 1981: 73–111; Vernant 1991: Chapter 8; Platt 2011: 90–1). See Van Straten 1981: 75 and Day 2010: 87–92 on *agalmata* that were not statues.

[92] I refer here to Plato's portrayal of Alcibiades.

[93] Platt 2011: 47. See also Burkert 1997; Steiner 2001: 80–5; Gaifman 2016: 249–80.

challenges and the same dangers for the viewers as his or her corporeal manifestation.[94]

To be sure, not every Greek saw a divine epiphany in a statue.[95] Still, statues could well manifest the living presence of the god.

Based on this epiphanic aspect of statues, one can argue that Alcibiades refers to the statues of the gods in Socrates' soul as a way of presenting his encounter with something divine. However, his revelation of Socrates as some sort of divine being turns out to be false. To clarify this point, I want to consider Alcibiades' views about Socrates' possession of knowledge. First, Alcibiades wrongly believes that Socrates has attained knowledge (Socrates himself has denied this[96]). He assumes that this knowledge can be transmitted as a doctrine and, indeed, exchanged as some sort of commodity. We see these ideas dramatized in Alcibiades' offer of his own beautiful body in exchange for Socrates' wisdom. Indeed, Socrates responds to Alcibiades' proposition by suggesting that this is in fact a greedy business exchange:

> if . . . you are attempting to strike a bargain (κοινώσασθαί) and to exchange (ἀλλάξασθαι) [your] beauty for [my] beauty, you are clearly intending to get the better of me in no small way. For you are trying to acquire true beauty in exchange for seeming beauty and, in truth, you are contriving to exchange bronze for gold. (218e–219a)

In claiming that Alcibiades offers bronze in exchange for gold, Socrates alludes to the famous scene in Homer's *Iliad* where Glaucus foolishly gives his enemy Diomedes golden armor in exchange for bronze (6.232–6). As Homer indicates, the two pieces of armor have radically different values: the bronze armor is worth 9 oxen and the gold 100 oxen (6.235–6). When Alcibiades sees someone who (seemingly) has divine wisdom, he responds by offering that individual a lowly and base object.

Second, Alcibiades fixates on the idea that Socrates has some sort of divine knowledge. Socrates warns Alcibiades that he may not have this knowledge and urges him to explore these issues further (219a). But Alcibiades ignores this warning and promptly jumps into bed with him. As Deborah Steiner rightly claims, Alcibiades engages in an idolatrous love affair: he desires the wrong object.[97]

---

[94] Petridou 2015: 50. Platt 2011: 90–105 et passim offers an excellent analysis of divine epiphanies in statues; see also Steiner 2001: 120–34, who discusses this topic in the context of the role and perception of Greek statues in general.

[95] As Petridou 2015: 50 rightly notes.   [96] As Alcibiades notes in 216d.

[97] Steiner 1996; see also Sheffield 2006: 204.

As a budding philosopher, Alcibiades should be aiming for truth, beauty, and knowledge, but he develops an obsessive attachment to a human being. Clearly, Alcibiades has no understanding of Socrates' philosophical project – he simply wants to get hold of the (putatively) divine wisdom of Socrates. Edmonds offers an interesting interpretation of this scene:

> Alcibiades' experience of his encounter with the divine [in Socrates] is, like the experience of the mysteries, a powerful imagistic experience that he cannot adequately frame in words, one that kindles his desire for the beauty that he has seen and impels him to action. Alcibiades, however, reacts in a characteristically wrong fashion to this experience, attempting to appropriate rather than to adore.[98]

As Edmonds argues, the beauty that Alcibiades saw in Socrates was in fact the Form of Beauty, but Alcibiades wrongly took Socrates to be the possessor of this beauty. But does Alcibiades see the divine Form of Beauty when he is in the presence of Socrates? He seems so fixated on getting Socrates' wisdom that he cannot even begin to ascend the Ladder of Love. There can be no doubt that Socrates had a very powerful effect on Alcibiades. But his false understanding of Socrates – and his own bad values – made Alcibiades interpret him in the wrong way. In my view, Alcibiades does not see a partial divine epiphany in Socrates' soul but rather an image of his own desires and projections.

Alcibiades, the profaner of mysteries, presents a false epiphanic experience. His vision of Socrates is utterly blinkered. He profanely imitates an Eleusinian hierophant and gives a speech that offers a false revelation of the mysteries of Socrates. Indeed, his account of the divine inner core of Socrates stands in stark opposition to Diotima's discourse on the philosophic *epoptês'* vision of the divine Form of Beauty. Just as he profaned the Eleusinian Mysteries by putting on a costume and imitating the hierophant's words, Alcibiades profanes philosophy by misunderstanding the nature of philosophic knowledge and offering his body in exchange for this wisdom. In Plato's view, no-one can gain a vision of the Forms by appropriating someone else's ideas,[99] and no-one who has seen the Forms can hand over his vision as some sort of doctrine. In Alcibiades' speech, Plato brings together a philosopher and a politician. Alcibiades sees the world in terms of power: he wants what Socrates has and offers something in exchange. Alicibiades' *pleonexia* shows itself in his effort to

---

[98] Edmonds 2017: 209.
[99] As we saw above, it is not clear if Socrates has seen the Forms. In Diotima's view, he is a mere *mustês*.

get "gold in exchange for bronze." Alcibiades' character and values make him unable to understand Socrates and to offer a revelation of this philosopher's inner core. In this scene in the *Symposium*, Plato portrays a power-hungry and pleonectic man presenting an account of a philosopher whom he does not understand. In this way, his hierophantic account of Socrates as some sort of divine person turns out to be yet another profanation of the mysteries. In this case, he profanes the mysteries of philosophy, which has as its object the divine Forms.

★★★★★★★★★★★★

The philosopher can offer an account of the essence of Beauty, but he cannot put his encounter with the divine into words. The epiphany of divine Beauty goes beyond human language. I want to close this chapter with a brief discussion of Leopardi's poem, *The Infinite*, which I cited in the epigraph to this chapter. I chose this poem to foreground Plato's struggles with language in his account of the soul's vision of Beauty. Leopardi did not treat the infinite in religious terms, but he pointed to the failure of language to capture the infinite. Here is the poem again:

> This lonely hill was always dear to me,
> And this hedgerow, which cuts off the view
> Of so much of the last horizon.
> But sitting here and gazing, I can see
> Beyond, in my mind's eye, unending spaces,
> And superhuman silences, and depthless calm,
> Till what I feel
> Is almost fear. And when I hear
> The wind stir in these branches, I begin
> Comparing that endless stillness with this noise:
> And the eternal comes to mind,
> And the dead seasons, and the present
> Living one, and how it sounds.
> So my mind sinks in this immensity:
> And foundering is sweet in such a sea.[100]

To describe the infinite, Leopardi breaks the sonnet form by adding a fifteenth line! In the first fourteen lines, the poet conjures up hills,

---

[100] Here is the poem in Italian: Sempre caro mi fu quest'ermo colle,/ e questa siepe, che da tanta parte/ dell'ultimo orizzonte il guardo esclude./ Ma sedendo e mirando, interminati/ spazi di là da quella, e sovrumani/ silenzi, e profondissima quïete/ io nel pensier mi fingo, ove per poco/ il cor non si spaura. E come il vento/ odo stormir tra queste piante, io quello/ infinito silenzio a questa voce/ vo comparando: e mi sovvien l'eterno,/ e le morte stagioni, e la presente/ e viva, e il suon di lei. Così tra questa/ immensità s'annega il pensier mio:/ e il naufragar m'è dolce in questo mare.

hedgerows, and wind blowing on the land; in the final line, he "founders" in the infinite as in a sea.

As Robert Harrison puts it so eloquently: "The 'foundering' of the last line refers to a shipwreck (*naufragar* in Italian), which we must understand as a purely psychic event that revolutionizes or overturns the perception of the landscape. What began as a land poem ends as a sea poem, as the differentiated boundaries of time's dimensions are liquefied by the imaginative activity that the poem tracks in the speaker's mind."[101] Plato takes the reader into the "great sea of beauty" and, from there, to the Form of Beauty. The philosopher does not "founder" when he sees Beauty, but he does encounter a "wondrous" and "divine" being that he cannot fully understand or put into words. In presenting Beauty in terms of a divine epiphany, Plato tries to revolutionize the reader's perception of the physical and intelligible realm. He asks the reader to move both into and beyond the self to see Beauty shining with divinity in the realm of the Forms.

[101]   Harrison, "The Magic of Leopardi," *New York Review of Books*, February 10, 2011.

CHAPTER 3

Dialogue of Self and Soul

> Meanwhile the mind, from pleasure less,
> Withdraws into its happiness;
> The mind, that ocean where each kind
> Does straight its own resemblance find,
> Yet it creates, transcending these,
> Far other worlds, and other seas;
> Annihilating all that's made
> To a green thought in a green shade.
>
> —Marvell, *The Garden*

> Soon wild commotions shook him and made flush
> All the immortal fairness of his limbs
> Into a hue more roseate than sweet pain
> Gives to a ravish'd nymph when her warm tears
> Gush luscious with no sob. Or more severe,–
> More like the struggle at the gate of death;
> Or liker still to one who should take leave
> Of pale immortal death, and with a pang
> As hot as death's is chill, with fierce convulse
> Die into life.
>
> —Keats, *Hyperion*

As his biological time ticks away, Socrates describes the everlasting life of his soul. His friends keep their eyes on the clock: Cebes reminds everyone to speak up now while Socrates is still alive (107a), and Crito urges Socrates to delay drinking the poison, since "the sun is on the mountains and has not yet set" (116e). But Socrates looks beyond the present to the future life of his soul. He presents four arguments for the immortality of the soul. In one argument, he says that the soul acquired knowledge of the Forms before it entered a body. As he claims: "souls existed previously . . . apart from bodies, before they took on human form, and they had intelligence" (76c).[1] By

---

[1] ἦσαν ἄρα ... αἱ ψυχαὶ καὶ πρότερον, πρὶν εἶναι ἐν ἀνθρώπου εἴδει, χωρὶς σωμάτων, καὶ φρόνησιν εἶχον.

pointing to a period of existence before incarnation, Socrates locates the soul outside of biological and historical time. And just as the soul's past stretches back interminably, its future extends forever: "if the soul is immortal, we need to care for it not only for the period of time that we call life, but for all time" (107c). In this dialogue, Socrates speaks as a mortal self about the immortal soul that dwells in his body.

In the *Phaedo*, Plato presents an account of immortality that differs radically from that of the *Symposium*. In particular, he conceives of the soul as immortal. The soul exists separately from the body – it can live in a body and reincarnate, but it can also dwell apart from the corporeal realm. As we saw in the last chapter, the human who desires immortality wants an eternal self – an "everlasting me." In the *Phaedo*, humans have immortal souls but will not get eternal selves. Plato's discourse in the *Phaedo* is psychocentric rather than anthropocentric. The soul, rather than the human being, maintains its identity over time. In this text, Socrates seeks to identify himself with his soul, not with his finite life as a human.

This dialogue's focus on the afterlife raises questions about Greek beliefs about death. In classical Greek texts, we find contradictory claims about the afterlife.[2] On the one hand, many texts refer to death as the final end of life. In the *Phaedo*, for example, Cebes says that the soul just scatters away like smoke after death (70a); in the *Republic*, Glaucon expresses great doubt over Socrates' claim that the soul is immortal and indestructible (608d). Other texts, however, refer to an afterlife in Hades that includes rewards and punishments. In Aristophanes' *Frogs*, for instance, Dionysus goes to Hades and finds a group of happy dead people (Eleusinian initiates) in one part of the underworld and miserable non-initiated people in another part.[3] As we saw in the last chapter, the initiates in the Eleusinian Mysteries had hope of gaining a good afterlife. But the operative word here is "hope."

As scholars have shown, aside from fringe groups like the Pythagoreans and Orphics, the Greeks had no real surety about the afterlife.[4] Although many literary texts represent Hades, this does not mean that the Greeks

---

[2] It is beyond the scope of this investigation to examine preplatonic Greek conceptions of the soul. Rather, I follow Bremmer (1983; see also 2002) and Long (2015), who have offered excellent accounts of the developing notions of the *psuchê* in ancient Greece.

[3] For discussions of the Eleusinian initiates in Hades in the *Frogs*, see Bowie 1993: 228–37; Lada-Richards 1999: 45–120.

[4] Sourvinou-Inwood 1981, 1988, and especially 1995; Johnston 1999; Bremmer 2002: 6–8; Bowden 2010: 23; Long 2015: chapter 1.

had a shared belief about the afterlife. As Jan Bremmer observes: "on the whole, the Athenian public did not firmly believe in rewards or punishments after death. In fact, they do not seem to have expected very much at all. 'After death every man is earth and shadow: nothing goes to nothing.'"[5] To cite one example, in Plato's *Apology*, Socrates takes an agnostic position: either he will have no existence at all after death or else his soul will migrate to another place where good judges preside over the dead (40c–41a).

In identifying the soul as immortal, Plato addresses the human fear of death. He presents four arguments for the immortality of the soul that aim to combat this fear. Indeed, he claims that the philosopher should "practice death" during his lifetime. He does this by separating his soul from his body and contemplating the Forms. In this dialogue, Plato elevates the immortal soul over the human individual. In addition, he represents the soul's life in a body as a hellish and punishing experience. However, as he states, the soul can gain release from this punishment: if it lives a good life as a philosopher, it leaves the body forever after death. At that point, the soul gets off the cycle of incarnation and dwells everlastingly with the Forms.

In the *Phaedo*, Plato presents the first detailed account of the soul and the Forms. He discusses these in a series of arguments for the immortality of the soul. Indeed, he braids the soul and the Forms together in almost every single argument. In Chapter 1, I analyzed the divinity-marker *theios* for the Forms in the *Phaedo*. In this chapter, I examine the divinity-markers that Plato uses for the soul. As we will see, Plato conceives of the soul as having a divine preincarnate life in the realm of the Forms. Even on earth, the soul is "godlike." I also analyze the passages that mark the Forms as divine. Not surprisingly, the soul's divine state depends on its contemplation of the divine Forms.

Plato repeatedly uses the Orphic divinity-marker for the soul and the Forms in this dialogue. To clarify this idea, I offer a detailed discussion of Orphic discourses and practices in Greece in the classical period. As I argue, Plato drew on the Orphic myths about the soul and the initiate's final resting place with the gods, but he recast this idea in philosophical terms: the "initiated" philosophic soul finds its resting place in the divine realm of the Forms. Plato also borrows the Orphic "story of the soul" to give his immortal soul a narrative: for the Orphics, the soul is divine but falls into bodies and gets reincarnated as a punishment for an originary crime. Once it purifies itself and gets initiated, the soul goes to dwell

---

[5] Bremmer 2002: 7. The quote is from Euripides' *Meleagros* (fr. 532 Nauck).

everlastingly with the gods. Plato's story of the soul follows this same narrative arc: after a divine beginning, it falls into the prison of the body and reincarnation; it can return to an incorporeal life in the divine realm of the Forms if it purifies itself by practicing philosophy.

3.1 The Double Narrative in the *Phaedo*

Plato constructs two narratives in this dialogue: the narrative of Socrates' life and death, and the narrative of the immortal soul before, during, and after bodily reincarnation. I call this the "double narrative." The narratives of Socrates the individual and of the immortal soul operate in different chronotopes (in Bakhtin's sense of this term[6]): while Socrates lives a single life on earth, the soul lives everlastingly and spends an endless period of time in the earthly realm and, ideally, in the realm of the Forms. Plato places Socrates' human narrative in the larger narrative of the soul. This larger story focuses on sin and salvation.

To bring these stories together, Plato creates a threshold narrative. He places Socrates at the threshold between life on earth and the afterlife. Or, to put this more clearly, he places the soul of Socrates at the end of its life on earth and at the beginning of its new life among the gods and Forms. In addition, Plato sets up an opposition between the "visible," physical realm and the "invisible" realm of the Forms. He dramatizes this opposition in the character of Socrates: Socrates will leave the hellish visible world after death and enter a good and divine invisible world.

In this double narrative, Plato places great emphasis on Hades. However, he turns the traditional idea of Hades upside-down: in fact, the embodied human soul on earth lives in a dark and punishing under-world; but there is a good "Hades" (*Haides*) where a soul can dwell, the "invisible (*aides*)" realm of the Forms.[7] In short, Plato creates and juxta-poses two kinds of Hades: (1) an underworld region that contains both embodied humans and human souls that are punished after each life,

---

[6] Bakhtin discusses the chronotope as it operates in literary narratives. As he indicates, the specific constructions of time and space (and their interaction) in narratives produce specific spatio-temporal configurations. These provide the ground for specific ways of representing human beings and their interaction with historical, social, and natural forces (1981: 85). Bakhtin describes the chronotope as follows: "in the literary artistic chronotope, spatial and temporal indicators are fused into one carefully thought-out, concrete whole. Time, as it were, thickens, takes on flesh, becomes artistically visible; likewise space becomes charged and responsive to the movements of time, plot, and history" (1981: 84). I discuss Bakhtin's theory in detail and the way that chronotopes operate in Plato's dialogue in Nightingale 2001.

[7] See 81a for this idea. I will discuss this in detail below.

and (2) a philosophic Hades that exists in the invisible realm of the Forms. Plato conceives of these two Hades spatially and portrays them on a vertical axis. The latter exists up above the physical world, while humans and punished souls dwell in a subterranean region. In this vertical scheme, the good philosophic souls live up above in a luminous realm, while ordinary and bad souls dwell below the earth in dark and hellish regions.

By creating narratives for the individual Socrates and his everlasting soul, Plato juxtaposes two different dramatic protagonists acting in two different dramas. To take a simple example, Plato uses identical images and terminology to bring together Socrates the mortal human and the immortal soul that occupies his body. On the last day of his life, Socrates lives in a "prison" (*desmôtêrion*), but the officials "release" (*luousi*; *lelumenon*) him from his fetters (*desmoi*) so that he can be readied for death (59e–60c); correlatively, his soul is "bound" (*dedemenos*) in the "prison" (*desmôtêrion*) of his body, and only the practice of philosophy can "release" it from these fetters (*lusis, louein*; 82d–e, 114b–c). In the two dramas, Socrates, the human who has just been released from physical bonds, speaks about his soul's imminent release from the prison of his body. By composing and entwining these two dramas, Plato places the soul in two different chronotopes: it can dwell in the incorporeal and eternal realm of the Forms or in a mortal and temporalized body.

The *Phaedo* goes back and forth between the human individual and the immortal soul. On the one hand, Socrates the individual has lived his life on earth as a philosopher and now prepares for death. His soul, by contrast, existed before this life and will supercede it after Socrates dies. Plato creates a sort of "dialogue of self and soul" in this text by having Socrates use the word "I" in relation both to himself and to his soul. Thus, when Crito asks him how to bury his body, Socrates responds: "however you please, if you can catch me and I do not get away from you" (115c). "I," Socrates, will get away from Crito and my body, while "I," the soul, will journey to the gods:

> Men, I cannot persuade Crito that I am this Socrates who is now conversing and arranging each of the things that have been said, but he thinks I am the man whom he will soon see as a corpse, and he asks how to bury me. As I long ago said in a long discourse, when I drink the poison, I will no longer remain with you, but I will go away to the joys of the blessed.[8] (115c–d)

---

[8] 115c–d: οὐ πείθω, ὦ ἄνδρες, Κρίτωνα, ὡς ἐγώ εἰμι οὗτος Σωκράτης, ὁ νυνὶ διαλεγόμενος καὶ διατάττων ἕκαστον τῶν λεγομένων, ἀλλ᾽ οἴεταί με ἐκεῖνον εἶναι ὃν ὄψεται ὀλίγον ὕστερον νεκρόν, καὶ ἐρωτᾷ δὴ πῶς με θάπτῃ. ὅτι δὲ ἐγὼ πάλαι πολὺν λόγον πεποίημαι, ὡς, ἐπειδὰν πίω τὸ φάρμακον, οὐκέτι ὑμῖν παραμενῶ, ἀλλ᾽ οἰχήσομαι ἀπιὼν εἰς μακάρων δή τινας εὐδαιμονίας.

In saying "I am this Socrates" but not the bodily man "whom he will soon see as corpse," Socrates refuses to identify himself with his body. Yet he still speaks in the first-person as a mortal human being – "this Socrates" who sits in the prison and has his final conversation with his friends. In the last line, however, he says that "I will no longer remain with you but I will go away to the joys of the blessed." Here, Socrates speaks as a soul, not as a human being. In short, Socrates uses the first-person singular "I" to speak both for himself and for his soul.

Plato has Socrates use this double "I" to indicate that, quite apart from its human incarnations, the soul has its own "I." As the center of consciousness, the soul must persist in its unity and singularity from one life to another. Indeed, the soul that now animates Socrates had gained knowledge of the Forms in its early preincarnate state, and it carries this with it to each human life.[9] The "I" of the soul, however, differs radically from the "I" of the human. The soul has its own agenda: it aims to escape the cycle of reincarnation and live forever contemplating the Forms. In addition, the soul that thinks, makes choices, moves a body, and contemplates the Forms, acts in both the visible and the invisible realms.

3.2 Plato's Conception of the Soul

In the *Phaedo*, Plato presents the first full account of the immortal soul. Although he regularly refers to the soul (*psuchê*) in earlier dialogues, he does not offer an account of its nature. In this text, he identifies the soul as an immortal and invisible entity that exists separately from the body. To be sure, in the eschatology in the *Gorgias*, Plato represented souls as being rewarded or punished after death, but he did not present an argument for the immortal soul in that dialogue. In the *Phaedo*, he sets forth detailed arguments and ideas about the soul. First, the soul is immortal, incorporeal, invisible, and the seat of reason. It can be incarnated and reincarnated in different bodies, both human and animal. The body is alien to the soul and pollutes it by turning it towards earthly activities and pleasures. The body is a "prison" for the soul, and the soul must endeavor to escape it by living a philosophical life. Indeed, the philosopher should separate his soul from his body by using his mind alone to contemplate the Forms. The

---

[9] As Socrates indicates in the eschatology, the soul will bring its "education and rearing" (*paideia kai trophê*) to Hades (107d). Based on the education it received in its last human life, the soul will fare well or badly in the afterlife: it receives punishment or reward for its moral and intellectual qualities. The punishment also includes incarnation in another body, possibly an animal.

philosopher "purifies" his soul by separating it from the body and grasping the Forms.

In this dialogue, Plato makes a number of philosophical claims about the soul:

(1) **The soul is immortal and separate from the body**. The former is "invisible" and indestructible; the latter is "visible" and destructible (79a–80b).

(2) **The soul animates the body** (105c–106d). Plato argues in the Final Argument that the soul has life as a necessary attribute, and thus brings life to human and animal bodies.[10] This capacity for animation does not involve cognition, emotion, or desire.

(3) **The soul has reason and possesses knowledge.** The soul's reason can contemplate the Forms. The soul is "like" and "akin to" the Forms in that it is invisible and incorporeal (80b). The soul has knowledge of the Forms that it gained in a preincarnate state; it can "recollect" the Forms during its human life. Bodily obstruction can affect the soul's reasoning.

(4) **The soul has moral agency.** The soul engages in practical reasoning (80a). It has autonomy. It has virtues and vices.

(5) **The soul has its own desires and pleasures**. The soul is not simply rational. It can desire wisdom but also be infected by the body with baser desires (it can "desire" the corporeal; 81d–e). Also, the soul has its own pleasures, such as the pleasure of learning (114e).

Plato packs a lot into the soul in the *Phaedo*. He does not separate it into parts, as he will do in later dialogues. In this text, the soul has many different capacities. At one time, it contemplates the Forms; at another, it animates the body; at yet another, it makes moral choices. I will not attempt to present a coherent account of these different aspects of the soul (an impossible feat). Rather, I want to examine Plato's ideas about the soul in the first three immortality arguments.[11] These arguments deal with different aspects of the soul.

I think of the Cyclical Argument, the Recollection Argument, and the Affinity Argument as the "where," "when," and "what" of the soul. The

---

[10] This is a terribly difficult argument. I follow Frede (1978), who argues that the soul is not a Form, and that fire and snow are entities in the physical world. To mention but one example, fire not only participates in the Form of Heat, but has heat as a necessary attribute. Likewise, the soul participates in the Form of Life and has life as a necessary attribute. It can never not be alive and bring life. From the claim that the soul is "deathless," Plato argues that it is "indestructible" and "immortal."

[11] The "Final Argument" focuses on the Forms, so I will not discuss this here.

Cyclical Argument focuses on the idea that the soul exists in Hades as well as on earth. This addresses the places "where" the soul dwells and sets up the idea that the soul can dwell in the realm of the Forms (a place separate from Hades and earth). The Recollection Argument emphasizes the temporality of the soul. Plato gives the soul a past "when" it existed before entering a body. This anticipates the "when" of its everlasting future. The Affinity Argument addresses "what" the soul is by placing the soul in relation to the Forms and to the bodily realm. The soul is "like" and "akin to" the Forms (though not identical to them); the body is "alien" to it. This argument treats the soul as a substance that differs from the Forms and the bodily realm. To be sure, Plato does not explicitly identify the soul as a substance that is ontologically separate from the Forms and from the bodily realm. But he makes this idea clear in his discussions of the soul in the middle-period dialogues.

Although I identify the where, when, and what of the soul in these three arguments, I want to emphasize that these aspects of the soul can all come up in a single argument (though one of them will dominate in a given argument). I separate these aspects as a heuristic device. This helps me to analyze Plato's claims about the nature and capacity of the soul.

The Cyclical Argument follows upon Socrates' claims that he will go to good gods after death. Cebes expresses serious doubt about this, and Socrates proceeds to quote an "old story" (*palaios logos*) to validate this idea: the souls "go from here to there, and then come back here again, and they are born again from the dead; and if it holds thus, and living people are born from the dead, then surely our souls would have to exist in that world" (70c–d). Plato uses the language of "here" and "there" to locate the souls on earth and in Hades. He posits the opposition of the living and the dead and claims that these come into being from one another. This supposedly proves that "our souls exist in Hades" (71e). This argument focuses on the ongoing and potentially everlasting existence of the soul. It also posits the doctrine of reincarnation. Finally, it indicates that the soul can dwell in different places (in Hades and on earth). To be sure, Plato does not mention the realm of the Forms in this argument – he does this later in the text, where he indicates that the perfected philosophical soul will leave the bodily realm altogether and dwell in the realm of the Forms.[12] By emphasizing the "where" or the *places* that the soul can dwell in the Cyclical Argument, Plato introduces the idea that the soul lives and acts

---

[12] I will discuss this in detail below.

in different realms. As we will see, the dwelling places for the soul play an important role in the dialogue.

In the Recollection Argument, Plato introduces the temporality of the soul. He had already implied this in the Cyclical Argument, but he did not take up this topic directly. Interestingly, it is Cebes who first brings up the doctrine of recollection, reminding Socrates that he and Simmias have heard him talk about this many times. Here, Plato subtly indicates that Cebes and Simmias have had long arguments about the soul and the Forms in the past. Indeed, Plato represents the characters as having agreed on the existence of the Forms. This means that he does not have to argue for this position: the existence of the Forms is a given.

What does the Recollection Argument tell us about the soul? Socrates states that when a person has perceived something, he knows not only the thing he perceives but also some other object he has perceived before: he recollects the former object (73c–d). The passing of time allows him to see something now and recall something from the past. Socrates now asks how people know that the Forms exist. To address this question, Socrates brings up the example of equal items on earth and their relation to the Form of Equality (74a–b): "Did we not, by seeing equal pieces of wood or stones or other such things, derive from them that object [the Form of Equal], which is different from them? . . . Don't equal stones and pieces of wood, being the very same ones, sometimes appear as equal and at other times not?" (74b).[13] Socrates takes the latter claim to prove that the soul had a previous knowledge of the Forms: "When someone sees something and thinks, 'this thing which I now see wants to be like one of the realities (*tôn ontôn*), but falls short (*endei*) of them and cannot be such as that reality is, but is inferior to it,' he who thinks this must necessarily have had previous knowledge of the thing which he says the other resembles but falls short of" (74d–e). Indeed, Socrates states, souls knew the Form of Equality before they first saw any equal things on earth, that is, before they entered the body (75a–b): "before we began to see, hear and perceive other things, we must have attained knowledge of the Equal itself" (75b).[14] As Socrates argues, we could not have gained this knowledge by way of our senses. He thus concludes that the soul had a preincarnate beginning.

---

[13] 74b: ἆρ' οὐκ ἐξ ὧν νυνδὴ ἐλέγομεν, ἢ ξύλα ἢ λίθους ἢ ἄλλα ἄττα ἰδόντες ἴσα, ἐκ τούτων ἐκεῖνο ἐνενοήσαμεν, ἕτερον ὂν τούτων; . . . .ἆρ' οὐ λίθοι μὲν ἴσοι καὶ ξύλα ἐνίοτε ταὐτὰ ὄντα τῷ μὲν ἴσα φαίνεται, τῷ δ' οὔ.

[14] 75b: πρὸ τοῦ ἄρα ἄρξασθαι ἡμᾶς ὁρᾶν καὶ ἀκούειν καὶ τἆλλα αἰσθάνεσθαι τυχεῖν ἔδει που εἰληφότας ἐπιστήμην αὐτοῦ τοῦ ἴσου.

This argument focuses on the soul's past and its first preincarnate beginnings with the Forms. Socrates emphasizes the time "when" the soul knew
the Forms before it entered the body: "our souls existed previously, separate
from bodies ... before they took on a human form, and they had intelligence" (ἦσαν ἄρα ... αἱ ψυχαὶ καὶ πρότερον, πρὶν εἶναι ἐν ἀνθρώπου εἴδει,
χωρὶς σωμάτων, καὶ φρόνησιν εἶχον; 76c). The soul, then, always had
intelligence and knowledge. Indeed, the soul possesses this knowledge even
if it has forgotten this when it lives in a body. As this argument implies, the
soul maintains its own identity over time: since the soul can recollect this
knowledge, it must have had continuous existence. In this argument, Plato
does not refer to the Forms as a place or realm. Still, given his claims about
the places where the soul dwells in the Cyclical Argument, the Recollection
Argument implies that the preincarnate souls lived in the realm of the
Forms. Plato will return to this idea later on.

In the Affinity Argument, Plato addresses the "what" of the soul. Rather
than offering a definition or account of what the soul is, Plato approaches this
indirectly by comparing the soul to the Forms and to the body. He posits "two
kinds of beings in the universe" (*eidê tôn ontôn*), the "visible and the invisible"
(*to men horaton, to de aidês*): "the invisible is always the same and the visible is
never the same" (τὸ μὲν ἀιδὲς ἀεὶ κατὰ ταὐτὰ ἔχον, τὸ δὲ ὁρατὸν μηδέποτε
κατὰ ταὐτά; 79a). Here, he divides the realm of the Forms, which I will call
"the invisible," from "the visible" (physical) realm, where things endlessly
change. Socrates claims that the soul is more like the Forms and less like
the body, and asks whether "the soul is visible or invisible." Cebes states that
the soul is invisible, "at least to humans" (79b). We must emphasize that the
invisibility of the soul to humans differs from "the invisible" realm of the
Forms. Based on Plato's distinction between "the invisible" and "the visible"
realms, we cannot simply place the unseen soul in the realm of "the invisible,"
where beings are "always the same." The soul does not stay the same, as the
Forms do. The soul changes for the better and worse over time, while the
Forms exist outside of change and temporality. In short, even though the soul
is unseen, it changes and moves everlastingly, while the Forms remain fixed
and unchanging in the invisible realm. For this reason, we cannot place the
soul squarely in "the invisible" realm. Still, the soul's invisibility provides
evidence for its incorporeality.

Based on the similarity of the "invisibility" of the soul and "the invisible"
realm of the Forms, Socrates identifies the soul as "like" the Forms: "the
soul is most like the divine, immortal, intelligible, uniform, indissoluble,
and ever unchanging; but the body is most like the human, mortal,
multiformed, unintelligible, dissoluble, and ever unconstant to itself"

(τῷ μὲν θείῳ καὶ ἀθανάτῳ καὶ νοητῷ καὶ μονοειδεῖ καὶ ἀδιαλύτῳ καὶ ἀεὶ ὡσαύτως κατὰ ταὐτὰ ἔχοντι ἑαυτῷ ὁμοιότατον εἶναι ψυχή, τῷ δὲ ἀνθρωπίνῳ καὶ θνητῷ καὶ πολυειδεῖ καὶ ἀνοήτῳ καὶ διαλυτῷ καὶ μηδέποτε κατὰ ταὐτὰ ἔχοντι ἑαυτῷ ὁμοιότατον αὖ εἶναι σῶμα; 80b). Here, Plato identifies the Forms by way of their attributes: divine, immortal, intelligible, singular in form, indissoluble, and unchanging. The soul, then, is "most like" the Forms even though it can inhabit bodies. By giving the Forms the *theios* divinity-marker and positing the soul's likeness to the Forms, Plato also marks the soul as having divine capacities.

Plato takes the likeness argument further by suggesting that the soul is "akin to" (*sungenês*) the Forms. Using the metaphor of kinship, he places the soul in a sort of family relationship with the Forms. The soul is most at home (as it were) when it separates from the body and contemplates the Forms:

> When the soul inquires, alone by itself, it goes thither to the pure, ever-existing, immortal, and unchanging; and, inasmuch as it is akin to this, it is always in its presence, that is, when [the soul] is by itself and when this is permitted. And [the soul] ceases from its wandering and stays with these [Beings], and remains always the same and constant, inasmuch as it lays hold of such things. And this state is called wisdom. (ὅταν δέ γε αὐτὴ καθ' αὑτὴν σκοπῇ, ἐκεῖσε οἴχεται εἰς τὸ καθαρόν τε καὶ ἀεὶ ὂν καὶ ἀθάνατον καὶ ὡσαύτως ἔχον, καὶ ὡς συγγενὴς οὖσα αὐτοῦ ἀεὶ μετ' ἐκείνου τε γίγνεται, ὅτανπερ αὐτὴ καθ' αὑτὴν γένηται καὶ ἐξῇ αὐτῇ, καὶ πέπαυταί τε τοῦ πλάνου καὶ περὶ ἐκεῖνα ἀεὶ κατὰ ταὐτὰ ὡσαύτως ἔχει, ἅτε τοιούτων ἐφαπτομένη: καὶ τοῦτο αὐτῆς τὸ πάθημα φρόνησις κέκληται; 79d)[15]

It may seem that the soul is "akin to" the Forms simply because it has the capacity to contemplate these realities. But the metaphor of kinship conjures up the idea that the soul gravitates to the Forms as though to its family members.[16] In short, the soul is naturally suited to be with its kindred beings, the Forms. Left by itself, it would do just that.

In spite of its affinity to the Forms, however, the soul has almost none of its attributes. First, the soul is changeable – it can become better or worse. Second, the soul can enter into bodies and live as a human or animal.

---

[15] See also 67a–b: "In this way, being pure and freeing ourselves from the foolishness of the body, we will very probably be with those [Beings] and know by ourselves everything that is pure, and this, perhaps, is the truth. For it is not permitted for the impure to lay hold of the pure" (καὶ οὕτω μὲν καθαροὶ ἀπαλλαττόμενοι τῆς τοῦ σώματος ἀφροσύνης, ὡς τὸ εἰκὸς μετὰ τοιούτων τε ἐσόμεθα καὶ γνωσόμεθα δι' ἡμῶν αὐτῶν πᾶν τὸ εἰλικρινές, τοῦτο δ' ἐστὶν ἴσως τὸ ἀληθές· μὴ καθαρῷ γὰρ καθαροῦ ἐφάπτεσθαι μὴ οὐ θεμιτὸν ᾖ).

[16] See especially Bostock 1986: 19–20.

Third, it has agency and, when embodied, can move certain bodily things around (its present body and physical items that it comes into contact with). Fourth, the soul is not "intelligible" in the way that the Forms are. The Forms are the ultimate objects of knowledge; the soul is the knower rather than the object of knowledge. Fifth, the soul is not "divine" in any simple sense: it can raise itself to the realm of the divine, but it can lower itself to an earthly state. In this way, it differs from the gods (who are always good) and the Forms. The soul, then, is "most like" the Forms, but this likeness has its limits. Plato likens the soul to the Forms because it is invisible, incorporeal, and naturally suited to contemplate the Forms. In addition, he indicates that the soul has the capacity to become divine for a time (during contemplation) or, in ideal circumstances, to become everlastingly divine. It is the soul's kinship to the divine Forms that allows it to achieve a divine state.

We have not yet finished with the Affinity Argument. For Socrates also suggests that the soul is "like the divine" (*homoion tôi theiôi*) in that it "rules" (*archein*) the body. As he claims, "the divine is of such a kind by nature to rule and lead, and the mortal to obey and be ruled" (80a). Here, he refers to the gods, not the Forms (since the Forms do not rule or lead). Like the gods, who rule over humans, the soul has the capacity to rule over its own body. If the soul rules the body properly, it does this by way of intelligence. In this argument, then, Plato gives the soul two divinity-markers: he likens the soul to the divine Forms and also to the gods. Still, he does not grant full divinity to the soul. The soul can raise only itself to a "godlike" status by contemplating the Forms and controlling the body.

Plato returns to the likeness of the soul to the gods in the passage where Socrates discusses "mind" (*nous*), both cosmic and individual.[17] Socrates speaks of his early discovery of Anaxagoras' claim that "mind" (*nous*) "orders and causes all things (νοῦς ἐστιν ὁ διακοσμῶν τε καὶ πάντων αἴτιος) in the heavens" (97c). When Socrates first took up Anaxagoras' book, he had expected to hear that the shape of the earth and its central position in the heavens was due to the fact that this was the "best" cosmic system (97d–e; 98a). What he found instead was a physicalist notion of causation. Socrates completely rejects this idea (99b).[18] As he claims,

---

[17] While he does not refer to the soul in this passage, he clearly considers the soul as having (or being) a mind.

[18] Socrates opposes Anaxagoras' claim that the earth is flat and rests on the air, and also the claim (probably Empedoclean) that a vortex surrounds the earth and keeps it stable (Aristotle *De caelo* 295a attributes this idea to Empedocles).

a mind that orders the heavens must make each thing in the cosmos "the best it can be" (97c). Indeed, he had been looking for a divine intelligence that ordered and ruled the universe:

> They [the natural philosophers] do not seek for the power that makes things placed as it is best for them to be placed, and they do not think that there is any divine force, but they believe they can discover an Atlas stronger, more immortal, and more all-encompassing than this, and in truth they do not think that the good and binding binds and holds things together. (τὴν δὲ τοῦ ὡς οἷόν τε βέλτιστα αὐτὰ τεθῆναι δύναμιν οὕτω νῦν κεῖσθαι, ταύτην οὔτε ζητοῦσιν οὔτε τινὰ οἴονται δαιμονίαν ἰσχὺν ἔχειν, ἀλλὰ ἡγοῦνται τούτου Ἄτλαντα ἄν ποτε ἰσχυρότερον καὶ ἀθανατώτερον καὶ μᾶλλον ἅπαντα συνέχοντα ἐξευρεῖν, καὶ ὡς ἀληθῶς τὸ ἀγαθὸν καὶ δέον συνδεῖν καὶ συνέχειν οὐδὲν οἴονται; 99c)

Although Socrates does not explain what he means by a "divine" power or force that directs all things, he clearly refers to a divine mind that rules the cosmos teleologically. As he puts it:

> I would never have thought that, when he [Anaxagoras] said that these things were cosmically ordered (*kekosmêsthai*) by intelligence, he would introduce any other cause than that it is best for them to be in this state. When he assigned the cause to each thing and to all things in common, I thought he would explain the best for the individual and the good for all things in common. (98a–b)[19]

Here, Socrates endorses the idea that a divine mind orders the heavens by aiming at the good. Unfortunately, he does not pursue this idea any further in this text.

Socrates now moves from macrocosm to microcosm: he discusses his own mind and its powers over his body. He claims that his decision to stay in the prison is the "true cause" of his present affairs. As he says, rather humorously, "my bones, being moved by an opinion (*doxa*) of what is best, would be in Megara or Boeotia, unless I thought it was more just (*dikaioteron*) to pay the penalty which was ordered by the city" (99a). Here, Socrates claims that his mind controls his body. As he observes:

> It seemed to me to be most of all as if someone should say that Socrates does all the things he does with his mind (*nous*) and then, when attempting to give the causes for each of the things I do, should state that I am sitting here

---

[19] 98a–b: οὐ γὰρ ἄν ποτε αὐτὸν ᾤμην, φάσκοντά γε ὑπὸ νοῦ αὐτὰ κεκοσμῆσθαι, ἄλλην τινὰ αὐτοῖς αἰτίαν ἐπενεγκεῖν ἢ ὅτι βέλτιστον αὐτὰ οὕτως ἔχειν ἐστὶν ὥσπερ ἔχει· ἑκάστῳ οὖν αὐτῶν ἀποδιδόντα τὴν αἰτίαν καὶ κοινῇ πᾶσι τὸ ἑκάστῳ βέλτιστον ᾤμην καὶ τὸ κοινὸν πᾶσιν ἐπεκδιηγήσεσθαι ἀγαθόν.

now on account of the fact that my body is made of bones and sinews, and
bones are hard and have joints that separate them from each another, and
sinews can be contracted and relaxed, and bones are held around by the flesh
and skin which surrounds them; and, with the bones hanging in the joints,
the sinews, slackening and tightening, make me able now to bend my legs,
and this is the cause of why I sit here with my legs bent. And if, in turn, he
mentions other such causes, like voice, air, hearing, and countless other
things, as the reason why I am conversing with you, in truth he fails to
mention the real causes, i.e., that the Athenians thought it was better to vote
against me, and therefore I have decided it is better for to me to sit here, and
I thought it more just that I remain here and pay the penalty which they
have ordered. (98c–e)[20]

Socrates indicates that his mind (and that of the Athenians) causes his
present situation. His body plays a secondary role – it cannot move itself
without the mind. Socrates uses his mind to judge that the present location
of his body is good and just.[21] Socrates judges and acts in relation to what
his mind thinks is right. Just as a divine mind would order and move the
heavens by aiming at the good, his own mind thinks and controls his body
by understanding the good. Of course the Athenians make a bad decision –
they have wrong ideas about the good. But they still act on what they think
is good.

In this passage, Plato clarifies the claim in the Affinity Argument that the
soul is "like" god. There, he likened the soul to the gods by way of its
capacity to rule the body. Here, he identifies a (hypothetical) divine mind
and compares this to the human mind, which has the capacity to consider
(and, in the case of the philosopher, to know) the good and to move its own
body. While Plato does not flesh this idea out in cosmological terms, he
does indicate that the soul's mind resembles the divine mind by way of its
intelligent rulership over the body. To be sure, he presents this idea
indirectly – Socrates himself claims that he himself never discovered

[20] καί μοι ἔδοξεν ὁμοιότατον πεπονθέναι ὥσπερ ἂν εἴ τις λέγων ὅτι Σωκράτης πάντα ὅσα πράττει νῷ
πράττει, κἄπειτα ἐπιχειρήσας λέγειν τὰς αἰτίας ἑκάστων ὧν πράττω, λέγοι πρῶτον μὲν ὅτι διὰ
ταῦτα νῦν ἐνθάδε κάθημαι, ὅτι σύγκειταί μου τὸ σῶμα ἐξ ὀστῶν καὶ νεύρων, καὶ τὰ μὲν ὀστᾶ ἐστιν
στερεὰ καὶ διαφυὰς ἔχει χωρὶς ἀπ' ἀλλήλων, τὰ δὲ νεῦρα οἷα ἐπιτείνεσθαι καὶ ἀνίεσθαι,
περιαμπέχοντα τὰ ὀστᾶ μετὰ τῶν σαρκῶν καὶ δέρματος ὃ συνέχει αὐτά· αἰωρουμένων οὖν τῶν
ὀστῶν ἐν ταῖς αὑτῶν συμβολαῖς χαλῶντα καὶ συντείνοντα τὰ νεῦρα κάμπτεσθαί που ποιεῖ οἷόν τ'
εἶναι ἐμὲ νῦν τὰ μέλη, καὶ διὰ ταύτην τὴν αἰτίαν συγκαμφθεὶς ἐνθάδε κάθημαι· καὶ αὖ περὶ τοῦ
διαλέγεσθαι ὑμῖν ἑτέρας τοιαύτας αἰτίας λέγοι, φωνάς τε καὶ ἀέρας καὶ ἀκοὰς καὶ ἄλλα μυρία
τοιαῦτα αἰτιώμενος, ἀμελήσας τὰς ὡς ἀληθῶς αἰτίας λέγειν, ὅτι, ἐπειδὴ Ἀθηναίοις ἔδοξε βέλτιον
εἶναι ἐμοῦ καταψηφίσασθαι, διὰ ταῦτα δὴ καὶ ἐμοὶ βέλτιον αὖ δέδοκται ἐνθάδε καθῆσθαι, καὶ
δικαιότερον παραμένοντα ὑπέχειν τὴν δίκην ἣν ἂν κελεύσωσιν.
[21] While Plato does not identify the soul as "self-moving motion" in this dialogue, i.e., the only agent
that can move bodies (human or cosmic), he does seem to be leaning in this direction.

a divine mind that would rule the cosmos (and he moves on to discuss the Forms as causes). But he does raise the idea of a divine power that would rule and move the cosmos, and he presents a macrocosm–microcosm analogy. In this argument, then, Plato posits the soul's likeness to god.[22]

Let me conclude this section by considering the Cyclical and Affinity arguments together. While the Cyclical Argument indicated that the soul could live on earth and in Hades, the Affinity argument adds a new, intelligible realm for the soul to visit or dwell in. In the argument for the soul's kinship to the Forms, Socrates says that the soul "goes thither" (*ekeise oichetai*) to the Forms when it separates itself from the body (79d). Here, Plato refers to the Forms as existing in a place that the soul can inhabit. The soul can also dwell in a body and live fully in that region. The realms of the Forms and the body, then, mark two key destinations for the soul. In the eschatology, Plato gestures towards a third region for the soul – the place where it gets punished and purified in a subterranean region in between lives on earth – but he presents this idea in very vague terms. What matters for Plato are the two dwelling places for the soul – the bodily and the intelligible realms. The goal of the soul is to depart from the body and dwell with the Forms. In conceiving of the Forms as a place or realm, Plato uses spatial language to talk about incorporeal beings. But Plato cannot avoid using imagistic language in his discussions of the Forms, and he regularly conceives of the Forms as a place in this and other dialogues.

Plato takes this idea further in the Affinity Argument. He identifies the realm of the Forms as the "true Hades," and contrasts this with the traditional "hellish Hades" (as I call it). As Socrates states, the invisible soul goes to the invisible and divine realm of the Forms:

> The soul, the invisible, goes to another such place, one that is noble and pure and invisible (*aidê*) – to "Hades" (*haidou*) in truth – and into the presence of a good and wise god (whither, if god wills, my soul must soon go) ... if the soul is delivered in a pure state – not dragging the body along with itself, inasmuch as it did not willingly associate with it in life, but fleeing it and gathering itself together alone to itself, since it has always cared for this – then it is doing nothing other than practicing philosophy rightly and really practicing death. (80d–81a)[23]

[22] In addition, as we see in the case of the Athenians, the soul can fail to realize its divine capacities by rejecting the practice of philosophy.
[23] 80d–81a: ἡ δὲ ψυχὴ ἄρα, τὸ ἀιδές, τὸ εἰς τοιοῦτον τόπον ἕτερον οἰχόμενον γενναῖον καὶ καθαρὸν καὶ ἀιδῆ, εἰς Ἅιδου ὡς ἀληθῶς, παρὰ τὸν ἀγαθὸν καὶ φρόνιμον θεόν, οἷ, ἂν θεὸς θέλῃ, αὐτίκα καὶ τῇ ἐμῇ ψυχῇ ἰτέον ... ἐὰν μὲν καθαρὰ ἀπαλλάττηται, μηδὲν τοῦ σώματος συνεφέλκουσα, ἅτε οὐδὲν κοινωνοῦσα αὐτῷ ἐν τῷ βίῳ ἑκοῦσα εἶναι, ἀλλὰ φεύγουσα αὐτὸ καὶ συνηθροισμένη αὐτὴ εἰς

By playing on the etymology of *aidês* ("invisible") and *haidês* ("Hades"), Plato identifies the invisible Forms as occupying a place, i.e., a "true Hades" for the philosophic soul.[24] The good philosophic souls go to this "place" (*topos*) after death.

Plato also represents both the hellish Hades and true Hades in the eschatology. In this myth, he creates an upside-down world. Humans now live in a hellish realm in hollows in the earth, while philosophic souls journey up to the "true Hades" of the Forms. Plato conceives of hellish Hades as the place where souls live in human and animal bodies, but also as a place of punishments for the soul after each embodied life. These are different aspects of hellish Hades: the soul's life in a human body differs from the soul's punishments in Hades in between incarnations. As I have suggested, Plato shows much more interest in the hellish life in a human body than the periods of punishments for the soul in between lives. In their earthly lives, the soul is, unbeknownst to itself, living in a hellish prison of the body, but it can go to a true Hades after death – the invisible realm of the Forms – if it masters philosophy when living in a human body. And even while it lives in a body, the soul can spend time in the realm of the Forms by separating itself from the body and contemplating the Forms.[25]

In the first three arguments for the immortality of the soul, then, Plato indicates that the soul is an invisible substance that has intelligence and the ability to know the Forms. In addition, it has memory that allows it to maintain its identity from its preincarnate life with the Forms. The soul is akin to the Forms and does not belong in the body. As we have seen, Plato creates different regions in which the soul can act and dwell, namely, the bodily and intelligible realms. And he also gives the soul a temporality that outlasts that of a human life. In the Affinity Argument and in Socrates' discussion of Anaxagoras' cosmic *nous*, Plato grants the soul divine capacities. Finally, the fact that the soul lived in the divine realm of the Forms before incarnation marks the soul as having some sort of divine status. In

---

ἑαυτήν, ἅτε μελετῶσα ἀεὶ τοῦτο – τὸ δὲ οὐδὲν ἄλλο ἐστὶν ἢ ὀρθῶς φιλοσοφοῦσα καὶ τῷ ὄντι τεθνάναι μελετῶσα ῥᾳδίως.

[24] Note that in Attic Greek, the first alpha in Ἅιδης has a rough breathing and is thus transliterated as *haidês*; in Epic (Homer) and Doric Greek, there is no rough breathing over the alpha, so the transliteration is *aidês*. Although Plato uses Attic Greek, he and the Athenians heard either *haidês* or *aidês* (Hades) in different poems and prose texts. In short, the words "invisible" and "Hades" were associated with each other. See, e.g., Homer *Iliad* 5.844–5, where Athena puts on the hat of "Hades" and makes herself "invisible."

[25] Of course the eschatology represents philosophers dwelling in a physical place in the aether rather than in the realm of the Forms. In terms of ontology, Plato puts this aethereal place below the incorporeal and changeless realm of the Forms. In this text, he chose to represent the second-best destination for the philosophic soul (more on this below).

short, Plato does not identify the soul as divine, but he does suggest that it can actualize its divine capacities by dwelling in the divine realm of the Forms.

3.3   Dwelling in Divine Regions in the Afterlife

As Plato suggests, the philosophic soul journeys to divine regions after it leaves its dead body. The soul can go to the divine realm of the gods or to the Forms. Since the Forms are ontologically higher than the gods, there is an important difference between "dwelling with the gods" and "dwelling with the Forms" in the afterlife. The philosophic soul goes to these two different places depending on whether it has reached a near-perfect or perfect state. We find these two destinations for the philosophic soul clearly demarcated in the eschatology: (1) the philosophic souls dwell in a body in the aethereal realm where gods actually live in their temples (111b–c); (2) the perfected philosopher leaves the bodily realm altogether and lives with the Forms (114c). I will discuss the eschatology in detail below; here, I will follow its basic idea that there are two destinations for the philosophical soul depending on whether it has perfected itself in the practice of philosophy. In this section, I will first examine the passages indicating that the soul goes to live with the gods after death, and then those where the soul goes to live with the Forms. I will also discuss Plato's use of one of the Orphic divinity-markers for the Forms.

Let us consider Socrates' claims that the philosophic soul goes to the gods after death. As he says about the afterlife of his soul (i.e., the soul that occupies his body):

> If I did not think that I would go, first, to other good and wise gods and, then, to men who have died that are better than those here, I would be wrong in my lack of consternation at death. But know well now that I expect to arrive among good men – though I would not affirm this with complete confidence. And know well that, if I would affirm any of these things confidently, it would be this, that I will go to the gods, my good masters. (εἰ μὲν μὴ ᾤμην ἥξειν πρῶτον μὲν παρὰ θεοὺς ἄλλους σοφούς τε καὶ ἀγαθούς, ἔπειτα καὶ παρ' ἀνθρώπους τετελευτηκότας ἀμείνους τῶν ἐνθάδε, ἠδίκουν ἂν οὐκ ἀγανακτῶν τῷ θανάτῳ· νῦν δὲ εὖ ἴστε ὅτι παρ' ἄνδρας τε ἐλπίζω ἀφίξεσθαι ἀγαθούς – καὶ τοῦτο μὲν οὐκ ἂν πάνυ διϊσχυρισαίμην – ὅτι μέντοι παρὰ θεοὺς δεσπότας πάνυ ἀγαθοὺς ἥξειν, εὖ ἴστε ὅτι εἴπερ τι ἄλλο τῶν τοιούτων διϊσχυρισαίμην ἂν καὶ τοῦτο; 63b–c)

Socrates says that his soul will migrate to a region where the gods dwell. However, in contrast to the traditional Greek deities, he conceives of the gods as "good and wise." He does not identify these gods by name. Indeed, Plato chose not to name the "good gods" in this dialogue – he shows much more interest in the Forms than in the gods.

Socrates also claims that philosophers will live with the *genos* of the gods in the afterlife: "it is not permitted for someone who has not practiced philosophy and is not wholly purified to depart and go to the tribe (*genos*) of the gods, but only the lover of knowledge" (εἰς δέ γε θεῶν γένος μὴ φιλοσοφήσαντι καὶ παντελῶς καθαρῷ ἀπιόντι οὐ θέμις ἀφικνεῖσθαι ἀλλ᾿ ἢ τῷ φιλομαθεῖ; 82b–c). The philosopher alone – who has purified himself by practicing philosophy – enters into the tribe of the gods after death. This indicates that the soul has "become like god" if it practices philosophy in a human life.

Finally, in the Affinity argument, Socrates says that the soul goes to the gods and also to the Forms after death:

> The soul, the invisible, goes to another place of that kind, one that is noble and pure and invisible – to "Hades" in truth – and into the presence of a good and wise god (*ton agathon phronimon theon*), whither, if god wills, my soul must soon go . . . if it is delivered in a pure state – not dragging the body along with itself, inasmuch as it did not willingly associate with it in life, but fleeing it and gathering itself together alone to itself, since it has always cared for this – it is doing nothing other than practicing philosophy rightly and really practicing death. (80d–81a)

The soul "departs" from the body after death and goes to live with "a good and wise god." In addition, since Socrates identifies the invisible "'Hades' in truth" with the realm of the Forms, the philosophic soul will also go to dwell with the Forms after death. Indeed, the philosophic soul can only be "delivered" (*apallattetai*) and live without a body "in a pure state" if it contemplates the Forms. In this passage, then, the soul goes both to the gods and the Forms in the afterlife. Socrates seems to refer to a single region here, so we can infer that the gods have a place in the realm of the Forms. We must emphasize, however, that the Forms are ontologically higher than the gods. The good and wise gods must necessarily contemplate the eternal and changeless Forms. But the gods also oversee humans and have tasks on earth.

Let me turn to the passages that refer to the soul going to the divine realm of the Forms (rather than to the gods) in the afterlife. As Socrates claims:

> [The philosopher's soul,] following reason and always being with it, *beholding what is true, divine, and not the object of opinion*, and being nourished by this, thinks that it must live in this way as long as it is alive and, when it dies,

going to what is akin to itself and of this kind, it is released from human evils. (ἑπομένη τῷ λογισμῷ καὶ ἀεὶ ἐν τούτῳ οὖσα, τὸ ἀληθὲς καὶ τὸ θεῖον καὶ τὸ ἀδόξαστον θεωμένη καὶ ὑπ' ἐκείνου τρεφομένη, ζῆν τε οἴεται οὕτω δεῖν ἕως ἂν ζῇ, καὶ ἐπειδὰν τελευτήσῃ, εἰς τὸ συγγενὲς καὶ εἰς τὸ τοιοῦτον ἀφικομένη ἀπηλλάχθαι τῶν ἀνθρωπίνων κακῶν; 84a–b, my italics)

How do we know that Plato refers to the Forms here? First, he identifies them by their attributes: they are "true," "divine," and "not the object of opinion." He also uses a common term for the philosopher grasping the Forms: the soul "beholds" the Forms. Finally, he uses the same kinship analogy that we saw in the Affinity Argument: when the soul of the philosopher dies, it goes to "what is akin (*sungenes*) to itself."[26] In this passage, then, the philosophic soul goes to the Forms, which are "true and divine." Here, Plato implies that the soul has some sort of divine capacity that allows it to contemplate the Forms and, if it perfects itself philosophically, to dwell with them forever.

Socrates expresses the same idea (formulated negatively) in a discussion of the afterlife of the non-philosophers:

Since it [the non-philosopher's soul] is compelled to have the same beliefs as the body and rejoices in these, and has the same habits and nurture, it can never go to Hades in purity, but it always departs full of the body, so that it quickly falls again into another body and grows in it, like a seed that is sown, and for this reason it has no portion of being-together with with the divine and pure and singular in form. (ἐκ γὰρ τοῦ ὁμοδοξεῖν τῷ σώματι καὶ τοῖς αὐτοῖς χαίρειν ἀναγκάζεται οἶμαι ὁμότροπός τε καὶ ὁμότροφος γίγνεσθαι καὶ οἷα μηδέποτε εἰς Ἅιδου καθαρῶς ἀφικέσθαι, ἀλλὰ ἀεὶ τοῦ σώματος ἀναπλέα ἐξιέναι, ὥστε ταχὺ πάλιν πίπτειν εἰς ἄλλο σῶμα καὶ ὥσπερ σπειρομένη ἐμφύεσθαι, καὶ ἐκ τούτων ἄμοιρος εἶναι τῆς τοῦ θείου τε καὶ καθαροῦ καὶ μονοειδοῦς συνουσίας; 83d–e)

In this passage, Plato identifies the Forms by the attributes "divine," "pure," and "singular in form." He also refers to Hades, that is, the invisible realm of the Forms (rather than the underworld). In this "true Hades," the philosophic soul has "a being-together with the divine and pure and singular in form." In addition, Socrates suggests that the philosophic souls who "go to Hades in purity" leave the cycle of reincarnation, while the unphilosophic souls will incarnate in another body. Finally, he uses the word *sunousia* to describe the soul's "being-together with" the Forms. The term *sunousia* brings together the being of the soul with the Being of the Forms. In this passage, Plato gives the *theios* divinity-marker to the Forms and indirectly grants the soul some sort of divine capacity.

---

[26] He uses the word "likeness" (*homoion*), not "kinship," for the soul's relation to the gods.

Let us look, finally, at a passage where Socrates refers to the Orphic doctrine of the afterlife and applies this to the philosophic soul's afterlife with the gods and the Forms. As he states:

> The soul, then, having this condition, goes away to that which is like itself – the *invisible, divine, immortal, and wise,* and the soul that goes there is happy, *released from wandering,* folly, fears, fierce desires, and other human evils; and, *as is said of the initiates, it truly lives for the rest of time with the gods.* (οὐκοῦν οὕτω μὲν ἔχουσα εἰς τὸ ὅμοιον αὐτῇ τὸ ἀιδὲς ἀπέρχεται, τὸ θεῖόν τε καὶ ἀθάνατον καὶ φρόνιμον, οἷ ἀφικομένη ὑπάρχει αὐτῇ εὐδαίμονι εἶναι, πλάνης καὶ ἀνοίας καὶ φόβων καὶ ἀγρίων ἐρώτων καὶ τῶν ἄλλων κακῶν τῶν ἀνθρωπείων ἀπηλλαγμένη, ὥσπερ δὲ λέγεται κατὰ τῶν μεμυημένων, ὡς ἀληθῶς τὸν λοιπὸν χρόνον μετὰ θεῶν διάγουσα; 81a, my italics)

The soul goes to beings that are "like" itself – the "invisible, divine, immortal, and wise." How do we know that Plato refers to the Forms rather than the gods here? First, he explicitly identifies the Forms with "the invisible," but does not use this term for the gods. Second, the claim that the soul "is released from wandering" picks up on the earlier statement that the soul "ceases from its wandering" when it contemplates the Forms: the soul "ceases from its wandering and stays with these Beings [the Forms] and remains always the same and constant, inasmuch as it lays hold of such things" (79d). The word "wise" (*phronimon*) in this passage, however, may give us pause, since it seems to refer to intelligent beings, i.e., the gods. But, as Christopher Rowe points out, "what is said to be like the soul, of course, is the Forms; and they are 'wise' insofar as they are the source of wisdom."[27]

In the last line of this passage, Plato refers to the Orphics ("as is said of the initiates") and their doctrine that the initiated soul will "live for the rest of time with the gods." Indeed, he seems to be quoting an Orphic line here. In this dialogue, Plato often uses the Orphic divinity-marker to discuss the afterlife of the philosophic soul. The Orphics believed that the soul of the initiated lives for the rest of time with the gods in Hades. In this passage, Plato suggests that the philosophic souls, like the Orphics, will live with the gods (and the Forms) after death.[28] But we need to examine Plato's use of this Orphic idea more deeply in order to interpret this passage correctly.

---

[27] Rowe 1993: 192. Cf. Hackforth 1972: 88, who states that Plato refers to the Gods, not the Forms, here. Gallop 1975: 143 claims that "in this section of the dialogue, God (or gods) and the Forms are spoken of interchangeably as the soul's destination. They are, in effect, identified, and divine attributes are applied to both alike."

[28] If this is the case, then Plato indicates, albeit indirectly, that the gods dwell in the presence of the Forms. As scholars have noted, Plato does not offer any clear sense of the relation of the gods to the cosmos or to the Forms in this text. He only hints at these connections.

In this dialogue, Plato adopts and also transforms Orphic doctrines. Consider the following passage, where Socrates presents a variant of the Orphic phrase that the soul "lives forever with the gods for the rest of time":

> It is likely that those who instituted the mystery rites are not wrong, but truly they long ago spoke a riddling discourse, saying that whoever goes to Hades uninitiated, without the rites, will lie in the mud, but he who has been purified and initiated *goes to dwell with the gods*. As the people who deal with the mystery rites say: "the thyrsus-bearers are many, but the *bacchoi* are few." These people, in my view, are no other than those who philosophize truly. (69b–d, my italics)[29]

This passage needs some unpacking. First, we must identify the people who "instituted the mystery rites." Socrates refers to them in two statements: (1) "whoever goes to Hades uninitiated will lie in the mud," and (2) "the thyrsus-bearers are many, but the *bacchoi* are few." As scholars agree, the ideas in the first passage come from the Orphic Mysteries. But the reference to *bacchoi* in the second passage seems to refer to the Bacchic mystery cult. As we will see below, however, the Orphic Mysteries had adopted key elements of the Bacchic cult in the classical period. We can therefore identify the *bacchoi* in this passage as Orphic initiates. Thus, in this passage, Plato does not refer to two separate mystery religions. Rather, both passages refer to a single "Orphic" or (as some scholars put it) "Orphic/Bacchic" religious movement.

Let us turn now to the question of how to interpret this passage. As Socrates claims, the originators of the Orphic Mysteries must be interpreted allegorically because they presented their ideas by way of a "riddling discourse" (αἰνίττεσθαι). Plato introduces an important point here: the Orphic poems and discourses should not be interpreted literally. The reader of Plato must be alert to the possibility that, when he uses Orphic

---

[29] 69b–d: τὸ δ᾽ ἀληθὲς τῷ ὄντι ἢ κάθαρσίς τις τῶν τοιούτων πάντων καὶ ἡ σωφροσύνη καὶ ἡ δικαιοσύνη καὶ ἀνδρεία, καὶ αὐτὴ ἡ φρόνησις μὴ καθαρμός τις ᾖ. καὶ κινδυνεύουσι καὶ οἱ τὰς τελετὰς ἡμῖν οὗτοι καταστήσαντες οὐ φαῦλοί τινες εἶναι, ἀλλὰ τῷ ὄντι πάλαι αἰνίττεσθαι ὅτι ὃς ἂν ἀμύητος καὶ ἀτέλεστος εἰς Ἅιδου ἀφίκηται ἐν βορβόρῳ κείσεται, ὁ δὲ κεκαθαρμένος τε καὶ τετελεσμένος ἐκεῖσε ἀφικόμενος μετὰ θεῶν οἰκήσει. εἰσὶν γὰρ δή, ὥς φασιν οἱ περὶ τὰς τελετάς, ᾽ναρθηκοφόροι μὲν πολλοί, βάκχοι δέ τε παῦροι·᾽ οὗτοι δ᾽ εἰσὶν κατὰ τὴν ἐμὴν δόξαν οὐκ ἄλλοι ἢ οἱ πεφιλοσοφηκότες ὀρθῶς. See Kingsley 1995: 117–23 for an excellent discussion of the Orphic conception that the uninitiated soul "lies in the mud"; Parker 1983: 286 notes that "lying in the mud" is also found in the Eleusinian Mysteries. There was a great deal of overlap in the Orphic and Eleusinian Mysteries in terms of their ideas about life in the underworld for the initiates and noninitiates. As Parker observes (282), "by the end of the fifth century at the latest, the public part of the Eleusinian 'promise' was expounded in 'Orphic' poems."

ideas to describe the philosopher, he does not do this in a straightforward way. In this passage, Socrates offers his own allegorical interpretation of *bacchoi*: these are not ordinary Orphic initiates but rather "those who philosophize rightly." In short, he takes the religious statements of the Orphics as speaking in a riddling way about philosophy.

How, then, should we interpret Socrates' reference to the Orphic claim that "he who has been purified and initiated goes to dwell with the gods" after death? Both Plato and the Orphics aim at the best afterlife for the soul. In the case of the Orphic initiate and the Platonic philosopher, the goal is to escape from the cycle of incarnation: the initiated Orphic soul is released from reincarnation and lives a happy eternal life with the gods in Hades; the perfected philosophic soul escapes from reincarnation and goes to dwell forever with the Forms. As we will see in the eschatology, an afterlife of the soul living with the gods in the realm of the aether is a great reward, but it is not the highest mode of life for the soul. In its most blessed state, the soul lives a disembodied life everlastingly with the Forms. Following his suggestion that the Orphic discourses should be read allegorically, I take Plato to be using the Orphic phrase "*the initiated goes to dwell with the gods*" to mean "*the philosophic soul goes to live with the divine Forms*" after death.[30] If this is on target, then Plato uses the Orphic divinity-marker for both the Forms and the soul in this passage: the Orphic gods mark the divinity of the Forms, and the initiated Orphic soul's everlasting life with the gods marks the philosophic soul's return to its divine and disembodied life with the Forms.

3.4 Pythagoreanism and Orphism in the *Phaedo*

The *Phaedo* features many references to the Orphics. To fully understand the Orphic divinity-marker, however, we must look at the Orphic Mysteries in detail. In this section, I will analyze the Orphic Mysteries in the classical period in Greece. But I first want to look briefly at the Pythagorean aspects of the *Phaedo*, since the Pythagoreans and Orphics share some doctrines even though they were different religious movements.

Plato put three Pythagorean characters into the *Phaedo* – Echecrates, Simmias, and Cebes – and he located the dialogue in Phlius, which had a large number of Pythagoreans.[31] Echecrates was a citizen of Phlius, and he

---

[30] As we saw in the Introduction, Plato marks the divinity of the Forms by using the "Gods divinity-marker." In this passage, then, Plato uses the Orphic gods as a divinity-marker for the Forms.

[31] See Guthrie 1962: 179–80; Sedley 1995. See also Horky 2013: chapter 5, who argues that this dialogue (among others) features Pythagorean mathematical metaphysics.

had studied with the Pythagorean Philolaus.[32] Echecrates appears in the frame dialogue, where he asks Phaedo to tell him how Socrates died. After asking Phaedo for a report, Echecrates remains mostly silent while Phaedo speaks. However, when Simmias and Cebes present the Pythagorean idea that the soul is a harmony, Echecrates speaks up, interrupting the main dialogue (88c–d). He says that he had taken the idea that the soul is a harmony very seriously. The Thebans Cebes and Simmias, who engage in the discussion with Socrates in the main dialogue, had also studied with Philolaus in Thebes (61d–e). Surprisingly, they present and argue for the idea that the soul is a harmony that lasts only until disharmony sets in (86b).[33] This contradicts the Pythagorean claim that the soul is immortal.[34] As Sedley suggests, "Plato wants us to see how inadequately Pythagoreanism has prepared his speakers for appreciation of the soul's immortality."[35] While Plato clearly took the Pythagoreans seriously, he seems to have found their soteriological ideas not fully coherent.

The Pythagoreans and the Orphics both believed in the immortality of the soul and reincarnation. Indeed, Herodotus brings these two religious movements together, claiming that they had similar rituals (2.81).[36] Some ancient Greeks even speculated that Pythagoreans wrote the Orphic poems (perhaps because Orpheus was a legendary figure and Pythagoras a historical individual). For example, the fifth-century writer Ion of Chios ascribed many of Orpheus' books to Pythagoras, and Epigenes made a similar move in his treatise "On Works Attributed to Orpheus" (OF 1128).[37] Of course we will never know who composed the Orphic poems. For this reason, I honor the ancient tradition that identifies the

---

[32] As Aristoxenus (fr. 19 Wehrli = DL 8.46) indicates.

[33] See Sedley 1995 for a discussion of whether the theory of harmony belonged to Philolaus. For an excellent discussion of Plato and Pythagoreanism, see Horky 2013. Horky focuses in particular on the mathematical theories of the Pythagoreans.

[34] Most scholars believe that the Pythagoreans conceived of the soul as immortal, but Horky (forthcoming) offers a persuasive argument against this idea.

[35] Sedley 1995: 12.

[36] Herodotus 2.81 links them together, claiming that the Pythagoreans and Orphics, following the Egyptians, buried their dead in wool. This claim does not take us very far. One of the key differences between the two is that the Orphics had mystic initiation rites, while the Pythagoreans did not. In addition, the Orphics had specific myths about the gods and the soul, and a promise of a good afterlife with the gods. See Betegh 2014, who offers an excellent discussion of Orphism and Pythagoreanism. I do not agree with him, however, that the Orphics did not believe in metempsychosis (more on this below).

[37] Clement of Alexandria, Strom. 5.8.49 and 1.21.131. As Clement claims, Epigenes attributed Orpheus' poems to two specific Pythagoreans. See Graf/Johnstone 2007: chapter 6 for a good discussion of this topic. See Betegh 2014: 151–2 for a discussion of the Greeks' questions about the authorship of the Orphic poems.

poems and doctrines as "Orphic." In particular, Plato often refers to the "Orphics" and mentions the "Orphic life" (*Orphikoi tines legomenoi bioi, Laws* 782c). Plato clearly distinguished the Orphics and the Pythagoreans.

To speak very generally, the Orphics believed that the soul had a divine beginning but fell from the gods due to an original crime. The soul enters bodies as a mode of punishment, and will continue to reincarnate unless it gets initiated into the mysteries during a human life. The soul of the initiate has a different afterlife than other people: it leaves the cycle of reincarnation and goes to dwell everlastingly with the gods in Hades. The Orphics placed great emphasis on the moment of death for the initiate: at this time, the soul left the body and entered its true life with the gods. The death of the initiated human being marks a key moment in the life of the soul. The Orphics focused in particular on the soul's movement across the threshold of death. The entire initiation ceremony prepared them for this transition. Indeed, as Riedweg has argued, they probably went through a ritual enactment of death during the initiation ceremony.[38] Like Plato's philosophers, they were "practicing death."

As I have suggested, Plato creates a threshold narrative in the *Phaedo*: Socrates stands on the threshold of death but looks forward to the next life of his soul. The Orphics positively celebrated the threshold moment when the body dies and the soul goes to Hades. Consider the following passages from a fourth-century Orphic gold leaf, which marks the transformative moment when the soul leaves the body and goes to the gods: "Now you have died and now you have come into being, oh thrice happy one, on this same day. Tell Persephone that Bacchios himself released you" (νῦν ἔθανες καὶ νῦν ἐγένου, τρισόλβιε, ἄματι τῷδε. εἰπεῖν Φερσεφόναι σ' ὅτι Β‹άκ›χιος αὐτὸς ἔλυσε; *OF* 485).[39] The repetition of "now" (*nun*) conjures up the very moment when the body dies and the soul goes to Hades. "On this same day" the soul experiences the death of its human body and begins a wondrous new life. In the Orphic rites, Dionysus Bacchios "releases" the soul when the human goes through initiation. However, the soul must prove that it has been initiated when it gets to Hades. Indeed, it first meets a guardian or god in Hades who presents a test: "And they [the guardians in Hades] will ask you for what need you have come; to them you should relate very well the whole truth. Say: 'I am the child of Earth and starry Heaven; Starry is my name'" (τοῖς δὲ σὺ εὖ μάλα πᾶσαν ἀληθείην

---

[38] Riedweg 2010: 227; see also Bernabé 2016: 28, who argues that, in the rituals of initiation, people engaged in an *imitatio mortis*.

[39] In this chapter, I use the translations and texts from Graf/Johnston 2007 (with minor alterations). I will discuss the Orphic leaves below.

καταλέξαι. εἰπεῖν· Γῆς παῖς εἰμι καὶ Οὐρανοῦ ἀστ‹ερόεντος›· Ἀστέριος ὄνομα; *OF* 477). By stating that it is the "child of earth and starry heaven," the soul cites the Orphic "password" that gives evidence of initiation.[40] In this gold leaf, then, the "I" who speaks here is the "I" of the soul rather than the human who has just died. And the soul has a new name: Starry. The soul who speaks here has taken on a divine status and identity.

The *Phaedo* shares the same concerns that the Orphics did: the immortal soul, its reincarnation in bodies, its imprisonment in the body and, in ideal cases, its happy afterlife with divine beings. The Orphic poems put these ideas about the soul into a narrative: the soul has a divine aspect but falls into a body due to an evil element in it; the body is a punishment for the soul; the soul can escape from reincarnation by getting purified and initiated into the mysteries; the initiated soul dwells happily for the rest of time with the gods in Hades. Plato follows this lead and places the soul in a narrative that has a beginning, middle, and everlasting end. If he did not give the soul's life a plot, it would just have one life after another in an endless succession. Plato used the Orphic narratives to create his own story of the soul. In the *Phaedo*, Plato provides the reader with all the pieces of the soul's story: its divine beginning with the Forms in a preincarnate state; its incarnation/reincarnations; and, for the purified soul of the philosopher, its everlasting life with the divine Forms. To be sure, in this dialogue, Plato does not present this story in a full way (as he will do in the *Phaedrus* and *Timaeus*). But one can find the different chapters of the story of the soul in specific passages in the dialogue.

In addition to using the Orphic narrative of the soul, Plato adopted their idea that life on earth is a punishment and death a blessed release. Indeed, he borrowed the Orphic vocabulary of purification (*kathairein*) and release (*lusis*). He makes extensive use of this terminology in his discussion of the philosopher's "purification" and "release" from the body (more on this below). Finally, Plato's emphasis on the impurities of the body also reflects the Orphics' negative conception of the body. Plato's use of the Orphic divinity-marker, then, is quite complex. The Orphics had a number of distinct doctrines, rituals, and myths, and Plato refers to one or another of these in different parts of the *Phaedo*. At times, he borrows a single Orphic idea or ritual practice as a divinity-marker for the soul; at other times, he alludes to the Orphic anthropology, which includes the soul's origin, its

---

[40] We find the word *symbola* ("passwords") in *OF* 484 (=Graf/Johnston 27). As Johnston in Graf/ Johnston 2007: 94 claims, the passwords were meant to be spoken by the soul in Hades – it "constitut[es] a sort of crib-sheet for the soul's most final of exams."

incarnation/reincarnation, and its final life with the gods. In the latter case, the Orphics provide a divinity-marker that applies to the Forms and the soul at the same time. In short, the Orphics offer a much broader divinity-marker than the others do. For this reason, I will look at both the individual Orphic divinity-markers and the broader markers found in the Orphic anthropology.

3.5 Orphism in the Classical Period

In this section, I will offer a detailed discussion of Orphism in the classical period. I do this so that other scholars can work more easily with this material. For those readers who simply want to focus on Plato, I would urge you to move to the next section in this chapter.

Although we can never know what was happening on the ground in ancient Greece, extant evidence gives us a fairly good idea of the basic elements of the Orphic mystery religion. But this evidence presents serious challenges for the interpreter. The scholarship on the Orphic mystery cult is vast: some scholars argue for a purely Orphic cult (Panorphism); others for an Orphic/Bacchic cult; and some reject Orphism as a coherent religious movement.[41] As many scholars have noted, the Orphic and Bacchic mysteries had converged by the mid-fifth century BCE in various parts of Greece.[42] But the Bacchic Mysteries still maintained their own cultic identity. Due to the paucity of evidence on this latter cult, we do not fully understand the Bacchic Mysteries. As Bremmer notes, "we are still

---

[41] In recent scholarship, Bernabé (2002, 2002a, 2009, and in his edition of the Orphic fragments) adopts the Panorphic position (see also Bernabé and Jiménez San Cristóbal 2008). Riedweg (1998, 2002, 2010), Graf/Johnston (2007), Betz (2010), and Bremmer (2014: Chapter 3) argue for some form of an "Orphic" mystery cult. Burkert (1985: 300) identified three schools within "the sphere of Orphica," the Eleusinian, Bacchic, and Pythagorean, and he later suggested that the Bacchic Mysteries may have substituted for the Eleusinian Mysteries, at least in some places (1987: 38–9; cf. Bianchi 1974; Parker 1983: chapter 10, 2011). Edmonds (2004, 2010) rejects the idea of a coherent Orphic movement, arguing instead that itinerant religious specialists initiated people in diverse ceremonies. Cole (2003: 202–3 and 2007: 339–41) argues that the gold leaves are not Orphic but Bacchic.

[42] Graf/Johnston 2007: 214–16; Bremmer 2014: 73. As Parker 2005: 368 notes, we have not found any gold leaves in Attic tombs (see also Parker 2011: 257); we do, however, have evidence for orpheotelists working in Athens. Santamaría (2012a) offers a useful survey of recent work on Orpheus and Orphism (see also 2012b on the Derveni papyrus). For the Orphic texts, see Scarpi 2002. Note Herodotus' reference to "those called Orphics and Bacchics" (2.81.2); see also Euripides' *Hippolytus*: "Boast now about your vegetarian diet, having Orpheus as your master, and engage in Bacchic revelling, honoring the trifles of many books" (ἤδη νυν αὔχει καὶ δι᾽ ἀψύχου βορᾶς σίτοις καπήλευ᾽ Ὀρφέα τ᾽ ἄνακτ᾽ ἔχων βάκχευε πολλῶν γραμμάτων τιμῶν καπνούς; 952–4). The latter is an angry taunt, and cannot be taken as firm evidence; still, the passage brings together the Orphic and Bacchic Mysteries.

badly informed about Bacchic mysteries in classical times and it may well be that we are dealing with a variety of mysteries, of which some assumed an Orphic colouring."[43] Still, the evidence points to an Orphic religion that differed from other cults of Dionysus.[44] Let me emphasize that my discussion of the Orphics brings together a variety of Orphic ideas and practices. The Orphics lived in different cultures in the Greek world and did not have a single cult with a specific set of doctrines. As Gabor Betegh rightly suggests, we cannot posit an "essentialist" Orphism, that is, the notion that the Orphic practitioners all had the same beliefs and ritual practices.[45] I will use the term "Orphic" to refer to a wide set of Orphic ideas and practices that included elements of the Dionysian Mysteries.

In terms of the evidence from the classical period, recent archaeological findings offer important material about the Orphic Mysteries: (1) The bone plaques found in graves in Olbia (late fifth century BCE). These use the phrases *Dionysos Orphiko(i)* and "life-death-life." (2) The inscribed gold leaves found in graves in various parts of Greece (the earliest date back to the late fifth century BCE). (3) The Derveni papyrus (dated between late-fifth and late fourth century; see below). In addition, Plato himself provides important early source material for Orphism.

I want to examine five key aspects of Orphism: the mystagogues or "orpheotelists" who offered initiation ceremonies; the Orphic theogony (which goes back to at least the early fifth century BCE); the Orphic myths about the gods and humans; the doctrine of the reincarnation of the soul; and the initiate's happy everlasting life with the gods in Hades after death. I focus on the myths and practices of the Orphic Mysteries in the fifth and fourth centuries BCE. This will allow us to locate Plato's ideas in a historical and religious context.

Individual mystagogues (*orpheotelestai* or "orpheotelists") taught the initiands and conducted the Orphic initiation ceremonies.[46] They used the poetic texts of "Orpheus" and "Musaeus," which were written in books. The orpheotelists worked all over Greece, offering education and initiation for payment, and had started working in Athens by the mid– to

---

[43] Bremmer 2014: 76. Graf says that the Orphic "adaptation of Dionysiac purification turns it into an instrument of personal psychic wellbeing and eschatological hopes" (Graf/Johnston 2007: 147).
[44] As Graf in Graf/Johnston (2007: 143) puts it: "among the ecstatic worshippers of Dionysus, then, there was a small, very special group, and Orpheus addressed only them – this at least was the self-definition of 'Orphic' Bacchic cults in the classical age."
[45] Betegh 2014: 153–4.
[46] As Bremmer shows (2014: 66–76), orpheotelists had set up shop in Athens and other parts of Greece in the mid to late fifth century. See Plato *Rep.* 364c–e and 365a–365b for attacks on the orpheotelists; see also Theophrastus *Char.* 16.12–13.

late fifth century BCE.[47] The orpheotelists used sacred poetic texts (*hieroi logoi*) in purification and initiation ceremonies. This practice flew in the face of traditional Greek religion, which did not have holy books. The main poetic texts in the Orphic cult were the *Descent to Hades* (*Katabasis*) and the *Theogony*.[48] There were multiple versions of these poems (in Greek culture, poems changed over time). But all of them dealt with the nature of the cosmos, the origin of humans, and the lot of the soul.

In terms of extant poems from the early period, we have good evidence of the Orphic myths from the Derveni papyrus (dated late fifth to late fourth century BCE). The anonymous author of this text cites poetic lines from Orphic poems. In addition, the author of the Derveni papyrus presents an allegorical commentary on the poetic lines that aims to decode the riddling text of Orpheus. In short, the Derveni papyrus takes the form of a detailed allegorical commentary of lines taken from two Orphic poems.[49] The author of the papyrus identifies the Orphic poems as containing hidden truths about the cosmos. He interprets the poems as presenting Anaxagorean philosophical ideas.[50] As he states, Orpheus was "speaking in riddles" (column vii.5: αἰνιγματώδης; vii.6: αἰν[ίγμα]τα, [αἰν] ίγμασ[ι]ν; ix.10: ἠινίζετο; xiii.6: αἰνίζεται). He proceeds to clarify these riddles by using the language of philosophy. He tacks back and forth between revealing the truths of the secret Orphic Mysteries and keeping them hidden from the "impure."[51]

The Derveni papyrus presents an early version of the Orphic theogonic myth. To put this very briefly, Night and Aether were the primordial

---

[47] These payments are mentioned in the Derveni papyrus (col. 20). See also Plato, *Rep.* 364b.

[48] Riedweg 2010 attempts to put together different lines from the gold leaves into a single *hieros logos*; see also Bremmer 2014: 62–6. Cf. Edmonds 2010, who argues that there was no *hieros logos* or an Orphic cult – rather, we are dealing with a variety of itinerant religious specialists. The Orphics also had a *Physika* (or *Peri phuseôs*) poem that brought together Orphic myths with sixth–fifth-century natural philosophers. Gagné 2007 offers an excellent analysis of the *Physika* and notes the way that the author(s) of this text used philosophic ideas about "air" and "wind" to set forth new cosmological ideas (see especially *OF* 800–803).

[49] The dating of the commentary in the papyrus is under debate: some scholars date it to the late fifth century BCE, others to the late fourth century BCE. Bernabé (2002 and 2007b: 99) dates the commentary in the Derveni papyrus to the late fifth century; Kouremenos, Parássoglou, and Tsantsanoglou (2006) date it between 340 BC and 320 BC.

[50] On the philosophic orientation of the Derveni papyrus, see Janko 1997 and 2001; Laks 1997; Most 1997; Betegh 2004; Bernabé 2007b. For a good discussion of the philosophy in the papyrus (and the way that it differs from Anaxagoras), see Laks 1997.

[51] For example, referring to a "well-chosen verse" of Orpheus, the author instructs people to "put doors on their ears": Orpheus only speaks to "those pure in hearing," i.e., initiands and initiates (col. vii.9–11). The author distinguishes between "those who know" (οἱ ὀρθῶς γινώσκοντες; ix.2) and "those who do not know" (οἱ οὐ γινώσκοντες; xii.5). He thus makes a double move: he utters some ideas openly to attract followers, but keeps others secret and closed to non-initiates.

deities.[52] Zeus went to the cave of Night to discover how he could become the major power in the cosmos; Zeus then swallowed the penis of Ouranos and "sprang from the Aether first" (col. xiii.4[53]). Zeus is "first" in the sense of "firstborn" by way of his new creation of the cosmos. In short, although Night and Aether were the primordial deities, and other gods existed before Zeus, once Zeus swallows the penis of Ouranos and takes over his power, he is the "first" god who springs from Aether. After that, he creates the cosmos out of himself.[54] Zeus thus becomes the primary god who recreates the cosmic system more or less from scratch. In his creation of the gods, Zeus rapes and impregnates his mother Rhea-Demeter, who gives birth to Kore/Persephone. The papyrus ends with Zeus' first rape; since it is partly burned, we do not have the full myth in this text. We find the rest of the myth in later sources.[55] The myth runs as follows: after Zeus rapes Demeter, who gives birth to Kore/Persephone, he then rapes Kore, who gives birth to Dionysus. The Titans kill Dionysus and eat him, and Zeus destroys them with the thunderbolt. Then Dionysus is reborn with the help of Athena.

The Orphic poems also presented a specific anthropogony. Humans came into being in the following way: the Titans killed, dismembered, and ate Dionysus; after Zeus destroyed the Titans with his thunderbolt, humans came into being from the soot of the thunderbolt. For this reason, humans are part divine and part earth. As Bernabé and Jiménez San Christóbal put it:

> We have something of Dionysus within us, namely the part that had been ingested by the Titans. This is our positive, divine part, which desires to reintegrate itself with its originary nature. On the other hand, we have within us the remains of the Titans. This is our sinful, proud, and wicked part, from which we must liberate ourselves.[56]

[52] See Betegh 2004: 154–6 for a discussion of "Aether" as a primordial deity that was equal in rank to "night." Cf. Bernabé 2011: 86, who claims that the primordial deities in Orphic myth were Night, Earth, and Heaven; he bases the myth on a large number of sources, most of which are postclassical. My focus is on the myths available to Plato.

[53] There are many difficulties with the phrase from the Orphic poem "ὃς αἰθέρα ἔχθορε πρῶτος" in column xiii.4. I follow Betegh 2004: 29, who says that Zeus "sprang from the aether first," i.e., as the new "firstborn" in the cosmos (with Aether as the primordial substance) after he swallows the penis of Ouranos. Betegh uses later Orphic myths and Greek cosmogonies to set forth this argument. Laks 1997: 122–3 argues that Ouranos is the "firstborn" who "springs into the aether" (but Zeus swallowed his penis and took over his power); Bernabé 1997: 107 claims that Ouranos "first created aether."

[54] Betegh 2004: 154–6 discusses the evidence for Zeus as the "first-born" from Aether.

[55] Since the evidence for the Orphics runs through late antiquity, the early myths were revised and changed over time. As Bernabé observes (2011: 85–93), most of the later myths indicate that Night, Heaven (Ouranos), and Earth were the original deities.

[56] Bernabé/Jiménez San Christóbal 2008: 41; see also Betegh 2004: 340–1. Scholars have debated whether humans were born from the Titans or from both the Titans and Dionysus. Bernabé 2002: 432 and 2008: 107, 112, Bernabé/Jiménez San Christóbal 2008: 31–2, and Bremmer 2014: 76 claim

Although it may seem that humans do not bear responsibility for Dionysus' death, they nonetheless share the guilt of the Titans.[57] Humans bear an original sin and must pay a penalty for this injustice. As a punishment, the human soul must dwell in a body and reincarnate forever unless it undergoes purification rites and initiation. After initiation, the soul will have "flown out of the heavy, difficult circle" of reincarnation (*OF* 488) and go to dwell with the gods. By undergoing these rituals, especially initiation, the soul pays the price for the original crime against Dionysus. When the initiate's human body dies, the purified soul goes to Hades and lives happily with the gods below.

Dionysus played the role of the "releasing" god in the Orphic Mysteries. The gold leaves present this idea clearly. For example, one states: "tell Persephone that Bacchios has released (ἔλυσε) you" (*OF* 485–6, quoted in full above). Dionysus Bacchios, the *theos lusios*, "released" the initiates in Hades from their guilt.[58] Since the human soul bears the responsibility for the murder of Dionysus, this god had to free them from guilt. When Dionysus releases the souls, Persephone allows them to dwell with her in a sacred meadow. As a fourth-century gold leaf puts it: "For I also claim to be of your happy race. I have paid the penalty for unrighteous deeds. Either Moira overcame me or the star-flinger of lightnings. Now I come as a suppliant to holy Persephone so that she may kindly send me to the seats of the pure" (*OF* 490.3–7). The initiate ends up living with Persephone and the other gods in a good region in Hades. In another fourth-century gold leaf, we find a set of instructions for the soul to follow when it first meets a daimon or god in Hades: "But as soon as the soul has left the light of the sun, go to the right [. . .], being very careful of all things. 'Greetings, you who have suffered the painful thing; you have never endured this before . . . . Journey on the right-hand road to the holy

---

that humans came from both the Titans and Dionysus. Burkert 1985: 298 and 1999: 100–1, Kahn 1997, and Johnston (Graf/Johnston 2007: 66–93) claim that humans were descendants of the Titans. Cf. Brisson 1992, who argues that there is not enough evidence for this anthropogony (see also Edmonds 2004: 75–80). Cf. Olympiodorus (a neoplatonic commentator on the *Phaedo* et al.), who claimed that humans are "a part" (*meros*) of Dionysus because the Titans had torn him apart and eaten his flesh and humans were also part of the soot of the burned Titans, who had been blasted by Zeus' thunderbolt (*in Phaed.* 1.1.3; *OF* 220).

[57] For useful discussions of this topic, see West 1983: 184–5; Seaford 1986: 4–6; Brisson 1992a; Edmonds 1999; Betegh 2004: 340–1 and passim; Bernabé 2001: 15, 57–8, 78, 90, 108, 114; Betz 2010; Bremmer 2014: 76; Rodriguez 2016: 206.

[58] Dionysus was associated with the underworld in the Orphic and Eleusinian Mysteries. For Dionysus as the god of many names and forms, see Csapo 2016; see also Otto 1933; Osborne 1997; Robertson 2003.

meadows and groves of Persephone'" (*hierous leimonas kai alsea Persephoneias*; *OF* 487). If the soul follows this itinerary, it ends up "dwelling with the gods" in Hades after death.

Unfortunately, we know very little about the initiation ceremonies of the Orphics. Scholars generally agree that an orpheotelist read from the *hieroi logoi* (i.e., the "sacred poems" about the gods, humans, reincarnation, etc.) in a night-time ceremony. But other rituals are less clear. The author of the Derveni papyrus says that "those going through the rites saw the holy things" (*ta hiera eidon*), and refers to "the things they saw or heard or learned" (*eidon ê êkousan ê emathon*; col. xx.1–8). This suggests that the initiands not only heard the Orphic discourses but saw sacred objects. Some scholars, emphasizing the Dionysian aspect of the cult, posit that the initiation was "ecstatic," and included wine and dancing.[59] Since Dionysus was the "god who comes," i.e., the god of epiphany, the initiands may have witnessed some sort of revelation. Finally, neo-ritualist scholars have attempted to find the *legomena* (things said) and the *dromena* (things done) at the initiation ceremony in the texts of the gold leaves.[60] Riedweg suggests (cautiously) that the initiation ceremony included a "ritual enactment of death."[61] This may have provided Plato with the idea of "practicing death."

The Orphic myths about gods and humans deviate from traditional Greek myths, which divide gods and humans in the firmest possible terms (with the exception of the ἥρωες). Indeed, the Orphic Mysteries operated outside traditional Greek religion. As Fritz Graf and Sarah Johnston observe, these Orphic Mysteries functioned as a "supplement" to traditional religious rites and festivals: "the marginality of [Orphic] groups . . . can better be understood as 'supplementarity' – that is, these groups offered additional benefits that mainstream cults did not. To authenticate and validate those benefits, as well as to preserve their traditions, such groups, which were not embedded in *ta patria* of mainstream cult, looked instead to *hieroi logoi*."[62] Mainstream cults took the form of civic festivals and they featured animal sacrifice. The Orphic Mysteries were run privately, and they rejected the sacrifice and eating of animals. Indeed, to attract clients, the orpheotelists had to convince people that they would

---

[59] Faraone 2010 argues that certain lines from the gold leaves refer to dancing at the initiation ceremony. Graf/Johnston 2007: 157 suggest that wine was drunk at the final initiation (and also in the afterlife); Bernabé/Jiménez San Cristóbal 2008: 84–9 argue for the presence of wine in this ceremony.

[60] See especially Riedweg 2010: 241.   [61] Riedweg 2010: 227.   [62] Graf/Johnston 2007: 179–80.

pay a severe penalty in Hades if they did not get initiated. As the author of the Derveni papyrus observes (column v), many people did not believe in the terrors of Hades. Clearly, the experts in the Orphic Mysteries had to offer persuasive accounts of the human soul's original sin, punishing reincarnations, and repeated trips to a bad part of Hades.

We can better understand the supplementary nature of the Orphic cult by observing its differences from the Eleusinian Mysteries. First, Athens ran the Eleusinian Mysteries as part of its public festival for Demeter and Persephone, while private individuals ran the Orphic Mysteries and charged a fee for purifications and initiations. Both of these mysteries featured initiation and offered a good afterlife, but the Orphic initiands visited the orpheotelists numerous times before getting initiated. As Theophrastus says in the "Superstitious Man": "he goes every month to the orpheotelists with his wife (but if she is not free, with the nurse and children) to participate in initiations" (καὶ τελεσθησόμενος πρὸς τοὺς Ὀρφεοτελεστὰς κατὰ μῆνα πορεύεσθαι μετὰ τῆς γυναικός — ἐὰν δὲ μὴ σχολάζῃ ἡ γυνή, μετὰ τῆς τίτθης — καὶ τῶν παιδίων *Char.* 16.11a). The author of the Derveni papyrus also notes the differences between the civic and private mystery cults (xx.1–8):

> I am not that surprised that people who have performed the rites and have been initiated in the cities ([ἐμ]πόλεσιν ἐπιτελέσαντες [τὰ ἱε]ρά) do not comprehend them (μὴ γινώσκειν); for it is impossible to hear what is said and to learn it simultaneously (ἀκοῦσαι ὁμοῦ καὶ μαθεῖν τὰ λεγόμενα). But those who [have been initiated] by someone who makes a profession of the rites (παρὰ τοῦ τέχνην ποιουμένου τὰ ἱερά) deserve amazement and pity: amazement because, although they suppose, before they go through the rite, that they will have knowledge (εἰδήσειν), after they have gone through it they go away without gaining knowledge (εἰδέναι), and make no further inquiries, as if they knew something about what they saw, heard, or learned (εἶδον ἢ ἤκουσαν ἢ ἔμαθον).

In the first part of this passage, the author suggests that initiates in the institutional cults like the Eleusinian Mysteries – "those initiated in the cities" – cannot comprehend what is going on because they are trying to "hear and learn what is said" at the time of the initiation ritual. In the Greater Eleusinian Mysteries, for example, there is only one initiation ceremony, and the initiands must take everything in all at once.[63] The author of the Derveni papyrus contrasts these civic rituals with initiation by religious specialists in the "discipline" (*technê*) of the Orphic Mysteries.

---

[63] Riedweg 1987: 6–11 offers a useful discussion of what the initiands learned and saw.

In the second part of this passage, the author of the papyrus takes aim at orpheotelists who claimed to teach Orphic doctrines and to get the initiands to "see, hear, and learn."[64] As a self-proclaimed Orphic expert, the author claims that the orpheotelists do not understand the truth of the Orphic Mysteries and cannot teach the correct doctrines. In short, the author attacks the orpheotelists because they did not have the special understanding of Orpheus that he himself did. The Orphic experts and orpheotelists had to compete against each other to get paying clients. Given this competitive environment, it is no surprise that they required that their clients visit them many times for instruction, purification, and initiation. All of this stands in stark contrast with the Eleusinian Mysteries.

The Orphics set forth specific ideas about the afterlife. Indeed, the gold tablets indicate that Hades had different regions for the initiated and uninitiated. In terms of the final abode for the initiated soul in Hades, some gold leaves from the fifth to fourth century BCE state that initiates dwell in "the holy meadows and groves of Persephone" (*OF* 487) or in the "holy seats of the pure" (*hedras euageiôn*; *OF* 490). Plato himself refers to Orphic initiates as engaging in "symposiums of the pure in Hades."[65] Clearly, the souls of the initiates go to a happy, albeit vaguely described, region in Hades. As Johnston observes:

> [The Orphics] don't say much about what ultimately awaits the initiate . . . what little they do say, however, aligns well with Hesiod's paradisiacal vision: the initiates expect to dwell among meadows and groves (3.6, 27.4), to enjoy abundant wine (26 a.6 and b.6), to be happy and blessed – gods instead of humans (5.9), and to dwell among the blessed.[66]

We must emphasize that, even though the souls of the initiates escape the cycle of reincarnation, they are not fully disembodied in Hades. The Orphics did not completely separate the soul from the body. As we can see in the passages above, they occupy space and enjoy carnal pleasures in the afterlife. Indeed, for the Greeks, even the gods had bodies. As Vernant has shown, the gods had immortal bodies that were radiant, powerful,

---

[64] The author of the Derveni papyrus criticizes the orpheotelists in order to showcase his own "correct" understanding of the Orphic Mysteries. As an expert interpreter and diviner, the author of the Derveni papyrus had to compete with other specialists. As Burkert observes, "this is the way specialists behave; their existence is dependent on the condition that they remain rare and exceptional" (Burkert 1982: 9; see also Obbink 1997: 48–9).

[65] On the "holy meadows" in the afterlife, see Graf/Johnston 2007: 9, 39, 100, 120; Bremmer 2014: 76. Bernabé and Jiménez San Cristóbal 2008: 21–8 offer a useful discussion of the meadows, trees, and fountains in Hades. On the "symposiums of the pure," see Plato, *Rep.* 363d.

[66] Graf/Johnston 2007: 116.

beautiful, and perfect; they ate and drank, had blood in their veins, slept, had sex, and so on.[67] In the Orphic Mysteries, then, the initiates got off the cycle of reincarnation but still ended up in some sort of body. Plato himself explicitly complains about the bodily state of the initiates at the "symposiums of the pure" in Hades: "Musaeus and his son offer goods that are finer than those given by the gods to the righteous. For, in their stories, they lead them to Hades and make them lie down on couches, setting up for them a symposium for the holy; and, these people [the initiates], wearing garlands, live in a state of drunkenness for the rest of time, believing that the best payment for virtue is everlasting inebriation"[68] (*Rep.* 363c–d).

Before Plato, the Greeks did not have a philosophical conception of an incorporeal soul or soul–body dualism. It is no surprise, then, that the souls of the initiates in the Orphic cult had some sort of embodiment in the afterlife.[69] Plato adopted the Orphic myths and rituals, but he applied these to the immortal, incorporeal soul and the Forms. Plato accepts the Orphic idea that the soul can escape the cycle of reincarnation, but he takes this a step further: in the final afterlife, the soul will be completely disembodied and dwell in the presence of the Forms. The divine realm of the Forms is incorporeal and invisible (as is the soul). Plato's perfected philosophic soul is "released" from the cycle of incarnation and leaves the

---

[67] Vernant 1991: 27–49.

[68] *Rep.* 363c–d: Μουσαῖος δὲ τούτων νεανικώτερα τἀγαθὰ καὶ ὁ ὑὸς αὐτοῦ παρὰ θεῶν διδόασιν τοῖς δικαίοις· εἰς Ἅιδου γὰρ ἀγαγόντες τῷ λόγῳ καὶ κατακλίναντες καὶ συμπόσιον τῶν ὁσίων κατασκευάσαντες ἐστεφανωμένους ποιοῦσιν τὸν ἅπαντα χρόνον ἤδη διάγειν μεθύοντας, ἡγησάμενοι κάλλιστον ἀρετῆς μισθὸν μέθην αἰώνιον.

[69] See Aristotle's claim in *On the Soul* 1.5 410b27 (=*OF* 421) that the "so-called Orphic poems" stated that "the soul enters from the universe into breathing beings, borne by the winds." This seems to identify the soul with air (see Sassi 2018: 123–8). Note also that the Orphic story of the human soul is one of a cluster of myths representing fallen divinities that reincarnated into bodily forms, suffered punishment, and returned to a blissful state. Empedocles, for example, set forth a similar tale. As he claimed, *daimones* were originally gods but committed some offense and had to "wander away from the abodes of the blessed for thrice ten thousand seasons, being born in all forms of mortal beings" (B 115.5–6; B 117). Indeed, the daimons have to "wander in darkness though the meadows of disaster" (*atê*; B 121). Reincarnation in mortal bodies is part of this punishment. But the daimons can return to the gods after a period of suffering and "share the hearth and the tables of the other gods, relieved of human distress, safe from destiny and invulnerable" (B 147). Where do humans fit into this scheme? Clearly, a daimon reincarnates into a human during part of its journey. Indeed, Empedocles claims that he himself has been a daimon who has lived as a girl and a boy (B 117). He identifies humans as paying for an earlier crime: "alas, oh wretched race of mortals, unblessed, you have been born from such strifes and groanings" (B 124). This might mean that humans came into being through the strife among the daimons, but one cannot push this passage too far. Indeed, we do not have evidence that all humans are housing a daimon and are therefore fallen daimons. Of course Empedocles also claims that he is now a god (B 112). He has presumably been recalled from exile and can now "share the table" of the gods (B 147). What we can say is that the daimon is a fallen god that can make its way back to immortal bliss. Whereas the Orphics focus on the human being, which is part divine and part earthly, Empedocles' daimons are divinities through and through.

body altogether. Plato thus transformed the vague conceptions of the soul advanced by his predecessors (including the Orphics) into a clear dualistic philosophy.

3.6 Plato's Adaptation of the Orphic Mysteries

It is tricky to comprehend Plato's use of the Orphics in his philosophy because he roundly rejected the orpheotelists and their rituals.[70] Let us look first at his negative comments on the Orphic mystagogues and their promises about the afterlife. At the opening of the *Republic* (330d–e), Cephalus expresses his "fear and anxiety" (*deos kai phrontis*) over "stories about Hades that say that one has to pay the penalty there for unjust deeds done here." After Cephalus says that he will use his great wealth to make the right sacrifices to the gods in the hopes of a good afterlife (331b), Socrates argues against this approach and hints that the redemption of one's soul should not be tied to wealth. Later in the dialogue, he mentions "poets and prophets" who claimed that a person would suffer in Hades for his or her crimes:

> [Adeimantus:] "But we will pay the penalty (*dikên dôsomen*) in Hades for the unjust actions we did here, either ourselves or our children's children."
> [Socrates:] "But surely, my friend, a calculating person will say that the rites and the delivering gods have great power, as the greatest cities claim, and [he will say that] the poets and prophets, sons of the gods, indicate that this is true." (366a–b)[71]

Socrates makes an ironic dig at the "calculating" person who has offered rites (*teletai*) that invoke gods who will "deliver" the initiate from his or her crimes. The phrase "delivering gods" (*lusioi theoi*) refers to the Orphic

---

[70] Note that Pindar used the terminology of the Orphic and Bacchic rites in his dithyrambs and threni. See Versnel/Frankfurter/Hahn 2009: 9–10: "the use of τελετά in Pindar's victory odes points towards a rather general meaning: a religious rite or ceremony of any nature: Panathenaea, Olympic games, theoxenia. On the other hand, the fragments of the Pindaric Dithyrambs and Threni, if they indeed belong to Pindar, show that he also used the term for mysteries and Dionysiac rites."

[71] 366a–b: ἀλλὰ γὰρ ἐν Ἅιδου δίκην δώσομεν ὧν ἂν ἐνθάδε ἀδικήσωμεν, ἢ αὐτοὶ ἢ παῖδες παίδων. ἀλλ᾽, ὦ φίλε, φήσει λογιζόμενος, αἱ τελεταί αὖ μέγα δύνανται καὶ οἱ λύσιοι θεοί, ὡς αἱ μέγισται πόλεις λέγουσι καὶ οἱ θεῶν παῖδες ποιηταὶ καὶ προφῆται τῶν θεῶν γενόμενοι, οἳ ταῦτα οὕτως ἔχειν μηνύουσι. See also *Rep.* 363c–d (quoted above) and *Laws* 870d–e: "Hearing from those in the mystic rites who are serious about these things, many are persuaded that there is vengeance for such acts in Hades, and that it is necessary for those returning back here to earth to pay the penalty in accordance with nature" (πολλοὶ λόγον τῶν ἐν ταῖς τελεταῖς περὶ τὰ τοιαῦτα ἐσπουδακότων ἀκούοντες σφόδρα πείθονται, τὸ τῶν τοιούτων τίσιν ἐν Ἅιδου γίγνεσθαι, καὶ πάλιν ἀφικομένοις δεῦρο ἀναγκαῖον εἶναι τὴν κατὰ φύσιν δίκην ἐκτεῖσαι).

notion that Dionysus and Persephone "delivered" the initiate from the cycle of reincarnation. Note, finally, that the calculating person invokes "poets and prophets, sons of the gods" as authorizing the claim that the initiation rites will release the initiand from his/her guilt. Here, Socrates refers to the poet/prophet Orpheus (among others), whom some considered to be the son of Apollo.[72] Plato himself suggests that Orpheus was the son of Selene and the Muses (*Rep.* 364e).

Not surprisingly, Plato attacks the people who sold salvation in this mystery cult. As Socrates states:

> Begging priests and prophets, going to the doors of the rich, persuade them that they have a power procured from the gods which they use in sacrifices and incantations, and if there is some evil deed done by himself or his ancestors, they can heal these with pleasurable festivals, and if a person wants to ruin an enemy, for a small expense he will harm the just along with the unjust by way of enchantments and binding spells, persuading the gods, as they say, to serve them. (364b–c)[73]

Plato objected to the people offering a good afterlife for a price. He considered these men ignorant and money-hungry. In spite of these attacks on the orpheolotelists, however, Plato adopted key elements of the Orphic myths.[74]

How, then, does Plato use and transform the Orphic mystery cult? Anyone who reads the *Phaedo* will quickly note the numerous references to "purification" (*katharsis, katharos,* and *kathairein*) and "release" (*lusis, louein, apallasein*). But they may not realize that Plato takes many of these ideas from the Orphics.[75] While the Greeks purified themselves in most religious rituals, the combination of "purification" and "release" has an Orphic basis. To give a few examples, in the *Republic*, after mentioning "begging priests and soothsayers who go to the doors of the rich" and claim to have acquired power from the gods, Socrates states:

---

[72] As Versnel, Frankfurter and Hahn 2009: 31 argue, the Greeks considered Orpheus to be the son of Apollo and a Muse; Graf/Johnston 2007: 145 make the same observation.

[73] 364b–c: ἀγύρται δὲ καὶ μάντεις ἐπὶ πλουσίων θύρας ἰόντες πείθουσιν ὡς ἔστι παρὰ σφίσι δύναμις ἐκ θεῶν ποριζομένη θυσίαις τε καὶ ἐπῳδαῖς, εἴτε τι ἀδίκημά του γέγονεν αὐτοῦ ἢ προγόνων, ἀκεῖσθαι μεθ' ἡδονῶν τε καὶ ἑορτῶν, ἐάντε τινὰ ἐχθρὸν πημῆναι ἐθέλῃ, μετὰ σμικρῶν δαπανῶν ὁμοίως δίκαιον ἀδίκῳ βλάψει ἐπαγωγαῖς τισιν καὶ καταδέσμοις, τοὺς θεούς, ὥς φασιν, πείθοντες σφίσιν ὑπηρετεῖν.

[74] Olympiodorus claimed that "Plato paraphrases Orpheus everywhere" (*Phd.* 7.10.10; παρῳδεῖ γὰρ πανταχοῦ τὰ Ὀρφέως). Of course this is an exaggeration, but it does point to Plato's approval of the Orphic myths.

[75] For a good discussion of purity and purification in the Orphics, see Petrovic and Petrovic 2016: Chapter 12. See also Parker 1983: chapter 10 on purification and salvation in Plato.

They furnish a noisy throng of books of Musaeus and Orpheus ... according to which they make sacrifices, and persuade not only private citizens but cities that there are *releases and purifications* (*luseis te kai katharmoi*) for unjust deeds, through burnt offerings and pleasant games for the living and for the dead, which they call mystic rites, which release (*apoluousin*) us from the evils there [in Hades], while terrible things await those who have not engaged in these sacrificial rituals. (*Rep.* 364e–365a)[76]

By putting "release and purification" together, and referring to Orpheus and Musaeus, Plato indicates that this idea comes from Orphism. He also quotes the Orphic term for "mystic rites" (*teletai*). We also find this terminology in book 7, wnere Socrates mentions the "release and healing from the bonds of ignorance" (αὐτῶν λύσιν τε καὶ ἴασιν τῶν δεσμῶν καὶ τῆς ἀφροσύνης; 515c). In the *Phaedo*, Plato refers to philosophy as bringing "release and purification" (λύσει τε καὶ καθαρμῷ; 82d).

Plato borrows the Orphic belief in ritual purification (*katharsis, katharos, kathairein*), but reconceives this in terms of the philosopher purifying himself by practicing philosophy. For the Orphics, purification included eating a vegetarian diet, bathing in a ritual manner, sprinkling themselves with lustral water, and offering libations of milk.[77] Plato does not suggest that philosophers should follow these Orphic prescriptions, but he does insist that they should refrain from bodily pleasures and live an ascetic lifestyle. Indeed, to purify themselves, philosophers must contemplate the Forms and put this knowledge into practice in daily life. As Socrates puts it, "the truth is really some sort of purification from all such things [pleasures/ desires], and temperance, justice, courage and wisdom itself are a kind of purification" (69b).

Plato also uses the Orphic idea that the gods "release" (*lusis, louein, apallasein*) the initiate from the cycle of incarnation at the moment of death. As we saw in the gold leaf above, the god Bacchios "releases" (*eluse*) the initiate so that it can escape the cycle of reincarnation at the moment of death (*OF* 485). In the *Phaedo*, Plato repeatedly refers to the philosophic soul's "release" from the body at death (*lusis, louein*; 62b, 64c, 64e–65a, 67d, 70a, 82d, 83a, 83b, 84a, 84b, 107c, 114c). As Socrates claims, the philosophers must "keep themselves pure from it [the body] until god

[76] 364e–365a: βίβλων δὲ ὅμαδον παρέχονται Μουσαίου καὶ Ὀρφέως ... καθ' ἃς θυηπολοῦσιν, πείθοντες οὐ μόνον ἰδιώτας ἀλλὰ καὶ πόλεις, ὡς ἄρα λύσεις τε καὶ καθαρμοὶ ἀδικημάτων διὰ θυσιῶν καὶ παιδιᾶς ἡδονῶν εἰσι μὲν ἔτι ζῶσιν, εἰσὶ δὲ καὶ τελευτήσασιν, ἃς δὴ τελετὰς καλοῦσιν, αἱ τῶν ἐκεῖ κακῶν ἀπολύουσιν ἡμᾶς, μὴ θύσαντας δὲ δεινὰ περιμένει.
[77] Herrero de Jáuregui 2010: 14–18 and passim. Eur. *Hipp* 953–5 suggests that the Orphics were vegetarians. Cf. Betegh 2014, who claims that the Orphics did not practice vegetarianism.

himself releases us" (ἕως ἂν ὁ θεὸς αὐτὸς ἀπολύσῃ ἡμᾶς; 67a). In the eschatology, moreover, he says that "those who have lived exceptionally holy lives are freed and released, as though from prisons, and go upwards to a pure dwelling" (ἀπαλλαττόμενοι ὥσπερ δεσμωτηρίων, ἄνω δὲ εἰς τὴν καθαρὰν οἴκησιν ἀφικνούμενοι; 114b–c). Indeed, the soul "is released [*ekloumenên*] from the body as though from chains (*desmôn*, 67d)." Here, Socrates refers to the Orphic conception of the body as a prison (more on this below).[78] In Plato's scenario, the philosopher uses reason to separate his soul from the body during life and thus releases his soul from the bodily realm at death. In ideal cases, the perfected philosopher will leave the body altogether and everlastingly contemplate the Forms.

3.7   The Orphic Divinity-Markers for the Soul

Plato does not simply adopt the Orphic notions of purification and release: he borrows key elements from the Orphic "story of the soul." The Orphic story has four chapters: the soul starts out as divine, falls into human bodies, gets initiated, and regains a life with the gods. Plato's story shares the narrative arc of the Orphic myth of the human soul.[79] First, as we saw above in the Recollection Argument, the soul lived with the Forms before it entered a body. Socrates reiterates this point later in the dialogue, claiming that the soul entered into the body as a prison after this early preincarnate state: "What do you say about the argument in which we stated that learning is recollection and that, since this is the case, our soul necessarily existed somewhere else before it was imprisoned in a body?" (τί οὖν . . . περὶ ἐκείνου τοῦ λόγου λέγετε ἐν ᾧ ἔφαμεν τὴν μάθησιν ἀνάμνησιν εἶναι, καὶ τούτου οὕτως ἔχοντος ἀναγκαίως ἔχειν ἄλλοθι πρότερον ἡμῶν εἶναι τὴν ψυχήν, πρὶν ἐν τῷ σώματι ἐνδεθῆναι; 91e–92a). The soul contemplated (and, as it seems, dwelled with) the Forms in a pre-incarnate state. Since Plato considers disembodied contemplation as the happiest state for

---

[78] Bernabé 2011: 118–46 offers a detailed analysis of the prison of the body in the context of early Orphic texts and ideas; as he notes, the Orphics see the body as the tomb of the soul, but Plato transposed this into the "prison" of the soul. Note that Clement of Alexandria said that the Pythagorean Philolaus (B 14 DK) was the first to claim that the body was the prison of the soul. As many scholars have noted, the Orphics borrowed ideas from the Pythagoreans. However, the Pythagoreans did not have mystic rites (which Plato mentions in this passage). See Casadesús 2000 and 2008; Edmonds 2004: 177; Bernabé 2011: 133–40; Horky 2013: 172–3; and Rodriguez 2016: 11 for discussions of the Orphic and Pythagorean sources for Plato's notion of the body as the prison of the soul. For Plato's comments on or use of Orphic material, see Bernabé 1997 and especially 2011; Kingsley 1995: 112–32.

[79] We can piece together Plato's story by bringing together the different passages in the text.

the soul (114c), we can infer that the original, pre-incarnate state was blissful.

The notion that the soul lived disembodied in the divine realm of the Forms points to a "divine" (*theios*) element in the soul. As we saw above, the soul is "like" the divine: since "the divine is of such a kind by nature to rule and lead" (τὸ μὲν θεῖον οἷον ἄρχειν τε καὶ ἡγεμονεύειν πεφυκέναι), and the soul naturally rules the body, the soul "resembles" (*eoiken*) the "divine" (*tôi theiôi*). Elsewhere, Socrates claims that "the soul . . . is more divine and excellent (*theioteron kai kallion*) than the body" and that it is "more divine" (*theioteron*) than harmony (91c–d). He also calls it "godlike" (*theioedes*; 95c). To be sure, Socrates never says outright that the soul is divine, and he clearly thinks that bad souls do not have this status. Still, the soul can achieve a godlike state when it has purified and perfected itself as a philosopher. Given that the soul contemplated the "kindred" Forms before it ever entered a body, it has the divine capacity to grasp and know these higher beings. To this extent, Plato's soul resembles that of the Orphics: it is partly divine but must be incarnated and reincarnated due to some evil element in it.

In this dialogue, Plato does not provide a reason for the original fall of the soul into a body. In the Orphic myths, humans come into the world with original sin even though they have divine origins. It may be that Plato's story envisaged some sort of similar beginning. Unfortunately, he says nothing in this dialogue about the soul's life before incarnation. He offers a more detailed story of the soul in the *Phaedrus* and *Timaeus*.

In the *Phaedo*, Plato indicates that incarnated souls live in a lower realm. Indeed, he represents the soul as moving downward and upward on a vertical scale. For example, in the eschatology, he places humans in hollows beneath the surface of the earth in a sort of Hades. He thus represents humans as living in a sort of hell during life; only by practicing philosophy and leaving the body behind at death can the soul go up to the blissful, invisible realm of "true Hades." As Socrates states, the bad soul "falls" into the body, which is an "impure" place for the soul: the vicious soul "being of such a kind, is *weighed down* and dragged back to the visible region by its fear of the invisible and of Hades" (ὃ δὴ καὶ ἔχουσα ἡ τοιαύτη ψυχὴ βαρύνεταί τε καὶ ἕλκεται πάλιν εἰς τὸν ὁρατὸν τόπον φόβῳ τοῦ ἀιδοῦς τε καὶ Ἅιδου; 81c, my italics). Indeed, the "contaminated" soul "falls" – *piptein* – into another body (83d). As in other dialogues, Plato creates a vertical hierarchy in which vicious souls descend to the lower parts of the earth and virtuous souls ascend to the Forms. In this dialogue on death and the afterlife, Plato explicitly refers to Hades but turns the traditional Greek notion of hell upside down: humans live in hell in the hollows of the earth, but the philosophic soul can move upwards to a higher and happier invisible realm after death.

Once the soul enters into the cycle of incarnation, it has the chance to improve its condition. In a human life, it can practice philosophy and eventually be released from reincarnation. Still, in these middle chapters of the story of the soul, the body serves as a punishment for the soul. As Socrates states:

> The *logos* spoken in the secret mysteries about these things, that we humans are in a prison and that it is not right to free oneself from this or to run away, seems to me to be a great and difficult matter to understand. But this, Cebes, seems to me to be spoken well, that the gods are our guardians and that we humans are the possessions of the god. (62b)[80]

Referring to the "secret mysteries" of the Orphics, Socrates mentions their belief that the body is the prison of the soul. As we have seen, in the Orphic myths, the soul carries with it the Titans' crime against the gods and is punished by incarnating into bodies. By adopting the idea that the body is the prison of the soul, Plato indicates that humans living on earth are in some sense paying a penalty for a primordial crime.

Plato explicitly mentions the Orphic notion that embodiment is a punishment for the soul in his discussion of the etymology of *sôma* ("body") in the *Cratylus*:

> I think that the people associated with Orpheus most of all gave this name [*sôma*] to the body, believing that the soul is undergoing a punishment for something, and it has this [the body] as an enclosure, like a prison, so that it is kept safe (*sôzêtai*), and that this is, as the word suggests, the "safekeeper" [*sôma*] for the soul until it pays the penalty. (400c)[81]

Plato does not mention the crime for which the soul must pay the penalty here. Still, he refers to incarnation (and, we infer, reincarnation) as a punishment for an early offence against the gods. Other thinkers in Plato's academy discussed the idea that the soul pays for an ancient crime by living in a human body. For example, Plato's disciple Xenocrates,

---

[80]   62b: ὁ μὲν οὖν ἐν ἀπορρήτοις λεγόμενος περὶ αὐτῶν λόγος, ὡς ἔν τινι φρουρᾷ ἐσμεν οἱ ἄνθρωποι καὶ οὐ δεῖ δὴ ἑαυτὸν ἐκ ταύτης λύειν οὐδ᾽ ἀποδιδράσκειν, μέγας τέ τίς μοι φαίνεται καὶ οὐ ῥᾴδιος διιδεῖν· οὐ μέντοι ἀλλὰ τόδε γέ μοι δοκεῖ, ὦ Κέβης, εὖ λέγεσθαι, τὸ θεοὺς εἶναι ἡμῶν τοὺς ἐπιμελουμένους καὶ ἡμᾶς τοὺς ἀνθρώπους ἓν τῶν κτημάτων τοῖς θεοῖς εἶναι.

[81]   *Crat.* 400c: δοκοῦσι μέντοι μοι μάλιστα θέσθαι οἱ ἀμφὶ Ὀρφέα τοῦτο τὸ ὄνομα, ὡς δίκην διδούσης τῆς ψυχῆς ὧν δὴ ἕνεκα δίδωσιν, τοῦτον δὲ περίβολον ἔχειν, ἵνα σῴζηται, δεσμωτηρίου εἰκόνα· εἶναι οὖν τῆς ψυχῆς τοῦτο, ὥσπερ αὐτὸ ὀνομάζεται, ἕως ἂν ἐκτείσῃ τὰ ὀφειλόμενα, τὸ ʼσῶμα.ʼ

commenting on *Phaedo* 62b, says that the body "is Titanic, and it culminates in Dionysus."[82] This refers to the Orphic claim that humans, as partial
descendants of the Titans, pay the penalty for the murder of Dionysus by
entering into bodies; the titanic element of the human soul comes to an
end ("culminates") when Dionysus forgives it and releases it from the cycle
of reincarnation. Aristotle also refers to the Orphic claim that the soul's life
in a body is a punishment for an ancient crime:

> We have been put together straightaway by nature, as they say in the
> mystery rites, as a punishment (*timoria*) for all of us. For the divinely
> inspired ancients say that the soul pays a penalty and that we live by way
> of a punishment for great ancient crimes. The yoking of the soul to the body
> looks very much like this. For as the Tyrrhenians are said to torture captives
> by chaining dead bodies face to face with the living, fitting each part to each
> part, so the soul seems to be stretched out and fastened onto all the sensing
> parts of the body.[83]

This passage offers an interesting representation of the Orphic "mystery
rites." In the *Phaedo*, Plato does not refer to the Titans or give humans
a titanic element, but he does treat human life as a punishment. In the
Laws, however, he identifies evil humans as titanic (701b–c): men who have
no respect for the gods "imitate the nature of the Titans." As I suggest, we
should locate Plato's reference to the body as a prison in the context of the
entire Orphic myth of the soul, with its divine beginning, fall, reincarnation, release from its cycle of reincarnation, and its final home with the
gods.

Finally, Plato borrows the Orphic notion that the soul that purifies itself
on earth will have a happy life with the gods when it leaves the human body
at death. As we have seen, the Orphic initiate may have gone through
a "ritual enactment of death" during the initiation ceremony.[84] The initiation served to purify the soul and prepare it to enter a good region of
Hades. In Plato, the philosopher "practices death" by separating his soul
from the body and contemplating the Forms. Practicing death has the
effect of purifying the philosopher's soul. In some sense, this is a ritual
enactment of death (though the philosopher does this repeatedly; there is
no single "initiation"). In addition, like the Orphic initiate, the pure

---

[82] Fr. 20 Heinze, from Damascius, *In Pl. Phaed.*, 1, par. 2 (ed. L. G. Westerink). On this passage, see
Boyancé 1948 and 1963.
[83] Fr. 60; Iamb. *Protr.* 8 (47. 21–48. 9 Pistelli). I take Aristotle's mention of the "mystery rites" and
"divinely inspired ancients" as referring to the Orphic doctrines.
[84] Riedweg 2010: 227.

philosophic soul goes to live either in the realm of the gods or in the divine realm of the Forms.

Plato's use of the Orphic divinity-marker for the soul and the Forms is very detailed and complex. As we have seen, the Orphics had a very rich set of myths, doctrines, and rituals. These influence a number of ideas in Plato's dialogue. Given that the *Phaedo* focuses on the death of Socrates and the immortality of the soul, it comes as no surprise that Plato used so much Orphic material in this text.

3.8 The Matter of Vision in the Eschatology

In the eschatology in the *Phaedo*, Plato represents near-perfect philosophers living on the "true earth" in the realm of "aether." Though this realm is divine, it is corporeal and does not mark the final end for the philosophic soul. Socrates speaks of a higher realm where the soul can dwell: "those who have purified themselves with philosophy live for the rest of time altogether without bodies, and they go to habitations even more beautiful than these" (οἱ φιλοσοφίᾳ ἱκανῶς καθηράμενοι ἄνευ τε σωμάτων ζῶσι τὸ παράπαν εἰς τὸν ἔπειτα χρόνον, καὶ εἰς οἰκήσεις ἔτι τούτων καλλίους ἀφικνοῦνται; 114c). In short, the near-perfect philosophers live with the gods in the aether and the perfected philosophic souls dwell with the Forms.

In this myth, Plato represents the second-best afterlife for the philosophers. Here, he focuses on the aethereal realm, which is located on the true surface of the earth. As Socrates states:

> We think that we live on the upper surface of the earth but do not perceive that we live in the hollows of the earth, just as if someone who lives in the depth of the sea should believe that he dwells on the surface of the ocean, and, seeing the sun and the stars through the water, should believe that the sea was the sky. This person, due to laziness or weakness, would never have reached the surface of the ocean and seen – by rising and lifting his head out of the sea into that region there – how much purer and more beautiful it is than the world he lived in . . . . But if anyone should journey to the top of the air or, being winged, should fly upwards, he would lift his head above it and see things in that upper world just as fishes push their heads out of the water and see the things in our world. And if he has a nature that can endure the sight (*theôrousa*), he would know that this is the true heaven and the true light and the true earth. (109b–110a)

By placing humans in a dark hollow in the earth, Plato effectively locates them in Hades as it was traditionally understood. If the soul practices philosophy in a human life, it can leave this hellish region and the prison of the body: "but those who appear to have lived an exceptionally holy life are freed from these regions in the earth and released as though from prisons, and they journey upwards to a pure home on the earth" (οἳ δὲ δὴ ἂν δόξωσι διαφερόντως πρὸς τὸ ὁσίως βιῶναι, οὗτοί εἰσιν οἱ τῶνδε μὲν τῶν τόπων τῶν ἐν τῇ γῇ ἐλευθερούμενοί τε καὶ ἀπαλλαττόμενοι ὥσπερ δεσμωτηρίων, ἄνω δὲ εἰς τὴν καθαρὰν οἴκησιν ἀφικνούμενοι καὶ ἐπὶ γῆς οἰκιζόμενοι; 114b–c). Indeed, the soul does not belong in the body at all and longs to escape this life. The philosopher wants to die because this will release his soul to experience its true and blissful life in the presence of the Forms.

Plato creates a hierarchy of places for the soul to dwell. In our present life, we live in the "hollows" beneath the surface of the earth and do not realize that there is a true earth "above" our own. As in the Ladder of Love in the *Symposium* and the Allegory of the Cave in the *Republic*, Plato sets up a vertical movement in this eschatology: people must practice philosophy to move "up" to the highest realm of the Forms. Here, Plato conveys the idea of this vertical ascent by using the image of fishes leaping above the water and terrestrial creatures growing wings. This ascent is, first and foremost, intellectual – the philosopher must practice dialectic to attain the vision of the Forms. But this ascent also has an ethical orientation: he must handle his body and his social affairs on earth in the correct way. In the vertical hierarchy in the *Phaedo*, Plato adds a geographical element that we do not find in the Ladder of Love or the Allegory of the Cave. Depending on its intellectual and ethical development, the soul dwells in a specific region in the cosmos and occupies a body that lives either in water, air, or aether.

I want to pose two questions about Plato's representation of life in the aether. First, why does Plato choose to put the near-perfect philosophers in the aether? Second, why does he focus on the physical vision of beauty rather than on moral acts or intellectual contemplation?

Let's look first at Plato's depiction of aether, the highest realm in the physical cosmos. As Socrates states, "the earth itself is pure and lies in the pure heaven (where the stars are), which many of those who customarily speak about such things call *aithêr*" (αὐτὴν δὲ τὴν γῆν καθαρὰν ἐν καθαρῷ κεῖσθαι τῷ οὐρανῷ ἐν ᾧπέρ ἐστι τὰ ἄστρα, ὃν δὴ αἰθέρα ὀνομάζειν τοὺς πολλοὺς τῶν περὶ τὰ τοιαῦτα εἰωθότων λέγειν; 109b–c). Who are the people who speak about "aether"? First, the Greek poets regularly referred to aether as the "upper air" where the gods and certain blessed people dwell.[85] In addition, many presocratics viewed aether as the upper air, though Anaxagoras (and, possibly Heraclitus and Empedocles) identified aether as fire.[86] Aether also features prominently in the Orphic poem quoted in the Derveni papyrus – it is a primordial deity, along with Night (however, in later Orphic myths, aether plays a minor role). Finally, some tragic dramas present the idea that souls end up in the aether after death.[87] I want to briefly examine these tragic texts, which have not been considered in the context of the *Phaedo*. Most if not all of them are Euripidean. As Eric Csapo has shown, Euripides' later tragedies "responded in part to the general expansion of Dionysian cultic activity in Athens (and elsewhere) both through the reception in Central Greece of Orphic Mysteries, and through the absorption of the ideas and imagery of such cults by the Eleusinian Mysteries."[88] These Euripidean passages about the soul's aethereal afterlife, however, may not reflect the Orphic Mysteries, since the souls of the Orphic initiates generally go to Hades.[89]

While the aethereal eschatologies in tragic texts are wonderfully various, most of them focus on the gods. Consider, first, the choral ode from Euripides' *Chrysippos* (E *TrGF* 839.1–14):

> Greatest Earth and Aether of Zeus – he [Aether] the begetter of humans and gods and she [Earth] receiving damp drops of spreading moisture, gives birth to mortal men, to plants, and to the races of beasts, from which she is rightly considered the mother of all. Those things born from earth go back to earth, and those growing from the aethereal seed return to the heavenly pole. (Γαῖα μεγίστη καὶ Διὸς Αἰθήρ, ὃ μὲν ἀνθρώπων καὶ θεῶν γενέτωρ, ἣ δ᾽ ὑγροβόλους σταγόνας νοτίας παραδεξαμένη τίκτει θνητούς, τίκτει

---

[85] On *aithēr* as the divine abode, see (e.g.,) Homer. *Iliad* 2.449, 4.413, 5.191–2, 8.555–7, 14.287; *Hymn to Demeter* 67, 70, 457; *Hymn to Apollo* 434; *Hymn to Ares* 551, 560; Sophocles, *Ajax* 1192, *OT* 867, *Antigone* 415, *OC* 1983; Aristophanes, *Birds* 685–6. Cf. Sedley (1989: 362–3), who claims that Plato borrows the notion of *aithēr* specifically from Anaxagoras, who is explicitly discussed and attacked earlier in the dialogue. This is problematic because (as Sedley himself notes) Anaxagoras associates *aithēr* with fire. Clearly, in this eschatology, Plato does not identify the aethereal region as fiery.

[86] Anaxagoras was the only presocratic who consistently said that aether was fire. Anaximines and Diogenes of Apollonia posit air (*aer*), not aether, as the primordial substance of the cosmos. As Vlastos 1993: 208.n.63 noted in his discussion of the early prosocratics, "the distinction between air and aether is hazy in the philosophers (for Heraclitus, cf. b 31 b 36, b 76; Emped. b 17.18 – 'air' is 'aether' and in b 71, while at b 38 aether=fire!)." Cf. Kingsley 1995: 13–23, who claims that Empedocles did not identify aether with fire.

[87] Csapo 2008 offers an excellent discussion of the aethereal afterlife, and claims that it reflects some amalgamation of the Orphic and Eleusinian Mysteries. See also Scodel 2011, who discusses Euripides' interest in Orphic texts and ideas.

[88] Csapo 2008: 263; see also Scodel 2011.

[89] Bernabé/Christóbal 2008: 42–5 note that there is one Orphic tombstone from the third century BC that says the dead initiate lives in the heaven, "elevated by his father among the heavenly stars" [SEG 28 no. 528 = PEG 2.1 466 T]. They see this as a deviation from the Orphic Mysteries.

βοτάνην φῦλά τε θηρῶν· ὅθεν οὐκ ἀδίκως μήτηρ πάντων νενόμισται. χωρεῖ
δ' ὀπίσω τὰ μὲν ἐκ γαίας φύντ' εἰς γαῖαν, τὰ δ' ἀπ' αἰθερίου βλαστόντα
γονῆς εἰς οὐράνιον πάλιν ἦλθε πόλον)

Here, the phrase "Aether of Zeus" links Zeus to aether. The primordial god
Aether is "the begetter of humans and gods."[90] If "Zeus' Aether" begets
humans and gods, and Earth "gives birth to mortal men," then humans
have both a divine and earthly nature. This has some resemblance to the
Orphic anthropology. As the last line of the fragment indicates, when
humans die, their bodies go to earth but their aethereal seed returns to
heaven. We find a similar passage in the *Pirithous* (written by Euripides or
Critias): "you, the self-generating, you who wove the nature of all things in
the circle of Aether, around which light and dark variegated night perpetually dance, and the countless throng of stars" (σὲ τὸν αὐτοφυᾶ, τὸν ἐν
αἰθερίῳ ῥύμβῳ πάντων φύσιν ἐμπλέξανθ', ὃν πέρι μὲν φῶς, πέρι δ' ὀρφναία
νὺξ αἰολόχρως, ἄκριτός τ' ἄστρων ὄχλος ἐνδελεχῶς ἀμφιχορεύει; E *TrGF*
593.1–5). We do not know the identity of the "self-generating" god, but
Aether seems to be a primordial deity, since it existed before the self-
generating god created "the nature of all things."

We also find passages where humans and demigods end up in aether
after death. In Euripides' *Suppliants*, when Theseus tells the Theban herald
that the dead Argive bodies require burial, he says that their breath will go
to the aether: "Let the dead now be buried in the earth, and let it return
there whence each thing came to the light – the soul-breath (*pneuma*) to
the aether, and the body to the earth" (ἐάσατ' ἤδη γῇ καλυφθῆναι νεκρούς,
ὅθεν δ' ἕκαστον ἐς τὸ φῶς ἀφίκετο ἐνταῦθ' ἀπελθεῖν, πνεῦμα μὲν πρὸς
αἰθέρα, τὸ σῶμα δ' ἐς γῆν; 531–4). Although the Greek word *pneuma* means
"breath," Theseus treats this as a special and distinct part of a person,
separate from his or her body – for this reason, I translate *pneuma* as "soul-
breath" in this passage. We find a similar idea in Euripides' *Erechtheus*,
where Athena claims that the souls of Erechtheus' dead daughters went to
the aether: "Their souls did not depart to Hades, but I have settled their
breath in the aether" (ψυχαὶ μὲν οὖν τῶνδ' οὐ βεβᾶσ' ['Αιδ]ην πάρα, εἰς δ'
αἰθέρ' αὐτῶν πνεῦμ' ἐγὼ [κ]ατῴκισα; E *TrGF* 370.71–2). Here again, the
poet identifies the soul (*psuchê*) with breath (*pneuma*). Aether is clearly
a higher and better place for the soul to dwell than in Hades.

We find an interesting reference to the aetherial afterlife in Euripides'
Helen. In the scene where the prophetess Theonoe serves as the judge of the

---

[90] Though one could also take "ὁ . . . γενέτωρ" as referring to Zeus. I take Aether as a primordial god
because the person/chorus speaking the quote addresses Aether alongside the goddess Earth.

rightness of the claims between Menelaus and her brother (who both want to have Helen), she states: "For there is retribution for these things, for the dead below and for all humans living above. The mind (*nous*) of the dead is not living [in a body] but it has conscious immortal thought since it falls into immortal aether" (καὶ γὰρ τίσις τῶνδ᾽ ἐστὶ τοῖς τε νερτέροις καὶ τοῖς ἄνωθεν πᾶσιν ἀνθρώποις· ὁ νοῦς τῶν κατθανόντων ζῇ μὲν οὔ, γνώμην δ᾽ ἔχει ἀθάνατον εἰς ἀθάνατον αἰθέρ᾽ ἐμπεσών; 1013–16). Though evil people will be punished for wrongdoing, the immortal mind (*nous*) – which either is or resembles the soul – will live in the aether after death.

Consider also Pylades' statement in Euripides' *Orestes*: "May the fruitful earth and the bright aether not receive me if I betray you and leave you after freeing myself" (μήθ᾽ αἷμά μου δέξαιτο κάρπιμον πέδον, μὴ λαμπρὸς αἰθήρ, εἴ σ᾽ ἐγὼ προδούς ποτε ἐλευθερώσας τοὐμὸν ἀπολίποιμι σέ; 1086–7). Here, Pylades suggests that his body will go to earth and his soul to the aether. Finally, we have one fragment from Euripides (probably from the *Phaethon*) in which the soul-breath belonging to the demigod Phaethon ends up in Aether: "he who was recently blooming in the flesh was quenched, falling like a star, and he released his soul-breath to the aether" (ὃ δ᾽ ἄρτι θάλλων σάρκα διοπετὴς ὅπως ἀστὴρ ἀπέσβη, πνεῦμ᾽ ἀφεὶς ἐς αἰθέρα; Plut. *Mor.* 416e, 1090c; E *TrGF* 971). Phaethon was the son of Helios and a mortal woman (or perhaps a nymph), and he had both a divine and earthly nature.

In these passages, the tragedians identify aether as a primordial deity and refer to certain souls (or soul-breaths) going to the aether as some sort of reward. In addition, an Athenian inscription from the fifth century, found at the base of the tomb for the Athenian soldiers who died in the battle of Potidea (432 BCE), seems to indicate that these men had a special place in Aether due to their heroism in the battle: "Aether received their souls, earth their bodies" (IG I3 1179, ll. 6–7: αἰθὲρ μὲμ φσυχὰς ὑπεδέχσατο, σόμ[ατα δὲ χθὸν] / τõνδε).[91] At least in this one case, the Athenians endorsed the notion of an aethereal afterlife (they did not refer to this on other graves). The Athenians in fifth-century Athens, then, had some sense of an aethereal eschatology. Since aether was the realm of the Olympian gods, not the chthonic gods, the Athenians seem to have believed that some souls would go to the gods in heaven rather than to Hades. Of course the Eleusinian

---

[91] Arrington (2015: 66) discusses this inscription in his book on the Athenian war dead. As he states: "this terminology is similar to the language that Euripides uses to describe the heroization of the Hyakinthides."

and Orphic initiates went to Hades, so the aethereal afterlife seems to mark a special and divine kind of reward.

Since the poets regularly represented the gods as living in the aether, the Greeks associated this realm with divinity. Following this tradition, Plato identifies the aethereal region as the place where gods dwell. As Socrates claims in his discourse on the aethereal region, the gods "truly dwell" (τῷ ὄντι οἰκητὰς θεούς) in the temples there (111b). This is the realm of the gods. Indeed, the philosophers who live there have direct contact with the gods: for these people, "there are groves and temples of the gods, in which the gods truly dwell, and there are utterances and prophecies and perceptions of the gods, and being-together with the gods takes place in a direct way" (111b–c)[92]. Here, the gods manifest themselves to the philosophers in visible epiphanies and in audible speech. The philosophers thus enjoy a direct "being-together" (*sunousia*) with the gods. Not suprisingly, the entire region on the true earth is a "sight for blessed spectators to behold" (αὐτὴν ἰδεῖν εἶναι θέαμα εὐδαιμόνων θεατῶν; 111a).

Even though they live in a divine region, the souls of the philosophers on the true earth have mortal human bodies. Socrates offers a brief description of these individuals and the various places that they live on the true earth:

> There are many animals and men there, some dwelling in the middle region, others on the coasts of the air (as we live on the coasts of the sea), and others on islands near the mainland, which the air flows around. What water and the sea are to us in terms of our needs, air is to them; and what air is to us, aether is to them. The seasons are mixed in such a way that people do not have diseases, and they live much longer than we do here. In sight, hearing, wisdom and other such things, they are superior to us in the way that air is superior to water, and aether is superior to air in terms of it purity. (111a–b)[93]

While the philosophers on the true earth have many good qualities that humans down in the hollows lack, they do have bodies that die. Indeed, although aether is a divine region, it does not mark the final destination for the philosophic soul: the mature philosophic soul will leave the body altogether and live with the Forms.

---

[92] 111b–c: καὶ δὴ καὶ θεῶν ἄλση τε καὶ ἱερὰ αὐτοῖς εἶναι, ἐν οἷς τῷ ὄντι οἰκητὰς θεοὺς εἶναι, καὶ φήμας τε καὶ μαντείας καὶ αἰσθήσεις τῶν θεῶν καὶ τοιαύτας συνουσίας γίγνεσθαι αὐτοῖς πρὸς αὐτούς.

[93] 111a–b: ζῷα δ' ἐπ' αὐτῇ εἶναι ἄλλα τε πολλὰ καὶ ἀνθρώπους, τοὺς μὲν ἐν μεσογαίᾳ οἰκοῦντας, τοὺς δὲ περὶ τὸν ἀέρα ὥσπερ ἡμεῖς περὶ τὴν θάλατταν, τοὺς δ' ἐν νήσοις ἃς περιρρεῖν τὸν ἀέρα πρὸς τῇ ἠπείρῳ οὔσας· καὶ ἑνὶ λόγῳ, ὅπερ ἡμῖν τὸ ὕδωρ τε καὶ ἡ θάλαττά ἐστι πρὸς τὴν ἡμετέραν χρείαν, τοῦτο ἐκεῖ τὸν ἀέρα, ὃ δὲ ἡμῖν ἀήρ, ἐκείνοις τὸν αἰθέρα. τὰς δὲ ὥρας αὐτοῖς κρᾶσιν ἔχειν τοιαύτην ὥστε ἐκείνους ἀνόσους εἶναι καὶ χρόνον τε ζῆν πολὺ πλείω τῶν ἐνθάδε, καὶ ὄψει καὶ ἀκοῇ καὶ φρονήσει καὶ πᾶσι τοῖς τοιούτοις ἡμῶν ἀφεστάναι τῇ αὐτῇ ἀποστάσει ᾗπερ ἀήρ τε ὕδατος ἀφέστηκεν καὶ αἰθὴρ ἀέρος πρὸς καθαρότητα.

3.9   Beauty and Vision

Plato places great emphasis on beauty, light, and the purity of nature in his discourse on the aether. First, he constructs three levels of physical life in the cosmos: the sea, the hollows in the earth, and the surface of the "true earth." The sea is the lowest and ugliest region of the cosmos: "the things in the sea are destroyed and eaten away by brine, and nothing of any account grows in the sea, and to speak generally there is nothing perfect but stones and sand and endless mud and filth" (110a).[94] Indeed, the sea contains nothing of beauty: "to judge in comparison with the beautiful things in our world, there is nothing worth anything there" (πρὸς τὰ παρ᾽ ἡμῖν κάλλη κρίνεσθαι οὐδ᾽ ὁπωστιοῦν ἄξια; 110a). "The hollows of the earth," where humans live now, make up the second realm. Here again, Plato emphasizes the rot and decay in the bodily realm: "this earth and the stones and the entire region here [in the hollows] are destroyed and eaten away" (ἥδε μὲν γὰρ ἡ γῆ καὶ οἱ λίθοι καὶ ἅπας ὁ τόπος ὁ ἐνθάδε διεφθαρμένα ἐστὶν καὶ καταβεβρωμένα; 110a).[95] In both the sea and the hollows in the earth, the material elements are rotten and corroded. In this scheme, the quality of matter runs along an aesthetic spectrum: the elements corroded by the sea have no beauty, and the elements in the hollows, though corroded by air, manifest some beauties. But the beauties in the hollows do not compare to the radiantly beautiful elements on the true earth.

The third realm, the "true earth" in the aether, is of course material – plants, animals, and humans live and die there. But Plato does not focus on bodily decay and corruption in this realm. Rather, he emphasizes the purity, perfection, and beauty of nature.[96] In contrast to Socrates' earlier attacks on the impure and corroded bodily realm that pulls the soul away from reason and goodness, the visible region on the true earth is pure and radiates beauty. Indeed, rather surprisingly, the materials in the aether do not erode or decay, as they do in the hollows. As Socrates states:

---

[94]   110a: διεφθαρμένα ἐστὶν καὶ καταβεβρωμένα ... τὰ ἐν τῇ θαλάττη ὑπὸ τῆς ἅλμης, καὶ οὔτε φύεται ἄξιον λόγου οὐδὲν ἐν τῇ θαλάττη, οὔτε τέλειον ὡς ἔπος εἰπεῖν οὐδέν ἐστι, σήραγγες δὲ καὶ ἄμμος καὶ πηλὸς ἀμήχανος καὶ βόρβοροί εἰσιν.

[95]   Because this region is dark and impure, it blocks our present view of the true earth and heavens. As Brill observes (2009: 18), "The perspective of one who occupies a hollow, like the perspective of one who lives under the sea, is not utterly erroneous; rather, it is flawed only because it is fragmentary. It is a perspective that does not yet take its own position under consideration."

[96]   As Rowe 1993: 275–6 suggests, the hierarchical ordering of the physical realm – with the true earth in the *aithēr*, the hollows in the air, and the water in the sea – indicates that each level of the cosmos is more or less distant from the Forms; he adds, rightly in my view, that the myth does not offer "any further useful information about the form-particular hypothesis."

The mountains and the stones are smooth and diaphanous and their colors are more beautiful. And the gems we so admire here – carnelians, jaspers, emeralds, and all such things – are fragments of the things there, and in that place there is nothing that is not of this kind and even more beautiful than these. And the cause of this is that the stones are pure and not devoured or destroyed (κατεδηδεσμένοι οὐδὲ διεφθαρμένοι) as they are here by decay and brine due to things flowing together, which bring ugliness and disease to stones, the earth, and to animals and plants. And the earth there is adorned (κεκοσμῆσθαι) with all such gems and with gold and silver and other such things. And these things are fully revealed, being abundant and large and everywhere (ἐκφανῆ γὰρ αὐτὰ πεφυκέναι, ὄντα πολλὰ πλήθει καὶ μεγάλα καὶ πανταχοῦ τῆς γῆς), so that the earth is a sight for blessed spectators to behold. (110d–111b)[97]

In contrast to the materials in the hollows, which are "destroyed and devoured" (διεφθαρμένα ἐστὶν καὶ καταβεβρωμένα), the stones in the aether do not get "devoured or destroyed" (κατεδηδεσμένοι οὐδὲ διεφθαρμένοι). The stones and elements on the true earth do not erode because this region, for the most part, lacks water and air, which can harm bodies. This suggests that matter, at its best, need not have bad qualities. Of course Plato does not want to posit a higher kind of matter – the stone and gems on the true earth comprise the same materials as those things below. Rather, he conjures up a region that stands at the border (as it were) between the physical and the intelligible realms. This divine region is "cosmically adorned" (κεκοσμῆσθαι) with gems, gold, and silver which are "abundant" (*polla plêthei*), "large" (*megala*), and visible "everywhere" (*pantachou*). Indeed, they are "fully revealed" (*ekphana*) to the spectators. This material revelation shows itself in a superabundance of beauty.

Vision plays an important role in this discourse. Plato places the reader in different points of view so that he/she can see different aspects of the true earth. First, Socrates presents the god's eye view of the earth:

The earth when seen from above looks like balls made up of twelve pieces of leather, variegated (ποικίλη) in appearance and divided into patches of color (χρώμασιν διειλημμένη) of which the colors we see here are samples (as it

---

[97] *Phaedo* 110d–111b: καὶ αὖ τὰ ὄρη ὡσαύτως καὶ τοὺς λίθους ἔχειν ... τήν τε λειότητα καὶ τὴν διαφάνειαν καὶ τὰ χρώματα καλλίω· ὧν καὶ τὰ ἐνθάδε λιθίδια εἶναι ταῦτα τὰ ἀγαπώμενα μόρια, σάρδιά τε καὶ ἰάσπιδας καὶ σμαράγδους καὶ πάντα τὰ τοιαῦτα· ἐκεῖ δὲ οὐδὲν ὅτι οὐ τοιοῦτον εἶναι καὶ ἔτι τούτων καλλίω. τὸ δ᾽ αἴτιον τούτου εἶναι ὅτι ἐκεῖνοι οἱ λίθοι εἰσὶ καθαροὶ καὶ οὐ κατεδηδεσμένοι οὐδὲ διεφθαρμένοι ὥσπερ οἱ ἐνθάδε ὑπὸ σηπεδόνος καὶ ἅλμης ὑπὸ τῶν δεῦρο συνερρυηκότων, ἃ καὶ λίθοις καὶ γῇ καὶ τοῖς ἄλλοις ζῴοις τε καὶ φυτοῖς αἴσχη τε καὶ νόσους παρέχει. τὴν δὲ γῆν αὐτὴν κεκοσμῆσθαι τούτοις τε ἅπασι καὶ ἔτι χρυσῷ τε καὶ ἀργύρῳ καὶ τοῖς ἄλλοις αὖ τοῖς τοιούτοις. ἐκφανῆ γὰρ αὐτὰ πεφυκέναι, ὄντα πολλὰ πλήθει καὶ μεγάλα καὶ πανταχοῦ τῆς γῆς, ὥστε αὐτὴν ἰδεῖν εἶναι θέαμα εὐδαιμόνων θεατῶν.

were) such as painters use. But there the whole earth is made of such colors
and of those that are shinier and purer (λαμπροτέρων καὶ καθαρωτέρων)
than those here. For one part is purple and wondrous in its beauty, and
another is golden, and yet another is white – whiter than chalk or snow. And
the earth is made up of other colors of a similar kind, which are more
numerous and more beautiful than those we see here. (110b–c)[98]

In this multicolored world, the earth takes on a variegated (*poikilê*) appearance due to the interaction of colors and light.[99] What does Plato mean by
"variegated" (*poikilê*)? Adeline Grand-Clément offers an excellent account
of the notion of *poikilia* in ancient Greece: "the creation [of a *poikilos*
object] lies in bringing heterogeneous elements together as a unified whole,
while they retain their own nature and keep interacting in a dynamic
fashion . . . . The characteristic of *poikilon* is to create strong connections,
to bond dissimilar elements."[100] As she suggests, it is the dissimilarity of the
elements that creates the beauty of variegation. In the *Republic* and other
dialogues, Plato attacks "variegation" and identifies it with the multiplicity
of base objects/actions and the vulgar pleasures that they induce.[101] In the
eschatology in the *Phaedo*, by contrast, he positively revels in the variegation of light and color.

After placing the reader in the god's eye view, Plato moves back to the
individual standing on the surface of the true earth. He starts with the
image of a person in our region in the hollows standing on the coastline
and looking down at the ocean, and then transfers this scenario to the
aethereal realm. In the latter case, the surface of the "ocean" is air rather
than water. The person standing on the coastline of the air-ocean, looking
down from the shore in the aether, gets a glimpse of the air and water
below: "these very hollows of the earth, being full of water and air, offer
some aspect of color as they glitter among the variegation of the other
colors [in the aether and air], so that its appearance is one of continuous
variegation" (καὶ γὰρ αὐτὰ ταῦτα τὰ κοῖλα αὐτῆς, ὕδατός τε καὶ ἀέρος
ἔκπλεα ὄντα, χρώματός τι εἶδος παρέχεσθαι στίλβοντα ἐν τῇ τῶν ἄλλων

98 110b–e: πρῶτον μὲν εἶναι τοιαύτη ἡ γῆ αὐτὴ ἰδεῖν, εἴ τις ἄνωθεν θεῷτο, ὥσπερ αἱ δωδεκάσκυτοι
    σφαῖραι, ποικίλη, χρώμασιν διειλημμένη, ὧν καὶ τὰ ἐνθάδε εἶναι χρώματα ὥσπερ δείγματα, οἷς δὴ
    οἱ γραφῆς καταχρῶνται. ἐκεῖ δὲ πᾶσαν τὴν γῆν ἐκ τοιούτων εἶναι, καὶ πολὺ ἔτι ἐκ λαμπροτέρων
    καὶ καθαρωτέρων ἢ τούτων· τὴν μὲν γὰρ ἁλουργῆ εἶναι καὶ θαυμαστὴν τὸ κάλλος, τὴν δὲ
    χρυσοειδῆ, τὴν δὲ ὅση λευκὴ γύψου ἢ χιόνος λευκοτέραν, καὶ ἐκ τῶν ἄλλων χρωμάτων
    συγκειμένην ὡσαύτως, καὶ ἔτι πλειόνων καὶ καλλιόνων ἢ ὅσα ἡμεῖς ἑωράκαμεν.
99 As I have suggested elsewhere (Nightingale 2018), this stands in stark contrast to the conception of
    the beauty of pure colors in the *Philebus*.
100 Grand-Clément 2015: 415.
101 On Plato's view of "variegation," see Liebert 2010: 110; Porter 2010: 87. See also Nightingale 2018 for
    a discussion of the eschatology in the *Phaedo* in terms of aesthetics.

χρωμάτων ποικιλία, ὥστε ἕν τι αὐτῆς εἶδος συνεχὲς ποικίλον φαντάζεσθαι; 110c–d). Since the hollows are located below the air-ocean, the viewer on the true earth sees the lower earthly elements as beautiful insofar as they interact with the colors in the aether. Those living below in the hollows, by contrast, see many of these phenomena as ugly and corroded. What is ugly in the lower realm glitters with beauty in the aethereal realm. Indeed, the philosopher on the true earth sees a "continuous variegation" (*suneches poikilon*) of beautiful elements.

Why does Plato place so much focus on physical beauty in this myth? Earlier in the dialogue, Socrates had argued that the Form of Beauty "causes" every beautiful particular: "if anyone says that something is beautiful by having a lovely color or shape or any other sort of thing, I let that go because I am confused by all these things, and I hold in a simple, artless, and perhaps foolish way that no other thing makes it beautiful except the presence or communion of Beauty itself (100c–d).[102] Indeed, the philosopher should transcend the "visible" (ὁρατόν) realm, which is "defiled" and "impure" (μεμιασμένη καὶ ἀκάθαρτος; 81b). In the arguments in the *Phaedo*, Plato treats the material realm as impure through and through. But in the eschatology, he applies the terms "corrupt" and "impure" only to the material elements in the sea and in the hollows (110e); on the true earth, the elements are pure. In the Recollection Argument, Socrates claimed that the particulars on earth "fall short of" or "are in need of" (*endei*) the Forms (74d–e). On the true earth, the near-perfect philosophers understand that the beauties they see around them partake of the Form of Beauty (they must surely have an intellectual grasp of the "deficiency" of the beautiful particulars in relation to the Form of Beauty, or they would not have graduated to this divine region). Even so, they behold with their eyes the superabundance of physical beauty everywhere they look. Here, Plato's discourse features plenitude rather than deficiency. How should we understand his move from the ontological deficiency of bodily entities to the plentitude of bodily beauty in the aether?[103] There is

---

[102] ἀλλ᾽ ἐάν τίς μοι λέγῃ δι᾽ ὅτι καλόν ἐστιν ὁτιοῦν, ἢ χρῶμα εὐανθὲς ἔχον ἢ σχῆμα ἢ ἄλλο ὁτιοῦν τῶν τοιούτων, τὰ μὲν ἄλλα χαίρειν ἐῶ, ταράττομαι γὰρ ἐν τοῖς ἄλλοις πᾶσι, τοῦτο δὲ ἁπλῶς καὶ ἀτέχνως καὶ ἴσως εὐήθως ἔχω παρ᾽ ἐμαυτῷ, ὅτι οὐκ ἄλλο τι ποιεῖ αὐτὸ καλὸν ἢ ἡ ἐκείνου τοῦ καλοῦ εἴτε παρουσία εἴτε κοινωνία. On Forms as "causes" in the *Phaedo*, see Vlastos' discussion of different ways of understanding *aitia* – as he notes, some conceptions of *aitia* are not causal in the strict sense (1971); cf. Mueller 1998, who argues that the Forms have causal efficacy. It is beyond the scope of this essay to discuss Plato's theory of Forms or the Forms as "causes."

[103] Porter (2016: 575) offers an interesting discussion of this discourse on beauty: "That this seductive appeal to the senses contradicts Plato's metaphysical asceticism and purism everywhere else in the same dialogue has been noted in the past. One solution to this contradiction, if it is that, is to say

something paradoxical about this region – the place is material but has an abundance of wondrous beauty.

Part of the paradox is that Plato depicts the physical beauty in the aethereal realm as divine. Indeed, he uses the terminology found in poetic narratives of divine epiphany to describe the aethereal region. Consider the language that Greek poets used to represent divine epiphanies: beauty, dazzling light, wondrousness, and *enargeia* (the clear presence of a god or goddess).[104] As Petridou has shown, epiphanies feature "the extreme, unbridled beauty, magnitude, and radiance of the god," and they appear as "wondrous."[105] Take, for example, Demeter's epiphany in the *Homeric Hymn to Demeter*. The goddess radiates with light as she reveals herself to the royal women in Eleusis: "a light shone from the immortal body of the goddess, and her golden hair spread down over her shoulders, and the firm house was filled with brightness like a bolt of lightning" (τῆλε δὲ φέγγος ἀπὸ χροὸς ἀθανάτοιο λάμπε θεᾶς, ξανθαὶ δὲ κόμαι κατενήνοθεν ὤμους, αὐγῆς δ᾽ ἐπλήσθη πυκινὸς δόμος ἀστεροπῆς ὥς; *HH* 2.278–81). At the same time, Demeter shakes off her disguise and "beauty breathed around her" (περί τ᾽ ἀμφί τε κάλλος ἄητο; 276). Again, in the *Homeric Hymn to Aphrodite*, the goddess appears to Anchises as "clad in a robe that shone more brightly than the light of fire and the most beautiful necklaces were around her tender throat–beautiful, golden, and richly variegated–and [the robe] radiated like the moon over her tender breasts, a wonder to behold" (πέπλον μὲν γὰρ ἔεστο φαεινότερον πυρὸς αὐγῆς . . . ὅρμοι, δ᾽ ἀμφ᾽ ἀπαλῇ δειρῇ περικαλλέες ἦσαν καλοὶ χρύσειοι παμποίκιλοι· ὡς δὲ σελήνη στήθεσιν ἀμφ᾽ ἀπαλοῖσιν ἐλάμπετο, θαῦμα ἰδέσθαι; *HH* 5.86–91). In this same hymn, "the cheeks [of Aphrodite] shone with ambrosial beauty" (κάλλος δὲ παρειάων ἀπέλαμπεν ἄμβροτον; *HH* 5.174–5). In these passages, the goddesses "shine" with radiant light.[106] The body of a god or goddess has a "wondrous" appearance.

Plato's discourse on the true earth features the poetic language of divine epiphanies. Let me give a few examples. "These things [on the true earth] are fully revealed (*ekphanê*), being abundant and large and everywhere, so that the earth is a sight for blessed spectators to behold." The air-ocean

---

that Plato, in this portion of the dialogue, is exploring the meaning of beauty, for instance by asking us to conceive of the Beautiful – its Idea and highest reality – by means of the imagination. Another possibility is that he is pointing out the inherent paradoxes in any attempt to do so." Porter treats Plato in terms of the aesthetics of the sublime rather than in theological terms (though he does note the "sacral" aspects of this myth).

[104] Platt 2011: 56–65; Petridou 2015: 36–7; see also Pfister 1924 on the key terminology that the Greeks used for epiphanic encounters.

[105] Petridou 2015: 36.

[106] On the discourse of radiance in archaic Greek texts, see Prier 1989: 50–9.

"glitters with light" (*stilbonta*; 110b). Colors are "wondrous in their beauty" (*thaumastên kallos*; 110c). The mountains and stones look "diaphanous" in the light (*diaphaneian*; 110d). Everything on earth sparkles in the "true light of the sun" (*to alêthinon phôs*; 109e). However, Plato uses this language for the entire region of the true earth, rather than for a single divine being. The true earth and its aethereal environs radiate "everywhere" (*pantachou*) with luminous beauty.

Plato gave a great deal of thought to beauty. As we have seen in earlier chapters, physical beauty has an immediate and pleasurable presence – one responds to this as soon as one sees it. However, beauty also has an aspect that we have not discussed: its presence to the beholder has a futural aspect. The person who sees beauty feels that it promises something more. As Nehamas has suggested, beauty offers a promise of happiness (though it does not generally deliver on this).[107] The experience of beauty creates a desire for something more. At the simplest level, a person who sees bodily beauty will want to see the same object day after day and have the same pleasure. But this experience can stoke one's desire for even greater beauties and pleasures. Plato created the plenitude of the aethereal realm as a way of promising something beyond it. He makes this clear by using comparative adjectives, emphasizing that objects in the aether are "more beautiful" than things below in the sea and air, and pointing to beings in a higher realm that are "more beautiful" than those in the aether (109b–110a, 110b–c, 110d–111b, 114c). The beauty of the aethereal region serves as a sort of placeholder for a higher and more divine beauty.

Rather than representing the philosophers on the true earth as seeing an epiphany of divine Beauty itself, as he does in the *Symposium* and *Phaedrus*, Plato offers a visual image that evokes the divine Form of Beauty but does not fully reveal it. His myth gestures towards a full (intelligible) epiphanic vision of the Form of Beauty. Plato gives the reader a visual image that points to the fullness and everlasting presence of divine Beauty. As we have seen, the divine aethereal region is the second-best place for the philosophic soul to dwell in. For Socrates mentions a higher and more beautiful realm than the one in the aether – the realm of the Forms (114c). Still, Plato gives the philosophers in the aethereal region a blessed status: "they see the sun, moon, and stars as they really are, and in all other ways their blessedness follows upon this" (τόν γε ἥλιον καὶ σελήνην καὶ ἄστρα ὁρᾶσθαι ὑπ' αὐτῶν οἷα τυγχάνει ὄντα, καὶ τὴν ἄλλην εὐδαιμονίαν τούτων ἀκόλουθον εἶναι; 111c). In this upper region, the philosophers see the heavenly bodies –

---

[107] Nehamas 2010.

the outer edges of the physical universe – in a true way, and this makes them blessed. This aethereal region, then, marks the last step for the philosophic soul before it perfects itself and leaves the bodily realm altogether. The philosophers can see and hear the gods in this region, and the gods themselves dwell in their temples. But this is not the highest realm in Plato's philosophy, and the gods are not the highest divinities.

CHAPTER 4

Wings of Desire

Glory be to God for dappled things –
    For skies of couple-colour as a brinded cow;
        For rose-moles all in stipple upon trout that swim;
Fresh-firecoal chestnut-falls; finches' wings;
        Landscape plotted and pieced – fold, fallow, and plough;
        And all trades, their gear and tackle and trim.

All things counter, original, spare, strange;
    Whatever is fickle, freckled (who knows how?)
        With swift, slow; sweet, sour; adazzle, dim;
He fathers-forth whose beauty is past change:
                Praise him.
                                    –Hopkins, "Pied Beauty"

But when I am consumed in the fire,
Give me new Phoenix wings to fly at my desire.
    –Keats, "On Sitting Down to Read King Lear Once Again"

In the *Phaedrus*, Plato composes another dialogue on love and beauty. Once again, he foregrounds metaphysical desire and shows how it lifts the soul to the Form of Beauty. He also represents the philosopher seeing an epiphany of divine Beauty. However, Plato offers a different conception of the soul in this text than he did in the *Symposium*: the soul is immortal, tripartite, and self-moving (245c–e). As the only "self-moving" entity in the cosmos, the soul initiates the motion in bodies. In addition, all souls have eros for the Forms, including the gods (who are divine souls). Because the gods themselves possess eros, I will refer to philosophic eros as "divine desire." Finally, in the *Phaedrus*, the divine souls of the gods govern the physical cosmos and play an important role in human life. This dialogue thus anticipates Plato's cosmology in the *Timaeus*.[1] In this

---

[1] See also *Laws* 10, which does not set forth a full cosmology, but focuses on souls as self-movers and argues that a divine soul moves and rules the cosmos.

chapter, I present a detailed discussion of the soul, focusing in particular on reason, eros, and the soul's relation to the gods and the Forms.

The *Phaedrus* features something we have not seen in earlier dialogues: it is replete with local divinities and the myths that surround them. Let me give a few examples. First, Socrates and Phaedrus have their conversation in a "sacred place" outside the city walls that has a shrine and an altar for the nymphs and the river Ilissus (aka Achelous). Second, Socrates mentions the altar of the wind god Boreas, located nearby, and discusses the Athenian myth of Boreas and Oreithuia. Later in the dialogue, Socrates claims that he has been "inspired by the nymphs" (*nympholeptos*). Finally, after his second speech, Socrates says that Pan and the river nymphs granted him the "art of speech" that enabled him to deliver the palinode. As I argue, Plato puts Socrates in a sacred placed filled with local Greek divinities to anticipate his theological discourse on the divine souls and the Forms in the palinode (Socrates' second speech in the dialogue). The local gods discussed in the early part of the dialogue proleptically anticipate the palinode, which presents the true divine beings in Plato's metaphysics.

Since the *Phaedrus* focuses on gods and divine beings, it is no surprise that Plato uses a good deal of mythic discourse in this text. Indeed, at the opening of the dialogue, he offers a small meditation on myth. We find this in Socrates and Phaedrus' discussion of the myth of the north-wind god Boreas. The two men sit down near an altar of Boreas that marked the place where, according to the Athenians, Boreas seized the maiden Oreithuia and snatched her into the heavens. Socrates asks whether they should follow the sophists who have naturalized this myth, claiming that a gust of wind blew Oreithuia over the rocks to her death. Socrates rejects this idea because it would mean naturalizing all the myths about the gods, which would effectively rob the world of gods and eliminate a great deal of mythic discourse. In this passage, Plato effectively valorizes myth and affirms the idea that a god can possess a human being. I analyze this scene and show that the myth itself contains an allegory of the soul's descent to a lower status due to its attachment to written texts. Even the spare, naturalized version of the myth – a gust of wind blows Oreithuia, who is playing with Pharmakeia, down over the rocks to her death – takes on new meaning when one sees its hidden allegory. As I argue, Plato takes a seemingly literal statement and turns it into a mythic story about the soul and its possible ascent or descent.

These early references to divine possession set up Socrates' discourse on divine inspiration (*mania*) in the palinode. In this speech, Socrates mentions four groups of people driven to madness by divine inspiration: priests/priestesses inspired by gods at oracular centers; people inspired in the Dionysian mystery cult; poets inspired by the Muses; and philosophers inspired by Eros. The ancient Greeks believed that either divine inspiration or natural causes could cause madness. In the case of divine inspiration, the gods could drive humans mad either to help or punish them. In this dialogue, Socrates focuses exclusively on the beneficial aspects of divinely inspired madness. To explicate this idea, I offer a detailed discussion of how the Greeks conceived of divine inspiration in oracular, poetic, and telestic contexts. As we will see, a god could alter an individual's ordinary rational capacity, albeit in different ways. I interpret Plato's notion of the philosopher possessed by eros in the context of these traditional modes of divine inspiration. As I argue, the love-maddened philosopher takes on a higher level of reason: eros does not obstruct his mind but rather enhances it.

I will also discuss the philosopher's epiphany of the divine Form of Beauty. Plato presents a detailed narrative of the soul's epiphany of the Form of Beauty. Indeed, he sets forth two epiphanic narratives in which the soul sees the Forms: in the first narrative, the soul sees the Forms before incarnation; in the second, the philosophic lover beholds the Form of Beauty as he looks at his beautiful beloved. As I argue, Plato borrows language from poetic accounts of epiphany to showcase the idea that the philosopher's vision of the Forms is epiphanic. In addition, he compares the soul's vision of the Forms to the highest initiate seeing a god in the Eleusinian Mysteries. In short, Plato uses two divinity-markers to present the idea that the philosopher sees an epiphany when he beholds the Form of Beauty: the Poetic Narratives of Epiphany divinity-marker and the Eleusinian Mysteries divinity-marker.

Finally, I analyze Socrates' assertions that he must speak "piously" and "truthfully" about divine beings, both the gods and the Forms. Given Plato's claim that the Forms are divine and the gods are perfectly good, he must offer a new mode of discourse for speaking about divinity. Just as the Greeks paid careful attention to speaking "piously" about the gods, Plato showcases the right and wrong ways of talking about divine beings.

4.1   The Soul

How does Plato conceive of the soul in this dialogue? First, he treats the soul as tripartite. Plato had already presented the tripartite soul in the *Republic*: there, he distinguishes between the rational part (*to logistikon*), the spirited part (*to thumoeides*), and the appetitive part (*to epithumêtikon*). The "spirited part" features emotions such as anger, righteous indignation, pride, and the love of honor; the "appetitive part" features desires for bodily pleasure and money.[2] Plato does not, however, place eros squarely in the appetitive part of the soul in the *Republic*. Rather, he speaks of eros in a rather incoherent way: at times, he identifies it as lust, which belongs in the appetite part of the soul (439d, 572e–573a); at other times, he identifies it as the philosophic desire for the Forms (490a–b). Plato presents a clearer picture of eros in the *Phaedrus*, representing it as the mind's metaphysical desire for the Forms. Eros does not belong in the appetitive part of the soul; rather, it is an aspect of the rational part of the soul. This raises the question whether the "rational part of the soul" is exclusively rational. In my view, we cannot identify Plato's erotic mind as "pure reason." Plato's conception of "reason" was richer and more complex than our own. I will continue to use the phrase "rational part of the soul" with the caveat that this includes eros.

In his mythic discourse on the tripartite soul, Plato represents the tripartite soul as a charioteer (reason) driving a pair of horses, one white (spirit) and one black (appetite). But he adds a dazzling new feature to the soul: wings. As I will argue, the wings represent the soul's metaphysical desire for the Forms. In adding wings to the rational part of the soul, Plato goes beyond the basic theory of the tripartite soul. In addition, this image of the soul applies to the gods as well as humans: divine and human souls all have a charioteer, two horses, and wings (although the divine souls, unlike the human soul, are perfect). Plato specifically identifies the wings with Eros. To cite one passage here, Socrates says that "mortals refer to him as winged Eros (*erota … potênon*), but the gods call him 'Winged' (*Pteros*) because of the necessity for the growth of wings" (252c). In the classical period, the Greeks represented Eros as winged in statuary and vase paintings.[3] We have a great deal of visual evidence from this period, and there can be little doubt that Plato had seen these images.[4]

Plato's charioteer-equine-avian image of the soul reflects his idea of the soul as "self-moving." Indeed, mobility plays an important role in this text. Plato even offers a proof of the immortality of the soul by referring to its self-motion. As Socrates states: the soul is the first principle of motion (*archê kinêseôs*) in the cosmos; bodies cannot move themselves but must be moved by souls; if souls stopped moving, then the whole cosmos would come to a standstill; since the cosmos continues to move, the soul is

---

[2] On Plato's conception of the soul in the *Republic*, see Robinson 1970; Annas 1981: 109–52; Bobonich 2002: 216–373; Lorenz 2006: 9–53.

[3] See Stafford 2013 for a discussion of the statues and vase paintings in the classical period.

[4] See Carson 1998 for a beautiful account of Eros in ancient Greece.

ungenerated and indestructible (245d–e). By identifying "self-motion" as the "essence" (*ousia*) of the soul, Plato views the soul in terms of its mobility (245e). For this reason, his image of the tripartite soul features mobile elements – the chariot, the horses, and the wings. The charioteer guides the soul in different directions, the horses move the soul forward, and the wings move it upwards.

Let us look more closely at the wings. As Socrates states, the Forms nurture both the charioteer and the wings: "The reason for the [soul's] eagerness to behold the plane of truth in its own region is that the fitting pasture for the best part of the soul comes from the meadow there, and the nature of the wing, by which the soul is lifted up, is nourished by this" (οὗ δ' ἕνεχ' ἡ πολλὴ σπουδὴ τὸ ἀληθείας ἰδεῖν πεδίον οὗ ἐστιν, ἥ τε δὴ προσήκουσα ψυχῆς τῷ ἀρίστῳ νομὴ ἐκ τοῦ ἐκεῖ λειμῶνος τυγχάνει οὖσα, ἥ τε τοῦ πτεροῦ φύσις, ᾧ ψυχὴ κουφίζεται, τούτῳ τρέφεται; 248b–c). Since the mind and wings feed on the Forms, they are necessarily allied to one another: eros is the metaphysical desire of the rational part of the soul.[5] Clearly, the wings give the soul an upward mobility. Indeed, the only job of the wings is to lift the soul up to the Forms. Since the wings (as well as reason) get nourishment from the Forms, we can say that the Forms fuel eros. Indeed, the rational contemplation of the Forms has the effect of heightening philosophic eros. Metaphysical desire does not slacken when the rational part of the soul sees the Forms; rather, eros yearns for them even more.

Plato's image of the wings lifting the mind up to the Forms clearly identifies the wings with the rational part of the soul. Indeed, Socrates refers to the soul of the gods as winged: "being perfect and winged, the soul (of a god) moves through the heavens and governs the whole cosmos" (τελέα μὲν οὖν οὖσα καὶ ἐπτερωμένη μετεωροπορεῖ τε καὶ πάντα τὸν κόσμον διοικεῖ; 246b–c). The gods rule the cosmos by way of their perfect reason. In addition, since the gods have wings, they must feel metaphysical desire for the Forms. For this reason, I identify eros in this dialogue as "divine desire." Plato thus moves beyond the "daimonic desire" of the *Symposium*. In the *Phaedrus*, eros is a fully divine element in the rational part of the soul.

In this dialogue, Plato conceives of the human soul as immortal and godlike. I say "godlike" because the souls, in their preincarnate state, traveled with the gods and engaged in the same rational activities as they did. In this early period of its life, the soul had a near-divine status. On

[5] To be sure, Plato offers inconsistent accounts of the location of the wings on the soul – he refers to the whole soul as feathered (251b), the horses as winged (256a), and the mind alone as winged (249c). Since he presents this idea in mythic discourse, we bump into a surplus of meaning.

earth, the philosopher can "become like god" by practicing philosophy and contemplating the Forms. Indeed, Plato indicates that the gods themselves are divine by virtue of their nearness to the Forms (249c). Of course the human soul does not have the perfection of the souls of the gods. The human soul has the rational capacity of the gods, but it can become better or worse depending on whether its reason can control the lower parts.

Plato also gives the human soul a story in the *Phaedrus*. He does this by way of a mythic narrative of the philosophic soul. As we have seen, in the *Symposium*, Plato presented a short narrative of a philosophic soul ascending the Ladder of Love and seeing an epiphany of the divine Form of Beauty. In that dialogue, however, he identified the soul as mortal. Once Plato conceived of the soul as immortal, he developed what I have called the "story of the soul." He had to impose a structure and plot on the interminable life of the soul. In the *Phaedo*, as I argued, the soul first lives in a preincarnate state in which it contemplates the Forms; it then falls into a human body and enters the cycle of incarnation; the perfected philosophic soul departs the body altogether and contemplates the Forms for the rest of time. Plato based this story of the soul on the Orphic myths. In the *Phaedrus*, he develops his own story: this has a similar structure as the one in the *Phaedo*, but it differs in some key ways.

In the first chapter of this story of the soul, Plato depicts the human souls living in a preincarnate state. Each of them follows a god and travels with it to the "edge" of the heaven (the fixed stars). There, the charioteer beholds the incorporeal realm of the Forms (248a). However, in contrast to the divine souls, human souls have unruly horses, and these impede the charioteer from contemplating the Forms. For this reason, the human souls cannot see the Forms properly: some souls see the Forms with difficulty, others not at all (248a–b). Of course the soul has not yet entered a human body, so it is hard to understand how its spirited and appetitive parts operate.

In the *Phaedo*, Plato modeled his story of the soul on the Orphic myths that ascribed the original sin of the human souls to their birth from the impious Titans. The souls have to pay a penalty for this crime by being imprisoned in a mortal body. Plato did not adopt the notion that the soul has a titanic ancestry, but he did represent the soul as falling into the prison of the body and entering the cycle of reincarnation. Unfortunately, he did not offer an account of the imperfection or original sin of the human soul. In his account of the preincarnate human soul in the *Phaedrus*, Plato gives several reasons for the imperfection of the soul: the "badness of the charioteer" (κακίᾳ ἡνιόχων; 248b), and the intense desires of the black horse, "the horse that has a share in badness" (ὁ τῆς κάκης ἵππος μετέχων; 247b). Indeed, even in this preincarnate state, the black horse "weighs [the soul] down, making it heavy and inclining it down toward the earth, for whatever charioteer whose [bad horse] is not well trained" (βρίθει γὰρ ὁ τῆς κάκης ἵππος μετέχων, ἐπὶ τὴν γῆν ῥέπων τε καὶ βαρύνων ᾧ μὴ καλῶς ἦν τεθραμμένος τῶν ἡνιόχων; 247b). The appetitive part of the soul already longs for a body down below on earth. In the human souls, then, the charioteer faces difficulty controlling the appetitive part of the soul.

In Plato's mythic narrative of the preincarnate human soul, the charioteers-cum-horses of the souls trample other souls in the heavens, breaking the legs and wings of the souls. As Socrates puts it, the soul, "suffering some misfortune and being filled with forgetfulness and evil, is weighed down, and growing heavy, it loses its wings and falls to earth" (τινι συντυχίᾳ χρησαμένη λήθης τε καὶ κακίας πλησθεῖσα βαρυνθῇ, βαρυνθεῖσα δὲ πτερορρυήσῃ τε καὶ ἐπὶ τὴν γῆν πέσῃ; 248c). Plato does not identify the "misfortune" that causes the fall of the soul to earth. At any rate, when the souls fall from the gods and enter a mortal body, they lose most of their wings. However, a "root" (rhiza) and "stalk" (kaulos) of the wings remains in the soul and can regrow. Later in the palinode, Plato portrays a philosophic lover beginning to grow back his wings as his vision of the beauty of his boyfriend leads him to recollect and see the Form of Beauty (251a–e).

In the final chapter of the story of the soul, the philosopher has the opportunity to return to his original life with the gods. Plato represents this in terms of the philosopher's soul regaining its wings. When the soul has regrown its wings, it will return to the gods (256b). As Socrates states, the soul that lives as a philosopher in three successive lives will become fully winged and leave the cycle of reincarnation (249a). And even philosophic lovers who have not fully controlled their sexual appetites have "now begun to go on their hyperouranion journey" to the Forms (ἐλθεῖν τοῖς κατηργμένοις ἤδη τῆς ὑπουρανίου πορείας; 256d).[6] They have started to regain their wings. Indeed, a soul that has lived an excellent philosophic life and been able to exercise control over its appetites will be "light and winged" (256b). Plato does not offer a full-blown eschatology in this text, but he does represent the souls as receiving punishment after each life and moving to another body (human or animal) during the next round of incarnation (249a–b; 257a). Not surprisingly, this story of the soul has

[6] In 247c, Plato uses the word hyperouranion to indicate the realm of the Forms.

a happy ending for the philosophers: they can leave the body and journey back to the Forms.

4.2 Divine Encounters in the *Phaedrus*

In the opening scene of the *Phaedrus*, Socrates and Phaedrus discuss a myth about a god who seized a maiden. Here, Plato offers a brief but important meditation on myth. Consider first the place where Socrates and Phaedrus converse, a "beautiful" (*pankalon*, 230b) spot outside the city walls along the Ilissus river. They enter a sacred place that has a shrine for the nymphs and the river-god:[7] as Socrates observes, "based on the female figurines (*korai*) and statues (*agalmata*), this place appears to be sacred (*hieron*) to the nymphs and the river" (230b). Socrates also notes that there is an altar nearby of Boreas, the wind-god that snatched Oreithuia and took her up to the heavens (according to the myth, she gave birth to the winged "Boreads," 229c). In short, this natural area has been ritually marked out as sacred to various deities. As Susan Cole has shown, for the Greeks, "the landscape was a living world, alive with the possibility of divinity."[8] Indeed, each Greek city-state marked out specific places as belonging to the gods by creating shrines and surrounding them with mythic narratives:

> Geographically based narratives, probably as old as the institutions they claim to explain, locate the individual community in its landscape and connect it to mythic representations of the larger universe. Anthropomorphic representations of divinity and personifications of features of the natural world encouraged the belief that the world of the gods and the world of nature were parts of a single continuum.[9]

In the *Phaedrus*, Socrates and Phaedrus sit down in a holy spot that features this "continuum" between the gods and nature.

Once they arrive in this sacred place, Socrates and Phaedrus engage in a discussion of the myth of the wind god Boreas snatching up and raping Oreithuia. The story of Boreas and Oreithuia had particular importance for the Athenians: in their civic theology, Boreas had "married" the

---

[7] Note that, in going to this "sacred place" outside the walls, Socrates is *atopos* (out of place). As Phaedrus says: "You are the most out of place (ἀτοπώτατός) man. Indeed you are like a stranger being guided around (ξεναγουμένῳ) and someone who is not from our country (οὐκ ἐπιχωρίῳ)" (230c–d). While Phaedrus attributes Socrates' unfamiliarity with the locale to the fact that he never leaves the city, we can attribute his out-of-placeness to the fact that his soul is at home in the region of the Forms (the *hyperouraios topos*). For discussions of this topic, see Griswold 1986: 21–5; Nightingale 2004: 157–8.

[8] Cole 2004: 14–15.   [9] Cole 2004: 21–2.

Athenian maiden Oreithuia and was thus a divine relative and helper of
Athens.[10] The Athenians had set up the altar for Boreas on the Ilissus River
because the god had responded to their prayers during wartime, providing
divine aid in two important battles.[11] The Athenians took this story very
seriously. Indeed, Aeschylus wrote a satyr play on Boreas and Oreithuia
(*Oreithuia*) and Sophocles also wrote a play on this topic (Strabo 7.3.1). In
the *Phaedrus*, then, Socrates and Phaedrus enter a place full of local
divinities to whom the Athenians have ascribed specific myths and
accounts. As we will see, the local divinities in this place play an important
role in the dialogue.

Let us examine Socrates' and Phaedrus' discussion of the myth of Boreas
and Oreithuia.[12] Phaedrus asks whether the story that Boreas seized
(ἁρπάσαι) Oreithuia and impregnated her with divine children is in fact
true (229c). Socrates responds:

> If I disbelieved, as the *sophoi* do, it would not be strange. Then I could say,
> offering a rational explanation (σοφιζόμενος), that a blast of the north wind
> pushed her down (κατά) over the nearby rocks when she was playing with
> Pharmakeia and then, having died in this way, she was said to have been
> snatched upward (ἀνάρπαστον) by the god Boreas. (229c–d)

Here, some unnamed "wise men" reduce the story of a divine–human
encounter to an event caused by natural elements. Socrates, by contrast,
"agrees with the customary account" (πειθόμενος δὲ τῷ νομιζομένῳ) of
Boreas and Oreithuia, and rejects the naturalistic approach to this story. As
he claims, the *sophoi* who use this approach must offer the same account of
"hordes" of gods such as the centaurs, Gorgon, Pegasus, Chimaera, and
other divine beings (229c–230a). In short, if one naturalizes a single story
about a god, one will have to do this for all the divinities. Indeed, the
naturalist interpretation effectively empties the world of divine and semi-
divine beings. In opposing the naturalistic account, Socrates objects to
a hermeneutic strategy that is rooted in a materialist conception of the
cosmos.

The naturalistic approach to stories of divinity not only raises questions
about the existence of the gods but also about the proper discourse to use in
discussing the nature of the gods and the cosmos. In the *Phaedrus*, Plato
identifies the gods as perfectly good and rational and considers the Forms

---

[10] See Herodotus 7.189 and Pausanias 1.19.5 for discussions of this Athenian myth.
[11] As Herodotus 7.189.3 indicates.
[12] For good discussions of the Boreas/Oreithuia scene, see Ferrari 1986: 9–12; Griswold 1986: 36–44;
Werner 2014: 19–38. These scholars do not discuss the theological aspects of this scene.

as the highest divinities in the universe. It is no surprise, then, that he opposes the men who offer naturalistic interpretations of stories about the gods. These interpreters effectively eliminate both the divine objects of the philosopher's quest (the gods and the Forms) as well as the linguistic medium that has the capacity to represent this realm (mythic discourse).[13] In Plato's view, the naturalistic interpretation is precisely the wrong way to talk about the cosmos and its divine beings. Indeed, the reduction of the gods to mere natural forces marks an "impious" use of language. The discussion of Boreas and Oreithuia, then, deals directly with the question of how to speak correctly about the gods.

4.3 Naturalistic and Allegorical Interpretations of the Boreas and Oreithuia Myth

In Socrates' statements on Boreas and Oreithuia, Plato encodes an allegory that anticipates the ideas about the gods, souls, and Forms set forth in the palinode. This allegory offers important material on Plato's conception of mythic discourse and his notion of divine inspiration in the palinode. As I suggest, Plato offers an allegory of both versions of the Boreas–Oreithuia encounter, i.e., (1) the customary story of Boreas and Oreithuia, and (2) the naturalized version of the story. In the customary story (1), Oreithuia was "snatched upwards (ἀνάρπαστον) by Boreas" and impregnated with divine children (229c–d). The men who naturalize this account view the customary story as (2) something that people "said" (λεχθῆναι) to dress up in mythic terms the "natural fact" that "a blast of the north wind pushed Oreithuia downwards (κατά) over the nearby rocks to her death when she was playing with Pharmakeia" (229d). Socrates uses the language of "up" (*ana*) and "down" (*kata*) in his discourse on the customary and naturalized accounts of the Boreas/Oreithuia story. As we will see, this terminology forms the framework for the allegory.

I want to look first at the customary account of Boreas' divine seizure and possession of Oreithuia ((1) above). Here, we can see an allegorical figuration of Eros "seizing" and "possessing" the love-mad philosopher and lifting him "upwards" to the higher realm of the Forms (247c). In the palinode, Socrates describes a philosophic soul on earth inspired by Eros in "the best of all possible divine inspirations" (αὕτη πασῶν τῶν ἐνθουσιάσεων ἀρίστη; 249d–e). Eros brings about the love-madness by

---

[13] Of course these naturalistic interpreters do not acknowledge the existence of Forms. Still, by eliminating the gods, they effectively get rid of divine beings.

which "someone, when seeing beauty here and recollecting true beauty, becomes feathered and raises his wings, longing to fly upwards" (ἤν ὅταν τὸ τῆδέ τις ὁρῶν κάλλος, τοῦ ἀληθοῦς ἀναμιμνησκόμενος, πτερῶταί τε καὶ ἀναπτερούμενος προθυμούμενος ἀναπτέσθαι; 249c, see also 253a). Eros "seizes" the philosopher's soul (ληφθεὶς, 252c3; ὅταν ὑπ᾽ Ἔρωτος ἁλῶσι, c5–6) and moves it upwards, just as Boreas "snatched Oreithuia upwards" (*anarpaston*).[14]

Socrates uses the terminology of "upwards" and "downwards" quite extensively in the palinode. Consider his portrayal of the preincarnate human souls who follow the gods up to the realm of the Forms:

> The souls travel upwards (πρὸς ἄναντες) to the vault of the heavens, where the chariots of the gods, being evenly balanced and controlled by the reins, travel with ease. But the others [soul-chariots] travel with difficulty: for the horse that has a share in badness weighs the soul down (βρίθει), making it heavy (βαρύνων) and inclining (ῥέπων) it down toward the earth. (247a–b)[15]

Some human souls fared better than others and were able to get a good look at the Forms: "the [human] soul that followed the god successfully and likened itself to god, raised up (ὑπερῆρεν) the head of its charioteer to the outer region" and there saw the "higher" realities (ἄνω; 248a). Even when the philosophic soul lives on earth, it can have this vision if it is seized by eros for a beautiful boy and regrows its wings: this will allow it to ascend to the divine Forms. In my view, the customary story of Boreas "snatching Oreithuia upwards" to the heavens contains an allegorical figuration of the philosophic soul seized by Eros and lifted up to the Forms.

I turn now to the naturalized version of the myth, where the north wind blows the maiden down over the rocks while she is playing with Pharmakeia ((2) above). As I argue, this contains an allegory of the fall of the soul that occupies itself with writing. Plato uses the term *pharmakon* in this dialogue exclusively in association with writing (230d6, 268c, 274e). Indeed, right after the Boreas/Oreithuia passage above, Socrates says that Phaedrus has lured him outside the city walls with a *pharmakon* that he identifies as "discourses written in books" (λόγους οὕτω προτείνων ἐν βιβλίοις; 230d). In my view, Plato chose the name Pharmakeia in order to link this scene to his notion of writing as

---

[14] For discussions of Plato's different conceptions of inspiration (prophetic, telestic, poetic, and erotic) in the *Phaedrus*, see Verdenius 1962: 134–40; Ferrari 1986: 140–90; Griswold 1986: 70–85; Rowe 1990; Mikalson 2010: 110–39; Morgan 2010a.

[15] See also the double reference to the soul's heavy weight, which pulls the soul down to earth: the soul "became heavy and weighed down" (βαρυνθῇ, βαρυνθεῖσα; 248c).

a *pharmakon* (scholars have not found any evidence of a character called Pharmakeia in antique lore). If we identify Pharmakeia as an allegorical figure of writing, then we can claim that the person who plays with the narcotic of the written word will fall into the realm of the dead. The naturalized reading of the Boreas/Oreithuia story, then, contains a clever allegory. For, in the seemingly natural event of the wind blowing the girl off the rocks to her death, Plato encodes an allegory of the fall of the soul due to its addiction to the narcotic of writing.

Let me offer evidence for this claim. In the discussion of writing later in the dialogue, Socrates suggests that writing contains words that are effectively dead. He begins with the comparison of the written text to a painting:

> Writing has this unusual effect, and is in truth similar to painting. For the offspring of painting stand there as though they are alive (ὡς ζῶντα), but if you ask them a question, they maintain a solemn silence. The same is the case with written texts. You would think that they speak as though they possessed knowledge, but if you ask a question about something, wishing to learn, they indicate one thing alone, the same thing again and again. (275d)

Like the painting, the written text seems as though it is alive but in fact sets forth words that say the same thing repeatedly. They cannot speak as a living person. Socrates makes the connection between writing and death even more clearly in his farmer/gardener analogy. Here, Socrates compares the written text to the gardens of Adonis used in the festival of the Adonia (276b). In this festival, women planted little gardens in pots, let the seeds push up their first green shoots, and then threw them into springs to celebrate the dying god Adonis.[16] In the gardens of Adonis, then, the seedlings die before they bear fruit. As Socrates claims, only the spoken word has "seeds" (ἔχοντες σπέρμα) that grow in other souls and bear fruit, whereas the seeds of written texts "do not bear fruit" (ἄκαρποι; 277a) and thus end up dying. In this passage about writing, then, Socrates identifies the written word as dead discourse. This bolsters my allegorical reading of the naturalist interpretation of the Boreas/Oreithuia myth: like Oreithuia falling down to her death while playing with Pharmakeia, the soul who spends time with the narcotic of writing encounters dead discourse that pulls him downwards and away from the Forms.

---

[16] As the paroemiographer Zenobius explains, the gardens "... are sown in clay vessels and grow only to the point of becoming green; they are carried away along with the dying god and are thrown into springs" (Zenobius 1.49; Leutsch/Schneidewin 1965: 19). On the Adonia festival, see Detienne 1977: 64–6, 78–80; Winkler 1990: 189–93.

We also see this "fall of the soul" in Socrates' account of writing in the Egyptian tale. There, in the character of Thamus, Socrates says that "[writing] will produce forgetfulness in the souls of its learners because they will neglect to exercise their memory (*mnêmê*); indeed, on account of the faith they place in writing they will recollect (*anamimnêskomenos*) things by way of alien marks external to them and not from within, themselves by themselves" (275a).[17] As we will see, memory plays a critical role in the philosopher's contemplation of the Forms: the act of recollection allows the embodied human soul to have a vision of the Forms. Socrates' claim that writing implants dead discourse in the soul and thus damages the memory offers yet more evidence that attaching oneself to written texts will bring about the "fall" of one's soul.

Finally, my allegorized reading of the naturalist version of the story plays an important role in the drama of Socrates and Phaedrus. Phaedrus has brought with him a written speech of Lysias that argues that a beautiful boy should grant sexual favors to a non-lover. Clearly, Phaedrus is entranced by Lysias' speech; indeed, he has spent the whole morning going over it and is attempting to memorize it (228a–b). Like Oreithuia, then, Phaedrus is "playing with pharmakeia," i.e., the *pharmakon* of writing. Phaedrus' attachment to the written word will drag his soul down if he carries on with this addiction. First, it will prevent him from being seized by Eros and swept upwards towards heaven (as Boreas sweeps Oreithuia up in the customary story). And, as Socrates states, there will be severe punishments for the person who attaches himself to written discourses like that of Lysias: his soul will "roll around on earth for 9000 years and then will live without reason (*anous*) beneath the earth (ὑπὸ γῆς) in Hades" (257a; see also 249a). As this passage indicates, the man addicted to writing will end up in the realm of the dead.

It is worth noting that others have found an allegory in this Boreas–Oreithuia passage. The Platonic scholiast Hermias of Alexandria, for example, offers a detailed allegorical reading of this story, and ends with the following claim:

> Let Oreithuia, then, be the soul of Phaedrus, and let Socrates be Boreas, snatching him and carrying him down (καταφέρων) towards a choiceworthy death. I say "carrying him down" (καταφέρων) and not "carrying him up" (ἀναφέρων) because if the soul is not humbled in an extraordinary way, it could not allow itself to be carried upwards.[18]

[17] For a detailed discussion of the passage on writing in the *Phaedrus*, see Nightingale 2013: 243–64.
[18] Hermias von Alexandrien, *In Platonis Phaedrum Scholia*, ed. P. Couvreur (Hildesheim/New York 1971) 28–9.

Although I read the story differently from Hermias, I agree that the question of being carried upwards or downwards has important philosophical and theological ramifications. For, in Socrates' second speech, Eros snatches and possesses the philosophical soul so that it moves up towards the Forms. This happens when the love-maddened philosopher remembers the Form of Beauty and begins to regrow his wings (more on this below). In addition, by planting an allegory in the spare, naturalized reading of the myth, Plato takes a simple literal claim and gives it a mythic and philosophical depth.

One does not need to pick up on this allegory to understand Plato's valorization of myth in this dialogue. Even in a straightforward reading of the Boreas/Oreithuia scene, one can see that Plato rejects a literal and materialist account of cosmos. To set forth his theological ideas, he cannot use literal language or even analytic argumentation. Plato needs myth to convey the idea that the gods move the cosmos by contemplating the Forms. Likewise, he must use myth to give the human soul a divine status and to represent the relation of the soul to the cosmic gods and the divine Forms.[19]

4.4 Nympholepsy

Plato creates two dramas in this text: in the main drama, Socrates and Phaedrus find a sacred place where they can converse; in the cosmic drama in the palinode, the souls of the gods and humans fly to the edge of the universe to grasp the Forms. These two dramas reinforce each other. To cite a few examples, in the main drama, Socrates and Phaedrus go outside the walls of Athens; in the cosmic drama, the souls go beyond the physical boundaries of heaven to contemplate the *hyperouranion* realm of the Forms. In the main drama, Socrates speaks about gods who have inspired humans (including, as he claims, himself); in the cosmic drama, Eros inspires the philosopher to ascend to the Forms. The events in the main drama, then, anticipate and reflect higher truths about the soul and the Forms.[20]

Let us look first at the main drama. As we have seen, Plato places Socrates in a "sacred place" outside the city walls (*hieron topon*, 230b–c; *theios topos*, 238d). He thus signals that this place is the site of possible divine inspiration

---

[19] For excellent accounts of Plato's mythic discourses in the *Phaedrus*, see Ferrari 1986: Chapter 5; Griswold 1986: Chapter 4; Morgan 2000: 155–241; Werner 2014.

[20] Of course, the local drama of Socrates and Phaedrus has many features that we do not find in the discourse on the soul and Forms in the palinode. Indeed, the local drama offers many important ideas that fall outside of Plato's metaphysics. In particular, they discuss topics about humans' social and political life on earth, including their false opinions and base desires.

and epiphanies. As Petridou has shown, "mountains, meadows, rivers, seashores, springs, and caves were traditionally perceived as places *in remotis*, that is, as ominous places charged with interstitiality and ambiguity that invite divine epiphanies."[21] Socrates has left the civic realm of Athens and sits in a place infused with divinity.[22] In Socrates' first speech, he refers to the local gods who inhabit this sacred place. In fact, as he says midway through the speech, he is on the verge of being "possessed by the nymphs" (νυμφόληπτος; 238d1). As he puts it, "truly this place seems to be divine (θεῖος ... ὁ τόπος), and therefore, if I am possessed by a nymph (*numpholêptos*) as my speech progresses, do not be surprised – for even now I am almost speaking in dithyrambs" (238c–d).[23]

In ancient Greece, nympholepsy was considered to be an actual religious phenomenon.[24] To cite but one example, Aristotle places nympholepsy in the category of divine possession. As he puts it in his discussion of happiness in the *Eudemian Ethics*: does *eudaimonia* come "when men are inspired by some god, like those possessed by a nymph or a god, or rather by fortune?" (ἤτοι καθάπερ οἱ νυμφόληπτοι καὶ θεόληπτοι τῶν ἀνθρώπων, ἐπιπνοίᾳ δαιμονίου τινὸς ὥσπερ ἐνθουσιάζοντες, ἢ διὰ τὴν τύχην; 1214a23–4). Nympholepsy was a distinct kind of divine possession, and it manifested itself in specific ways. As Robert Connor has shown, in ancient Greece, a nympholept showed a "heightened fluency and awareness, a concentration of faculties, an elevation of expression, and ultimately the reorganization of personality into a new identity and a new social role."[25] Presumably, the nympholept had to convey to others that the nymphs had inspired him and that this was the reason why he exhibited unusual fluency. Clearly, the Greeks did accept at least some of these claims: for, as Connor observes, some nympholepts became "wise men" (*sophoi*) and others prophets.[26]

In her book on nympholepsy, Corinne Pache offers an interesting comment on this scene in the *Phaedrus*:

---

[21] Petridou 2015: 227–8.

[22] Socrates also prays to Pan at the end of the dialogue. We do not find the presence of local gods in other dialogues: although Socrates might refer to the gods, he does not address them directly or pray to them by name. Socrates does of course refer to Apollo in the *Apology* and the *Phaedo*, but does not address him directly. The same goes for Asclepius, whom he mentions at the end of the *Phaedo*.

[23] Dithyrambs were choral poetry used for the worship of Dionysus. Note that, at the end of his first speech, Socrates says that he is speaking in hexameters rather than dithyrambs (241e). He also says in reference to Phaedrus' speech that he is in a state of Bacchic and Corbantic frenzy (συγκορυβαντιῶντα, 228b; συνεβάκχευσα, 234d).

[24] See Pache 2010 for an excellent book-length account of nympholepsy.

[25] Connor 1988; see also Pache 2010: Chapter 2.   [26] Connor 1988: 160–2.

When he evokes the possibility of becoming a *nympholêptos*, Socrates evokes both the cause, the divinity of the place, and the consequences, the shift to poetry . . . . Although the shrine of Achelous and the nymphs is not, as far as is known, associated with any particular nympholept, Socrates describes the sanctuary on the banks of the Ilissus as having the power to transform him into a nympholept. The shrine is located in a landscape permeated with stories of encounters between the divine and mortal realm.[27]

Plato created just this kind of landscape in the *Phaedrus*, and even added the myth of Boreas and Oreithuia. He also gave Socrates the capacities of a nympholept – a higher level of fluency and authority. Socrates' elevated discourse in the first and especially the second speech follows this pattern. Even in Socrates' first speech, Phaedrus comments that "an unusual fluency has taken hold of you" (παρὰ τὸ εἰωθὸς εὔροιά τίς σε εἴληφεν; 238c). At the end of this speech, Socrates notes that he is speaking in hexameters (238b; 241e) and wonders if the nymphs will take hold of him, though "this will be up to the gods" (ταῦτα μὲν οὖν θεῷ μελήσει; 238d). Thus, at the end of his first speech – in which he blames the lover – Socrates has not yet been possessed by the nymphs (241e). As he remarks, "if I begin to praise the non-lover, I will clearly be possessed by the nymphs (ὑπὸ τῶν Νυμφῶν . . . σαφῶς ἐνθουσιάσω) to whom you have purposely exposed me" (241e).[28]

In his first speech, Socrates attacks the lover for his bad treatment of the beloved boy. But he does not praise the non-lover, as Phaedrus (and the reader) expects him to do. Socrates' *daimonion* stops him from finishing the speech, and he gives the palinode instead. In the palinode, he takes back the false and pernicious claims he made in his first speech and sets out instead to praise Eros and the lover. Since Socrates refuses to praise the non-lover in his first speech, this may indicate that he will avoid possession by the nymphs. But he claims at the end of the palinode that the nymphs and Pan have given him the ability to give this speech. Thus, after delivering the palinode, Socrates asks Phaedrus: "Because I was divinely inspired (διὰ τὸ ἐνθουσιαστικόν), I do not remember, so tell me this: did I define love at the beginning of my speech?" (263d). Phaedrus says that he did present a definition, and Socrates proceeds to give the nymphs and Pan the credit for his speech: "how much more skilled in the art of speech are the nymphs, the daughters of Achelous, and Pan, son of Hermes, than Lysias,

---

[27] Pache 2010: Chapter 2.
[28] Here, Socrates suggests that the nymphs could inspire him and make him fluent in a discourse that could well be false and pernicious (praising the non-lover would be impious). Like the gods, the nymphs could possess a person for good or for ill.

son of Cephalus" (263d).[29] Here, Socrates suggests that the nymphs and Pan gave him the "art of speech" that he used in the palinode.

To be sure, Socrates' behavior and discourse in his first speech are very playful. We cannot take seriously his suggestions that he is divinely inspired. But we should acknowledge that Plato focuses on divine inspiration in several scenes that precede the palinode. Plato creates a sacred place and a philosophical character who claims to have been (or almost been) inspired in order to draw parallels between the main drama and the drama of the human soul in the palinode. By introducing nympholepsy into the text, Plato sets up his discourse on the four kinds of divine possession and especially on erotic inspiration.

4.5 Pious Philosophical Discourse

The passage on the proper interpretation of the Boreas/Oreithuia myth and the references to nympholepsy in the *Phaedrus* foreground a key issue in this dialogue: the right way to talk about divinities. Socrates makes a number of claims about pious discourse in this dialogue. As Socrates says after his first speech, which praised the non-lover, he feels troubled that his discourse was "impious" (*asebê*, 242d). Indeed, he worries that "I may be purchasing honor among men by committing a crime against the gods" (μή τι παρὰ θεοῖς ἀμβλακὼν τιμὰν πρὸς ἀνθρώπων ἀμείψω; 242c–d).[30] Socrates makes it clear that it is better to honor the gods than to seek honor among men. In his first speech, then, he had "committed a crime" against the god Eros,[31] and now he needs to "purify himself from guilt" (ἀφοσιώσωμαι) before the gods punish him (242c–243b). To appease the god Eros, Socrates chooses to give a "palinode" that takes the first speech back. He feels that he has to rectify – and, indeed, purify (καθήρασθαι) – his language (243a). Socrates specifically says that his discourse "spoke evilly (κακηγορίαν) about Eros" (243b). He needs to get his discourse right – he must speak piously about Eros.

---

[29] See also 262d: "I hold the gods of this place responsible. Perhaps the prophets of the Muses, the songs inspiring us from over our heads, have inspired us with this gift. For I do not have any share in the art of speaking." Thus, Socrates is not possessed by the nymphs in his first, impious, speech: the inspiration applies only to the palinode. There, Socrates adds Pan, the son of Hermes, to the divine mix, thus suggesting (rather playfully) that he is inspired by all the gods of the place (note also that Socrates ends the dialogue with a prayer to Pan; 279b).

[30] Socrates quotes Ibycus here. See Ibycus fr. 24, Bergk.

[31] He uses the words "commit a crime" – ἁμάρτημα, ἡμαρτηκότα – three times in the space of a few sentences (242c–d; see also 243a).

In this passage, Socrates sets out to speak piously about the god Eros. Of course, in the palinode, he does talk about Eros, but he also discusses the cosmic gods, the godlike human souls, and the divine Forms. His "pious" discourse covers all of the divine beings in Plato's metaphysics. By placing so much focus on piety, Plato reminds the reader that his metaphysical ideas are, in part, a *theologia*. Socrates also focuses on speaking in a pious way about divine beings later in the dialogue. As he says in the palinode: "let these things be as it is pleasing to the god, and let them be spoken of accordingly" (ἀλλὰ ταῦτα μὲν δή, ὅπῃ τῷ θεῷ φίλον, ταύτῃ ἐχέτω τε καὶ λεγέσθω; 246d). Socrates also prays to Eros "to have forgiveness" (συγγνώμην) for his former evil words and "to be kind and gracious" (εὐμενὴς καὶ ἵλεως) to him on account of his second speech (257a). Finally, Socrates calls his palinode a pious hymn to the god Eros: "we sang a mythical hymn of praise to our master Eros in a measured and pious manner" (μυθικόν τινα ὕμνον προσεπαίσαμεν μετρίως τε καὶ εὐφήμως τὸν ἐμόν τε καὶ σὸν δεσπότην Ἔρωτα; 265c). Once again, Socrates adverts to the notion of speaking piously (εὐφήμως) about the gods.[32]

Although Socrates has spoken in prose, he calls his speech a "hymn." As Platt points out, "the conventions of hymnic diction and performance mark a transition from secular to sacred behaviour and expectations."[33] Indeed, "the hymn performs the difficult balancing act of incorporating the god into mortal space and activity, acculturating his or her divine *eidos* through acts of representation, while simultaneously recognizing the God's power to transcend the limitations of sanctuary, human speech and material form."[34] Socrates' hymnic speech, then, is designed to emphasize the divine aspects of Plato's metaphysics.

Finally, in the discussion of rhetoric in the second half of the dialogue, Socrates claims that the true rhetorician (i.e., the philosophical rhetorician) must utter all of his discourses first and foremost to the audience of the gods. He must not simply speak properly *about* the gods, but he must utter all his discourse *to and for* the gods. As Socrates puts it:

> If someone does not enumerate the sorts of characters of his audience, and divide everything according to its kinds, and if he is not able to grasp each single thing by means of one Form, he will never have the art of speaking in so far as this is possible for men. And no one can acquire these things without a great deal of study. A man of sound mind must toil at these studies not for the sake of speaking and acting for men, but so that he can speak

---

[32] Note that Socrates says that Stesichorus is the son of "Euphemus," i.e., of "Pious Speech" (244a).
[33] Platt 2011: 61.   [34] Platt 2011: 64.

things that are pleasing to the gods and can perform every action pleasingly to the gods to the extent that this is possible (ἣν οὐχ ἕνεκα τοῦ λέγειν καὶ πράττειν πρὸς ἀνθρώπους δεῖ διαπονεῖσθαι τὸν σώφρονα, ἀλλὰ τοῦ θεοῖς κεχαρισμένα μὲν λέγειν δύνασθαι, κεχαρισμένως δὲ πράττειν τὸ πᾶν εἰς δύναμιν). For, Teisias, men wiser than ourselves say that it is not right for an intelligent man to attend to his fellow slaves, except as a side effect (πάρεργον), but to his good and noble masters. (273e–274a)

Using the language of masters and slaves to emphasize humans' servile status vis-à-vis the gods, Socrates insists that the true rhetorician must speak all of his discourses primarily to please the gods. Surprisingly, the philosophical rhetorician speaks to humans merely as an aside, a *parergon* (247a). In short, the philosopher's discourse should only address humans in passing.[35] As Socrates states, Phaedrus needs to discover "how he can most of all please god when acting or speaking about rhetoric" (ὅπη μάλιστα θεῷ χαριῇ λόγων πέρι πράττων ἢ λέγων; 274b). These claims go back to Socrates' quote from Ibycus at the beginning of the palinode: he fears that "[he] may be purchasing honor among men by committing a crime against the gods" (μή τι παρὰ θεοῖς ἀμβλακὼν τιμὰν πρὸς ἀνθρώπων ἀμείψω). Although one thinks of rhetoric as a matter of humans addressing humans, Socrates argues that one must speak correctly and piously to the audience of the gods. Not surprisingly, the dialogue closes with Socrates saying a prayer to "Pan and all the other gods of this place." In these passages, Plato showcases the proper way for the philosopher to use discourse.

As we will see, the right way to speak to and about the gods is rooted in Platonic philosophy, which Socrates sets forth in the palinode. This includes Socrates' claims that (1) the soul is immortal and godlike; (2) the rational part of the soul has eros for the Forms; (3) the souls of the gods are perfect, good, rational, and they continually contemplate the Forms; and (4) the Forms are the highest and most divine beings.

4.6 Souls, Gods, Forms

It is beyond the scope of this work to offer a full analysis of Plato's metaphysics and cosmology in the *Phaedrus*. However, to ground my argument, I will present a brief account of Socrates' discussion of the soul and the Forms in the palinode. Socrates begins this speech by focusing on the nature of the soul. As he claims, all souls – divine and human – are

---

[35] Note that the scene with the cicadas suggests that the gods are overseeing the discourses and actions of the humans (see especially 259d).

immortal. He demonstrates this by stating that the soul alone is "self-moving" and the "origin of all motion" (*archê kinêseôs*) in the cosmos. Since the cosmos keeps on moving, the "ever moving" soul must be immortal (245c–246a).

Socrates never fully explains how the "self-moving" soul controls the cosmos. But he does state that the soul initiates movement in bodies, including heavenly bodies: "All soul cares for that which is without soul, and it moves around the entire heaven, at one time being in one form and at another in a different form. The soul that is perfect and fully winged travels through the heavens and governs the entire cosmos" (246b–c).[36] Of course only the gods have "perfect and fully winged" souls. As Socrates says, eleven of the twelve Greek gods lead bands of souls in the heavens, each attending to his or her own cosmic duties (Hestia stays at home in the "house of the gods," presumably to maintain the hearth; 247a). In addition, these gods are ethically good (242d; see also 247e, "there is no envy among them"). And, since all of them ascend together to the edge of the heaven and contemplate the Forms, they all have perfected intellects (247b). Here, Plato adumbrates the cosmology he will set forth in the *Timaeus*, where the divine cosmic soul contemplates the Forms with its perfect intellect and also moves and controls its cosmic body.

In Socrates' narrative, human souls follow the gods. In this preincarnate state, the souls attend one or another god in the heavens.[37] When the souls of the gods contemplate the Forms, the human souls attempt to do the same. As Socrates claims: "of the other souls [i.e., human souls], that which followed god in the best way and likened itself to the god (ἄριστα θεῷ ἑπομένη καὶ εἰκασμένη) raised the head of its charioteer to that place outside the heavens," that is, to the realm of the Forms (248a). Here, Socrates indicates that the good human soul has the potential to be divine. Still, the human souls cannot see the Forms as well as the gods do (because their horses impede them). Indeed, some human souls get a better look at the Forms than others (248a–b).

---

[36] 246b–c: ψυχὴ πᾶσα παντὸς ἐπιμελεῖται τοῦ ἀψύχου, πάντα δὲ οὐρανὸν περιπολεῖ, ἄλλοτ᾽ ἐν ἄλλοις εἴδεσι γιγνομένη. τελέα μὲν οὖν οὖσα καὶ ἐπτερωμένη μετεωροπορεῖ τε καὶ πάντα τὸν κόσμον διοικεῖ.

[37] Note that Plato includes a group of gods that have different personalities (Zeus is kinglike, Ares is warlike, etc.). Given Plato's notion that the gods are good, one must assume that these gods have perfectly good souls. As Sedley observes (1999: 315): "It might seem hard to imagine that Plato would ultimately endorse so radical a form of polytheism (one more reminiscent of Euthyphro's theology, which accepts the Homeric picture of gods morally divided against each other). But the myth has made it clear that all these different gods are alike guided by a complete grasp of the moral Forms."

Let us look now at Plato's portrayal of the soul's relationship to the Forms. We have seen that the rational part of the soul has eros for the Forms. The divine Forms, in turn, serve to nourish the rational part of the soul. As Socrates states: "the divine is beautiful, wise, good, and all things of this kind: by these the wings of the soul are most of all nourished and grow" (τὸ δὲ θεῖον καλόν, σοφόν, ἀγαθόν, καὶ πᾶν ὅτι τοιοῦτον· τούτοις δὴ τρέφεταί τε καὶ αὔξεται μάλιστά γε τὸ τῆς ψυχῆς πτέρωμα; 246e). I take Plato to be referring to the Forms – Beauty, Wisdom, the Good, and "all other things of this kind" – because he repeatedly uses the metaphor of the "nourishment" of the soul only in the context of the soul contemplating the Forms (246e, 247a–c, 248b–c).[38] If this is on target, then "the divine" is instantiated by Beauty, Wisdom, and Goodness, and these nourish the rational part of the soul. Indeed, the soul feeds on these divine beings and thus becomes divine.

Plato offers a fuller picture of the soul's relation to the Forms by constructing a cosmic narrative that represents the souls' ascent to the incorporeal Forms. Using the image of the soul as a winged charioteer driving horses, he portrays the souls – both divine and human – as flying up to the edge of the physical heaven and taking a stand on its outer surface (247c). The circular motion of the heavens (i.e., the fixed stars that mark the boundary of the heavens) carry the souls around in a full revolution. During this time, the rational part of their souls (figured by the charioteer) look out at the divine "realities" outside the physical realm. There they "behold" (theorousi) the "place beyond the heavens" (hyperouranios topos, 247c). Plato uses the metaphor of vision to describe the soul's apprehension of the Forms.

Plato describes the divine souls' encounter with the Forms as follows:

> The colorless, shapeless, and intangible Being that really is what it is (ousia ontôs ousa) holds this region, visible only to the mind (nous), the pilot of the soul, and is the object of all true knowledge (epistêmê). Since the god's intellect (dianoia) is nourished on knowledge (epistêmê) and mind (nous) – as is the intellect of every soul that is concerned to receive what is appropriate to it – it rejoices when it sees Being over a period of time (dia chronou to on), and seeing these truths it is nourished and happy, until the revolution [of the heavens] carries it in a circle back to where it started. And in this revolution it sees Justice in itself, it sees Self-Control, and it sees Knowledge – not that in which change (genesis) is present or that which differs in different circumstances, being [knowledge] of things we on earth

---

[38] I discussed this passage in Chapter 1. As I noted, the "wings of the soul," i.e., the rational desire of the soul, "nourishes itself" on the Forms, not the gods.

call real – but the knowledge oriented towards what really is what it is. And [the soul], after gazing in this way on other beings that are truly real and feasting on them, sinks back inside the heavens and goes home. (247c–e)

The mind of the gods (and of every soul that can achieve this feat) "beholds" the Forms and gains nourishment from these higher Beings. I say "higher" because, in the spatial logic of the myth, the gods fly upward to the edge of the heavens; the Forms are "above" the gods. To be sure, the realm of the Forms does not occupy space and cannot, strictly speaking, exist "above" the bodily realm. Still, Plato regularly conveys the idea that the soul (including the divine souls of the gods) ascends to the Forms.

We must emphasize that there is a big ontological difference between the soul and the Forms. First, the souls move, while the Forms do not move or change. Second, the souls are temporalized, while the Forms exist outside of time. The divine souls contemplate the Forms "over a period of time" (note the verbal collocation – and ontological confrontation – of the temporalized divine soul and eternal Being in the phrase "διὰ χρόνου τὸ ὄν"). Thus, the time-bound soul confronts the timeless and changeless Forms. Even more importantly, Plato suggests that souls are divine by virtue of their contemplation of the Forms. As Socrates states: the philosopher gets "as close as possible, by way of recollection, to those things [the Forms] *by being close to which god is divine*" (πρὸς γὰρ ἐκείνοις ἀεί ἐστιν μνήμῃ κατὰ δύναμιν, πρὸς οἷσπερ θεὸς ὢν θεῖός ἐστιν; 249c, my italics). The gods are divine because they can everlastingly contemplate the Forms. The philosophic soul can become divine in the same way. Thus, the divinity of the souls derives from the Forms. Plato's cosmological scheme, then, has three divine elements: the human souls, the gods, and the realm of the Forms.[39]

4.7 Inspiration, Madness, and Enhanced Reason

When he gives his second speech – the palinode – Socrates takes back the things he said in his first speech.[40] He explicitly refers to Stesichorus' palinode, where the poet took back the things he had said about Helen. Indeed, Socrates quotes a line from that poem: "this discourse is not true" (οὐκ ἔστ᾽ ἔτυμος λόγος οὗτος; 243a). In his own palinode, Socrates places

---

[39] Of course the human souls have a lower level of divinity than the gods.
[40] Some scholars have suggested that Plato is also "taking back" the things he said about eros and the soul in the *Symposium*. As I have suggested, Plato develops his ideas from dialogue to dialogue.

Stesichorus' lines in the context of his speech of praise for the sane non-lover:

> It must be said that "the discourse is not true" which says that one should favor the non-lover more than the lover, when he is at hand, because the lover is mad and the other is sane. For if madness were simply an evil, this would have been spoken truly. But in fact the greatest goods come to us from madness when it is given as a gift from the gods. (λεκτέος δὲ ὧδε, ὅτι οὐκ ἔστ᾽ ἔτυμος λόγος ὃς ἂν παρόντος ἐραστοῦ τῷ μὴ ἐρῶντι μᾶλλον φῇ δεῖν χαρίζεσθαι, διότι δὴ ὁ μὲν μαίνεται, ὁ δὲ σωφρονεῖ. εἰ μὲν γὰρ ἦν ἁπλοῦν τὸ μανίαν κακὸν εἶναι, καλῶς ἂν ἐλέγετο· νῦν δὲ τὰ μέγιστα τῶν ἀγαθῶν ἡμῖν γίγνεται διὰ μανίας, θείᾳ μέντοι δόσει διδομένης; 244a–b)

In the palinode, Socrates rejects his earlier claim that the beloved boy should choose the "sane and thoughtful" (*sôphrôn*) non-lover over the lover, whose sick "madness" (*mania*) will do him harm. Both Lysias' speech and Socrates' first speech used the topos of the "mad lover" who hurts his beloved with his obsessive demands, and the "sane and thoughtful" non-lover who confers benefits on the boy in a sensible exchange for sex.[41] Indeed, those speeches set up a clear dichotomy between the non-lover's "intelligence and good sense" and the lover's "erotic madness" (νοῦν καὶ σωφροσύνην ἀντ᾽ ἔρωτος καὶ μανίας; 241a). In his second speech, Socrates turns this on its head. Rejecting this simple dichotomy, he argues that divinely inspired madness brings the greatest benefits to mankind.

Socrates lists four kinds of divinely inspired madness that have helped humanity. Before I examine this account, however, I want to briefly consider Greek views on madness. The Greeks in the classical period considered madness (*mania*) as deriving from two possible causes – divine or natural. In the former case, a god could drive a person mad as a punishment or as a great gift, depending on his/her divine predilection. Of course, the Greeks did not always know which of the two causes was operating in a given case. Thus, in literary texts, we find characters pondering whether a person's

---

[41] See, e.g., 231d: "For [the lovers] themselves agree that they are sick, rather than of sound mind, and they know that they are thinking in the wrong way and are unable to control themselves: therefore, how could they think, when they have come to their senses, that those acts were good which they decided on when being in such a condition?" (καὶ γὰρ αὐτοὶ ὁμολογοῦσι νοσεῖν μᾶλλον ἢ σωφρονεῖν, καὶ εἰδέναι ὅτι κακῶς φρονοῦσιν, ἀλλ᾽ οὐ δύνασθαι αὐτῶν κρατεῖν· ὥστε πῶς ἂν εὖ φρονήσαντες ταῦτα καλῶς ἔχειν ἡγήσαιντο περὶ ὧν οὕτω διακείμενοι βουλεύονται;). See also 232a, 233b–c. As Socrates says before the first speech: "Who do you think, in arguing that it is right to favor the non-lover over the lover, could omit praising the former for being sensible and blame the latter for his lack of reason?" (τίνα οἴει λέγοντα ὡς χρὴ μὴ ἐρῶντι μᾶλλον ἢ ἐρῶντι χαρίζεσθαι, παρέντα τοῦ μὲν τὸ φρόνιμον ἐγκωμιάζειν, τοῦ δὲ τὸ ἄφρον ψέγειν; 235e–236a). In his first speech, Socrates also refers to the "illness" of the lover (238e).

madness has come from the gods or from a physical malady. For example, Herodotus suggests that Cambyses' madness could have been caused either by a natural illness or by the gods; he does not come down on one side or the other (3.33–4). In Euripides' *Hippolytus*, the chorus wonders if Phaedra has been possessed by a god or is simply manifesting the sort of madness that normally afflicts females (141–7, 159, 161). In the *Bacchae*, Teiresias thinks that Pentheus has been driven mad by some sort of drug, though the Greek audience of the play knows that Dionysus has brought about the madness (327). To be sure, scientific thinkers like the Hippocratic writers and Aristotle claimed that madness had a natural cause. In *The Sacred Disease*, for example, the author attacks diviners and healers who claimed that madness comes from the gods; he argues that *mania* comes from a defect in the brain.[42] However, these scientific thinkers made up a tiny minority in Greek culture.

In terms of divinely sent madness, the gods could "inspire" an individual either by possessing him/her from within or from the outside. As Yulia Ustinova observes:

> A mortal could be possessed by a god (*theolêptos* or *katochos*), and her or his state would be described as possession, *katochê* . . . . One could also have the god inside, literally "be engodded" (*entheos*); in this case, the super-human compulsion was supposedly felt as an invasive power within one's body or mind. Every god could enthuse a mortal with *enthousiasmos*, "engodded-ness" or *epipnoia*, "inspiration." . . . However, the difference between "possession from the outside" and "invasion from the inside" was subtle and inconsistent, and the word usage hardly reflects a contrast in the human experience of approaching the divine: the same deities, in particular Apollo and the Muses, could both "seize" and "inspire" mortals, and quite often the words *katochos* and *entheos* were used synonymously.[43]

Perhaps the most famous example of a god possessing ("enthousing") individuals for good and for ill is found in Euripides' *Bacchae*: in this play, the chorus of Dionysus' followers enjoy a blissful manic state, while Pentheus and his family go mad in ways that lead to utter destruction. Euripides' literary portrayal of Dionysus presents both the positive and negative aspects of this god.[44]

---

[42] The Hippocratic *De morbo sacro* tacks back and forth between rejecting healers who used traditional or telestic rituals to heal mad people and discussing the dysfunctions of the brain that cause madness. Aristotle discusses madness in *EN* 1147a15 and *PA* 651b1–8. For discussions of Greek approaches to madness in the archaic and classical periods, see Padel 1981; Lloyd 1987: 23–4; Jouanna 2013; Ustinova 2017.

[43] Ustinova 2017: 9–10 (see also 2009: 9–11).

[44] One should not identify the events in this play, which was written for the public Athenian festival for Dionysus, with the Dionysian Mysteries. As we will see, this secret mystery cult featured night-

In spite of their belief that gods could inspire people and drive them mad in positive ways, the Greeks still stigmatized madness. In Athenian texts in the classical period, we find many examples of people looking down on mad individuals. In some cases, they even attempted to confine mad people in the house or in prison (see, e.g., Aristophanes *Wasps* 69–70; Xenophon *Mem.* 1.2.50; Plato *Laws* 11.934c–d). However, when mad people manifested a heightened kind of verbal fluency and power, the Greeks attributed this *mania* to divine inspiration.

As we saw in the passage on nympholepsy, the nympholept could become more charismatic and fluent in speech. Xenophon presents a similar idea in the *Symposium* (1.9.10):

> All those possessed by the gods are worthy to gaze upon. Those who have been inspired by gods other than Eros are prone to be sterner in appearance, more terrifying in voice, and more vehement, while those inspired by the modest god Eros have tenderness in their face, speak in a gentler voice and bear their bodies in the most noble way. Thus Callias acted at that time on account of Eros, and he was worthy to be looked upon by those initiated by the god.[45]

Xenophon suggests that people inspired by the gods display either a more forceful or gentle demeanor than they usually have. He clearly considers this a positive state. We can infer that, in political and military contexts, divinely inspired men could strike fear into crowds by their charisma and power, while love-mad people could exert a powerful attraction. Xenophon finds these individuals "worthy to gaze upon" rather than disgusting or frightening.

In the *Phaedrus*, Socrates presents four kinds of divinely sent madness (*mania*) – oracular, poetic, telestic, and erotic.[46] I want to examine each of these different kinds of inspiration in the context of Greek culture and religion. In the first kind of madness, gods inspired prophets and priests in oracular contexts. As Socrates claims: "For the prophetess in Delphi and

---

time rituals of initiation that included dance and music that, at least in principle, drove people to a maddened state of mind in order to create healing. In the Dionysian Mysteries, people volunteered to participate in the rituals, including initiation, to gain healing from some sort of personal malady.

[45] 1.9.10: πάντες μὲν οὖν οἱ ἐκ θεῶν του κατεχόμενοι ἀξιοθέατοι δοκοῦσιν εἶναι· ἀλλ' οἱ μὲν ἐξ ἄλλων πρὸς τὸ γοργότεροί τε ὁρᾶσθαι καὶ φοβερώτερον φθέγγεσθαι καὶ σφοδρότεροι εἶναι φέρονται, οἱ δ' ὑπὸ τοῦ σώφρονος ἔρωτος ἔνθεοι τά τε ὄμματα φιλοφρονεστέρως ἔχουσι καὶ τὴν φωνὴν πραοτέραν ποιοῦνται καὶ τὰ σχήματα εἰς τὸ ἐλευθεριώτερον ἄγουσιν. ἃ δὴ καὶ Καλλίας τότε διὰ τὸν ἔρωτα πράττων ἀξιοθέατος ἦν τοῖς τετελεσμένοις τούτῳ τῷ θεῷ.

[46] Plato offers positive views about divine inspiration in *Apol.* 33c; *Ion* 536d, 542a; *Rep.* 366c–d, 493a; *Phaedrus* 244a–245b; and *Laws* 719c–d. See Büttner 2011 for an excellent analysis of Plato's views on divine inspiration.

the priestesses at Dodona, in their maddened state, brought about many great things in Greece, both in private and in public matters" (ἥ τε γὰρ δὴ ἐν Δελφοῖς προφῆτις αἵ τ᾽ ἐν Δωδώνῃ ἱέρειαι μανεῖσαι μὲν πολλὰ δὴ καὶ καλὰ ἰδίᾳ τε καὶ δημοσίᾳ τὴν Ἑλλάδα ἠργάσαντο; 244a–b). The most famous example of this is the priestess Pythia's "madness" at the Oracle at Delphi.[47] According to the Greeks, the god Apollo inspired the Pythia with a divine form of madness so that she could receive and report his messages. In the classical period, the Greeks accepted this oracle as one of the most authoritative in Greece. In their view, when someone consulted this oracle, Apollo sent a message to this individual through the medium of the Pythia. To be sure, a few ancient writers wondered if the Pythia really went mad; others looked for natural causes of her *mania*. Several writers argued that some sort of gas or natural element brought about this madness.[48] Even so, most Greeks accepted that the Pythia spoke for Apollo.

Not surprisingly, modern scholars have tried to understand the Pythia's madness. Using cross-cultural anthropological studies on spirit possession, Lisa Maurizio offers a helpful way to understand the Pythia's altered state of mind. As she observes, in cultures that practice spirit possession, the possessed individual exhibits an altered state of consciousness that operates within a specific set of religious institutions and cultural expectations.[49] In the case of the Pythia, Maurizio claims, her manifestation of divine

---

[47] The literature on divination in general and on the Delphic oracle in particular is vast. See, e.g., Dodds 1951: chapter 3; Fontenrose 1978; Parker 1985; C. Morgan 1989; Dietrich 1990; Maurizio 1995, 1997; Rosenberger 2001; Bowden 2005; Flower 2008: 215–39; Eidinow 2007, especially Chapters 1, 3; Johnston 2008; Graf 2009; M. Scott 2010, 2014; Bonnechere 2011; Beerden 2013; Trampedach 2015; Kindt 2016. For an excellent discussion on the scholarship on divination, see Johnston 2008: chapter 1. Of course divine inspiration was not confined to the Delphic Oracle. For a good discussion of inspiration at different oracular sites, see Graf 2009: 595–8 and passim.

[48] Later Greek writers discussed the Pythia's inspiration and posited both gods and material elements as creating the Pythia's inspired trance. For example, in the first century CE, Plutarch claims that the Pythia did not, in the past or present, rant or rave but felt "calm and peaceful" after a consultation (*Mor.* 759b). He also argues that *pneuma*, i.e., breath or wind, played a role in the Pythia's inspired trance (*Mor.* 42c–48d). Indeed, Plutarch declares that the gods had abandoned the Greeks in his own period due to their moral degeneracy. For this reason, he claims, there was less *pneuma* in Delphi. Strabo, a first-century CE geographer, also says that *pneuma* gave the Pythia her ability to declare oracles (9.3.5). Although she "rages," he adds, she speaks with perfect coherence. Another first-century writer (and rhetorician), Lucian, claims that the Pythia is possessed by the god by inhaling vapors and then raves (5.65.164). We must note that these writers had different agendas and spoke of the Pythia's altered state of mind in different ways.

[49] Maurizio 1995. See especially pp. 74–5: "Since members of cultures where spirit possession is practised and institutionalized often have complex and nuanced interpretations of the validity and meaning of spirit possession, it follows that the behaviours associated with altered states of consciousness are culturally determined. That is, the behaviours exhibited by individuals in an altered state, as unexpected and uncontrollable as they may appear to the observer, are stereotypical

possession during oracular consultations was culturally determined: "neither a raving hysteric nor a prop of priests who duped the public, the Pythia at Delphi produced utterances that are a genuine expression of a cultural system which believed in and codified behaviour and speech that it understood as indicating the presence of the divine."[50]

Greek individuals and city-states as a whole almost always accepted the oracle's pronouncements. They did at times debate the true meaning of an oracular statement, but this did not affect its divine authority.[51] Of course we can never know what really happened when the Pythia sat on the tripod. We can say, however, that the Greeks did not consider her altered state of consciousness as a mental illness. Indeed, the Pythia's altered mental state manifested itself only when she was giving oracular consultations.

We come now to the second kind of divinely inspired madness in Socrates' account of *mania*: telestic madness. The term "telestic" (*telestikos*) refers to mystery rites. What mystery cult does Socrates have in mind here? As he states:

> When there have been diseases and immense troubles in certain families, which come from some ancient guilt, [divine] madness comes on and provides prophetic interpretations, and it discovers a deliverance for those who need this. This madness, taking refuge in prayers and service to the gods, and finding purifications and mystic rites, has made the man that it touches safe and sound both in the present and the future. [Divine *mania*] discovers a release from present evils for the person who is mad and possessed in the right way. (244d–245a)[52]

Evidently, people chose to engage in these mystery rites to get rid of the troubles that afflicted themselves or their families. Socrates explicitly identifies this mystery cult with "the mystic madness of Dionysus" (Διονύσου δὲ τελεστικήν ... μανίαν; 265b). Here, he refers to the

and fairly uniform within a culture." Note that Maurizio locates the Pythia in the wider genre of spirit possession, which features a person whose behavior differs markedly from everyday life but nonetheless differs "in a stereotypical way." The Pythia's behavior is "stereotypical" in that her utterances operate within a religious institution and her behavior has a relative uniformity (1995: 74–5). See also Crapanzo/Garrison 1977 on spirit possession.
[50] Maurizio 1995: 79.
[51] See, for example, Herodotus' account of the Athenians' debate over the exact nature of the "wooden walls" that were referred to in an oracular pronouncement from Delphi (7.142–3). The Athenians offered radically different interpretations of the pronouncement, but they clearly took this to be an authoritative divine message.
[52] 244d–245a: ἀλλὰ μὴν νόσων γε καὶ πόνων τῶν μεγίστων, ἃ δὴ παλαιῶν ἐκ μηνιμάτων ποθὲν ἔν τισι τῶν γενῶν ἡ μανία ἐγγενομένη καὶ προφητεύσασα, οἷς ἔδει ἀπαλλαγὴν ηὕρετο, καταφυγοῦσα πρὸς θεῶν εὐχάς τε καὶ λατρείας, ὅθεν δὴ καθαρμῶν τε καὶ τελετῶν τυχοῦσα ἐξάντη ἐποίησε τὸν (ἑαυτῆς) ἔχοντα πρός τε τὸν παρόντα καὶ τὸν ἔπειτα χρόνον, λύσιν τῷ ὀρθῶς μανέντι τε καὶ κατασχομένῳ τῶν παρόντων κακῶν εὑρομένη.

Dionysian Mysteries, which included initiation and rituals that created madness during the ceremonies. We may wonder who participated in the mysteries. Socrates speaks of individuals or families afflicted by troubles caused by some ancestral guilt. These individuals sought healing from the Dionysian Mysteries. Anyone, male or female, could go through the initiation and rituals that brought on a temporary madness that had curative effects. As Graf observes, "the detailed analysis of our evidence for Bacchic initiation rites showed that they were understood as having a cathartic function."[53]

Herodotus offers a useful account of a person experiencing the "madness" of the Dionysian Mysteries. As he claims, the Scythian king Scyles admired Greek culture and went to the Greek city Borysthenes, where he dressed and lived as a Greek without the Scythians knowing this. He then decided to get initiated into the Dionysian Mysteries (Διονύσῳ Βακχείῳ τελεσθῆναι) and be driven into a maddened state (μαίνεσθαι). When the Scythians discovered that Scyles was living in the Greek city of Borysthenes, they went there and watched him participating in the Dionysian Mysteries. As Herodotus claims, they "scorned the Greeks for Bacchic revelling" (βακχεύειν) and opposed the god who "took hold of" (λαμβάνει) men and made them "mad" (μαίνεσθαι; 4.78.3–79.4).[54] Of course the Scythians saw and judged this event as cultural outsiders. As a Greek, Herodotus does not treat this mystery cult in a negative light. Indeed, he seems to take it for granted that his Greek readers understood the benefits of the Dionysian Mysteries.

In Plato's *Laws*, we find a description of the healing rituals in the Dionysian cult. He focuses in particular on the music and bodily motion featured in the mystic rites:

> The nurses of small children and those applying healing rituals in the case of the Corybants find this [motion] useful. When mothers want to get their badly sleeping children to rest, they apply not restfulness but its opposite, motion. They always rock them in their arms and apply a certain kind of melody rather than silence, as though they were charming (*kataulousi*) their children with flute music, just as in the case of the healing of divinely maddened bacchants, who use this dancing motion and music simultaneously . . . . In both of these cases, the sufferings are a form of fear, and fears are due to a poor condition of the soul. Thus, when someone applies a shaking to such people, the motion applied from the outside conquers

---

[53] Graf/Johnston 2007: 144.
[54] Of course the Scythians perceived this as non-Greek outsiders who did not understand the cult (and they did not want their king to adopt alien religious practices). Herodotus wrote for Greek readers who understood and accepted this mystery cult.

the fear and the manic motion on the inside, and this conquering action manifestly brings about a peaceful calmness in the soul for each person who has a troublesome leaping of the heart, and it produces a welcome result. For it makes the children go to sleep. In the awakened bacchants, who dance and are charmed by the flutes (*auloumenos*) in the presence of the gods to whom each of them worships and sacrifices with good omens, this [the dancing motion and music] produces a sane condition instead of a maddened state. (790d–791b)[55]

In this long and complex passage, Plato compares mothers soothing their babies with rocking and singing to troubled people dancing to music in mystery cults in order to achieve a calm state. Plato refers to two different mystery cults here. First, the cult of the Corybants, who worshipped the Phrygian mother goddess Cybele. Second, the Dionysian Mysteries, where bacchants danced in night-time ceremonies to high-pitched music and thus achieved a maddened state. In both cults, the participants went through a series of rituals in order to achieve a madness that brought about healing. In using the words *kataulein* and *aulein*, Plato refers to the *aulos*-playing in the rituals in the Dionysian Mysteries.[56] The participants went into an altered state of consciousness for a period of time and, at least in principle, ended up in a healthier state of mind.

These two mystery cults had a good deal of overlap. Indeed, as Graf claims, an ancient Greek myth brought together the Corybants and Bacchants. In this myth, Hera drove the young Dionysus mad, and then he went to Rhea (aka Cybele) and was healed and given the telestic rites.[57] As Graf observes:

---

[55] 790d–791b: χρήσιμον αἵ τε τροφοὶ τῶν σμικρῶν καὶ αἱ περὶ τὰ τῶν Κορυβάντων ἰάματα τελοῦσαι. ἡνίκα γὰρ ἄν που βουληθῶσιν κατακοιμίζειν τὰ δυσυπνοῦντα τῶν παιδίων αἱ μητέρες, οὐχ ἡσυχίαν αὐτοῖς προσφέρουσιν ἀλλὰ τοὐναντίον κίνησιν, ἐν ταῖς ἀγκάλαις ἀεὶ σείουσαι, καὶ οὐ σιγὴν ἀλλά τινα μελῳδίαν, καὶ ἀτεχνῶς οἷον καταυλοῦσι τῶν παιδίων, καθάπερ ἡ τῶν ἐκφρόνων βακχειῶν ἰάσεις, ταύτῃ τῇ τῆς κινήσεως ἅμα χορείᾳ καὶ μούσῃ χρώμεναι . . . . δειμαίνειν ἐστίν που ταῦτ' ἀμφότερα τὰ πάθη, καὶ ἔστι δείματα δι' ἕξιν φαύλην τῆς ψυχῆς τινα. ὅταν οὖν ἔξωθέν τις προσφέρῃ τοῖς τοιούτοις πάθεσι σεισμόν, ἡ τῶν ἔξωθεν κρατεῖ κίνησις προσφερομένη τὴν ἐντὸς φοβερὰν οὖσαν καὶ μανικὴν κίνησιν, κρατήσασα δέ, γαλήνην ἡσυχίαν τε ἐν τῇ ψυχῇ φαίνεσθαι ἀπεργασαμένη τῆς περὶ τὰ τῆς καρδίας χαλεπῆς γενομένης ἑκάστων πηδήσεως, παντάπασιν ἀγαπητόν τι, τοὺς μὲν ὕπνου λαγχάνειν ποιεῖ, τοὺς δ' ἐγρηγορότας ὀρχουμένους τε καὶ αὐλουμένους μετὰ θεῶν, οἷς ἂν καλλιεροῦντες ἕκαστοι θύωσι, κατηργάσατο ἀντὶ μανικῶν ἡμῖν διαθέσεων ἕξεις ἔμφρονας ἔχειν. See also *Ion* 536c: "just as the Corybantian worshippers perceive that tune alone which belongs to the god who possesses them, and they are full of gestures and phrases for that tune, but do not pay attention to any other" (ὥσπερ οἱ κορυβαντιῶντες ἐκείνου μόνου αἰσθάνονται τοῦ μέλους ὀξέως ὃ ἂν ᾖ τοῦ θεοῦ ἐξ ὅτου ἂν κατέχωνται, καὶ εἰς ἐκεῖνο τὸ μέλος καὶ σχημάτων καὶ ῥημάτων εὐποροῦσι, τῶν δὲ ἄλλων οὐ φροντίζουσιν).

[56] See Wilson's excellent discussion of flute music in Greece, especially in Athens (1999).

[57] Graf/Johnston 2007: 146. Graf cites Apollodorus' account of this story (*Library* 3.5.1 = 3.33) and refers to a line from the early epic poem, *Europia*, which states that Dionysus was purified by Rhea and given the mystic rites.

This myth connects ritual purification and the teaching of initiatory rites: it is the etiological myth for Dionysiac initiation. To outside observers, this [Dionysian] ritual appeared to be not very different from the rituals of Rhea-Cybele. Both rituals aimed at an altered state of consciousness for the participants. In both cults, this state expressed itself in the same way, in orgiastic, ecstatic song, music, and dance, and the two divinities and their cults were connected during the fifth century BCE at the latest.[58]

We can see, then, why Plato brings together the telestic rites of Cybele and Dionysus in the *Laws*.

Socrates' discussion of telestic madness in the *Phaedrus* focuses on the Dionysian Mysteries. As Plato suggests in the *Laws* passage, the mystic rites of the Dionysian Mysteries "produce a sane condition instead of a maddened state" (791b). In short, the dancing and music in this ceremony were designed to bring about an altered state of consciousness that eventually led to healing.[59] One goes mad to become sane. To be sure, considered from the outside perspective, the night-time revelers engaging in orgiastic dancing may seem to resemble mentally ill people. But this madness occurred in ritually controlled contexts where individuals were led into a trance by music and dance.

We find a bit more evidence for the Dionysian mystery cult in Aristotle's *Politics*, where he discusses the divine inspiration that brings about purification (*catharsis*). He refers to this kind of mystery cult in his analysis of the proper ways to use different kinds of music:

> It is clear that we should use all the harmonies, but not in the same way, i.e., the ethical harmonies for education ... and the active and enthusiastic ones (*enthousiastikais*) for listening to when others perform them. For the emotions that come to some souls strongly also occur in all souls, though this differs in terms of greater or lesser intensity, as in the case of pity and fear, and also divine inspiration (*enthousiasmos*): for some people are possessed (*katochôchimoi*) by this motion, and we see them under the influence of sacred songs (*ierôn melôn*) when they use melodies that excite their souls into a mystic trance (*exorgiazousi*), and they are brought into a state so as to get healing treatments and purification (*iatreias kai katharseôs*).[60] (*Pol.* 8.7, 1342a1–11)

---

[58] Graf/Johnston 2007: 246–7.   [59] See Ustinova 2017.

[60] φανερὸν ὅτι χρηστέον μὲν πάσαις ταῖς ἁρμονίαις, οὐ τὸν αὐτὸν δὲ τρόπον πάσαις χρηστέον, ἀλλὰ πρὸς μὲν τὴν παιδείαν ταῖς ἠθικωτάταις, πρὸς δὲ ἀκρόασιν ἑτέρων χειρουργούντων καὶ ταῖς πρακτικαῖς καὶ ταῖς ἐνθουσιαστικαῖς. ὃ γὰρ περὶ ἐνίας συμβαίνει πάθος ψυχὰς ἰσχυρῶς, τοῦτο ἐν πάσαις ὑπάρχει, τῷ δὲ ἧττον διαφέρει καὶ τῷ μᾶλλον, οἷον ἔλεος καὶ φόβος, ἔτι δ' ἐνθουσιασμός· καὶ γὰρ ὑπὸ ταύτης τῆς κινήσεως κατοκώχιμοί τινές εἰσιν, ἐκ τῶν δ' ἱερῶν μελῶν ὁρῶμεν τούτους, ὅταν χρήσωνται τοῖς ἐξοργιάζουσι τὴν ψυχὴν μέλεσι, καθισταμένους ὥσπερ ἰατρείας τυχόντας καὶ καθάρσεως.

Although Aristotle does not mention the Dionysian Mysteries explicitly here, he refers to all the key elements of the cult: "divine inspiration" (*enthousiasmos*), "possession" (*katochôchimoi*), "sacred songs" (*ierôn melôn*), music that "excites souls into a mystic trance" (*exorgiazousi*), and "healing treatments and purification" (*iatreias kai katharseôs*). Finally, he asserts that people subject to strong emotions gain relief by way of this possessed state: they get "treatment and purification" for these troubled emotions. We find all of these rituals and activities in the Dionysian Mysteries.

In the second kind of madness in the *Phaedrus*, then, Dionysus both inspires and heals troubled individuals. As Socrates observes, the troubled psyche of the participant "goes mad" and gains *katharsis* (καθαρμῶν, 244e). Of course the individuals taking part in these telestic rites achieved an altered state of consciousness only for the period of the ceremony. This was not a lasting kind of madness. Note, finally, that in the Dionysian Mysteries, the god "possessed" a group of people: this differs from the divine inspiration of select individuals in the case of oracular inspiration.

We come now to Socrates' third kind of divine madness: the Muses' inspiration of the poets. The textual evidence for this kind of inspiration starts with Homer and Hesiod and runs through the poetic tradition. As scholars have noted, the early poets considered the poet and Muse as co-operating in the act of composition and/or performance: the poet used his own skills even as the Muse inspired him to speak with exceptional eloquence. Even in the fifth century BCE, when some Greeks identified the Muses' inspiration of the poet as driving him into an ecstatic state, they still considered the poet to be fully able to use his own ideas and skills.[61] Plato went further in claiming that the Muses or some other god com-pletely took over the mind and voice of the poet: the poet's own skills and wisdom play no role in his poetic compositions. As Murray observes: "it was Plato who, so far as we know, first opposed the concepts of poetic inspiration and technique."[62] In short, Plato's philosophical ideas about poetic inspiration did not reflect ordinary Greek views. In particular, he created a firm boundary between poetic inspiration and poetry as a craft that derived from the poet's knowledge. Plato discusses poetic inspiration in a number of texts. In the early dialogues, he affirms the idea that the Muses inspire the poets but emphasizes that the poets do not understand the things they speak about. For example, as Socrates says in the *Apology*:

---

[61] See Tigerstedt 1970 and Murray 1981, who rightly claim that the notion of the poets achieving an ecstatic madness due to the inspiration of the Muses was first posited in the late fifth century BCE.
[62] Murray 1981: 99–100.

"In a short time I understood this about the poets, that they do not compose what they compose by way of wisdom, but by nature, and because they were divinely possessed (*enthousiazontes*), like the inspired prophets and speakers of oracles. For these men too say may fine things, but they do not have knowledge of any of the things they speak about" (22b3–c). Though these men did not possess knowledge, "they spoke many fine things." In the *Ion*, Plato indicates that the god actually speaks through the poets: "The god used the poets, the speakers of oracles, and the prophets as servants, taking away their *nous*; thus, we who hear the poets know that they are not speaking these extremely worthy things, since *nous* is not in them, but the god himself is the one speaking, and through these men he gives utterances to us" (διὰ ταῦτα δὲ ὁ θεὸς ἐξαιρούμενος τούτων τὸν νοῦν τούτοις χρῆται ὑπηρέταις καὶ τοῖς χρησμῳδοῖς καὶ τοῖς μάντεσι τοῖς θείοις, ἵνα ἡμεῖς οἱ ἀκούοντες εἰδῶμεν ὅτι οὐχ οὗτοί εἰσιν οἱ ταῦτα λέγοντες οὕτω πολλοῦ ἄξια, οἷς νοῦς μὴ πάρεστιν, ἀλλ᾽ ὁ θεὸς αὐτός ἐστιν ὁ λέγων, διὰ τούτων δὲ φθέγγεται πρὸς ἡμᾶς; 534c–d). As this passage indicates, the god somehow divests the poet (and also the prophet) of *nous*. Here, Plato makes a strong claim about the intellectual capacities of the poet: not only does he lack knowledge of the things he speaks about, but he (temporarily) loses his reason. The poet does of course utter comprehensible and, indeed, elevated language. But he is "outside of himself" (*exô seautou*; *Ion* 535c). For this reason, Plato treats him as "mad" (but not mentally ill).[63]

In sum, each kind of inspiration on Socrates' list in the *Phaedrus* differs according to the god, the religious context, and the type of individual who is inspired. As we have seen, the Greeks understood divine inspiration by way of cultural expectations that were rooted in their religious systems and its attendant discourses and practices. To attempt to understand this in modern or scientific terms is methodologically problematic. As anthropologists put it, we are "etic" rather than "emic": we investigate the Greeks as outsiders to their social groups, religious beliefs, and cultural practices rather than as people living inside the culture.

---

[63] Although Plato praises possession by the Muses, he has not changed his negative views about the poets in the *Phaedrus*. When Socrates puts the human souls into nine categories based on how much of the Forms each kind of soul saw in its preincarnate state, he places the philosophers in group one and the poets in group seven, just above the sophists and demagogues (group eight) and the tyrants (group nine, 248e). While he celebrates the blessings that come from poetic inspiration, he denigrates poets insofar as they lack knowledge. For useful discussions of Plato's conception of the Muses' inspiration of the poets, see Burnyeat 1977; Murray 1992; Nancy 2001; Halliwell 2002: Chapter 4; Ledbetter 2003: 87–94; Harris 2004; Scott 2011; Büttner 2011; Collobert 2011.

In the *Phaedrus*, Plato lists three traditional kinds of divine inspiration (oracular, telestic, poetic) to set up his claim that Eros inspires the philosopher. Here, the eros-inspired philosopher has a *mania* that puts him into an altered state of consciousness. Indeed, erotic inspiration enhances his reason. This allows the philosopher to recollect and contemplate the Forms. As Socrates states:

> My whole speech up to this point has been concerned with the fourth kind of madness – that which someone experiences when he sees beauty here and recollects true Beauty; then he takes wing and flutters eagerly in his desire to fly upwards, but he cannot do this – he gazes upward like a bird and neglects things below, and the reason for this is that he is in a maddened state. [My speech has shown that,] of all kinds of inspiration, this is the best kind of madness and comes from the best source to him who has it and shares in it, and he who loves beautiful objects and partakes in this madness is called a lover. (249d–e)[64]

Erotic inspiration resembles the other three kinds of divine possession in that the love-maddened individual achieves an altered state of consciousness. But erotic inspiration has its own special aspect. In the first three kinds of inspiration, a god acts from the outside on a human being. In erotic inspiration, by contrast, eros exists within every soul, divine and human. Eros does not function as a god who lives and acts externally to humans. Indeed, as I will claim, Plato treats Eros in purely mythopoetic terms when he describes the soul's desire for the Forms.

To examine this issue, let me briefly recall my discussion of the status of the daimon Eros in the *Symposium*. There, Plato used mythic discourse to indicate that daimons dwell in the middle realm between gods and humans: through them alone can humans connect with the gods. Daimonic eros enables the philosopher to reach the divine Forms. While the soul is mortal in the *Symposium*, it has the rational capacity to contemplate the Forms. But it needs daimonic eros to move it up to this divine realm. In the *Symposium*, there is no evidence that Plato conceived of the daimon Eros as an actual divine being. Rather, he used mythopoetic discourse to foreground the idea that the philosopher's reason has a daimonic desire for the divine Forms. Plato makes a similar move in

---

[64] 249d–e: ἔστι δὴ οὖν δεῦρο ὁ πᾶς ἥκων λόγος περὶ τῆς τετάρτης μανίας – ἣν ὅταν τὸ τῇδέ τις ὁρῶν κάλλος, τοῦ ἀληθοῦς ἀναμιμνησκόμενος, πτερῶταί τε καὶ ἀναπτερούμενος προθυμούμενος ἀναπτέσθαι, ἀδυνατῶν δέ, ὄρνιθος δίκην βλέπων ἄνω, τῶν κάτω δὲ ἀμελῶν, αἰτίαν ἔχει ὡς μανικῶς διακείμενος – ὡς ἄρα αὕτη πασῶν τῶν ἐνθουσιάσεων ἀρίστη τε καὶ ἐξ ἀρίστων τῷ τε ἔχοντι καὶ τῷ κοινωνοῦντι αὐτῆς γίγνεται, καὶ ὅτι ταύτης μετέχων τῆς μανίας ὁ ἐρῶν τῶν καλῶν ἐραστὴς καλεῖται.

his discussion of eros in the *Phaedrus*. He uses mythic language to articulate the idea that eros exists within the soul rather than in the realm of the gods.

To be sure, in the *Phaedrus*, Socrates identifies Eros as a god and offers a hymnic speech to him. He also places erotic inspiration in the category of traditional kinds of inspiration. Given the parallel that Socrates draws between these kinds of divine possession and erotic inspiration, he seems at first glance to identify Eros as an actual god who works upon a person externally. Two pieces of evidence lead me to reject this idea.

(1)   Plato does not place Eros among the gods ruling the heavens in the cosmological scheme. Indeed, he gives the gods in the cosmos the wings of desire: these divine souls have eros! This eros works together with reason so that the god's mind maintains a constant connection with the divine Forms. In addition, the godlike human souls possessed wings in their preincarnate state and thus had metaphysical desire from the get-go. They did not need divine inspiration at that point, yet they already possessed eros.

(2)   Once he begins his speech, Socrates does not represent Eros as an actual god who inspires the soul from without. To be sure, before the palinode, he gets Phaedrus to agree that Eros is a god, the son of Aphrodite (242d). But he then offers two possible ideas about Eros: "if Eros is (as indeed he is) either a god or something divine, he cannot be evil" (εἰ δ᾽ ἔστιν, ὥσπερ οὖν ἔστι, θεὸς ἤ τι θεῖον ὁ Ἔρως, οὐδὲν ἂν κακὸν εἴη; 242d). Here, he indicates that eros may not be an actual god but rather "something divine." As I argue, eros is this "something divine" in the soul.

In the speech itself, Socrates has very little to say about the god Eros. At the beginning of the palinode, he says rather vaguely that love comes "from the gods" (*ek theôn*, 245b; *para theôn*, 245c). And he also says that people do not realize that the philosophic lover "has a god in him" (*enthousiazôn*) (249c–d). This does not, however, explain how this inspiration actually operates. Indeed, Socrates only refers to Eros as a god once after that, and this in a comic discussion of his name: "some Homeridai speak two lines on Eros that come from the hidden poems of Homer ... : 'mortals call him *Love with Wings* (*erôta potênon*) but the gods call him *Winged* (*Pteros*) because of the necessity for growing wings'" (λέγουσι δὲ οἶμαί τινες Ὁμηριδῶν ἐκ τῶν ἀποθέτων ἐπῶν δύο ἔπη εἰς τὸν Ἔρωτ ... τὸν δ᾽ ἤτοι θνητοὶ μὲν Ἔρωτα καλοῦσι ποτηνόν, ἀθάνατοι δὲ Πτέρωτα, διὰ πτεροφύτορ᾽ ἀνάγκην; 252c). This does not deal with Eros as a god who inspires humans. Indeed, as we have seen, in Plato's image of the charioteer, the wings represent philosophic eros (metaphysical desire for the Forms). The invented "Homeric" lines in fact bolster Plato's own image of the soul as having wings. This indicates that eros is an aspect of the soul, not a god acting from without.[65]

In sum, Socrates never portrays Eros as an external god who inspires the philosopher. Indeed, after the single explicit reference to Eros in his speech quoted above, he only brings up the god after the speech. There, he prays to Eros to forgive him for his first speech and to grant him favor. To be sure, Socrates does pray to an actual god here, but this prayer lies outside the palinode proper, which represents Plato's views on the divine realm of the Forms and the gods ruling the cosmos. For this reason, I argue, Plato does not identify Eros as an actual god separate from the soul itself.[66] Rather, he conceives of eros as a divine element in the soul. This "divine desire," when it operates fully in the human soul, gives it a higher state of consciousness.[67]

In my discussion of the *Symposium*, I claimed that the philosopher contemplating the Forms transcends himself during this activity. Plato presents a similar idea in the *Phaedrus*. His erotically maddened philosopher rises above earthly concerns and recollects the Forms. As Socrates observes, the philosophic souls are "stricken with amazement and are outside themselves" (ἐκπλήττονται καὶ οὐκέτ' <ἐν> αὑτῶν γίγνονται) – literally, "not in themselves" – when they see a good image of a Form on earth (250a). Indeed, the philosopher, "standing outside of (*existamenos*) human pursuits and being near the divine (*pros tôi theiôi*), is scorned by the many, who see him as crazy and do not realize that he is possessed by a god (*enthousiazôn*)" (249c–d).[68] Here, the philosopher transcends himself by turning away from human pursuits and being "near the divine," i.e., the Forms. In contrast to the inspired poets in the *Ion*, the philosopher who is "outside himself" is in full possession of his *nous*.

Plato uses mythopoetic discourse to represent eros and the soul's erotic ascent to the divine Forms. In suggesting that eros inspires the philosopher, Plato refers to the divine desire that is an aspect of the rational part of the soul. Thus, the love-mad philosopher does resemble other inspired

[65] Note also that when Socrates discusses the love-inspired philosopher, he focuses only on his maddened state and the internal conflicts within his soul. He does not represent Eros the god as acting on the lover in this scene.
[66] Of course Plato does acknowledge that Eros is a god in the traditional Greek pantheon. My focus here, however, is on Plato's philosophical psychology.
[67] Non-philosophers, however, do not act upon this desire – their worldly desires override this one.
[68] 249c–d: ἐξιστάμενος δὲ τῶν ἀνθρωπίνων σπουδασμάτων καὶ πρὸς τῷ θείῳ γιγνόμενος, νουθετεῖται μὲν ὑπὸ τῶν πολλῶν ὡς παρακινῶν, ἐνθουσιάζων δὲ λέληθεν τοὺς πολλούς.

individuals, but only in certain ways. From the point of view of other humans, the philosopher achieves an altered state of consciousness. He has separated himself from the human realm. From the point of view of the philosopher, however, his soul has transcended its human self and has a being-together with (*sunousia*) the divine Forms. The soul of the philosopher is most of all "in its mind" during contemplation even though, qua human, the philosopher is "outside himself."

4.8   Two Epiphanies of the Form of Beauty

How did the Greeks describe the experience of a divine epiphany? As Platt claims, "in the vocabulary of archaic Greek experience, an epiphany functions as the ultimate form of *thauma*, a 'wonder,' in which divine presence, or *eidos*, is asserted in profoundly physical terms ... it has a powerful, often transformative affect upon its witnesses and their surroundings."[69] As we will see, the philosophic lover in Plato's epiphanic narrative reacts to the vision of the Form with astonishment, fear, and religious reverence. The lover goes through a profound transformation that makes him see that earthly beauty has a divine source.

We must note first that Socrates depicts two epiphanies of the Forms in the palinode. These epiphanies occur in two different phases of the life of the human soul: one when the soul is preincarnate and the other when it lives on earth. Let us look at the first epiphany, where the preincarnate human soul sees the Forms. As Socrates says, the preincarnate human souls journeyed together with the gods to the edge of the heavens and contemplated the Form of Beauty:

> Beauty was brilliantly shining to look upon (κάλλος δὲ τότ᾽ ἦν ἰδεῖν λαμπρόν) when the souls – we with the blessed chorus following with Zeus and others following with other gods – saw that blessed sight and vision (μακαρίαν ὄψιν τε καὶ θέαν) and were initiated into the mysteries that are rightly called the most blessed. And in a perfect state we celebrated as mystic initiates (ὠργιάζομεν), being free from the evils that awaited us at a later time. And as the highest initiates (μυούμενοί τε καὶ ἐποπτεύοντες) we viewed in a pure light perfect and simple and calm and happy visions (φάσματα). (250b–c)[70]

[69] Platt 2011: 56–7. For useful discussions of divine epiphanies in ancient Greece, see Cancik 1990: 290–6; Graf 2004: 111–30; Platt 2011; Petridou 2015.

[70] 250b–c: κάλλος δὲ τότ᾽ ἦν ἰδεῖν λαμπρόν, ὅτε σὺν εὐδαίμονι χορῷ μακαρίαν ὄψιν τε καὶ θέαν, ἑπόμενοι μετὰ μὲν Διὸς ἡμεῖς, ἄλλοι δὲ μετ᾽ ἄλλου θεῶν, εἶδόν τε καὶ ἐτελοῦντο τῶν τελετῶν ἣν θέμις λέγειν μακαριωτάτην, ἣν ὠργιάζομεν ὁλόκληροι μὲν αὐτοὶ ὄντες καὶ ἀπαθεῖς κακῶν ὅσα ἡμᾶς ἐν

As Socrates suggests, the preincarnate souls had a relatively direct view of the Forms, which are divine in nature.[71] He refers to the souls as the "highest initiates" (*epopteuontes*), and thus conjures up the initiates at the Eleusinian Mysteries. As we have seen, in the Eleusinian Mysteries, a festival for Demeter and Persephone, people seeking initiation performed and experienced rituals of purification that enabled them to see sacred objects and have an epiphany of the goddess. In the final ceremony, the celebrants stood in the darkness of night in a building called the Telesterion; there, hundreds of torches were lit and a blaze of light filled the area.[72] The flickering fires added to the visual effects of the religious rituals. In addition, the hierophants acted out the "sacred drama" and held images of the gods. In these rituals and incantations, they conjured up an epiphany. In the passage above, the preincarnate souls, as *epoptai*, "celebrated as mystic initiates" (*ôrgiazomen*) as they beheld the divine Forms. The souls worshipped the Forms as divinities.

Plato also compares the preincarnate soul's epiphany of the Forms to the Eleusinian Mysteries in other ways. The souls saw the "blessed sight and vision" (μακαρίαν ὄψιν τε καὶ θέαν) just as the initiates did at the climax of the Eleusinian festival. And, just as the blazing torches illuminated the climax of the initiation ceremony, the souls' vision of the Forms took place "in a pure light" (ἐν αὐγῇ καθαρᾷ). Note in particular the reference to the "perfect and simple and calm and happy visions (*phasmata*)" that the soul experienced in this first epiphany. As Petridou has shown, ancient Greek texts "are rife with epiphanies of gods and heroes that manifest themselves in the form of a *phasma*."[73] This kind of epiphany differs from those in which the gods manifested themselves in anthropomorphic bodies or statues: "when Greek authors describe a divine manifestation in a *phasma* form, they mean a spectral appearance that has a more ethereal bodily quality than, let us say, the presence of a god or a hero in person."[74] In short, *phasmata* have a supernatural and other-worldly nature. As Petridou notes, the epiphany of the god or goddess in the form of a *phasma* took

---

ὑστέρῳ χρόνῳ ὑπέμενεν, ὁλόκληρα δὲ καὶ ἁπλᾶ καὶ ἀτρεμῆ καὶ εὐδαίμονα φάσματα μυούμενοί τε καὶ ἐποπτεύοντες ἐν αὐγῇ καθαρᾷ. I translate "ὠργιάζομεν" as "we celebrated as mystic initiates" to capture the language from the Eleusinian Mysteries that Plato uses here. We find this same verb in passages on the mysteries of Dionysus and Cybele (see the passages on the *Laws* 790b–c and Aristotle *Pol.* 8.7, 1342a1–11 above).
[71] Although the conflicts in their souls prevented them from having a clear and ongoing vision (248a).
[72] See Chapter 1 for a detailed discussion of the Eleusinian Mysteries. For an excellent account of Plato's use of the discourse of the Eleusinian Mysteries, see Riedweg 1987: 17–37, 47–69; see also Nightingale 2004: Chapter 2.
[73] Graf 2004: 126; Petridou 2015: 64.   [74] Petridou 2015: 66.

place in initiatory festivals that featured night-time rituals.[75] As we have seen, in the Eleusinian Mysteries, torchlights illuminated the nocturnal performances and the sacred objects that set the stage for the epiphany.[76] In using the discourse of *phasmata* and referring to the Eleusinian Mysteries, Plato conjures up the other-worldly nature of the preincarnate souls' contemplation of the Forms. In short, Plato uses the Eleusinian Divinity-Marker to represent the Forms as divine.

I want to look now at Plato's second narrative of epiphany, where the philosophic lover on earth has a vision of the Forms. The philosopher has an epiphany of the Forms by way of recollection. As Socrates states:

> It is necessary for a person to gain an understanding of a general conception in accordance with the Form, moving from many sensible perceptions and collecting these into a unity by way of reason. This is the recollection (ἀνάμνησις) of those things which our soul saw then, when it journeyed together with the god and lifted its vision above the things which we now say exist, and looked up to real being. Wherefore it is just to say that the mind of the philosopher is winged. For it gets as close as possible, by way of memory, to those things [the Forms] by being close to which the gods are divine. And that man alone who makes use of these memories, and is initiated in the ever-perfect mysteries, becomes truly perfect. (ὑπομνήμασιν ὀρθῶς χρώμενος, τελέους ἀεὶ τελετὰς τελούμενος, τέλεος ὄντως μόνος γίγνεται; 249b–c)[77]

Socrates uses the terminology of "then" and "now" to emphasize the difference between (1) the past time when the preincarnate soul viewed the Forms more or less directly, and (2) the present time when the philosopher recollects those earlier visions. As Socrates notes, most people on earth have forgotten their preincarnate life due to the demands of the body (250a); only a few people, the philosophers, have adequate memories of their earlier vision of the Forms. If the philosopher "uses these memories rightly," he will be "initiated in the ever-perfect mysteries" (249d). Since the philosophic soul was already an initiate (*epoptês*) in its preincarnate life, it effectively undergoes a re-initiation when it recollects the Forms in

---

[75] Petridou 2015: 65.

[76] Clinton 2004. For the ritual mechanisms used in the Eleusinian festivals to evoke epiphanic manifestations, see Graf 2004: 124; see also Versnel 1987: 42–55.

[77] Here is the full Greek passage (249b–c): δεῖ γὰρ ἄνθρωπον συνιέναι κατ᾽ εἶδος λεγόμενον, ἐκ πολλῶν ἰὸν αἰσθήσεων εἰς ἓν λογισμῷ συναιρούμενον· τοῦτο δ᾽ ἐστὶν ἀνάμνησις ἐκείνων ἃ ποτ᾽ εἶδεν ἡμῶν ἡ ψυχὴ συμπορευθεῖσα θεῷ καὶ ὑπεριδοῦσα ἃ νῦν εἶναί φαμεν, καὶ ἀνακύψασα εἰς τὸ ὂν ὄντως. διὸ δὴ δικαίως μόνη πτεροῦται ἡ τοῦ φιλοσόφου διάνοια· πρὸς γὰρ ἐκείνοις ἀεί ἐστιν μνήμῃ κατὰ δύναμιν, πρὸς οἷσπερ θεὸς ὢν θεῖός ἐστιν. τοῖς δὲ δὴ τοιούτοις ἀνὴρ ὑπομνήμασιν ὀρθῶς χρώμενος, τελέους ἀεὶ τελετὰς τελούμενος, τέλεος ὄντως μόνος γίγνεται.

a human life on earth. The philosophic soul that recollects the Forms sees them (again) in the present.

In the first epiphany, the preincarnate human souls had a relatively direct view of the divine Forms. Socrates portrays this vision in terms of a group of souls, so his account does not have the power of an epiphanic narrative that focuses on a single individual responding to a divine revelation. We find this narrative in the second epiphany, where the lover recollects the Form of Beauty as he looks at his beloved. Socrates sets up the second epiphany by offering a lengthy account of the love affair that leads to the vision of Beauty. This provides a rhetorical build-up for the divine revelation. Socrates represents the philosopher who loves a beautiful boy as going mad with desire (both physical and psychic). In particular, the agonizing experience of the growth of his soul's wings drives him into *mania* (251a–252d).

To understand this epiphanic narrative more clearly, we must first look at the words and tropes used in poetic narratives of epiphanies. As Platt notes, Greek literary accounts of divine epiphany focus on the radiance, beauty, and *enargeia* (full presence) of the god/goddess, and the fearful and astonished reaction of the human viewer.[78] As we will see, Plato uses all of these elements in his account of the philosophic lover's epiphanic vision of divine Beauty. Indeed, he uses the Poetic Narratives of Epiphany divinity-marker quite extensively. Consider the language of beauty and radiant light in poetic narratives of epiphany. In the Homeric hymns, a god manifests him or herself by emanating beauty and brilliant light. For example, in the *Homeric Hymn to Demeter*, Demeter radiates with light as she reveals herself to the royal women in Eleusis: "a light shone from the immortal body of the goddess, and her golden hair spread down over her shoulders, and the firm house was filled with brightness like a bolt of lightning" (τῆλε δὲ φέγγος ἀπὸ χροὸς ἀθανάτοιο λάμπε θεᾶς, ξάνθαι δὲ κόμαι κατενήνοθεν ὤμους, αὐγῆς δ᾽ ἐπλήσθη πυκινὸς δόμος ἀστερωπῆς ὥς; *HH* 2.278–81). At the same time, the goddess shakes off her disguise and "beauty breathed around her" (περί τ᾽ ἀμφί τε κάλλος ἄητο; 276). Again, in the *Homeric Hymn to Aphrodite*, the goddess appears to Anchises "clad in a robe that shone more brightly than the light of fire and the most beautiful necklaces were around her tender throat–beautiful, golden, and richly variegated– and [the robe] radiated like the moon over her tender breasts, a wonder to behold" (πέπλον μὲν γὰρ ἔεστο φαεινότερον πυρὸς αὐγῆς ... ὅρμοι δ᾽

---

[78] Platt 2011: 56–65. See F. Pfister 1924 on the key terminology that the Greeks used for epiphanic encounters.

ἀμφ' ἁπαλῇ δειρῇ περικαλλέες ἦσαν καλοὶ χρύσειοι παμποίκιλοι, δὲ σελήνη στήθεσιν ἀμφ' ἁπαλοῖσιν ἐλάμπετο, θαῦμα ἰδέσθαι; *HH* 5.86–91). In addition, "the cheeks [of Aphrodite] shone with ambrosial beauty" (κάλλος δὲ παρειάων ἀπέλαμπεν ἄμβροτον, *HH* 5.174–5). In these passages, the goddesses shine with an almost unearthly light.[79] Indeed, the poet compares this light to lightning bolts and the shimmering moon.

Plato uses this same language of light, radiance, and beauty in both narratives of epiphany. For example, in the depiction of the preincarnate human soul seeing the Forms, Socrates says that "Beauty then was radiant to look upon" (κάλλος δὲ τότ' ἦν ἰδεῖν λαμπρόν; 250b). Indeed, the Form of Beauty has a special status here on earth: "Beauty shone radiantly (ἔλαμπεν) in its being among the Forms there; and coming here we have grasped it as it shines (στίλβον) most clearly (ἐναργέστατα) through the clearest (ἐναργεστάτης) of our senses" (250d). Beauty has its own special light. Unlike other value Forms (like Justice, Self-Control, Courage, etc.), Beauty hits the viewer and immediately grabs his or her attention. Plato captures this idea by saying that Beauty shines most brightly among the Forms. He also emphasizes the *enargeia* (clear presence) of Beauty: both the sense of sight and the beauty of the object allow for the "clearest" (*enargestatê*) manifestation of the Form of Beauty.

In poetic narratives of epiphany, the human viewers responded to the god with fear and awe. In the *Hymn to Demeter*, for example, "the goddess walked to the threshold, and her head reached the roof, and she filled the doorway with divine light; then awe, reverence, and pale fear took hold of Metaneira" (ἡ δ' ἄρ' ἐπ' οὐδὸν ἔβη ποσὶ καί ῥα μελάθρου κῦρε κάρη, πλῆσεν δὲ θύρας σέλαος θείοιο. τὴν δ' αἰδώς τε σέβας τε ἰδὲ χλωρὸν δέος εἷλεν; *HH* 2.188–90). Later in the hymn, when Demeter throws off her disguise and fully reveals her divinity, Metaneira once again reacts with fear and astonishment: her "knees were loosed and she remained speechless" (τῆς δ' αὐτίκα γούνατ' ἔλυντο, δηρὸν δ' ἄφθογγος γένετο χρόνον; *HH* 2.281–2). We find the same fearful reaction in the *Hymn to Aphrodite*: "when Anchises saw the neck and lovely eyes of Aphrodite, he was afraid (τάρβησέν) and turned his eyes away" (*HH* 5.182). In these passages, the sight of the goddess generates a powerful bodily reaction: a person feels weak-kneed, loses speech, or turns away from the overwhelming sight.[80] In the *Iliad*, Achilles reacts to an epiphany of Athena as follows: "Achilles felt

---

[79] On the discourse of radiance in archaic Greek texts, see Prier 1989: 50–9.
[80] See also *HH* 7.37: "amazement" (*taphos*), seizes the sailors when they see the wonders of Dionysus.

astonishment, and he turned around and immediately recognized Pallas Athena. Her eyes shone terribly" (θάμβησεν δ᾽ Ἀχιλεύς, μετὰ δ᾽ ἐτράπετ᾽, αὐτίκα δ᾽ ἔγνω Παλλάδ᾽ Ἀθηναίην· δεινὼ δέ οἱ ὄσσε φάανθεν; *Il.* 1.199–200). Athena's eyes have a terrifying power. Amazingly, even animals feel terror at a divine epiphany: when Athena appears to Odysseus and his dogs, "Odysseus and the dogs saw her, and the dogs did not bark, but fled in fear (φόβηθεν) to the other side of the farmstead, whimpering" (16.159–64). As these passages show, the viewers react with fear, wonder, and reverence.

Let us look more closely at the second narrative of epiphany in Socrates' palinode. Before the lover recollects the Form of Beauty, he sees divine beauty in the boy's face:

> But he who is recently initiated, having seen many of the realities then, when he saw a godlike face or the form of a body that is a good imitation (εὖ μεμιμημένον) of Beauty, at first he shuddered (ἔφριξε) and some of the former fear took hold of him (τι τῶν τότε ὑπῆλθεν αὐτὸν δειμάτων); then, as he looks at him he reveres him like a god (ὡς θεὸν σέβεται) and, if he didn't fear that he would be thought completely mad, he would sacrifice to the boy as though to a divine statue and a god (ὡς ἀγάλματι καὶ θεῷ). (251a)

The lover feels the "former fear" that he experienced when he saw the divine Form of Beauty in a preincarnate state. Even then, the godlike human soul felt fear when it beheld the Forms. Here on earth, the philosopher responds with religious reverence, though he initially reveres the boy rather than the Form. Indeed, he wants to offer sacrifices to him as though to a god. Once again, the philosopher reacts with fear: "when the lover sees the beautiful boy, he is overwhelmed by fear (φόβῳ διόλλυται), so that from then on the soul of the lover follows the beloved in reverence and fear (αἰδουμένην τε καὶ δεδιυῖαν)" (254e). Plato uses the same language of fear and reverence found in poetic epiphanies of the gods.

At the climax of this narrative, the philosopher finally sees the Form when he looks upon the beautiful boy. As Socrates states:

> [The lover] saw the face of the beloved, which was flashing like lightning (ἀστράπτουσαν). And the memory of the charioteer, as he looked at him, was carried to the true nature of Beauty, and he saw it standing with Self-Control upon a holy pedestal. When he saw this, he felt terror and fell backward in reverence. (εἶδον τὴν ὄψιν τὴν τῶν παιδικῶν ἀστράπτουσαν. ἰδόντος δὲ τοῦ ἡνιόχου ἡ μνήμη πρὸς τὴν τοῦ κάλλους φύσιν ἠνέχθη, καὶ

πάλιν εἶδεν αὐτὴν μετὰ σωφροσύνης ἐν ἁγνῷ βάθρῳ βεβῶσαν· ἰδοῦσα δὲ ἔδεισέ τε καὶ σεφθεῖσα ἀνέπεσεν ὑπτία; 254b–c)[81]

Here, the "he" who sees the Forms is the rational part of the philosopher's soul. The philosopher's reason metaphorically falls backwards in reverence. The soul reacts to the divinity of Beauty just as a human reacts to a god in poetic narratives of epiphany. Indeed, the beloved boy's face flashes like a lightning bolt just as Demeter fills the house like a bolt of lightning when she reveals herself to the people of Eleusis in the *Hymn to Demeter* (*HH* 2.281). The beautiful boy's hyper-radiant face makes the philosopher's soul recollect and behold the divine Form of Beauty. In these passages, Plato uses the Eleusinian divinity-marker and the Poetic Narratives of Epiphany divinity-marker to emphasize the divinity of the Forms.

Seeing divine Beauty generates fear, wonder, and reverence. As I have suggested, the divine aspect of the Forms goes beyond language and philosophic comprehension. The philosophic soul can attain knowledge of the essence of Beauty, but it cannot fully apprehend its divinity. It thus reacts to Beauty with fear and reverence. By depicting the soul as "falling backwards" at the sight of Beauty, Plato conjures up the ontological gap between the soul and the Forms. He also shows that the philosopher reacts to the Form of Beauty with religious reverence.

Clearly, this "present" epiphany occurs by way of recollection and recognition. The lover recognizes the Form of Beauty radiating through the boy's face because his soul has seen this before, when it lived in a pure and disembodied state. This epiphany works when the soul "brings together" the vision "now" and the vision "then." The man seeing his beautiful beloved in the present understands that the Form of Beauty was the true object of his love all along. While Plato borrows from poetic accounts of epiphany, his epiphanic narrative differs from those of his predecessors in an important way: his individual viewer sees the divine Form of Beauty by recollecting an earlier epiphany. He sees the Form in two time-zones, as it were. The philosophic soul's experience of the first, preincarnate epiphany allows him to *recognize* the divine Form when he sees it in his earthly life. As Platt observes, in poetic epiphanies, the human viewer must be able to recognize the god when he/she appears: "as many epiphanic narratives suggest, the visual manifestation of a god, often signified by the use of *phainesthai* or *enargês*, requires a *corresponding process of perception and recognition*

---

[81] Riedweg 1987: 61–2 offers an interesting discussion of the religious aspects of the Greek word *bathron* ("pedestal"). He suggests that this word may refer to the Eleusinian Mysteries.

(*noêsis* and *anagnôrisis*) from its mortal witnesses."[82] Plato dramatizes this recognition scene in the second epiphany by showing the philosopher as recollecting the Form (rather than just seeing it, which he also does). By setting forth the two epiphanies and linking them together in the moment of recollection, Plato builds the recognition process into his account. We must emphasize, however, that the philosopher does not simply remember something he saw in the past: he sees this as manifesting itself in the present. It is precisely the divine presence of Beauty that generates his stunned reaction.

Let me close this chapter by examining one more religious element in Plato's epiphanic discourse: statues of the gods. As we have seen, Socrates says that the lover who sees the beauty in his beloved wants to worship him "like a statue (*agalma*) or a god" (251a; see also 252d–e). Here, the lover feels confusion over the nature of the beauty he beholds in his beloved: is he seeing a statue of the divinity or divinity itself? We find this oscillation again later in Socrates' speech, when he says that the lover "fashions [the beloved] and adorns him like a statue, as though he were his god, so that he can honor and worship him" (ὡς θεὸν αὐτὸν ἐκεῖνον ὄντα ἑαυτῷ οἷον ἄγαλμα τεκταίνεταί τε καὶ κατακοσμεῖ, ὡς τιμήσων τε καὶ ὀργιάσων; 252d–e). The lover sees his beloved as a statue (*agalma*) of Beauty and, at the same time, sees the divine Form of Beauty in the body-statue. The lover's confused response to the boy's "statuesque" body represents a common Greek religious experience: in looking at a statue of a god, the Greeks could at times see the presence of the god itself. As Platt observes, the statues of the gods "have the potential to be viewed as epiphanic embodiments of the deities they represent. They can simultaneously symbolize and constitute divine presence."[83] In the passages above, Plato portrays the lover as having the Greeks' dual response to seeing the statue of a god in a ritualized context: the statue both symbolizes and manifests the god.[84] The Greeks could see divinity in these statues by way of the rituals that surrounded the sanctuaries, festivals, and statues themselves.[85] As Jaś Elsner has shown, this ritualized mode of viewing "denies the appropriateness . . . of interpreting images through the rules and desires

[82] Platt 2011: 57, my italics.
[83] Platt 2011: 47. See also Burkert 1997; Steiner 2001: 80–5; Gaifman 2016: 249–80.
[84] As Vernant claims, the statues of the gods had the effect of "making the invisible visible, assigning a place in our world to entities from the other world. In the representational enterprise, this paradoxical aspiration exists in order to inscribe absence in presence, to insert the other, the elsewhere, into our familiar universe" (1991: 153).
[85] See my discussion of the Alcibiades scene in the *Symposium* in Chapter 2.

of everyday life. It constructs a ritual barrier to the identifications and objectifications of the screen of [social] discourse and posits a sacred possibility for vision."[86] One could argue that Plato uses religious discourse in both epiphanies to discursively "ritualize" the vision of the Forms.

Finally, the lover sees the epiphany of the Form of Beauty "standing on a holy pedestal" (*bathron*).[87] In classical Greek, the word *bathron* refers to the pedestal of a statue of a god.[88] Why does Plato place the Form of Beauty on a pedestal, as though it is a statue? First, he needs to create a visual image for the reader: he could not depict the invisible Form without providing some sort of visual aid. But he may also have based this image on the *hedos* or "seat" of the gods. In this context, the Greek word *hedos* did not refer to a physical "seat" but rather to a conceptual container of gods. As Platt claims:

> Whereas *agalma* and *xoanon* evoke the artefactual, created nature of images, *hedos* refers to their function as "vessels" or "receptacles" of divine presence . . . . The *hedos* makes concrete the idea that the sacred images operate as a kind of frame; they provide a physical object to act as a "container" of divinity, and even indicate the form the God might take. Yet by indicating the possibility of absence and mobility, a concept of the image as "seat" also expresses the idea that divinity operates beyond the framework of ritual and representation that constitutes his or her worship in a specific location.[89]

Plato reached for the "pedestal" (*bathron*), then, to create a "frame" for the Forms. The *bathron* acts as a "seat" that contains a divinity that is uncontainable. In adding this pedestal, Plato foregrounds the divinity of the Forms.

As I have argued in this chapter, Plato sets forth a new conception of metaphysical desire in the *Phaedrus*. Eros is a "divine desire" felt by all souls. Indeed, the rational part of the soul has its own desire. Plato represents this desire by creating an image of a charioteer, two horses, and wings. The wings represent metaphysical desire: they lift the soul up to contemplate the divine Forms. When the human souls fall to earth, they lose most if not all of their memory of the Forms, and also their winged divine desire. The soul regains the wings of desire by practicing philosophy.

---

[86] Elsner 2000: 45–63.
[87] It is possible that the Form of Self-Control is also standing on the pedestal. But the participle *bebôsan* is in the singular and modifies *tên tou kallous phusin*. This suggests that Beauty alone stands on the pedestal.
[88] See, e.g., Herodotus 1.183.1, 5.85.1–2; Aeschylus, *Persians* 812; Sophocles, *Antigone* 854.
[89] Platt 2011: 104.

Plato compares eros' "maddening" power over the soul to three traditional kinds of divine inspiration (oracular, poetic, telestic). While the philosopher does achieve an altered state of consciousness (as this is perceived by humans), he does not in fact lose his mind. Indeed, his mind is enhanced. During contemplation, he is most of all "in his mind" even though he has transcended his human self and thus appears "mad."

Plato uses the Poetic Narratives of Epiphany divinity-marker to introduce divinities that were not recognized as such by ordinary Greeks. He also uses the Eleusinian divinity-marker to present the idea that the philosopher sees a divine epiphany in the Form of Beauty. In Socrates' palinode, Plato repeatedly emphasizes the divinity of the realm of the Forms. He also shows the ontological chasm between the time-bound individual and the ever-present and unchanging Form: as a temporalized soul, the philosophic lover recollects a divine Being that he once saw "then" in the passing "now." As a self-moving and temporalized soul, the human confronts a changeless and eternal divinity.

CHAPTER 5

The Gods Made Visible

But how can you look at something and set your own ego aside? Whose eyes are doing the looking? As a rule, you think of the ego as one who is peering out of your own eyes as if leaning on a window sill, looking at the world stretching out before him in all its immensity. So, then: a window looks out on the world. The world is out there; and in here, what do we have? The world still – what else could there be? With a little effort of concentration, Mr. Palomar manages to shift the world from in front of him and set it on the sill, looking out. Now, beyond the windows, what do we have? The world is also there, and for the occasion has been split into a looking world and a world looked at. And what about him, also known as "I," namely Mr. Palomar? Is he not a piece of the world that is looking at another piece of the world? Or else, given that there is world that side of the window and world this side, perhaps the "I," the ego, is simply the window through which the world looks at the world. To look at itself the world needs the eyes (and the eyeglasses) of Mr. Palomar.

– Italo Calvino, *Mr. Palomar*

In the *Timaeus*, one god creates another: the Demiurge makes the cosmos, an animal god that has a divine soul and body. The Demiurge forms this cosmic "animal" as a copy of the "Form of Animal" (the *noêton zôon* or "intelligible animal"). While the Form of Animal is unchanging and eternal, the cosmic animal moves and changes over time. In his account of the Demiurge's cosmic theopoiesis (as it were), Plato presents a new philosophical theology. He introduces new gods.

To bring this innovation into clearer focus, let us briefly juxtapose Plato's accounts of the soul and body in the *Phaedo* and *Phaedrus* to the one he sets forth in the *Timaeus*. In the *Phaedo*, the soul is immortal and godlike but incarnates in mortal bodies as some sort of punishment; it longs to leave the alien body and dwell with its kindred Forms. Plato treats the body in highly negative terms in the *Phaedo* – it imprisons the soul and forces it to engage in bad actions. Although he does locate the spherical earth at the center of a spherical cosmos, which hints at a divine order, he does not posit a cosmic god (108e–109a). In the *Phaedrus*, Plato identifies the soul as immortal, divine, self-moving, and capable of reincarnation. In addition, he conceives of the gods as divine souls that govern the physical universe. He does not, however, place these souls firmly in the cosmic body or the stars. In addition, he does not posit a Demiurge who created the divine souls and the cosmos. Rather, the souls of the gods are divine simply by virtue of their ongoing contemplation of the divine Forms. In the *Timaeus*, by contrast, the divinity of the cosmic, astral, and human souls does not depend on their contemplation of the Forms; rather, they get their divinity from their demiurgic creator.

In the middle-period dialogues, Plato presented his key metaphysical and theological ideas about the Forms, the soul, and the bodily realm. There, he emphasized the soul's relationship to the divine realm of the Forms, the gods, and the body. In the *Timaeus*, he focuses primarily on the soul and the cosmos. To be sure, he nests his cosmology in the ontology of the Forms and particulars. But this takes a back seat in this dialogue. Indeed, Plato does not even represent the soul contemplating the Forms in this text, even though this is the ultimate object of *nous*, both for gods and humans. Rather, the cosmos and its denizens take center stage.

This difficult and wondrous dialogue has generated a vast number of interpretations, starting in antiquity and carrying on to the present day. The *Timaeus* presents a number of interpretive challenges for the reader. First, the discourse in the *Timaeus* is an *eikôs logos* (or an *eikôs muthos*) – a "likely/appropriate" account.[1] Second, the dialogue features many metaphorical and mythic passages. And, third, the text contains a number of technical and, at times, confusing arguments. To understand this dialogue, we will have to look at many passages and examine these in some detail.

In this chapter, I analyze the ideas and themes that I addressed in earlier chapters: the rational soul's relation to the Forms; the ontological status of the human soul; the immortal soul's life in mortal bodies; the story of the soul; and divine epiphany. I also discuss the divine beings in this cosmology: the Demiurge, the cosmic soul, the star gods, the ancillary gods, and

---

[1] There is a great deal of scholarship on the *eikôs logos* and *eikôs muthos*. See, e.g., Taylor 1928: 59–60, 73–4, 440–2; Cornford 1956: 28–32; Burnyeat 2005; Johansen 2008: Chapter 3; Betegh 2010; Mourelatos 2010; Broadie 2012: 31–52. I follow Burnyeat's account.

the human soul. I refer to the latter as the "rational human soul" to emphasize that this soul is purely rational.

I will first investigate the divine beings in this cosmology. In the beginning, the Demiurge creates the entire cosmos. As an intelligent "cause" (*aitia*), he designs and builds the universe (28a–b). The Demiurge makes the cosmos by contemplating the Form of Animal. This Form provides the paradigm for the physical cosmos. He creates a divine cosmic soul that moves and governs its own cosmic body.[2] The Demiurge places the cosmic soul or "World-Soul" in the entire body of the universe: "the [World-] Soul was woven [into the body] in every way from the center through the extremity, and enveloping it as a circle on the outside" (36d–e).[3] In a very basic sense, "all things are full of god" in this cosmology. In addition, the cosmic soul moves in circles – the psychic movement of its mind has the effect of moving its cosmic body in a circle and keeping the fixed stars rotating in the universe in perfect rotations.

The rational human soul, too, is divine. In the *Phaedo*, Plato identified the rational soul (or the rational aspect of the soul) as "godlike"; in his mythic discourse in the *Phaedrus*, he placed human souls among the gods, giving them a divine status. In the *Timaeus*, Plato makes the rational human soul fully divine (though it does not have the level of divinity that the cosmos does). Since the Demiurge creates the human rational soul out of the same materials and in the same structure as the cosmic soul, it can engage in the same rational activities as the gods: it moves its mind in circles and can contemplate the Forms. In addition, the rational human soul has the unique status of being able to live in different bodies – astral, human, and animal. To be sure, when it incarnates in a mortal body, it encounters a veritable onslaught of change. It does not sit easily in a body whose movement is rectilinear. Indeed, the human soul living in mortal bodies longs to return to its native star.

After discussing the cosmic and human souls, I will examine the bodily realm and the receptacle. To put this very generally, all bodies come into being and pass away in the receptacle. Although these are mere "images" of the Forms, certain bodies have a special status in the cosmos. First,

---

[2] See 37b5, where "discourse" (*logos*) is said to go on "within the thing that is self-moved" (ἐν τῷ κινουμένῳ ὑφ᾽ αὑτοῦ φερόμενος). See also 89a, where Timaeus says that the World-Soul (and souls in general) is self-moving: "of all motions that is the best which is produced in a thing by itself" (τῶν δ᾽ αὖ κινήσεων ἡ ἐν ἑαυτῷ ὑφ᾽ αὑτοῦ ἀρίστη κίνησις). On the self-moving soul, see Cornford 1956: 95n.2; Taylor 1928: 148, 178; Mohr 1985: 174.

[3] πᾶν τὸ σωματοειδὲς ἐντὸς αὐτῆς ἐτεκταίνετο καὶ μέσον μέσῃ συναγαγὼν προσήρμοττεν· ἡ δ᾽ ἐκ μέσου πρὸς τὸν ἔσχατον οὐρανὸν πάντη διαπλακεῖσα κύκλῳ τε αὐτὸν ἔξωθεν περικαλύψασα.

the cosmic body (the "World-Body") as a whole is perfect, imperishable, and beautiful. In terms of the structure of the cosmic body, the fixed stars mark its outer edge. Inside this outer circle, the planets move in perfect spirals at different levels of altitude, and the sun and moon move in circles around the earth (which sits at the center of the cosmos). Second, the star-gods have perfect and beautiful bodies: unlike other bodies in the universe, they do not change in size or structure or die away. The Demiurge makes bodies, including the cosmic body, out of atomic triangles. He creates these triangles out of the chaotic "stuff" in the receptacle, giving them different shapes (scalene, isosceles) and different sizes. The atomic triangles endlessly attach themselves to each other and form the molecules of the four elements (air, water, fire, earth). The four elements, in turn, conglomerate to make up the bodies in the visible realm. Finally, due to the self-motion of the cosmic soul (and, to a lesser extent, the astral and human souls), the atomic triangles are made to move all the time. By forming the atoms into triangles, the Demiurge gave the cosmos a geometric and rational structure. Paradoxically, the cosmos has a "perfect" body that never changes even though it contains atoms, elements, and bodies that undergo constant change. As we will see, Plato presents a much more positive account of the bodily realm in this dialogue.

The *Timaeus* stands out from earlier dialogues in its emphasis on motion. Plato describes in lavish detail the motions of the cosmic Soul, the cosmic Body, the stars, the human souls, and the atomic triangles. The World-Soul has one motion, which is circular. It moves its spherical World-Body in everlasting circles. This maintains the order and harmony of the universe. Plato famously valorized circular motion over rectilinear motion: the first is orderly, the second disorderly. While the cosmos as a whole moves the stars and planets in circular rotations, the atoms, elements, and sublunar bodies move in rectilinear motions. The cosmic soul does not create or direct these rectilinear motions – it simply keeps the entire cosmos moving by way of its circular motion.

The Demiurge designed the cosmos to be seen and admired. For this reason, vision plays a central role in this text. As Timaeus states, the god gives the gift of vision to humans not simply to enable them to live mortal lives but to allow them to learn numbers, mathematics, and philosophy. Indeed, the ultimate goal of human vision is to study the heavens and see it as a divinely beautiful spectacle. In conjunction with this teleological account of vision, Plato presents a complex theory of how vision comes about at the atomic level. He shows how the triangular atoms and the molecules of the four elements operate within the eye and the objects of sight, and explains how the eye sees its objects through the medium of light. I will examine this theory to show how embodied rational human souls apprehend the world as a visual phenomenon.

The rational human soul takes on new roles in this dialogue. This soul has its own individual mission, but it also contributes to the perfection of the cosmos. It does this in two ways. First, the cosmos becomes the best possible instantiation of the Form of Animal only if it includes mortal creatures. Indeed, the Demiurge structures the bodily realm of the cosmos for the purpose of making the best copy of the Form of Animal. Only the human soul can live in the mortal bodies of humans and animals (animals are declensions of humans because the bad human souls reincarnate in animals). The human soul perfects the cosmos, then, by living in mortal bodies.

Second, I suggest, the human soul perfects the cosmos by perceiving it at the physical level. The Demiurge designed the cosmos to be seen. The rational human soul is the only creature in the universe that can perceive the cosmos – the cosmic soul and star gods do not inhabit bodies that have a sensory apparatus. In short, the cosmos manifests itself as a meaningful physical phenomenon only to human beings. Without humans, the physical cosmos would be an orderly "becoming" but not a phenomenon.[4] Of course, the rational human soul must learn how to see the world in the right way. Only the philosophers can view the cosmos rightly, as a divine phenomenon. The cosmos manifests its divinity to humans through the "visible gods" of the stars (*horatoi theoi*, 40d, 92c). These appear to the human viewer as moving in beautiful and harmonious revolutions. While every human can admire the beauty of the stars, only the philosopher can see the heavens as they truly are, namely, a god manifesting its divinity to human eyes. In viewing the heavens as a divine phenomenon, humans serve to perfect the cosmos. The cosmos can only see itself (as it were) through the eyes of the philosopher.

Plato places great emphasis on vision and beauty in this text. At the beginning of Timaeus' account of the creation, the Demiurge makes the cosmic soul and body and then views this beautiful artwork with pleasure. In addition, humans bear witness to the cosmos and its beauty. In particular, the philosopher who has mastered astronomy sees the beauty, divinity, and goodness of the cosmos on both the intellectual and visual level. The divine cosmos discloses its divinity to this individual through the "visible

---

[4] To be sure, animals sense things in the world but they cannot perceive the cosmos as a cosmos.

gods" (*horatoi theoi*) in the heavens. In viewing the heavens, the philosopher sees a divine epiphany.

This kind of epiphany differs dramatically from the epiphany of the divine Forms. In the *Timaeus*, Plato does not offer a literary depiction of the philosophers ascending to the Forms (though they can of course contemplate the Forms). Rather, he focuses on the visible epiphany of the star gods. To be sure, Plato identifies two kinds of divine epiphanies in the *Timaeus*: "those gods who revolve in the heavens manifestly (*phanerôs*) and those gods who appear whenever they wish" (πάντες ὅσοι τε περιπολοῦσιν φανερῶς καὶ ὅσοι φαίνονται καθ' ὅσον ἂν ἐθέλωσιν θεοί; 41a). Here, he separates the star gods in the heavens and traditional gods on earth. In this dialogue, Plato focuses almost exclusively on the epiphany of the star gods. Even in the case of the star gods, however, Plato follows the traditional conception of epiphany, where a god manifests him/herself in a bodily form. To be sure, Plato's visible gods do not appear in a human or animal form as the Greek gods did. However, the Greek gods could also appear in the form of heavenly bodies. Thus, in the Homeric *Hymn to Apollo*, Apollo appears as a radiant star shining in the middle of the day (440–2). Plato reaches for this traditional mode of divine epiphany in his discourse on the divine cosmos. The philosopher sees a divine epiphany that is visible to the eye when he looks at the heavens. Indeed, he can see epiphanies all night long! Not surprisingly, the gods appear as beautiful and radiant with light. Here again Plato uses the language of poetic epiphanies.

The rational human soul is arguably the centerpiece of this text.[5] It can occupy different bodies and apprehend the cosmos at different levels. Plato presents a complex teleology designed to give the embodied human soul a chance to better its situation. Each individual soul wants to leave mortal life on earth and return to its native star. To do this, it must live as a philosopher who practices mathematics, astronomy, and dialectic. In earlier texts, Plato's philosopher did not study the stars; in the *Timaeus*, he must master astronomy. Indeed, Timaeus himself is "most expert in astronomy" and "has made it his primary task to know the nature of the universe" (27a). The philosopher has to examine the movements of the

---

[5] As Sedley observes (2008: 124): "Human beings play an absolutely pivotal role in the hierarchy of life. For it is uniquely when it reaches human embodiment that the rational soul becomes capable of attaining the purification that can, at least ideally, lead on to its release from incarnation and attainment of discarnate bliss. Both the human body and the world around us have been so constructed as to make this possible, and it is scarcely an exaggeration to say that the entire teleological structure of nature converges on this single purpose."

stars and planets to grasp the mathematical principles of these motions.[6] In doing this, he comes to understand that the orderly and perfect motions in the heavens manifest the activity of the divine cosmic soul.

While the philosophic soul bears witness to the harmony and beauty of the universe at the cosmic level, it also examines the stars to fulfill its own individual mission: to become like god. The philosopher studies the circular revolutions of the stars in order to imitate the cosmic soul's rational circles in his own mind. The philosopher can do this because his rational human soul moves in circles just as the World-Soul does. As we have seen, the human soul is divine, but it has a lower status of divinity than the cosmic soul. Once embodied in a mortal creature, however, its rational activity is obstructed by its body. On earth, it must work to regain its perfect <i>nous</i>. In viewing the heavens, the human mind looks at the divine mind: mind sees mind. Of course the philosopher must also investigate the Demiurge and his model (the Form of Animal) to grasp the primary principles of the cosmos. But it becomes like god primarily by imitating the cosmic soul.

As I will argue, studying the heavens also allows the philosopher to dwell in "divine time." I distinguish between earthly and divine time. The World-Soul that moves the cosmos in circles creates time's forward arrow, which makes mortal creatures on earth age and die. However, time's forward arrow does not have this effect on the cosmos or the stars. These divinities dwell in circular time or, as I call it, "divine time." Even though the astral gods have bodies that move over time, they do not age or suffer changes brought about by the forward movement of time. By contrast, humans experience time's forward arrow in their daily lives on earth. The human soul lives in mortal bodies that age, get sick, and die. The philosopher must learn to set his psychic clock to divine time. He can do this because the rational part of his soul operates in the same way as the cosmic soul; also, since it lived in a star before incarnation, it originally dwelled in divine time. By adjusting his psychic clock to divine time, the philosopher "becomes like god."

[6] Compare Plato's brief discussion of astronomical study in the <i>Republic</i>. As Socrates says, anyone who seeks to learn the truth by examining the physical world – even if he looks up at the stars – is in fact turning his intellectual gaze downwards (7.529b–c). To be sure, the heavens are beautiful, but one cannot apprehend real speed, slowness, true number, or its ratios by studying the heavens. Indeed, one cannot understand the proportional measurement of days to months and months to years, since the heavenly bodies do not move "always in the same way, without deviation" (529d–530b). The philosopher must practice astronomy "by means of problems, just as in the study of geometry." If he practices astronomy in the proper philosophic fashion, he must "leave the things in the heavens alone" (τὰ δ' ἐν τῷ οὐρανῷ ἐάσομεν 530b).

I will also discuss the story of the human soul in this dialogue. This story resembles those we found in the *Phaedo* and *Phaedrus*, but it also has some new features. The rational human soul starts out its life in a star. In this period of its life, its sees "the nature of the all," that is, the universe and its intelligible model, and it gets instructions for living the right kind of mortal life. At this point, the rational human soul does not perceive the physical phenomena of the cosmos. It has no sensory organs and can only apprehend the "nature of the universe" at the intelligible level. Plato relates this first chapter of the story of the soul very briefly, and this raises difficult questions. What did the soul apprehend in this period? What objects did it grasp? In the second chapter of the story of the soul, the rational human soul incarnates in human bodies. The soul does not fall into a body, however, due to some sort of inherent fault. Rather, it must live in mortal creatures so that the cosmos can fully imitate the Intelligible Animal. While the human soul plays a key role in the cosmic whole, it also has its own personal mission: to practice philosophy so that it can leave the mortal realm. In the last chapter of the story, the perfected philosophic soul returns to its native star.

I will conclude this chapter by examining how Plato presents the cosmos as a religious artifact. In setting forth the "dance of the stars" (40c), Plato refers to dances at religious festivals. Indeed, he identifies the cosmos with its heavenly bodies as a beautiful "choric dance" (40c). This dance reflects the incorporeal, changeless, and eternal being of the Form. In presenting this astral "choric dance," Plato refers to a cultural practice that was central to religious life in ancient Greece: circular dances performed for the gods at religious festivals. As we will see, the rituals at the festival enabled the Greek spectators watching the dance to briefly unite with the god. I will discuss the religious practice of circular dances at festivals for the gods in order to explicate Plato's choric star dance. Plato's star dance resembles traditional dances but also differs in important ways. Like ordinary spectators of choric dances, the philosophic viewers unite with the cosmic god by beholding the dance of the stars. But Plato's philosophic spectators see gods rather than humans dancing in circles. And the philosophers can actually "become like god" as they watch the star dance – an idea that stands in stark contrast to Greek spectators at religious festivals. Finally, I examine the claim that the cosmos is an "*agalma* of the eternal gods." As I argue, Plato uses the notion of statues of the gods to suggest that the cosmos is a religious image of the divine Forms.

5.1 Timaeus as a Religious Exegete

Timaeus not only discourses on the divine cosmos but directs prayers to this god. In this section, I will examine the way that Timaeus uses religious language in his speech. Timaeus opens his speech with the following prayer:

> Socrates, all those who have even a small share of wisdom always call upon god at the beginning of every undertaking, whether small or large. We who are going to give an account of the universe (*tou pantos*) – how it has come into being or else is uncreated – if we are not utterly crazy, must necessarily pray to and call upon the gods and goddesses that the things that we say are most of all acceptable to them and, after that, to ourselves. (27c–d)[7]

At this point, Timaeus directs his prayers to gods and goddesses, whom we can infer are the traditional Greek gods. Timaeus makes it clear that his discourse must first and foremost please the gods. As we have seen, the *Phaedrus* featured a meditation on the proper way to talk both to and about divinities (the gods and the Forms). There, Socrates identified the gods as the true audience of all discourse, be it rhetorical or philosophical. And he also prayed to the gods Eros and Pan. In the *Timaeus*, we find a similar claim: men must pray to the gods in every undertaking and articulate ideas that are suitable to the gods.

Timaeus also closes his speech with a prayer:

> Now I utter a prayer to the god who was created just now in my speech (although in fact this happened long ago) that he will grant salvation to those things that were said fittingly, but if we unwittingly said something out of tune, that he will impose the fitting penalty. And the proper justice is to make what is out of tune harmonious. So that in the future we speak discourses about the origin of the gods correctly, we pray that he gives us the medicine that is most perfect and best, that is, knowledge. (106a–b)[8]

Timaeus prays to the cosmos itself to grant divine approval and knowledge. The cosmic god has effectively supplanted the Greek gods. In the earlier

---

[7] ἀλλ', ὦ Σώκρατες, τοῦτό γε δὴ πάντες ὅσοι καὶ κατὰ βραχὺ σωφροσύνης μετέχουσιν, ἐπὶ παντὸς ὁρμῇ καὶ σμικροῦ καὶ μεγάλου πράγματος θεὸν ἀεί που καλοῦσιν· ἡμᾶς δὲ τοὺς περὶ τοῦ παντὸς λόγους ποιεῖσθαί πῃ μέλλοντας, ᾗ γέγονεν ἢ καὶ ἀγενές ἐστιν, εἰ μὴ παντάπασι παραλλάττομεν, ἀνάγκη θεούς τε καὶ θεὰς ἐπικαλουμένους εὔχεσθαι πάντα κατὰ νοῦν ἐκείνοις μὲν μάλιστα, ἑπομένως δὲ ἡμῖν εἰπεῖν. Note that Socrates prays to the sun in the *Symposium* 220d and prays to Pan at the end of the *Phaedrus*.

[8] He delivers this prayer at the opening of the *Critias* (106a–b): τῷ δὲ πρὶν μὲν πάλαι ποτ' ἔργῳ, νῦν δὲ λόγοις ἄρτι θεῷ γεγονότι προσεύχομαι, τῶν ῥηθέντων ὅσα μὲν ἐρρήθη μετρίως, σωτηρίαν ἡμῖν αὐτὸν αὐτῶν διδόναι, παρὰ μέλος δὲ εἴ τι περὶ αὐτῶν ἄκοντες εἴπομεν, δίκην τὴν πρέπουσαν ἐπιτιθέναι. δίκη δὲ ὀρθὴ τὸν πλημμελοῦντα ἐμμελῆ ποιεῖν· ἵν' οὖν τὸ λοιπὸν τοὺς περὶ θεῶν γενέσεως ὀρθῶς λέγωμεν λόγους, φάρμακον ἡμῖν αὐτὸν τελεώτατον καὶ ἄριστον φαρμάκων ἐπιστήμην εὐχόμεθα διδόναι.

prayer, when he addressed the traditional Greek gods, Timaeus had not introduced this new cosmic god. Once he goes through the creation of the cosmos, he can pray to this divine being. While the philosopher must cultivate his reason and "become like god," he must also worship the cosmic god.

Midway through the dialogue, when he first introduces the receptacle, Timaeus utters another prayer. He says that he will make a new beginning because he must add the third element of the universe, the receptacle, to the other two (the Intelligible Animal and the cosmos): "Now too, at the start of the account, we begin again to speak by calling upon god the savior to bring us safely through this out-of-place (*atopou*) and strange narration to the belief about what is appropriate/likely" (θεὸν δὴ καὶ νῦν ἐπ᾽ ἀρχῇ τῶν λεγομένων σωτῆρα ἐξ ἀτόπου καὶ ἀήθους διηγήσεως πρὸς τὸ τῶν εἰκότων δόγμα διασῴζειν ἡμᾶς ἐπικαλεσάμενοι πάλιν ἀρχώμεθα λέγειν; 48d–e).[9] Here again, Timaeus utters a prayer, invoking a god who will keep his discourse on the right course. Timaeus does not identify this god, but it must surely be the cosmic god: only a Platonic god could guide Timaeus' discourse on the receptacle. Indeed, he uses very similar language in this prayer as he does in his final prayer to the cosmos. In both prayers, he refers to the cosmos as a "savior" god: (1) "[I pray to] god the savior . . . to bring us safely" (σωτῆρα . . . διασῴζειν ἡμᾶς, 48e); (2) "[I pray that god] will grant salvation to those things that were said fittingly" (σωτηρίαν ἡμῖν αὐτὸν αὐτῶν διδόναι; 106a).[10]

As these prayers indicate, Timaeus wants to speak piously both to the gods themselves and also about the divine universe or, as he puts it, "the all" (*to pan*). Indeed, he considers his discourse as an "exegetical" interpretation of divine matters. He makes this point early in the speech, when he says that the cosmos is a "copy" or "likeness" (*eikôn*) of the Intelligible Animal. As Timaeus states:

> Thus, one should distinguish between the likeness and its model, inasmuch as accounts (*logoi*) are akin to those things of which they are exegetes (*exêgêtai*). On the one hand, [accounts exegetical] of that which is permanent, stable, and manifest to reason (*meta nou kataphanous*) are themselves permanent and unchangeable. To the extent that it is possible and fitting for accounts to be irrefutable and invincible, one must necessarily not fall short of this. On the other hand, [accounts exegetical] of that which is a likeness of

---

[9] Note that his "out of place" discussion of the receptacle focuses on space and place. Indeed, the passage on the receptacle effectively displaces the reader from his/her most basic ideas about the world. I will discuss the receptacle below.

[10] I am grateful to my student Thomas Slabon for showing me this verbal parallel.

that other [i.e. the model], being itself a likeness, are themselves likely/
appropriate (*eikotas*[11]) according to this analogy: as being is to becoming, so
is truth to conviction. If therefore, Socrates, in discussing all these things
regarding the gods and the generation of the universe, we are not able to give
accounts completely and in every way in agreement with each other as well
as accurate, do not be surprised. But if we can furnish likely/appropriate
(*eikotas*) accounts that are inferior to none, we must be pleased, remember-
ing that I the speaker and you the judges possess human nature. Therefore,
about these things, it is fitting to accept the *eikôs muthos* and not to search
for anything beyond this. (29b–d)[12]

I will not examine Timaeus' famous claim that his speech is an *eikôs logos*
(or an *eikôs muthos*). Rather, I want to note that he refers to his discourses
on the Forms and the cosmos as "exegetes." The word *exêgêtai* has a distinct
religious valence. As Myles Burnyeat observes:

> Not only is ἐξηγηταί a striking and solemn word in itself, but everywhere
> else it refers to a person: most commonly, the exegete who expounds an
> oracle, explains a dream, tells you the meaning of a ritual ceremony or
> advises on problems of expiation. . . . In later Greek ἐξηγηταί also refers to
> the guide who takes you round a sanctuary or temple (Pausanias V.15.10,
> SIG 1021.20); it would not be inappropriate to think of Timaeus as our
> guide to the beautiful design of the cosmos we inhabit. Thus the accounts
> (*logoi*) we are talking about are not any old statements, arguments, or
> discourses about the physical world. They are very special accounts personi-
> fied as the exegetes who expound or explain the unobvious significance of an
> object like a dream, ritual, or oracle which does not bear its meaning on its
> surface, because it comes from, or has some important connection with, the
> divine.[13]

Timaeus, then, serves as a religious "exegete" who speaks of divine matters.
Given that he presents the Demiurge's reasoning in terms of his creation of

---

[11] I follow Burnyeat 2005, who points out that *eikôs* can mean "reasonable," "appropriate,"
"likely," and "probable." Given the range of this word, I chose to translate it as "likely/
appropriate."

[12] 29b–d: ὧδε οὖν περί τε εἰκόνος καὶ περὶ τοῦ παραδείγματος αὐτῆς διοριστέον, ὡς ἄρα τοὺς λόγους,
ὧνπέρ εἰσιν ἐξηγηταί, τούτων αὐτῶν καὶ συγγενεῖς ὄντας· τοῦ μὲν οὖν μονίμου καὶ βεβαίου καὶ
μετὰ νοῦ καταφανοῦς μονίμους καὶ ἀμεταπτώτους – καθ᾽ ὅσον οἷόν τε καὶ ἀνελέγκτοις προσήκει
λόγοις εἶναι καὶ ἀνικήτοις, τούτου δεῖ μηδὲν ἐλλείπειν – τοὺς δὲ τοῦ πρὸς μὲν ἐκεῖνο ἀπεικασθέντος,
ὄντος δὲ εἰκόνος εἰκότας ἀνὰ λόγον τε ἐκείνων ὄντας· ὅτιπερ πρὸς γένεσιν οὐσία, τοῦτο πρὸς πίστιν
ἀλήθεια. ἐὰν οὖν, ὦ Σώκρατες, πολλὰ πολλῶν πέρι, θεῶν καὶ τῆς τοῦ παντὸς γενέσεως, μὴ δυνατοὶ
γιγνώμεθα πάντη πάντως αὐτοὺς ἑαυτοῖς ὁμολογουμένους λόγους καὶ ἀπηκριβωμένους
ἀποδοῦναι, μὴ θαυμάσῃς· ἀλλ᾽ ἐὰν ἄρα μηδενὸς ἧττον παρεχώμεθα εἰκότας, ἀγαπᾶν χρή,
μεμνημένους ὡς ὁ λέγων ἐγὼ ὑμεῖς τε οἱ κριταὶ φύσιν ἀνθρωπίνην ἔχομεν, ὥστε περὶ τούτων τὸν
εἰκότα μῦθον ἀποδεχομένους πρέπει τούτου μηδὲν ἔτι πέρα ζητεῖν.

[13] Burnyeat 2005: 149.

the cosmos, he does not simply describe the physical universe and its divinities (and, indirectly, the Intelligible Animal), but serves as an interpreter of the Demiurge's thoughts. In addition, by describing the physical universe and its divinities, Timaeus acts as an exegete speaking about divine matters.

In his discourse on the creation of the cosmos, Timaeus does not discover the Demiurge's thinking by examining empirical data. Rather, he focuses directly on the divine reasoning that went into the creation of the universe. He sets forth three claims that he takes as axioms: the universe is the most beautiful (*kallistos*) of all created things, the creator is the best (*aristos*) of all causes, and the cosmos is a copy of an intelligible model (29a–b). He then enters the mind of the creator: "for God (*theos*), willing (*boulêtheis*) that all things be good and nothing base, as far as possible, taking over all that was visible, which was not at rest but moving in an unharmonious and disordered way, led it into order out of disorder, considering (*hêgêsamenos*) that this was in every way better than before" (30a). Timaeus articulates a good part of the creator's reasoning by way of his own reason.

In sum, Timaeus not only prays to the gods but serves in some sense as the "exegete" of divine reasoning. His philosophic and scientific discourse should be considered, at least in part, as a religious exegesis.

5.2   Divinities in the Cosmos

I now want to discuss the various divine figures that populate the universe, beginning with the Demiurge. I put these divinities into different sections to make my ideas clear.

5.2.1   The Demiurge

Timaeus presents the Demiurge as a being of such an exalted status that he is almost impossible to understand: "to discover the maker and father of the universe is indeed a task; and, having discovered him, to relate this to all men is impossible" (28c). In spite of this disclaimer, Timaeus does offer some key ideas about this super-divinity. First, he says, the Demiurge "was good (*agathos*), and in him who is good no envy ever arises" (ἀγαθὸς ἦν, ἀγαθῷ δὲ οὐδεὶς περὶ οὐδενὸς οὐδέποτε ἐγγίγνεται φθόνος; 29e). Second, the Demiurge engages in a specific set of creative acts. In particular, he is the primary "cause" of the cosmos (*aitia*, 37a, 30b–c).

Plato's account of the Demiurge has generated many different interpretations. In particular, his notion of a Demiurge creating the cosmos has received a huge amount of criticism, beginning with Aristotle. Many thinkers have questioned the idea that the eternal universe has a beginning (while it has no ending). Some scholars have found a way to resolve this problem: they read the creation of the cosmos in metaphorical terms. They treat the Demiurge as the personification of the World-Soul. As they argue, Plato used this literary device to show the World-Soul functioning in its causal (demiurgic) aspects. Cornford, for example, uses this approach to argue that the World-Soul is the only cause of/in the cosmos.[14] Other scholars argue that we must read the dialogue literally. They do not see the creation of the eternal universe as a problem to solve. According to this position, the Demiurge, a transcendental cause, created the World-Soul. The Demiurge works from the outside to design and create the cosmos; the cosmic soul, by contrast, is immanent in the cosmos and acts solely on its own body.[15] Finally, some scholars treat the Demiurge as the personification of the Form of the Good (once again using the metaphorical approach to the creation story). As we saw in Chapter 1, in the *Republic*, Plato treats the Good as generating the Forms as well as the bodily realm. In the *Timaeus*, however, the Demiurge does not create the region of the Forms. For this reason, I reject the idea that the Demiurge is a mythical enactment of the Form of the Good. That said, the Good and the Demiurge intersect in important ways. We need to keep this in mind as we examine the *Timaeus*.

Let me emphasize that all scholars who work on the *Timaeus* acknowledge that it has a good deal of myth and metaphor. But it is one thing to address these literary aspects of the dialogue in one's interpretation of the dialogue, and quite another to treat the whole creation story in metaphorical terms. I find it best to read the dialogue as literally as possible. To interpret Plato's account of the creation of the cosmos metaphorically leads one into the realm of (wild) speculation.

Let me briefly set forth the key ideas in Plato's account of the Demiurge. As Timaeus states, "everything that comes into being necessarily comes from a cause" (πᾶν δὲ αὖ τὸ γιγνόμενον ὑπ' αἰτίου τινὸς ἐξ ἀνάγκης γίγνεσθαι), and the Demiurge is this cause (28a, 28c, 29d). Indeed, the

---

[14] Cornford 1956: 38.

[15] As Mohr observed in 1985, ever since Cherniss' *Aristotle's Criticism of Plato and the Academy*, vol. 1, "there has been nearly universal agreement among critics that Plato's God or divine Demiurge is a soul" (p. 178). Mohr gives a cogent argument against this view (pp. 178–83). The present scholarly consensus, however, is that we should read the dialogue literally. Broadie presents an excellent argument for the idea that the Demiurge is the transcendent cause of the cosmos (2012: 7–26). See also Brisson 1974: 32 and 1997; Menn 1995: 6–11; Sedley 2008: Chapter 4, and Johansen 2008: Chapter 4, who adopt the literalist reading.

Demiurge is the "best of all causes" (ὁ δ᾽ ἄριστος τῶν αἰτίων; 29a). The Demiurge created the cosmos because he "wanted all things to be most like himself" (πάντα ... μάλιστα ἐβουλήθη γενέσθαι παραπλήσια ἑαυτῷ; 29e). He is "the most supreme originator of becoming and the cosmos" (ταύτην δὴ γενέσεως καὶ κόσμου μάλιστ᾽ ... ἀρχὴν κυριωτάτην; 29e–30a). To create the universe, the Demiurge "fixed his gaze on the eternal" (πρὸς τὸ ἀίδιον ἔβλεπεν), i.e., the intelligible realm of the Forms (29a). The visible cosmos is a "copy" or "image" (eikôn) of the Intelligible Animal (noêton zôon, 29a–b), which contains all the "intelligible animals" (noêta zôa). The Demiurge took over all that was visible, which was in a state of disorder and unrest, and brought it into an order that was "better" (ameinon) and "most beautiful" (kalliston, 30a). He saw that what has nous is "more beautiful" (kallion) than that which is irrational (anoêton), and that "nous cannot be present in anything devoid of soul" (30b). Putting nous in the cosmic soul, and the soul in the cosmic body, he created the "most beautiful" and "best" cosmos (30c). The Demiurge also puts together the cosmic body, using all the elements of earth, air, fire, and water to create a "harmonic" whole (32c). He made the cosmic body "perfect" (teleion), ageless, and free of disease (32e–33a). The Demiurge also shaped it as a sphere (kukloeides) because this is "supremely perfect" (teleiotaton) and "more beautiful" (kallion) than all other shapes (33b). He gives the cosmos circular motion because this is "the motion most of all associated with intelligence (nous) and reason (phronesis)" (34a).[16]

Let us pause here to ask why Plato links reason (nous) with circular motion, especially the circular motion of the heavens. Not surprisingly, philosophers (beginning with Aristotle) have found this idea quite bizarre. Plato does not present arguments for this idea but simply sets forth some basic (and questionable) claims. First, he considers the sphere the best shape of all because it is equidistant from the center in every direction and therefore "self-similar" (homoios heautôi, 33c). He returns to this idea in Laws 10, where he discusses the "motion of reason" (kinêsis tou nou) in the context of the divine soul's movement of the cosmos. There, as he indicates, the motion that always moves in one place around a center, i.e., a circle, has the closest possible kinship to nous (897d–898a). As the Athenian puts it: "both [nous and the cosmos] move regularly, uniformly, within the same compass, around the same center and in the same direction, according to one formula and one ordering plan" (τὸ κατὰ ταὐτὰ

---

[16] Plato regularly opposes circular and rectilinear motion. The rectilinear motions are forward, backward, right, left, up, and down (43b).

δήπου καὶ ὡσαύτως καὶ ἐν τῷ αὐτῷ καὶ περὶ τὰ αὐτὰ καὶ πρὸς τὰ αὐτὰ καὶ ἕνα λόγον καὶ τάξιν μίαν ἄμφω κινεῖσθαι λέγοντες; 898a). Likewise, Plato assimilates the absence of intelligence to disorderly movement: "motion which is never uniform or regular, never in the same compass, around the same center, in the same direction or in a single place – motion which has no order, plan, or formula – is akin to unreason of every kind" (898b–c).[17] Plato thus associates order and harmony with rationality, and he sees the circle as maximally harmonious.[18] Since the heavenly bodies move in harmonious circular rotations, this must indicate that divine reason orders the heavens. Although Plato could not prove this idea, he used it as a basic postulate in his cosmology.

5.2.2   *The Cosmic Soul and Body*

The cosmos has a divine soul and body: the "World-Soul" and the "World-Body." The Demiurge creates the cosmic soul by mixing three elements: Being (*ousia*), the Same (*to auton*), and the Different (*to heteron*, 35a–b). After putting these three together, he created two bands of soul-stuff, attached crosswise, and bent them into circles moving along different axes. He thus created the Circle of the Same and the Circle of the Different. The Circle of the Same dominates the Circle of the Different, which moves along the diagonal inside of it. The cosmic soul moves itself in terms of thought (*nous*), and its self-motion moves the heavenly bodies.[19] Finally, the Demiurge attaches the World-Soul to the World-Body: "putting the soul in the midst of this he stretched this throughout the whole, and wrapped it around the body on the outside, and created the unique and solitary heaven as a circle rotating in a circle" (34b). The cosmic soul does not just occupy its body from the inside – it surrounds the cosmic body on the outside as well.

The World-Soul has ongoing contact with the Forms or Being (*to on*; *ousia*) and also with the physical realm of becoming (*ta gignomena*; 37a–b,

---

[17] For a good investigation of the *nous*-circular motion analogy, see Lee 1976. Note also Aristotle's attack on this analogy in *DA* I.3.407a2–b11.

[18] As Plato argues, the stars move in circular rotations while the planets move in spirals (and do not "wander," as they seem to do, 36c–d). Here, Plato followed Eudoxus' theory. For a detailed discussion of planetary motion in the *Timaeus*, see Cornford 1956: 72–90.

[19] Plato mentions the self-motion of the cosmic soul at 89a, where Timaeus says that "of all motions that is the best which is produced in a thing by itself, for it is most akin to the motion of thought and of the universe." Cornford 1956: 95n.2, citing the reference at 37b5 to "the thing that is self-moved," says that "the self-moved thing is the Heaven as a whole, which, as a living creature, is self-moved by its own self-moving soul" (see also Taylor 1928: 148, 178; cf. Mohr 1985: 174).

38a). Since the cosmos is a rational soul, we can easily understand its contemplation of the Forms. But how does the cosmic soul apprehend its own body? Timaeus offers a vague and confusing answer to this question. First, he says, the cosmic soul "touches" (*epaphêtai*) both the Forms and the particulars (37a–b).[20] However, when he expands on this idea, he refers to the "discourse" (*logos*) in the cosmic soul. This *logos* "concerns itself" with either the perceptible or intelligible realm:

> Whenever the discourse – being equally true whether it concerns that which is different or that which is the same, being born within that which is self-moved [the cosmic soul] without speech or sound – is concerned with the perceptible realm, and the Circle of the Different moves rightly and makes announcements to the whole of its soul, then firm and true opinions and beliefs come about. But when discourse is concerned with the object of reason and the Circle of the Same, rolling rightly, declares these things, then intelligence (*nous*) and knowledge (*epistêmê*) necessarily result. (λόγος δὲ ὁ κατὰ ταὐτὸν ἀληθὴς γιγνόμενος περί τε θάτερον ὂν καὶ περὶ τὸ ταὐτόν, ἐν τῷ κινουμένῳ ὑφ᾽ αὑτοῦ φερόμενος ἄνευ φθόγγου καὶ ἠχῆς, ὅταν μὲν περὶ τὸ αἰσθητὸν γίγνηται καὶ ὁ τοῦ θατέρου κύκλος ὀρθὸς ἰὼν εἰς πᾶσαν αὑτοῦ τὴν ψυχὴν διαγγείλῃ, δόξαι καὶ πίστεις γίγνονται βέβαιοι καὶ ἀληθεῖς, ὅταν δὲ αὖ περὶ τὸ λογιστικὸν ᾖ καὶ ὁ τοῦ ταὐτοῦ κύκλος εὔτροχος ὢν αὐτὰ μηνύσῃ, νοῦς ἐπιστήμη τε ἐξ ἀνάγκης ἀποτελεῖται; 37b–c)

In terms of its truth status, "discourse" manifests itself in the soul as true opinion or knowledge depending on the object it focuses on. When it concerns itself with the intelligible realm of the Forms, it has knowledge; when it deals with the perceptible realm (i.e. its own body), it has true opinion. In addition, Timaeus links the Circle of the Same with the realm of Being and the Circle of the Different with the realm of becoming.

Timaeus does not explain how discourse functions in the World-Soul. We can hesitantly suggest that the Circles of the Same and the Different first touch the Forms and the physical realm (respectively) and proclaim its

---

[20] Note also the following difficult passage: "Inasmuch as [the World-Soul] is blended together out of these three portions – with the nature of the Same and the Different and Being divided and bound together proportionally – it revolves back around itself. When it touches something whose being is scattered or else something whose being is indivisible, it moves through its whole soul and announces what it [the object] is the same as, or what it is different from, and in what respect, and how and when, it comes about that each thing exists and is acted upon both in the realm of becoming and in the realm of the ever-uniform" (ἅτε οὖν ἐκ τῆς ταὐτοῦ καὶ τῆς θατέρου φύσεως ἔκ τε οὐσίας τριῶν τούτων συγκραθεῖσα μοιρῶν, καὶ ἀνὰ λόγον μερισθεῖσα καὶ συνδεθεῖσα, αὐτή τε ἀνακυκλουμένη πρὸς αὑτήν, ὅταν οὐσίαν σκεδαστὴν ἔχοντός τινος ἐφάπτηται καὶ ὅταν ἀμέριστον, λέγει κινουμένη διὰ πάσης ἑαυτῆς ὅτῳ τ᾽ ἄν τι ταὐτὸν ᾖ καὶ ὅτου ἂν ἕτερον, πρὸς ὅτι τε μάλιστα καὶ ὅπη καὶ ὅπως καὶ ὁπότε συμβαίνει κατὰ τὰ γιγνόμενά τε πρὸς ἕκαστον ἕκαστα εἶναι καὶ πάσχειν καὶ πρὸς τὰ κατὰ ταὐτὰ ἔχοντα ἀεί; 37a–b).

findings via language. We can state that the cosmic soul's apprehension of its own body does not operate by way of an analogy to our own sense of our bodies. The cosmos does not have a sensory apparatus or inner organs. Rather, as Gretchen Reydams-Schils suggests, the cosmic soul gets ongoing information about the bodily realm through "a kind of self-awareness in the sense of purely internal cognition."[21] Of course Plato cannot offer a satisfying account for the way that the soul "touches" its body. We must simply accept that the World-Soul grasps the Forms and the bodily realm, and that it has two epistemic states, opinion/belief and knowledge.

5.2.3 Star Gods

After discussing the cosmic soul and body, Timaeus identifies four classes of living beings in the cosmos – terrestrial, winged, aquatic, and divine (40a). By the "divine," he means the star gods:

> The greatest class, that of the divine, he made out of fire, in order that this would be the shiniest and most beautiful to behold, and he made it well rounded (likening it to the universe), and he put this into the intelligence of the strongest [i.e., the Circle of the Same] so that it would follow together with this. He apportioned this [the class of the divine] around the entire circular heaven, to be a true cosmos-adornment (*kosmos*) for it, intricately woven throughout the whole. (40a)[22]

Each star god – which includes the sun and moon – has two motions. First, as a self-moving soul, the soul of the star moves its own star body "in the same spot uniformly, and it always thinks the same things about the same objects" (ἐν ταὐτῷ κατὰ ταὐτά, περὶ τῶν αὐτῶν ἀεὶ τὰ αὐτὰ ἑαυτῷ διανοουμένῳ; 40a–b). In short, it moves its own body endlessly in a circle. Second, the cosmic soul's Circle of the Same moves the stars around the heavens in its own rotation. The stars move in a "forward motion due to being dominated by the revolution of the Same and Similar" (τὴν δὲ εἰς τὸ πρόσθεν, ὑπὸ τῆς ταὐτοῦ καὶ ὁμοίου περιφορᾶς κρατουμένῳ; 40b). In sum, "the living divinities of the stars exist eternally and abide forever, revolving without variation in the same spot" (τῶν ἄστρων ζῷα θεῖα ὄντα καὶ ἀίδια καὶ κατὰ ταὐτὰ ἐν ταὐτῷ στρεφόμενα ἀεὶ μένει; 40b). As we will see, the stars play a key role in human life.

---

[21] Reydams-Schils 1997: 263.
[22] 40a: τοῦ μὲν οὖν θείου τὴν πλείστην ἰδέαν ἐκ πυρὸς ἀπηργάζετο, ὅπως ὅτι λαμπρότατον ἰδεῖν τε κάλλιστον εἴη, τῷ δὲ παντὶ προσεικάζων εὔκυκλον ἐποίει, τίθησίν τε εἰς τὴν τοῦ κρατίστου φρόνησιν ἐκείνῳ συνεπόμενον, νείμας περὶ πάντα κύκλῳ τὸν οὐρανόν, κόσμον ἀληθινὸν αὐτῷ πεποικιλμένον εἶναι καθ' ὅλον.

5.2.4   Ancillary Gods

As Timaeus indicates, the Demiurge creates the ancillary gods to aid him in
his design (41c). Due to his high ontological status, the Demiurge cannot
create mortal beings. He thus commands the ancillary gods to carry out
this task. What exactly are these gods and how do they operate? Sarah
Broadie argues that their goodness and divinity derive from the Demiurge
and questions whether they are separate gods or in some sense identical to
the Demiurge. She raises this idea this in part because Timaeus moves from
plural to singular in his discussion of the ancillary gods.[23] This may indicate
that the ancillary gods are co-workers of the Demiurge or, alternatively,
that they are in some strange way plural manifestations of this one
superdivinity.

This raises the question of whether the ancillary gods operate from outside
the cosmos or dwell within it. We find evidence for both of these positions in
the text. First, the Demiurge commands these gods to engage in the
demiourgia of the mortals: "imitate my power in my creation of you"
(μιμούμενοι τὴν ἐμὴν δύναμιν περὶ τὴν ὑμετέραν γένεσιν, 41c; see also
44d, 69c). Like the Demiurge, the ancillary gods have the skills of artisans:
they mix and sift and knead and weld the elements.[24] This suggests that they
act from without upon given materials. We can thus identify these gods as
co-workers of the Demiurge. As Broadie claims, the ancillary gods do not
animate a body but create many different things from the outside.[25]

Second, the Demiurge tells the ancillary gods to "give [mortals] nurture
and make them grow, and receive them back to yourselves after they have
died" (τροφήν τε διδόντες αὐξάνετε καὶ φθίνοντα πάλιν δέχεσθε; 41c).
When Timaeus says that the creator gods will "receive" mortals back when

---

[23] Timaeus refers to the ancillary gods now in the plural and now in the singular: μηχανώμενοι (70c),
ἔδοσαν, εἰδότες (71a), μεμνημένοι γὰρ τῆς τοῦ πατρὸς ἐπιστολῆς οἱ συστήσαντες ἡμᾶς (71d),
θεὸς ... δέδωκεν (71e), ἤδεσαν οἱ συντιθέντες (72e), ὁ θεὸς ... ἀποκρίνων ... μειγνύς ...
μηχανώμενος ... ἀπηργάσατο (73b–c), συνέστησεν (75a), ἐκόλλησεν ... συνέδησεν; διεκόσμησαν
οἱ διακοσμοῦντες (75d), ἀπηργάσατο τὴν κεφαλὴν ὁ ποιῶν (76c), ἠπίσταντο οἱ συνιστάντες ἡμᾶς
(76e), θεοὶ μηχανῶνται (77a), ταῦτα δὴ τὰ γένη πάντα φυτεύσαντες οἱ κρείττους (77c), τούτοις
οὖν κατεχρήσατο ὁ θεὸς (78b).

[24] At 73b8, for example, an ancillary god is said to take the atomic triangles that were straight and
smooth and create bone marrow by separating off the most perfect triangles and mingling them in
the proper proportion. Again, at 73d–e, a god makes bone by sifting pure and smooth earth,
kneading and wetting it with marrow, and dipping it in fire and water, and at 77a, the gods "mingle"
the elements to create trees and plants. Brisson 1974: 27–106 discusses the *demiourgos* in early
antiquity, and offers a detailed analysis of Plato's Demiurge as a craftsman. Brumbaugh 1989:
chapter 16 offers a useful analysis of Plato's attitudes to the "arts and crafts."

[25] Broadie 2012: 18; see also Sedley 2008: chapter 4; cf. Johansen 2008: chapter 4; Carone 2005:
chapter 3.

they have died, he seems to indicate that the ancillary gods dwell and act inside of nature. That is, the cosmos "receives" the dead bodies of humans and animals into its bodily elements. If we accept the latter idea, then we must see the ancillary gods as living in the cosmos and working along with the cosmic soul. I find this idea problematic. The text gives no evidence that the cosmic soul has demiurgic capacities. The Demiurge acts only at the beginning of creation. The cosmic soul, by contrast, lives immanently in its own body and controls the cosmos. Conceptually speaking, the cosmos cannot be fully up and running until the universe has been completed. In spite of Plato's less than consistent claims, it seems likely that the ancillary gods act before the cosmos comes into being.

Let me mention, finally, the "other divinities" (*alloi daimones*) that Timaeus adds to his account as a sort of addendum. Though he refers to these as *daimones* rather than *theoi*, he clearly means the traditional Greek gods. He explicitly mentions Earth and Ouranos, Phorcys, Chronos, Rhea, Zeus, Hera, and "their descendants" (40e–41a). Timaeus says that it is hard to know their origin (*gnônai tên genesin*), but he then suggests that we should believe the descendants of these gods, who assert their existence. Surprisingly, Timaeus ascribes the entire existence of the traditional gods to a biased group of human authorities. This rather ironic claim signals some level of doubt on his part: why should we accept the views of men who claim to be the descendants of the gods? In my view, Plato mentions these gods and daimons to maintain a connection with deeply held traditional ideas about the gods. He does not, however, weave these deities into his creation narrative.

Timaeus differentiates the cosmic gods and the traditional Greek gods as (1) "the gods who revolve manifestly" (*peripolousin phanerôs*), i.e., the star gods, and (2) "those who appear (*phainontai*) whenever they choose" (41a). Here, he presents two kinds of divine epiphany, platonic and traditional: the cosmic gods, later called the "visible gods," manifest themselves regularly every night, while the traditional Greek gods manifest themselves at random times. Given Plato's emphatic claims in the *Republic* that the gods never change, the traditional gods should not fit into the cosmology. Still, Plato wants to retain the traditional Greek gods in his account.

5.2.5 *Rational Human Souls*

The human soul is purely rational. Only after incarnation does it take on the lower two parts of the tripartite soul (spirit and appetite). In this text, only the rational human soul is immortal and divine. Timaeus has much to say about this soul. First, the Demiurge created it in the same structure and out of the same materials as the cosmic soul, and he used the same mathematical ratios and intervals as he did in the cosmic soul (35b–36b, 43d). The rational human soul, like the World-Soul, has a Circle of the Same and a Circle of the Different (42c, 43d). Of course the rational human soul differs from the World-Soul in important ways. In particular, the Demiurge makes it out of materials "left over" (*hupoloipa*) from the creation of divine souls, thus giving it a lower degree of purity (41d–e). In addition, the rational human soul can inhabit different bodies (astral, human, animal). This gives the human soul a unique status in the universe.

5.3   Heavenly Bodies: Radiant and Shadowy

To provide the context for my discussion of human beings, In this section, I want to examine the cosmic body and its atomic make-up. Plato presents different views of the cosmic body. At the ontological level, the cosmic body as a whole and the individual heavenly bodies are mere images of the Form of Animal that appear in the receptacle. At the cosmological level, however, the cosmic body is perfect, divine, and completely unchanging, and the heavenly bodies are perfect, divine and do not undergo any significant change. In short, in the ontological account, the cosmic body and the heavenly bodies of the star gods have a shadowy status; in the cosmological account, they are radiant bodies that do not change like other bodies in the universe.

I want to discuss these different conceptions of the cosmic body. Let us first consider the cosmic body in the cosmological account. As Timaeus claims, the cosmic body is perfect and divine. The Demiurge "made it smooth, uniform, and everywhere equidistant from its center, a whole and perfect body made out of perfect bodies" (λεῖον καὶ ὁμαλὸν πανταχῇ τε ἐκ μέσου ἴσον καὶ ὅλον καὶ τέλεον ἐκ τελέων σωμάτων σῶμα ἐποίησεν; 34b).[26] The cosmic body has a special status in the universe: it does not age or suffer any kind of deterioration. Nothing exists outside the cosmos and, for this reason, the cosmic body cannot be harmed by external materials (32e–33a). In addition, the cosmos is a sphere (*kukloeides*), "the most perfect" (*teleiotaton*) shape and "more beautiful" (*kallion*) than other forms (33b). Finally, the circular motion of the cosmic body is "the motion most of all associated with intelligence (*nous*) and reason (*phronêsis*)" (43b).

[26] Note that the word *teleos* can mean "complete" or "perfect." The "perfect bodies" from which the cosmic body is constructed are composed of the triangles that make up the physical cosmos. One could argue that each triangle is "complete," but Plato does not refer to them individually. For this reason, I see "perfect" as the better translation.

The cosmic body is made out of perfect and unchanging triangular atoms (as I call them) that come in different shapes.[27] The atoms, which are subject to constant motion, join together in different ways to form four differently shaped molecules.[28] The four molecules are the microscopic bodies of the four elements (air, water, fire, and earth). The four elements, in turn, mix together to create all perceptible bodies in the cosmos. Unlike the atoms, however, the molecules of the four elements are not perfect bodies: they are regularly broken down by atoms and molecules that strike them from the outside. The molecules undergo constant change. While the cosmic body is perfect and unchanging, then, it consists of the ever-moving bodies of the atoms and the ever-moving and ever-changing bodies of the molecules. Paradoxically, the perfect cosmic body is made up of perfect atoms that endlessly move and imperfect molecules that endlessly change.

Let us turn now to examine the cosmic and heavenly bodies in the ontological account. The cosmic body and the star bodies, like all bodies in the universe, are mere images of the Forms. From this point of view, the cosmic body has a low ontological status. To understand this idea, we must examine the receptacle, where bodies in the realm of becoming (*gignomena*) appear and disappear (49e–51e). Plato's discourse on the receptacle presents many interpretive difficulties, so I will discuss this in some detail. First, the receptacle existed even in the primordial chaos, prior to creation. The receptacle is the nurse and mother of all becoming, and it also "partakes" in the intelligible Forms (49a, 51a–b).

Plato sets forth two very different ideas about the receptacle in the *Timaeus*. (1) The receptacle is the "place/space" in which visible bodies come into being and perish. He identifies the receptacle as that "in which" things appear and disappear (49e, 50d). He also calls it a "place" or "space" (*topos*, 52a; *chora* 52a–b; *hedra*, 52b). (2) The receptacle is the formless material substrate that makes up all bodies in the universe. Plato presents this idea in two analogies. In the first analogy, he uses the example of a chunk of gold that is shaped into different objects (50a–c); in the second, he refers to the odorless liquid that serves as the basis of all perfumes (50e). By comparing the receptacle to these two material entities, Plato suggests

---

[27] The triangles are either isosceles or scalene – since scalene triangles come in different forms, the triangles have a number of shapes. In addition, for purposes of clarity, I will use "atom" for the triangles and "molecule" for a group of atoms that come together to form one of the four elements at a microscopic level. These are not Plato's terms.

[28] All motion in the cosmos derives from the cosmic, astral, and human souls (animals are mere declensions of humans) – atoms and molecules do not move themselves. The cosmic soul endlessly puts pressure on the cosmic body from the outside, and this keeps the atoms in motion.

that the receptacle is the material substrate from which bodies come into being and perish. Is the receptacle space, matter, or some combination of the two? This question has generated a vast amount of scholarship. Rather than entering into this debate, I want to focus on the ontological status of the bodily particulars that appear and disappear in the receptacle (whether it be space or a material substrate or a combination of the two).

In his discussions of the Forms and particulars in the middle-period dialogues, Plato suggested that bodily particulars "have a share in" the Forms; he also identified them as "likenesses," "imitations," and "copies" of the Forms.[29] We find this same terminology in the *Timaeus*. Let me cite a few passages to make the Form–particular relation clear. First, Timaeus claims that there is an "intelligible Form of each thing" (*eidos hekastou noêton*, 53c). Second, he says that the bodily particulars are "imitations of Beings" (τῶν ὄντων ἀεὶ μιμήματα), i.e., the Forms (50c). He also identifies them as "likenesses of intelligible objects and of eternally existent beings" (τὰ τῶν νοητῶν ἀεί τε ὄντων κατὰ ... ἀφομοιώματα; 51a).[30]

As in earlier texts, Plato emphasizes the low ontological status of the bodily "images" of the Forms. For example, Timaeus speaks of the particulars in the receptacle as "images" (*eikones*) that barely have any existence at all:

> It is therefore fitting for the image – since that very thing [the Form] for which it comes into being does not belong to it, but it is always moved around as a phantasm of something else – to come into being *in* something else, somehow clinging to Being or else being nothing at all. (ὡς εἰκόνι μέν, ἐπείπερ οὐδ' αὐτὸ τοῦτο ἐφ' ᾧ γέγονεν ἑαυτῆς ἐστιν, ἑτέρου δέ τινος ἀεὶ φέρεται φάντασμα, διὰ ταῦτα ἐν ἑτέρῳ προσήκει τινὶ γίγνεσθαι, οὐσίας ἁμωσγέπως ἀντεχομένην, ἢ μηδὲν τὸ παράπαν αὐτὴν εἶναι; 52c, my italics)

The bodily particulars appear as "phantasms of something else." They must cling to Being in order to have any substance.

In this account, the bodily particulars have a fleeting and shadowy quality. Indeed, as Timaeus claims, one should not even refer to the particulars in the receptacle as a "this" or "that":

> Whatever we see coming into being at different times, such as fire, we must never refer to it, i.e., fire, as "this" (*touto*) but as "suchlike" (*toiouton*), and we must never speak of water as "this" but always as "suchlike." And we should

---

[29] The *Parmenides*, a late middle-period dialogue, marks an important exception to this claim. In this dialogue, Plato presents a refutation of the idea that particulars "participate in" and are "images" of the Forms (although he hints that these ideas can somehow be rescued). Given his criticisms of the Forms in this text, it comes as a surprise to see Plato returning to some of his old ideas in the *Timaeus*.

[30] I accept Cornford's conjecture (1956: 186).

never call anything else "this," as though it had some stability. And when we point to things and use the phrases "this" and "that," we should never believe that we refer to some definite thing. (ἀεὶ ὃ καθορῶμεν ἄλλοτε ἄλλῃ γιγνόμενον, ὡς πῦρ, μὴ τοῦτο ἀλλὰ τὸ τοιοῦτον ἑκάστοτε προσαγορεύειν πῦρ, μηδὲ ὕδωρ τοῦτο ἀλλὰ τὸ τοιοῦτον ἀεί, μηδὲ ἄλλο ποτὲ μηδὲν ὡς τινα ἔχον βεβαιότητα, ὅσα δεικνύντες τῷ ῥήματι τῷ τόδε καὶ τοῦτο προσχρώμενοι δηλοῦν ἡγούμεθά τι; 49d–e)

This is a very bold claim. Does Plato really mean that we should not say, for example, "this is a wildfire"?[31] Should we refer to each particular as "of such a kind"? In the case of a wildfire, should we say "I see something appearing as a fiery kind"? Timaeus makes this even worse by stating that we must use "this" and "that" in reference to the receptacle: "But that [i.e., the receptacle] in which each of these things, always coming into being, appears, and from which, in turn, each thing perishes – of this alone we should use the expression 'this' and 'that'" (ἐν ᾧ δὲ ἐγγιγνόμενα ἀεὶ ἕκαστα αὐτῶν φαντάζεται καὶ πάλιν ἐκεῖθεν ἀπόλλυται, μόνον ἐκεῖνο αὖ προσαγορεύειν τῷ τε τοῦτο καὶ τῷ τόδε προσχρωμένους ὀνόματι; 49e–50a). It seems bizarre, if not impossible, to refer to the receptacle every time one speaks of a particular object. But this is precisely what Timaeus argues. We should not point to a particular "this"; rather, we should see "this" receptacle as appearing in "such and such" a way. Or we can say that "this" or "that" *region* of the receptacle appears in "such" a way. Thus, in the case of a wildfire, we can say that the receptacle "appears as fiery in this region of the receptacle."

Several passages in the text bolster this strange mode of discourse. For example, the receptacle "turning moist and fiery and receiving the character of earth and air, and experiencing all other properties that follow these, appears to the eye in many varieties" (ὑγραινομένην καὶ πυρουμένην καὶ τὰς γῆς τε καὶ ἀέρος μορφὰς δεχομένην, καὶ ὅσα ἄλλα τούτοις πάθη συνέπεται πάσχουσαν, παντοδαπὴν μὲν ἰδεῖν φαίνεσθαι, 52d–e; see also 51b). This shows us a way to refer to the receptacle (and not the particulars) when we speak: "the receptacle turning moist and fiery appears." In addition, Timaeus indicates that the receptacle has specific regions where each of the four elements congregates. In his discussion of chaos, for example, the bits of stuff in the receptacle collect together to form "traces" (*ichnê*) of the four elements, and these traces of the four elements appear in a different "place" (*chôran*) in the receptacle (53a–b). Timaeus also speaks of the heavens as "that region (*topôi*) of the universe where the nature of fire

---

[31] Note that Timaeus refers to the Form of Fire and other "self-subsisting realities" at 51c.

most of all has its allotment, and where also the bulk of it gathers together, and towards which it moves" (ἐν τῷ τοῦ παντὸς τόπῳ καθ᾽ ὃν ἡ τοῦ πυρὸς εἴληχε μάλιστα φύσις, οὗ καὶ πλεῖστον ἂν ἠθροισμένον εἴη πρὸς ὃ φέρεται; 63b). There seem to be special regions in the receptacle where the elements have a natural province. If we accept these claims, then we should refer to a particular, e.g., a wildfire, as follows: "this region of the receptacle appears as fiery."

Of course if one referred to the receptacle and to bodily particulars in this way, then one would have to use language in a radically different way. For the purposes of communication, however, this would not work. Plato surely does not want to suggest that we use this kind of language in real life: rather, he wants to keep the reader alert to the facts that (1) bodily particulars are mere images of the Forms, and (2) these images appear in the receptacle. In short, he wants to emphasize the low ontological status of the bodily particulars in relation to the Forms and to the receptacle.

In this ontology, all bodily particulars are images or phantasms of the Forms, including the cosmic body as a whole and the bodies of the star-gods. Let us examine this idea in terms of the heavenly bodies of the sun and stars (the sun is a star). As we have seen, the divine soul of the stars, like the cosmic soul, keeps its round fiery body moving everlastingly in a circle. But, in contrast to the cosmic body, which has nothing outside of it, the fiery bodies of the stars and the sun have an external environment where atoms and molecules of other elements collide with each other. The sun/star bodies are made up of atoms and molecules (especially molecules of fire) that endlessly come together and separate in this region of the receptacle. According to Plato's theory of atomic motion, the triangles strike and are struck by each other continually (ditto for the molecules of the four elements). In principle, the atoms, molecules, and elements that surround the sun/stars should affect the consistency of the star-bodies over time. But the sun and stars maintain a relatively constant amount of fire even though they are surrounded by air and other elements. Plato does not offer an account of why the bodies of the sun and stars do not change over time. We must simply accept this as part of the Demiurge's design.[32]

---

[32] Since the heavens are the proper province of fire, we can assume that fire molecules abound in this region: this means that the stars will never die out. In addition, huge molecule clusters presumably have greater resistance to being dissolved by other kinds of atoms and molecules. Still, this does not offer a sufficient account of why the stars maintain their star bodies even though they are separated from one another by air. We could also speculate that the circular motion of the star (powered by the star god) may function to keep the fire molecules in a tight, circular formation.

In Plato's ontological scheme, then, the bodies of the sun/star gods appear in the receptacle as images of the Forms of Fire and of Circle.[33] As images or phantasms, the heavenly bodies have a very low ontological status. We cannot rightly refer to them as "this" but as "of such a kind." In Plato's cosmological scheme, however, the sun and stars do not change like other bodies in the universe. The heavenly bodies are gods that make up the beautiful and perfect cosmic body. In short, in the ontological account, the bodies of the sun and star gods have a shadowy status; in the cosmological account, these bodies are changeless, ageless, and divine. Indeed, the perfect sun and star bodies make them "visible gods." While both the ontological and cosmological accounts are true, we must emphasize that heavenly bodies have a special status in this text.

In Plato's teleological scheme, the cosmos was designed to be viewed and studied. The very fire of the heavenly bodies allows humans to see the world. Even though the bodies of the sun and stars are mere images of the Forms that appear in the receptacle, they grant a vision of divinity to the philosophic viewer. As visible gods, the stars appear to the philosophers as an epiphanic manifestation of divinity. In short, the heavenly bodies and their motions are a "saturated phenomenon." They radiate with divinity.

5.4 The Cosmos Looks at Itself through Human Eyes

The rational human soul has the unique status of being able to live in different bodies. It first lives in a star, but then reincarnates in male human bodies, female human bodies and, in most if not all cases, animals.[34] By contrast, the cosmic soul has one body forever – a body that it can control easily since it has no external environment. Indeed, the cosmos has no bodily needs or desires. This soul does not need to "master" an unruly body

---

[33] Plato does not mention a Form of Circle in this text. I am adding this because the Demiurge, who has just looked at the Form of Animal, makes the cosmos "round" and "spherical," which is the "most perfect of all shapes" (33b). It is not clear whether the Intelligible Animal included a Form of Star. Plato does not tell us very much about the Intelligible Animal. He does mention the Form of Fire (51b–c).

[34] I take it that the rational human soul lives *in* a star body, not *on* the star. Note that Plato says that the human soul "returns to the its home in the star, its partner" (πάλιν εἰς τὴν τοῦ συννόμου πορευθεὶς οἴκησιν ἄστρου; 42b). The idea that the star god has the human soul as its "partner" in this "home," the star body, suggests that the human soul lives in the star. See also the discussion of the divine soul moving the sun in cosmology in *Laws* 899a: "Whether [the soul] drives the sun over all things from within a chariot, or from without, or in some other way, one must believe that it is a god" (εἴτε ἐν ἅρμασιν ἔχουσα ἡμῖν ἥλιον ἄγει φῶς τοῖς ἅπασιν, εἴτε ἔξωθεν, εἴθ' ὅπως εἴθ' ὅπῃ, θεὸν ἡγεῖσθαι χρεὼν πάντα ἄνδρα). In the chariot image, the soul rides *in* the sun as a chariot.

but rather to maintain the order built into the universe by the Demiurge.[35] The human soul is quite different: it does not live in a single body but dwells in different bodies, including human and animal bodies. These mortal bodies massively obstruct its rational activity. The human soul has a difficult life on earth, but it also plays a special role in the cosmos.

As Timaeus suggests, the ancillary gods created the human body in such a way that the soul could exercise its rationality under mortal conditions. In particular, the rational human soul is placed in the head – "the most divine part and the ruler over all other parts of us." The spherical head contains the rational soul with its circular motions (44d). The gods locate the head above the earth so that it extends up to heaven. And, crucially, humans have eyes. As Timaeus states:

> Vision (*opsis*) is the cause of the greatest benefit to humans, since none of the present accounts of the universe could ever have been given if men had not seen the stars, sun, or heaven. The vision of day and night, and the months and the revolutions of the years, and the equinoxes and turnings of the year have brought about the invention of number, and it has given us the cogitation of time and the ability to investigate the nature of the universe. From these, we have procured philosophy, and no greater good has come or will come to mortals as a gift from the gods. (47a–b)[36]

Viewing the heavens over the year gives humans numerical calculation and the "cogitation" (*ennoia*) of time. Indeed, one does not just gain a sense of time by way of vision but the capacity to measure time. Vision also invites humans to engage in a serious study of the heavens. Clearly, one must use one's mind in conjunction with vision to engage in this study. Still, the mortal human could not take the first step without eyes.[37]

Plato presents a teleological account of vision: the creator gods made eyes so that men could contemplate the heavens, learn mathematics and astronomy, and become fully fledged philosophers.[38] Let me discuss these activities in order. First, in viewing the heavens, the philosopher must

---

[35] As Mohr observes (2006), the World-Soul has the task of "maintaining order against an inherent tendency of the corporeal to be chaotic."

[36] ὄψις … αἰτία τῆς μεγίστης ὠφελίας γέγονεν ἡμῖν, ὅτι τῶν νῦν λόγων περὶ τοῦ παντὸς λεγομένων οὐδεὶς ἄν ποτε ἐρρήθη μήτε ἄστρα μήτε ἥλιον μήτε οὐρανὸν ἰδόντων. νῦν δ' ἡμέρα τε καὶ νὺξ ὀφθεῖσαι μῆνές τε καὶ ἐνιαυτῶν περίοδοι καὶ ἰσημερίαι καὶ τροπαὶ μεμηχάνηνται μὲν ἀριθμόν, χρόνου δὲ ἔννοιαν περί τε τῆς τοῦ παντὸς φύσεως ζήτησιν ἔδοσαν· ἐξ ὧν ἐπορισάμεθα φιλοσοφίας γένος, οὗ μεῖζον ἀγαθὸν οὔτ' ἦλθεν οὔτε ἥξει ποτὲ τῷ θνητῷ γένει δωρηθὲν ἐκ θεῶν.

[37] Johansen 2008: Chapter 8 suggests that perception on its own offers little in terms of content, and does not play a role in knowledge. Remes 2014 offers a powerful refutation of this claim.

[38] As Sedley 1989: 377 suggests, in the *Timaeus* "astronomy becomes *par excellence* the discipline which can bridge the gulf between the sensible and intelligible worlds" (see also Sedley 1999). Mathematical reasoning allows the philosopher to find circular motion in the stars and to infer from this that

master mathematics and come to see that the stars and planets all move in circles or spirals (ideally, he should study under Eudoxus or his students). Once he apprehends this mathematically, he can infer that the sun, moon, planets, and fixed stars are moved by reason. He then understands that the cosmos is itself divine and that the stars are "visible gods" (*theoi horatoi*, 40d, 92c), not just random fiery objects in the sky. Finally, he must grasp that he has the same rational faculty as the divine rationality that moves the heavens. Here, he recognizes his own rational activity in the movement of the heavens. The philosopher sees the divinity in the cosmos by way of his own divine reason.

In his theory of vision, Plato takes the reader down to the very atoms and molecules that make human vision possible. He offers a detailed account of how the sensory organ (the eye), the particular object of vision, and light interact so that humans can see phenomena (and see them in color!). In this theory, humans sense the world by way of ongoing influxes and effluxes of atoms and elemental molecules.[39] As Timaeus claims, humans possess "light-bearing eyes" (φωσφόρα ... ὄμματα).[40] The eye contains within it a "pure fire which is akin (ἀδελφόν) to the light of day" (45b). This light

> flows out through the eyes (διὰ τῶν ὀμμάτων) in a smooth and dense stream ... and whenever the stream of vision is surrounded by daylight, like flows out to like; by coalescing with this [i.e., the daylight], the stream of vision forms a single body (σῶμα) along the eyes' visual path, wherever the fire streaming out from within makes contact with the light which meets it from without. (45b–d)

The human eye sends forth its inner light out into the world. The eye's "light" flows forth in a stream and meets with the "light of day," which is "akin" to it.[41] Because of this kinship, the light coming from the eye is able to coalesce with the light of the sun to form a "single body" or, to put it differently, a single "beam" of light. What happens when this single beam of light comes in contact with bodily objects? Once again, fire plays the leading role: bodily objects have molecules of fire in them and they

---

a divine soul orders the heavens. Of course Plato condemned astronomers who look at the stars in the *Republic* (540b).

[39] In addition to creating perception, these influxes and effluxes also generate nutrition, desires, and the emotions (42a–b).

[40] Here, Plato follows Empedocles, who claimed that the eyes were a "lantern" bearing light (DK B84); he conceived of the eyes as sending "effluences" of light into the world. See Plato, *Meno* 76c–d, where Socrates offers a brief discussion of Empedocles' theory of effluences.

[41] It is "similar in its properties because of its similar nature" (45d). On "likeness" and "similarity" in Plato's *Timaeus*, see Bryan 2012: 114–60.

continually emit this fire. These fiery molecules, depending on the size of the triangles, "contract" (*sunkrinonta*) or "dilate" (*diakrinonta*) the beam: larger triangles of fire contract the beam and smaller triangles dilate it. Finally, the beam itself "distributes the motions of every object" to the eye (45d). Strangely, the beam of light does not touch the material object itself but rather its fiery elements.[42]

How does the visual beam transmit the motions of the object to the human perceiver? To understand this, we must look at Timaeus' account of the "affections" (*pathêmata*) that make sensation possible.[43] These "affections" are caused by molecules moving from the object through the beam of light and hitting the eyes of the viewer. Depending on their speed, structure, and quantity, the molecules create different "affections" on the eye.[44] From there, the specific affection moves to the center of intelligence (*to phronimon*), the soul. Since the soul is incorporeal, we cannot understand how the sensory organ communicates the *pathêmata* to the soul. Timaeus simply states that the eye takes these in via the beam, and the mind of the perceiver "grasps the object and identifies it."[45]

Plato presents this theory of vision in the teleological context of his cosmology. He does not simply aim to explain how vision works: he wants humans to learn to see the world in the right way. Of course only the philosophers can achieve this – they alone can apprehend the cosmos as a beautiful, animate, and divine phenomenon. As I suggest, in order to perfect the cosmos, the philosopher must see the divine soul operating in the heavens. The cosmos would lack perfection if it did not have creatures bearing witness to the beauty and divinity of the universe at the physical

---

[42] For useful discussions of Plato's theory of vision, see Brisson 1997; Ierodiakonou 2005; Remes 2014.

[43] Sensations create "affects" (*pathêmata*) in the soul, some quite violent, especially when a person is an infant but also throughout his or her adult life (42b–d). These *pathêmata* are a necessary aspect of visual perception (64a).

[44] As Timaeus puts it: "when even a small affect (*pathos*) hits that which is mobile by nature, it passes on particles (*moria*) in a chain reaction, with some particles passing on this same affection to others until it reaches the center of intelligence (*to phronimon*) and announces the property of the object" (τὸ μὲν γὰρ κατὰ φύσιν εὐκίνητον, ὅταν καὶ βραχὺ πάθος εἰς αὐτὸ ἐμπίπτῃ, διαδίδωσιν κύκλῳ μόρια ἕτερα ἑτέροις ταὐτὸν ἀπεργαζόμενα, μέχριπερ ἂν ἐπὶ τὸ φρόνιμον ἐλθόντα ἐξαγγείλῃ τοῦ ποιήσαντος τὴν δύναμιν; 64b).

[45] Given his dualistic notion of body and soul, Plato cannot account for the soul's grasp of the physical realm. In a difficult passage in the *Timaeus* (37a–b), he claims that the rational part of the soul (which is made of two circles, the "Circle of the Same" and the "Circle of the Other") is a self-moving being that "touches" (ἐφάπτεται) the bodily realm through sensation: "when the soul is concerned with that which is sensible, and the Circle of the Other – moving in an upright course – announces [a perception] to the whole of the Soul, opinions and beliefs come into being which are firm and true." We can infer that a vicious soul has a Circle of the Other that does not move aright and thus forms the wrong opinions.

level. And humans alone have the sensory and intellectual equipment to see the cosmos in its full glory. The Demiurge designed the cosmos to be seen. As Timaeus claims: "that which comes into being must have bodily form and be visible and tangible, but *nothing could ever be visible without fire*, and nothing tangible without solidity, and there is nothing solid without earth" (σωματοειδὲς δὲ δὴ καὶ ὁρατὸν ἁπτόν τε δεῖ τὸ γενόμενον εἶναι, χωρισθὲν δὲ πυρὸς οὐδὲν ἄν ποτε ὁρατὸν γένοιτο, οὐδὲ ἁπτὸν ἄνευ τινὸς στερεοῦ, στερεὸν δὲ οὐκ ἄνευ γῆς; 31b, my italics).

In the cosmos, only mortal creatures can see. And humans alone can grasp the cosmos as a meaningful phenomenon. The cosmos itself lacks eyes and a sensory apparatus: it does not have eyes or ears because there is nothing outside of it to see or hear (33c). Only humans can perceive things in the world and apprehend this rationally. In short, humans were designed to bear witness to the cosmos. As Broadie observes, "the cosmic god would presumably have remained fundamentally unfulfilled if it did not harbour mortal percipients to activate the possibilities for touch and vision that define the very materials of which its divine body is made."[46] Indeed, humans are not simply meant to see the world that the Demiurge made, but to see the cosmos as a beautiful and divine being.

To be sure, Plato does not set forth an explicit claim that humans perfect the cosmos by seeing it as a beautiful and divine object at the physical level. But he spends a surprising amount of time explaining the operations of vision. Indeed, he even presents an account of how humans see things in color. As I suggest, we must link Plato's theory of vision to his views on the perfection of the cosmos. In particular, his celebration of the physical beauty of the universe invites us to bring together the perfection of the universe and the rational human souls who bear witness to its beauty and divine order when they live in human bodies.

Let me briefly describe Plato's theory of how we see the world in color. Two key factors go into the sensation of color. (1) Bodily motion. At the microlevel, the triangles that make up the four elements in the cosmos are ceaselessly moving and bringing about change. On the human level, bodily things around us move, and we move our own bodies through this environment. These different moving bodies affect the human eye and determine the things that it sees. (2) The element of fire. The humans' "lightbearing eyes" contain an inner fire that does not burn, and the beam coming out of the eyes meets up with the external fire that creates light (the sun, fires, etc.). In addition, most bodies contain some element of fire in

---

[46] Broadie 2012: 91.

their makeup (whether a little or a lot). A person sees different colors depending on the quantity of fire in the constitution of a given object. To understand the perception of color, then, one must take into account the fire in the human eye, the fire in the external light, and the fire in the bodily objects that the human perceives. Depending on the quantity of fire in the object and the quality of external light at a given time, one sees different colors.

Let us consider how this works in the case of the color "shiny" (*lampron*). This is the color of the stars (among other things). In Plato's theory, "shiny" is one of the four basic colors, along with white, red, and black (all other colors come from these four).[47] As Timaeus states:

> When something moving rapidly falls upon [the beam of light] and pene-trates it up to the point of the eyes themselves, it pushes through the passages of the eyes and melts them; this movement pushes out from the eyes a cluster of fire and water, which we call tears. And when this moving element, being fire, encounters fire coming from the opposite direction – one firestream leaping out [of the eyes] like a lightning bolt and the other firestream coming in and being quenched by the moisture [in the eyes] – colors of all kinds come into being through this mixture. We call the experience of this "sparklings," and we call that object producing this "shiny" and "glittery." (67e–68a)[48]

Timaeus begins by mentioning "rapidly moving" fire, which clearly refers to intense sunlight. The fire moves from the sun to the eye and encounters the fire in a person's eye as well as its moisture. This makes the person see the specific color "shiny." To fully understand the fire moving from the sun to the eye, we must look at the scalene triangles that create corpuscles of fire at the microlevel. As Timaeus claims, the triangles that make up fire are the "sharpest," "fastest," and "lightest," and they have the effect of "piercing" other bodies, which comprise other kinds of triangles (56c–d). The triangles that generate molecules of fire are constantly moving throughout the cosmos and piercing other bodies. These triangles can either harm the body or element that they come into contact with or, alternatively, attach

---

[47] See Sassi 2015 for an excellent discussion of Plato's views on color; for the claim that "shiny" (or, as she translates it, "brilliant") is one the four basic colors in Plato, see p. 265.

[48] 67e–68a: τὴν δὲ ὀξυτέραν φορὰν καὶ γένους πυρὸς ἑτέρου προσπίπτουσαν καὶ διακρίνουσαν τὴν ὄψιν μέχρι τῶν ὀμμάτων, αὐτάς τε τῶν ὀφθαλμῶν τὰς διεξόδους βίᾳ διωθοῦσαν καὶ τήκουσαν, πῦρ μὲν ἀθρόον καὶ ὕδωρ, ὃ δάκρυον καλοῦμεν, ἐκεῖθεν ἐκχέουσαν, αὐτὴν δὲ οὖσαν πῦρ ἐξ ἐναντίας ἀπαντῶσαν, καὶ τοῦ μὲν ἐκπηδῶντος πυρὸς οἷον ἀπ' ἀστραπῆς, τοῦ δ' εἰσιόντος καὶ περὶ τὸ νοτερὸν κατασβεννυμένου, παντοδαπῶν ἐν τῇ κινήσει ταύτῃ γιγνομένων χρωμάτων, μαρμαρυγὰς μὲν τὸ πάθος προσείπομεν, τὸ δὲ τοῦτο ἀπεργαζόμενον λαμπρόν τε καὶ στίλβον ἐπωνομάσαμεν.

themselves to these things and become part of a different body. Indeed, the majority of bodies in the phenomenal realm contain portions of fire (albeit in different degrees).[49]

In the earthly realm, a human being is surrounded by the endless motion of bodies (micro or macro) and the presence of external light (brighter or dimmer). In addition, his or her "lightbearing eyes" emit their own fire ongoingly. In cases where the eyes are pierced by the intense fire of the sun, they shed a small degree of tears (adding moisture to the equation).[50] In the passage above, the combination of external fiery light, the fire leaping out of the eyes, and the fiery elements in the object brings about the sensation of the color "shiny." Timaeus also says that the movements of atoms and molecules of fire create "all kinds of colors." Thus, an object can be "shiny" and also have other colors; indeed, most bodies feature many colors.

Why do humans need to see the world in color? Plato does not provide a reason for this, but he does suggest that color adds to the beauty of the cosmos. To take one example, his detailed account of the color "shiny" (*lampron*) picks up on his earlier claims that the stars are the "shiniest" and most beautiful of all objects. As Timaeus stated, the Demiurge made the divine sun and stars "so that they would be the shiniest to behold (*lamprotaton idein*) and the most beautiful (*kallistos*)" (40a). Indeed, it is not just the shiny sun and stars that make the cosmos beautiful: all four elements – fire, water, air, and earth – are exceedingly beautiful to behold: "We must state what will be the four most beautiful bodies, which will differ from one another but can be produced from each other by way of dissolution . . . . For we would not agree with anyone that there are visible bodies more beautiful than these" (δεῖ δὴ λέγειν ποῖα κάλλιστα σώματα γένοιτ᾽ ἂν τέτταρα, ἀνόμοια μὲν ἑαυτοῖς, δυνατὰ δὲ ἐξ ἀλλήλων αὐτῶν ἄττα διαλυόμενα γίγνεσθαι . . . τόδε γὰρ οὐδενὶ συγχωρησόμεθα, καλλίω τούτων ὁρώμενα σώματα εἶναι; 53d–e).

In this dialogue, Plato places great emphasis on the beauty of the physical cosmos. As Timaeus says in the last lines of the dialogue: "a visible god (*theos aisthêtos*) came into being, the greatest, best, most beautiful (*kallistos*), and most perfect cosmos – this one cosmos, the sole of its kind" (θεὸς αἰσθητός, μέγιστος καὶ ἄριστος κάλλιστός τε καὶ τελεώτατος γέγονεν εἷς οὐρανὸς ὅδε μονογενὴς ὤν; 92c). Here again, Plato directly

---

[49]   The quantity of fire in a given body brings about our sensation of the color(s) of an object. In addition, different objects have different classes (*genê*) of fire in them, and these affect the visual beam in different ways (67e).

[50]   I take it that one would not see all that many colors if one was actively crying.

links the visibility of the cosmos with beauty and, in particular, with the divine beauties seen in the heavens. In my view, the cosmos would be less perfect if its physical beauty were not seen. Humans contribute to the perfection of the cosmos by seeing the cosmos as a physical phenomenon. The cosmos sees itself, as it were, through the eyes of the philosopher.

Finally, the philosopher will see not only beauty in the heavens but a physical epiphany of the gods. After all, the cosmos and the heavenly bodies are "visible gods" (40d, 92c). A god that manifests itself visibly to humans appears epiphanically. In earlier dialogues, Plato used the language of epiphany to refer to the rational human soul's contemplation of the divine Forms, while rejecting the idea that the gods appeared to humans in bodily epiphanies. In the *Timaeus*, he makes the divine appear visibly as well as intelligibly. Of course, in the *Timaeus*, only philosophers can see the stars as "visible gods" and thus experience a divine epiphany. As we saw in Chapter 2, in the Greek imaginary, gods could appear in the presence of humans but not be recognized: they manifest their divinity to humans only when they choose to do this. For example, in the *Hymn to Demeter*, the women of Eleusis do not at first recognize Demeter: "none of the men or deep-girdled women who saw her recognized her" (οὐδέ τις ἀνδρῶν εἰσορόων γίγνωσκε βαθυζώνων τε γυναικῶν; *HH* 2.94–5). Later in the poem, Metaneira sees a partial revelation of the goddess (188–90), and then a full epiphany (268–76). And, later on, the royal women in Eleusis see a full epiphany: "a light shone from the immortal body of the goddess, and her golden hair spread down over her shoulders, and the firm house was filled with brightness like a bolt of lightning" (τῆλε δὲ φέγγος ἀπὸ χροὸς ἀθανάτοιο λάμπε θεᾶς, ξανθαὶ δὲ κόμαι κατενήνοθεν ὤμους, αὐγῆς δ' ἐπλήσθη πυκινὸς δόμος ἀστεροπῆς ὥς; *HH* 2.278–81).

In the *Timaeus*, the philosophers who have mastered astronomy will see divine epiphanies in the stars when they behold the heavens. Through their sparkling radiance and perfect rotations, the stars manifest their divinity. The philosopher who studies the heavens comes to see the heavenly bodies as manifest gods. In this dialogue, Plato makes the gods visible.

5.5   Peregrinations of the Human Soul

In the *Timaeus*, Plato sets forth a new story of the human soul. This resembles the stories in the *Phaedo* and *Phaedrus* but differs in key ways. All human souls begin their lives in the body of a star. After this period, they are put into mortal bodies in order to make the cosmos perfect. Still, each individual soul has its own mission – to return to its native star.

Let us look first at the mythic passage that deals with the creation and destiny of the human soul:

> Going back to the mixing bowl in which he had mixed together the soul of the universe, he [the Demiurge] poured the remains of the previous material, mixing them together pretty much in the same way, but these remains no longer had an invariable and uniform purity, but were second and third in degrees of purity. And, putting this together in its entirety, he divided it into a number of souls equal in number to the stars, and he assigned each soul to each star and, placing them in there as though in a chariot, he showed them the nature of the universe and told them the laws of destiny. [As he told them,] one and the same initial birth would be assigned to all of them, so that no-one would be slighted by him. And it would be necessary for them, once they were sown into the fitting organs of time, to be by nature the most god-respecting creature. And since human nature is twofold, the superior class would hereafter be called "man." And when they [the souls] would be implanted in bodies according to necessity, there would be influx and efflux in their bodies, and the following would necessarily come into being – first, sensation that is innate and common to all, which comes from violent affections; and second, desire mingled with pleasure and pain and, in addition, fear and anger and all such things that naturally follow or oppose these. If they [the rational human souls] should master these, they would live justly, but if they should be conquered by these, they would live unjustly. And if a person lives well for the appropriate period of time, his soul would return to his home in the star, its partner, and live a blessed and congenial life. (41d–42b)[51]

This passage presents the story of the soul in three chapters: its beginning, its incarnation/reincarnations, and its possible return to its native star. Plato gives the rational human soul a strange status in the cosmos. Though immortal, it will be incarnated again and again. It can live in different bodies, even though its proper home (*oikêsis*) is in a star. As we will see,

---

[51] 41d–42b: καὶ πάλιν ἐπὶ τὸν πρότερον κρατῆρα, ἐν ᾧ τὴν τοῦ παντὸς ψυχὴν κεραννὺς ἔμισγεν, τὰ τῶν πρόσθεν ὑπόλοιπα κατεχεῖτο μίσγων τρόπον μέν τινα τὸν αὐτόν, ἀκήρατα δὲ οὐκέτι κατὰ ταὐτὰ ὡσαύτως, ἀλλὰ δεύτερα καὶ τρίτα. συστήσας δὲ τὸ πᾶν διεῖλεν ψυχὰς ἰσαρίθμους τοῖς ἄστροις, ἔνειμέν θ' ἑκάστην πρὸς ἕκαστον, καὶ ἐμβιβάσας ὡς ἐς ὄχημα τὴν τοῦ παντὸς φύσιν ἔδειξεν, νόμους τε τοὺς εἱμαρμένους εἶπεν αὐταῖς, ὅτι γένεσις πρώτη μὲν ἔσοιτο τεταγμένη μία πᾶσιν, ἵνα μήτις ἐλαττοῖτο ὑπ' αὐτοῦ, δέοι δὲ σπαρείσας αὐτὰς εἰς τὰ προσήκοντα ἑκάσταις ἕκαστα ὄργανα χρόνων φῦναι ζῴων τὸ θεοσεβέστατον, διπλῆς δὲ οὔσης τῆς ἀνθρωπίνης φύσεως, τὸ κρεῖττον τοιοῦτον εἴη γένος ὃ καὶ ἔπειτα κεκλήσοιτο ἀνήρ. ὁπότε δὴ σώμασιν ἐμφυτευθεῖεν ἐξ ἀνάγκης, καὶ τὸ μὲν προσίοι, τὸ δ' ἀπίοι τοῦ σώματος αὐτῶν, πρῶτον μὲν αἴσθησιν ἀναγκαῖον εἴη μίαν πᾶσιν ἐκ βιαίων παθημάτων σύμφυτον γίγνεσθαι, δεύτερον δὲ ἡδονῇ καὶ λύπῃ μεμειγμένον ἔρωτα, πρὸς δὲ τούτοις φόβον καὶ θυμὸν ὅσα τε ἑπόμενα αὐτοῖς καὶ ὁπόσα ἐναντίως πέφυκε διεστηκότα· ὧν εἰ μὲν κρατήσοιεν, δίκῃ βιώσοιντο, κρατηθέντες δὲ ἀδικίᾳ. καὶ ὁ μὲν εὖ τὸν προσήκοντα χρόνον βιούς, πάλιν εἰς τὴν τοῦ συννόμου πορευθεὶς οἴκησιν ἄστρου, βίον εὐδαίμονα καὶ συνήθη ἕξοι.

when it lives in a star, the rational human soul first has a purely intellectual apprehension of the cosmos; after incarnation in a mortal body, it views the cosmos both visibly and intellectually.

Timaeus recounts the rational human soul's first life on its star rather briefly. As he states, when this soul lives in a star, the Demiurge shows it the universe: "placing them there [in the star] as though in a chariot, he showed them (*edeixen*) the nature of the all" (ἐμβιβάσας ὡς ἐς ὄχημα τὴν τοῦ παντὸς φύσιν ἔδειξεν; 41e).⁵² What exactly is "the nature of the all"? And what do the human souls apprehend in this vision? Timaeus regularly uses "the all" (*to pan*) to refer to the created cosmos, with its bodies and souls.⁵³ However, in this passage, he cannot be referring to the visible cosmos because the rational human souls are not yet incarnate in mortal bodies and do not have a sensory apparatus. They apprehend "the nature of the all" rationally.

How should we understand this first intellectual apprehension of the universe? What exactly does the rational human soul grasp in this early period? Later in the dialogue, Timaeus brings up the "original nature" of the rational human soul and speaks about the objects of its knowledge:

> The appropriate motions for the divine part in us are the thoughts and revolutions of the universe. We must follow these motions, correcting the motions in our head that were harmed during birth, and by learning the harmonies and revolutions of the universe, liken the thinking part to the object of thought in accordance with *our original nature*. (τῷ δ' ἐν ἡμῖν θείῳ συγγενεῖς εἰσιν κινήσεις αἱ τοῦ παντὸς διανοήσεις καὶ περιφοραί· ταύταις δὴ συνεπόμενον ἕκαστον δεῖ, τὰς περὶ τὴν γένεσιν ἐν τῇ κεφαλῇ διεφθαρμένας ἡμῶν περιόδους ἐξορθοῦντα διὰ τὸ καταμανθάνειν τὰς τοῦ παντὸς ἁρμονίας τε καὶ περιφοράς, τῷ κατανοουμένῳ τὸ κατανοοῦν ἐξομοιῶσαι κατὰ τὴν ἀρχαίαν φύσιν; 90c-d, my italics)

By the "original nature" of the soul, Timaeus refers to its first life in a star. If the philosopher perfects the motions in his mind, he can achieve the same knowledge that his soul had when it dwelled in a star. To achieve this, he must liken his thinking to the object of thought, i.e., the "thoughts and the revolutions of the universe." What, then, are the thoughts of the universe? As we saw above, when the cosmic soul thinks, it contemplates the realm of Being (the Forms) and of becoming (37b). In the latter case, it apprehends physical events unfolding in its own cosmic body. The rational human soul, however, does not inhabit the cosmic body. Since it lives in

---

⁵² The image of the chariot hearkens back to the image of the preincarnate human souls as a charioteer guiding a team of horses in the *Phaedrus*. But, in the *Timaeus*, the rational human soul does not have lower parts – these are created later, when the body is formed. Here, the rational part exists on its own.

⁵³ See, e.g., 27a, 27c, 28b, 29d, 30b, 41a, 47a, 53a–b, 90c, 92c.

a star body, however, it can presumably apprehend its own body. In principle, then, when the rational human soul grasps divine thoughts, it should be able to "think" Being, soul, and, in a limited way, becoming.

Here, I will set forth a maximalist position for what the soul sees in its first life in a star. To be sure, this is pure speculation. Given the lack of textual evidence, we must proceed with caution. However, I do want to take seriously the idea that the soul viewed the cosmos rationally in this period of its life. The rational human souls did not just "see the planetary motions" (Johansen) or get "a vision of the universe" (Broadie).

In grasping "the nature of the all" rationally, the human soul apprehends a wide range of objects. (1) The human soul sees the Form of Animal (the "Intelligible Animal") and all the living beings contained in this Form, i.e., the Forms of the four classes of living beings (divine, winged, terrestrial, aquatic). In the Forms, it also apprehends being and eternity. (2) Since the cosmos is good and features rational and mathematical order, the human soul must rationally apprehend order, proportionality, goodness, harmony, and beauty; and it must also comprehend the elements of mathematics and harmonics. (3) Since the cosmos is a living being that moves itself, the human soul must rationally apprehend life, soul, *nous*, the soul's relation to a body, divine causality, motion, and the relation of *nous* to circular motion. (4) Since the World-Soul moves and controls its own body, and moves it according to measure and number, the human soul must grasp, at least to some extent, time, space, and the relation between soul and body. (5) Finally, the rational human soul may have had some grasp of the realm of becoming by way of its star body. This would include apprehending the triangles and molecules that create the four elements (fire, air, water, earth), and the way that these come together to form three-dimensional figures. I do not consider this list to be comprehensive. I set forth these ideas to invite readers to reconsider the claim that the human soul rationally apprehends "the nature of the all" in its first life in a star.

In terms of this first grasp of the universe, some scholars have suggested that, when the human soul sees "the nature of the all," this allows it to recollect the Forms when it lives in a mortal human body on earth. According to this view, the rational human souls apprehended the intelligible realm in this first stage in their life and they retain this knowledge after incarnation on earth.[54] Plato does not, however, mention the doctrine

---

[54] Brisson 1974: 440 argues in favor of the doctrine of recollection; cf. Vlastos 1994: 97. Johanson 2008: Chapter 8 offers an excellent examination of perception in general and the question of whether the *Timaeus* features the doctrine of recollection (he rejects the idea that the soul recollects the Forms).

of recollection in this dialogue. He never suggests that the incarnated human soul remembers this first rational vision of the nature of the all. For this reason, I do not think that the doctrine of recollection operates in Plato's cosmology. Rather, the rational human soul has the same capacity to apprehend the universe that it had when it lived in a star.

During this period of the rational human soul's life, the Demiurge gives it information about its future life on earth. As he states, all human souls will first incarnate in a male human body; if they live badly, they will be punished by moving downwards to women and animals. However, if they live justly and well for an apportioned time on earth (i.e., through a series of reincarnations as a male), they can depart from the mortal realm. At this point, the rational human soul will return to its native star and live a "blessed life" (*bion eudaimona*, 42b). Here, it returns to "its first and best state" (42d).

In spite of these claims about life in the stars, Broadie argues that the human soul did not experience bliss when it lived in the heavens. She focuses in particular on the brevity of the soul's inhabitation of a star:

> A soul that does well enough to rejoin its star will not be returning to a paradisal situation which it actually enjoyed at leisure before it was somehow ousted. On the contrary, the pre-carnate interval is dedicated to providing the souls with a basic moral outfit for mortal life. This means that their mortal embodiment will come as a fulfillment, even though one fraught with dangers.[55]

Contrary to Broadie, I do not see this first state as a minor "interval." This is the first chapter in the story of the soul. Indeed, the logic of the story has a specific structure: the human soul has a happy and purely rational beginning that includes a rational apprehension of "the nature of the all"; it goes through a series of painful and difficult incarnations in mortal bodies; and, in the cases when it practices philosophy over a specific period of time on earth, it finally returns to its star. We found a very similar story of the soul in the *Phaedo* and *Phaedrus*. However, in those dialogues, the soul aimed to leave the bodily realm altogether and return to the realm of the Forms. In the *Timaeus*, the soul has a similar mission, but it does not leave the bodily realm entirely. In Plato's cosmology, all souls live in bodies. The rational human soul will dwell in a star.

What happens to the rational human soul when it enters an animal body? As Timaeus states:

---

[55] Broadie 2012: 107.

[The soul] would be changed again into a wild animal according to the similarity of its nature, and in this transformation it would not cease from its woes until it drags that great mass of fire and water and earth and air (which later adhered to him), which is tumultuous and irrational, into conformity with the Circle of the Same and similar within him; if it dominates this by reason, [the soul] would return again to the form of its first and best state. (42c–d)[56]

The rational human soul, as it seems, must continue to work on developing its reason even when it is incarnated in an animal! In short, during its life as an animal, it must conform itself to the Circle of the Same. However, later in the text, Timaeus presents a quite different account of the human soul's life in lower creatures: "In this way all living creatures, then and now, exchange places with one another, changing positions by the loss or gain of understanding, or the loss or gain of foolishness" (καὶ κατὰ ταῦτα δὴ πάντα τότε καὶ νῦν διαμείβεται τὰ ζῷα εἰς ἄλληλα, νοῦ καὶ ἀνοίας ἀποβολῇ καὶ κτήσει μεταβαλλόμενα; 92c). The soul exercises its reason less and less as it moves down from male humans to women, birds, land animals, and fish. Thus, the souls that occupy women may attempt to use their reason, but many will fail and then move downwards into animals (presumably some souls in women do exercise reason and move upwards). In this scenario, the rational human soul would effectively go dim while it lives in the bodies of terrestrial animals (and get dimmer as it moves downwards to fish). In this period, the soul endures a punishment that takes the form of an obstruction of its reason.[57] To be sure, Timaeus does not offer a detailed or consistent account of the soul's activity in animal bodies, but the latter scenario seems more likely. According to this teleological cosmic scheme, the bad human soul can move up to human bodies after a period of punishment in an animal body.

Timaeus emphasizes that the human soul gets punished for its vicious actions and poor use of reason (86b–87b). Souls in male bodies who live "unjustly" (*adikêi*) will reincarnate into women; those who "are not evil (*akakoi*) but foolish (*kouphoi*)" and who view the cosmos "with the belief that the most solid proofs of the heavens come by sight" turn into birds; souls who have not practiced philosophy or studied the heavens, "because they are no longer using the circles in their minds," move into terrestrial

---

[56] 42c–d: κατὰ τὴν ὁμοιότητα τῆς τοῦ τρόπου γενέσεως εἴς τινα τοιαύτην ἀεὶ μεταβαλοῖ θήρειον φύσιν, ἀλλάττων τε οὐ πρότερον πόνων λήξοι, πρὶν τῇ ταὐτοῦ καὶ ὁμοίου περιόδῳ τῇ ἐν αὐτῷ συνεπισπώμενος τὸν πολὺν ὄχλον καὶ ὕστερον προσφύντα ἐκ πυρὸς καὶ ὕδατος καὶ ἀέρος καὶ γῆς, θορυβώδη καὶ ἄλογον ὄντα, λόγῳ κρατήσας εἰς τὸ τῆς πρώτης καὶ ἀρίστης ἀφίκοιτο εἶδος ἕξεως.

[57] The obstructions of reason get worse as the soul moves downward in the animal realm.

animals; and the most "thoughtless and unlearned" (*anoêtatôn kai amathestatôn*) souls, made impure by all kinds of bad actions (*plêmmeleias*), live in aquatic creatures (90e–92b). Here, Timaeus mentions three different factors that affect reincarnation: the soul's moral goodness or badness; its use or non-use of its reason; and its practice of astronomy and philosophy. However, even if the soul is not morally bad (*akakos*) in a given life, it must develop its reason to improve its lot in the next life. And, to live well, it must practice astronomy and philosophy (and do this in the right way). Not surprisingly, only a few men can live this excellent life. As Timaeus notes, "all men partake in true opinion while only a few partake in the *nous* of the gods" (51e). Incarnation in a human body presents immense difficulties for the rational human soul. But Plato promises them the possibility of returning up to their native star.

In this story of the soul, Plato uses the language of vertical movement (up and down). However, as Broadie rightly notes, incarnation in the mortal body is not a "fall": rational human souls must necessarily live in human and animal bodies so that the cosmos can be the best image of the Form of Animal.[58] In contrast to the Orphic tale of the fallen human soul that informs the story of the soul in the *Phaedo*, and the *Phaedrus*' account of human souls falling from the heavens, the *Timaeus* represents the incarnation of the soul into a mortal body as necessary to the perfection of the cosmos.

5.6   Becoming like God

In the *Theaetetus*, Socrates famously articulates the notion of "becoming like god": "Therefore it is necessary to attempt to flee from this place as quickly as possible. This escape is to become like god as far as this is possible; and this likening is to become just and holy with the aid of wisdom" (διὸ καὶ πειρᾶσθαι χρὴ ἐνθένδε ἐκεῖσε φεύγειν ὅτι τάχιστα. φυγὴ δὲ ὁμοίωσις θεῷ κατὰ τὸ δυνατόν· ὁμοίωσις δὲ δίκαιον καὶ ὅσιον μετὰ φρονήσεως γενέσθαι; 176a–b).[59] In this dialogue, Plato emphasizes ethical virtues, especially justice: god is "the most just" (*dikaiotatos*, 176c), so philosophers should seek to make themselves just.[60] In the *Timaeus*,

---

[58] Broadie 2012: 103–4.
[59] See Sedley 1999 for an excellent discussion of "becoming like god" in the *Theatetus* and the *Timaeus* (see also Carone 2005: 68–77). I agree with Sedley (1999), who claims that the ultimate goal for the philosopher is to contemplate the Forms (though the philosopher must use practical reason to engage in this kind of reason); cf. Broadie (2012: 111–12), who argues that the telos of the philosopher is to exercise and master practical reasoning.
[60] The question of the date of the *Theaetetus* is beyond the scope of this investigation.

---

however, Plato presents a different account of becoming like god. In particular, the philosopher must liken himself to the cosmic soul. Since the rational human soul is divine and moves in a circular motion, philosophers must study the stars to perfect their own minds.[61]

Timaeus emphasizes the divine nature of the rational human soul even in its life in mortal bodies on earth:

> Concerning the most sovereign part of our soul, we must understand this in the following way: god gave to each of us, as a daimon, that which dwells in the topmost part of our body and lifts us up from the earth to our kindred in heaven, since we are not a terrestrial plant but a heavenly plant (*phuton . . . ouranion*), if we speak in the most correct way: for from there, whence our soul was originally born, the divine [part of the soul] suspends our head, that is, our root, and keeps our body upright. (90a–b)[62]

On earth, humans are upside-down plants that have their roots in heaven. Humans are heavenly, not earthly plants. The Demiurge designed the rational human soul to aspire and ascend to the heavens.

To become like god, the philosophers must think divine thoughts:

> The person who has been zealous about the love of learning and true wisdom, and has most of all exercised those parts of himself, necessarily thinks immortal and divine thoughts (*phronein athanata kai theia*). And, insofar as it is possible for human nature to partake of immortality, he cannot fail to achieve this if indeed he lays hold of truth. Inasmuch as he always tends to his divine part and cosmically adorns (*kekosmêmenon*) the divine spirit that dwells in him, he is exceptionally happy. (90b–c)[63]

---

[61] In particular, the philosopher needs to prove by mathematical calculation that the stars move in circular motions (along different axes and in different diameters) and that the planets move in spirals. Note that Timaeus claims that one can practice astronomy incorrectly: one must not study the heavens in the belief that "the most sure proofs about these matters come through sight" (91e). For useful analyses of Greek astronomy, see Dicks 1970; G.E.R. Lloyd 1979: 169–225, 1987: 235–41, 304–19. On Plato's approach to astronomy, see Vlastos 1980; Sedley 1989: 377; and Mueller 1992: 192–4 (cf. Mourelatos 1981, who claims that Plato's astronomy focuses on kinematics rather than the study of celestial motions).

[62] 90a–b: τὸ δὲ δὴ περὶ τοῦ κυριωτάτου παρ' ἡμῖν ψυχῆς εἴδους διανοεῖσθαι δεῖ τῇδε, ὡς ἄρα αὐτὸ δαίμονα θεὸς ἑκάστῳ δέδωκεν, τοῦτο ὃ δή φαμεν οἰκεῖν μὲν ἡμῶν ἐπ' ἄκρῳ τῷ σώματι, πρὸς δὲ τὴν ἐν οὐρανῷ συγγένειαν ἀπὸ γῆς ἡμᾶς αἴρειν ὡς ὄντας φυτὸν οὐκ ἔγγειον ἀλλὰ οὐράνιον, ὀρθότατα λέγοντες· ἐκεῖθεν γάρ, ὅθεν ἡ πρώτη τῆς ψυχῆς γένεσις ἔφυ, τὸ θεῖον τὴν κεφαλὴν καὶ ῥίζαν ἡμῶν ἀνακρεμαννὺν ὀρθοῖ πᾶν τὸ σῶμα.

[63] 90b–c: τῷ δὲ περὶ φιλομαθίαν καὶ περὶ τὰς ἀληθεῖς φρονήσεις ἐσπουδακότι καὶ ταῦτα μάλιστα τῶν αὑτοῦ γεγυμνασμένῳ φρονεῖν μὲν ἀθάνατα καὶ θεῖα, ἄνπερ ἀληθείας ἐφάπτηται, πᾶσα ἀνάγκη που, καθ' ὅσον δ' αὖ μετασχεῖν ἀνθρωπίνη φύσει ἀθανασίας ἐνδέχεται, τούτου μηδὲν μέρος ἀπολείπειν, ἅτε δὲ ἀεὶ θεραπεύοντα τὸ θεῖον ἔχοντά τε αὐτὸν εὖ κεκοσμημένον τὸν δαίμονα σύνοικον ἑαυτῷ, διαφερόντως εὐδαίμονα εἶναι.

Plato brings together the human and the universe by forging a microcosm–macrocosm analogy: the philosopher must "cosmically adorn" (*kekosmêmenon*) the rational part of his soul. That is, he must make his reason into an ordered and perfect "cosmos" and thereby think divine thoughts. The divine order of the motion of the stars provides an objective correlative for the "cosmos" in his soul.

Timaeus also indicates that philosophers should become like god by studying both the divine and the necessary "causes" in the cosmos:

> We must therefore distinguish two kinds of causes, the necessary and the divine. We must seek the divine cause in all things in order to attain a blessed life, to the extent that our nature allows, and seek the necessary for the sake of the divine. Our reason is that, without these [necessary causes], those other objects that we zealously pursue cannot on their own be apprehended, grasped, or partaken of in any other way. (68e–69a)[64]

What does Timaeus mean by the divine cause? There are two divine causes in this text: the Demiurge, the first and highest cause, and the cosmic soul. In studying the divine causes, we can infer, the philosopher must analyze both the Demiurge and the cosmic soul. First, the philosopher must analyze the Demiurge's creation to understand the overall design of the cosmos. Second, he must examine the cosmic soul's causation of the movement of the heavenly bodies.

In this passage, Timaeus indicates that the philosopher "must seek the necessary causes" because he cannot discover or grasp the divine causes without them. This is a strong statement. In earlier dialogues, Plato indicated that the philosopher should ignore the bodily realm as much as possible and seek out the Forms. In the *Timaeus*, the philosopher must start by investigating the realm of becoming in order to ascend to the realm of Being.[65] He does this to actualize his capacity for thinking divine thoughts.

---

[64] 68e–69a: διὸ δὴ χρὴ δύ᾽ αἰτίας εἴδη διορίζεσθαι, τὸ μὲν ἀναγκαῖον, τὸ δὲ θεῖον, καὶ τὸ μὲν θεῖον ἐν ἅπασιν ζητεῖν κτήσεως ἕνεκα εὐδαίμονος βίου, καθ᾽ ὅσον ἡμῶν ἡ φύσις ἐνδέχεται, τὸ δὲ ἀναγκαῖον ἐκείνων χάριν, λογιζόμενον ὡς ἄνευ τούτων οὐ δυνατὰ αὐτὰ ἐκεῖνα ἐφ᾽ οἷς σπουδάζομεν μόνα κατανοεῖν οὐδ᾽ αὖ λαβεῖν οὐδ᾽ ἄλλως πως μετασχεῖν.

[65] How does the study of the bodily realm help the philosopher to grasp divine causes? The philosopher apprehends the orbits of the stars and planets and examines this order in astronomical and mathematical terms. In this way, he grasps the divine cosmic soul that moves them. In addition, in his everyday life, he can see (for example) that water evaporates into the air, air condenses and rains, fire produces smoke, or erupts in lava, and so on. At the level of the four elements, the philosopher understands that atomic triangles fit together in different ways to make up molecules of the four elements which, in turn, make up bodies. This grasp of the necessary causes includes understanding the interaction of the four elements and the way that they produce visible bodily forms.

5.7   Earthly and Divine Time

To fully understand how the rational human soul becomes like god, we must examine the operation of time in this dialogue. Plato famously claims that time is the "moving image of eternity" (εἰκὼ ... κινητόν τινα αἰῶνος, 37d). As Timaeus states:

> Since this [the intelligible Form of Animal] is an eternal living being, he [the Demiurge] set to work to make the universe, so far as he could, of a like kind. Since the nature of the Animal was eternal, he was not able to give this [eternity] entirely to the generated universe. He contrived to create a moving image of eternity; and, at the same time as he ordered the cosmos, he created an eternal image of the eternal Being that abides in unity – an image that moves according to number. And we call this time. (37d)[66]

To construct the cosmos, the Demiurge splinters the unity and eternity of the Form of Animal into the plurality of heavenly bodies that move everlastingly and harmoniously in the medium of time. Though the physical cosmos must move, its everlasting and perfect motions operate according to rational and mathematical principles: it "moves according to number" (37d–e). These mathematical principles make the movements of the heavens perfectly orderly. The divine cosmic soul endessly moves the star bodies in orderly circles to trace out an eternal image of eternity.

Rather paradoxically, Plato brings time and eternity – that is, the eternity of the Form of Animal – very close together. To achieve this, he gives the cosmos a body that is "perfect and ageless and unailing" (τέλεον καὶ ἀγήρων καὶ ἄνοσον; 33a) and makes the divine cosmic soul move its heavenly bodies in perfect circular revolutions. Unlike mortal bodies, the cosmic body does not get old or die; it changes only insofar as it moves in circles. To this extent, it does not have the negative qualities associated with the transience and death of bodies in the earthly realm. To be sure, the cosmic body moves in time's forward arrow – indeed, the cosmic soul marks out time's forward arrow by moving the heavenly bodies – but it does not change or pass away like other bodily phenomena. For this reason, the cosmos does not experience finitude.

Of course Plato fully understands that linear, forward-moving time brings about generation, growth, and death in the mortal realm. Indeed,

[66] 37d: καθάπερ οὖν αὐτὸ τυγχάνει ζῷον ἀΐδιον ὄν, καὶ τόδε τὸ πᾶν οὕτως εἰς δύναμιν ἐπεχείρησε τοιοῦτον ἀποτελεῖν. ἡ μὲν οὖν τοῦ ζῴου φύσις ἐτύγχανεν οὖσα αἰώνιος, καὶ τοῦτο μὲν δὴ τῷ γεννητῷ παντελῶς προσάπτειν οὐκ ἦν δυνατόν· εἰκὼ δ' ἐπενόει κινητόν τινα αἰῶνος ποιῆσαι, καὶ διακοσμῶν ἅμα οὐρανὸν ποιεῖ μένοντος αἰῶνος ἐν ἑνὶ κατ' ἀριθμὸν ἰοῦσαν αἰώνιον εἰκόνα, τοῦτον ὃν δὴ χρόνον ὠνομάκαμεν.

as he notes, even our use of language emphasizes passing of human life. The different tenses in our speech reflect our sense of the past and future. As Timaeus observes:

> Days, nights, months, and years did not exist before heaven, but he [the Demiurge] made them come into being at the same time as heaven was created. All these are parts of time, and the "was" and the "will be" came into being as elements [of time]. We do not notice that we apply these terms to eternal Being, which is not right. For we say (λέγομεν) "it was," "it is," and "it will be," but for this [Being] "it is" alone is fitting according to correct discourse. But it is right to speak of the "was" and the "will be" in reference to that which comes into being as it moves in time. (τὸ δὲ ἦν τό τ᾽ ἔσται περὶ τὴν ἐν χρόνῳ γένεσιν ἰοῦσαν πρέπει λέγεσθαι; 37e–38a)

Time passes in the linear movements of "days, nights, months, and years." This kind of time brings about the birth, aging, and death of mortal creatures. Plato emphasizes the temporality of human beings by giving them voice: *"we say"* (*legomen*) words like "was" and "will be." In putting one word after another to form sentences, human speech unfolds in linear time. In this passage, Plato emphasizes the linear time that determines human and mortal life.

Plato works with two different kinds of time in this dialogue. First, circular time: as a "moving image of eternity," the cosmic soul dwells in this cyclic temporality. Although the cosmos does have a beginning, it does not experience its life in terms of a past or a future. It has a perfect body that endlessly moves in circles. For this reason, the cosmos does not change in time's linear and forward motion. I call this "divine time." In identifying time as an eternal moving image of eternity, Plato links time directly to the eternal Forms rather than to the physical realm of decay and death. Second, linear time: mortals live in a temporality that moves forward in terms of days, months, and years. Humans and other mortals experience life in the mode of linear time. I call this "earthly time." In this case, Plato emphasizes the radical disparity between time and eternity.

As we have seen, the philosopher looks to the stars to perfect the rational "circles" in his mind. To achieve this, he must master mathematics, which enables him to understand the movements in the heavens, and comprehend that the cosmos itself and its heavenly bodies are perfect, eternal, and not subject to finitude. They dwell in divine time. To become like god, the philosopher must turn away from the mortal world, which is subject to earthly time, and identify himself as a rational soul whose "original nature" (ἀρχαίαν φύσιν, 90d) is divine. Given that the rational human soul had its first home in a star, it lived in divine time at the beginning of its life. The philosopher on earth, then, must imitate the motion of the cosmos and the stars and thereby dwell in divine time. To become like god and perfect the motions of his reason, the rational human soul must set its clock (as it were) to divine time.

5.8   The Cosmos as a Beautiful Religious Artifact

In Plato's cosmology, the Demiurge takes over all the chaotic stuff in the receptacle, which moved in disorderly ways, and brings it into an order that is "most beautiful" (*kalliston*, 30a). He creates a cosmos that is "the most beautiful of all things that come into being" (*kallistos tôn gegonotôn*, 29a). In the *Timaeus*, Plato celebrates the beauty of the cosmos in its largest and smallest elements. The shape of the cosmic sphere is "more beautiful" than all other forms (*kallion*), and the atomic triangles that make up the cosmos are "most beautiful" (*kalliston, kallistos*, 33b, 54a). The four elements, too, are "most beautiful" and "excelling in beauty" (*kallistos, kalliôn, diapheronta kallei*, 53e). In introducing the creator of the universe as a divine craftsman, Plato identifies the cosmos as a beautiful work of art. As I argue, he treats the cosmos as a religious artifact. First, he compares the movements of the stars to a choric dance at a religious festival. Second, he identifies the cosmos as a statue or divine image (*agalma*) of the divine Form of Animal.

5.8.1   The Cosmos as a Divine Dance at a Religious Festival

In the *Timaeus*, Plato compares the circular motion of the stars to a "choric dance" (*choreia*, 40c). In using the word *choreia*, Plato compares the motion of the stars to choric dances at religious festivals. He sets forth the complex choreography of the stars in some detail. Timaeus mentions the "stars' crossings with one another, and the returnings and partings of their circlings, and those [star gods] who move in relation to one another by coming together and those who move in opposing positions, and what [star gods] pass before each other and the times when each is hidden from view and when they come into view again."[67] Timaeus uses the language of dance movements – circling, coming together, pulling apart, moving in

---

[67]   40c: χορείας δὲ τούτων αὐτῶν καὶ παραβολὰς ἀλλήλων, καὶ [περὶ] τὰς τῶν κύκλων πρὸς ἑαυτοὺς ἐπανακυκλήσεις καὶ προχωρήσεις, ἔν τε ταῖς συνάψεσιν ὁποῖοι τῶν θεῶν κατ᾽ ἀλλήλους γιγνόμενοι καὶ ὅσοι καταντικρύ, μεθ᾽ οὕστινάς τε ἐπίπροσθεν ἀλλήλοις ἡμῖν τε κατὰ χρόνους οὕστινας ἕκαστοι κατακαλύπτονται καὶ πάλιν ἀναφαινόμενοι.

order, etc. – to depict the movements of the stars. Indeed, he says that "the movements of these bodies are wondrously variegated" (πεποικιλμένας δὲ θαυμαστῶς) (39d). Although the stars and planets move in circles and spirals, which are simple motions, their collective movements make up a beautiful and variegated dance. Of course the philosophic viewer must not see the stars as a random group. Rather, he must understand that the star gods move together in a choric dance, a *choreia* (40c).

The Greeks conceived of *choreia* in terms of dances at religious festivals. The choreographers for the festivals set out to create radiantly beautiful dances. As Steiner observes:

> Members of the choruses are adorned much in the manner of works of art, decked out in the same brilliant garments and exhibiting the same jewelry and polychrome sandals displayed by sculpted *korai* . . . . Radiance is also a *sine qua non* of a richly ornamented dancing group whose sparkle emanates with particular intensity from the feet that execute the steps.[68]

The costumes and the dances for religious festivals were designed to generate sparkly and dazzling visual effects that would give pleasure both to the gods and the human spectators.

When Plato identifies the spectacle of the circling stars as a *choreia*, he conjures up the artistry of choric dance with its harmonious, shiny, and sparkling movements.[69] Consider first how the color "shiny" (*lampron*), which I discussed above, manifests itself in the star dance. Note, first, that Plato regularly uses the word "shiny" (*lampron*) when he speaks of divine beauty and radiance (*Phd.* 109b, 110c; *Rep.* 616b–617b; *Tim.* 40a; *Crit.* 116c[70]). Indeed, he associates the color shiny with the gods. In the *Timaeus*, the Demiurge makes the bodies of the star gods out of fire so they "would be the *shiniest to behold* (*lamprotaton idein*) and the most beautiful" (40a, my italics). The heavenly bodies were designed to be viewed and marveled at. Indeed, they generate a specific response in the viewer. In particular, the color "shiny" creates the effect of "sparklings" (*marmarugas*): "we call the experience (*pathos*) of this [color] 'sparklings' (*marmarugas*) and we call the object producing this 'shiny' and 'glittery'" (*lampron kai stilbon*, 69a). What does it mean to experience the color "shiny" as "sparklings"

---

[68] Steiner 2014: 32. See also Kurke 2012: 223–4.

[69] Some choruses danced in circles, others in linear or rectangular formations. Csapo 2008 offers a good discussion of this topic.

[70] In *Critias* 116c, the wall of the acropolis, which contains the temple of Poseidon and Cleito, is made of "orichalcum, which had fiery sparklings (*marmarugas*)." To be sure, the "sparklings" themselves are not divine: in this case, the colors of the walls of the acropolis, which enclose the temples for the gods, produce these sparklings.

(*marmarugas*)? As scholars have noted, the word *marmarugas* is difficult to translate because it brings together color and movement.[71] For example, in poetic texts, *marmarugas* describes the visual effects of the movements of dancers in shiny costumes.[72] To cite a few examples, in the *Odyssey*, Odysseus watches the Phaeacian dancers and marvels as he "gazes at the sparklings (*marmarugas*) of their feet" (8.260–5). In the Homeric *Hymn to Apollo*, shining lights flash out from the dance of Apollo and the chorus of gods on Olympus: "Apollo plays his lyre stepping high and fitly, and a radiance shines around him and the sparklings of his feet and his close-woven vest [shine around him]" (3.201–3: ὁ Φοῖβος Ἀπόλλων ἐγκιθαρίζει καλὰ καὶ ὕψι βιβάς, αἴγλη δέ μιν ἀμφιφαείνει μαρμαρυγαί τε ποδῶν καὶ ἐϋκλώστοιο χιτῶνος; translation by Evelyn-White, slightly modified). The word *marmarugê* refers to light that sparkles when people move together in dance.[73] As a Homeric scholiast puts it: "*marmarugê* denotes the emission of light (*apostilpsis*) and the sort of brilliance (*lampêdon*) that derives from intense movement."[74] In the *Timaeus*, then, the human experience of the "sparklings" of the star dance is produced in part by motion: first, by the invisible motions of the fiery molecules that make objects "shiny" and "radiant"; second, by the motion of the shiny, radiant stars moving in the heavens. Plato thus links the star dance to the radiant and shiny dances at religious festivals.

Plato found the idea of the "dance of the stars" in fifth-century drama and Pythagorean thought.[75] Let me cite a few examples. In Euripides' *Electra*, the chorus refers to "the aethereal choruses of the stars" (ἄστρων τ' αἰθέριοι χοροί; 467). In a more detailed passage in the *Pirithous* (by Euripides or Critias), the chorus addresses an unnamed god around whom the sun and stars dance: "You, the self-generating, you who wove the nature of all things in the circle of Aether, around which light and dark variegated night perpetually dance, and the countless throng of stars" (σὲ τὸν αὐτοφυῆ, τὸν ἐν αἰθερίῳ ῥύμβῳ πάντων φύσιν ἐμπλέξανθ᾽, ὃν πέρι μὲν

---

[71] See Irwin 1974: 205–16; Sassi 2015: 266–7.

[72] As Peponi has noted in her discussion of ancient dances (2015: 212–13). See also Kurke 2012: 228; Steiner 2014: 32.

[73] On *marmarugê* in the context of the "light" that shone out in dances, see Peponi 2004: 302–8; 2015: 212–13 (see also Kurke 2012: 228–9, who associates *marmarugê* with the glimmering of metals as they shine in the sun).

[74] Scholia BPQV on *Odyssey* 8.265.

[75] Csapo 2008 discusses the "dance of the stars" in the context of cult, myth, poetry, and philosophy. As he points out, the tragic and comic choruses danced in a rectangular formation (in contrast to the dithyrambic circular choruses). Thus, the tragic choruses' references to stars dancing in circles are not meant to be self-referential.

φῶς, πέρι δ᾽ ὀρφναία νὺξ αἰολόχρως ἄκριτός τ᾽ ἄστρων ὄχλος ἐνδελεχῶς ἀμφιχορεύει; E *TrGF* 593.1–5).[76] Finally, Philolaus, a fifth-century Pythagorean, claimed that the stars, sun, moon, earth and counter-earth "dance" (*choreuein*) around the hearth of the universe.[77] Plato was no doubt aware of these poetic and philosophic discourses (he had a great affinity for Pythagorean ideas). However, in contrast to his predecessors, Plato's star gods perform a dance at a sort of cosmic religious festival designed for philosophic spectators.

By referring to the "choric dance" of the stars in the heavens, Plato uses a cultural practice that was central to religious life in ancient Greece: circular dances at religious festivals. The Greeks created these dances first and foremost to invoke the presence of the god being celebrated at the festival. As Kurke observes: "a beautiful choral performance was thought to conjure divine presence at a festival, while for the space of the song and dance, the chorus and human audience *fused or merged*, and both were briefly assimilated with the divine."[78] Both the dancers and viewers at a religious festival could feel the presence of the god and, under the right circumstances, "merge" and assimilate with this god for a time. We find a very similar phenomenon in Plato's dance of the stars: the philosopher "merges" with the gods when he views the star dance in the heavens.[79] Of course the philosophic soul merges with its god in a unique way, "by learning the harmonies and revolutions of the universe" and likening "its thinking part to the object of thought" (90c–d; quoted above). Indeed, the entire task of the philosopher is to imitate and identify with the cosmic god. He does this, in part, by watching the beautiful and radiant dance of the star gods.

Plato's dance of the stars differs from the circular dances at religious festivals. First, his gods have little in common with the traditional Greek

---

[76] Note also the references to star dances in Soph. *Antigone* 1146–53; Eur. *Ion* 1078–9; Eur. *Phaethon* 63–6 (see also Csapo 2008).

[77] DK 44 A16: πῦρ ἐν μέσῳ περὶ τὸ κέντρον, ὅπερ ἑστίαν τοῦ παντὸς καλεῖ . . . περὶ δὲ τοῦτο δέκα σώματα θεῖα χορεύειν; DK 44 A16). As Aristotle noted in the *De caelo* (283a), the Pythagoreans believed that the stars and earth revolved around a central fire. Note that Plato puts earth (not fire) at the center of the universe in the *Timaeus* (see also *Phaedrus* 247a, where the gods are called a "divine chorus" that move around the "hearth" of the earth).

[78] Kurke 2012: 222 (my italics). Kurke makes a similar point in 2012: 223: "there is abundant ancient evidence that choruses were imagined to enable a collapse of *time*, whereby the singing, dancing choreuts were fully merged or identified with the gods and heroes whose stories they sang"; see also Kowalzig 2007.

[79] Of course, the philosopher can only "merge" with the gods if he views the heavenly bodies correctly. This individual apprehends divine *nous* moving the stars in perfect rotations. But he must first do a huge amount of intellectual leg-work to apprehend this harmony.

gods celebrated at these festivals. Second, the chorus members in Plato's star dance are divine, and a hyperdivine craftsman creates the choreography.[80] Finally, the perfected philosopher who successfully imitates the circular motions of the cosmic soul "becomes like god" for the rest of his life. By contrast, ordinary Greeks watching dances at festivals merged with a god very briefly, in a ritualized context. Still, we find important parallels between Greek religious dances and Plato's star dance. In referring to the "choric dance" of the stars, Plato used a traditional religious art form to conjure up the philosopher's "religious" viewing of the heavens.

5.8.2 The Cosmos as an Agalma of the Forms

In addition to portraying the motion of the stars as a beautifully orchestrated dance, Plato identifies the cosmos as an *agalma*. The Greeks used the word *agalma* to refer to statues or artworks created for religious contexts. In the classical period, the word *agalma* primarily meant statues and images of the gods.[81] In referring to the cosmos as an *agalma*, then, Plato identifies it as a work of religious art.

Timaeus refers to the cosmos as an *agalma* at a specific moment in the Demiurge's creation. When the Demiurge first creates the soul and the body of the cosmos (35a–37c), and before he creates the star gods or mortal creatures, he stops to admire his creation: "when the creator-father saw that it [the cosmos] was moving and alive, an *agalma* of eternal gods/divine beings, he rejoiced" (ὡς δὲ κινηθὲν αὐτὸ καὶ ζῶν ἐνόησεν τῶν ἀιδίων θεῶν γεγονὸς ἄγαλμα ὁ γεννήσας πατήρ, ἠγάσθη; 37c).

What does Plato mean by identifying the divine cosmos (minus the star-gods and mortals) as "an *agalma* of the eternal gods" (τῶν ἀιδίων θεῶν . . . ἄγαλμα)? Who exactly are the gods here and what is the meaning of *agalma*? Scholars have wrestled with this passage. How can the cosmos be a religious image of the gods? Most argue that the cosmos-as-*agalma* is

---

[80] Strictly speaking, the cosmic soul moves all the stars and is the "performer" of the dance; but Plato refers to the stars as individual dancers.

[81] As Lewis and Stroud 1979: 193 point out, in the archaic period, the term *agalma* referred to a wide range of statues and images, whereas in the classical period it primarily designated sacred images. On *agalmata* and sacred images, see Gernet 1981: 73–111; Osborne 1988: chapter 5; Vernant 1991: chapter 8. Steiner 2001 offers a wide-ranging discussion of statues in the archaic and classical periods (see especially 31–2 on *agalma*). See also Kurke 2012: 223–4. For a discussion of *agalmata* or statues of victors in the games in the archaic period (which possessed a talismanic quality akin to the images of gods), see Kurke 1993. Osborne 1994 analyzes *agalmata* of *korai* (and their viewing audiences) in the archaic period.

an image or statue *for* the eternal gods.[82] According to this view, the cosmos-as-*agalma* is not an image *of* divine beings but rather a religious votary *for* the gods. I do not find this argument persuasive. First, Plato uses *agalma* in other dialogues to refer to a statue of the gods or humans.[83] He never refers to an *agalma* as a "statue *for* the gods." Second, at this point in the creation story, Timaeus has mentioned only two divinities – the Demiurge and the cosmos (minus the star gods). We can hardly bunch the Demiurge and the divine cosmos together and call them "the eternal gods" (*tôn aidiôn theôn*) to whom this votary gift has been given. Indeed, if this is a votive gift for the gods, the Demiurge would have created this gift for himself or for the cosmic god. But the cosmos *is* the *agalma*.

Finally, the Demiurge creates the cosmos *as an image* (*eikôn*) of the Form of Animal, and the bodies in the cosmos are treated as images (*eikones*) of various Forms. Timaeus makes this point repeatedly (29a–b, 37c–d, 51a, 52c). Given Plato's insistence that the soul, the bodily realm, and all the particulars are images of the Forms, it seems more reasonable to take cosmos-as-*agalma* as an image of the Forms. The whole notion of the cosmos as a material votive gift for the cosmic god (or the Demiurge) makes little sense here.

In my view, the cosmos is an artful image of the divine Form of Animal. I would translate *tôn aidiôn theôn agalma* as "an *agalma* of eternal *divine beings*" to underline that the physical cosmos is an image of the divine Forms (rather than a gift for the gods). It makes better sense to apply the Greek notion of an *agalma as a statue of a god* to the *cosmos as an "image" of the "eternal" (aidiôn) divine Forms*. After all, Timaeus has just stated (twice)

---

[82] Taylor 1928: 184–7 suggested some possible emendations of this strange passage, but claimed that he was unsure of the correct reading (of course he considered this dialogue to be Pythagorean, and not truly platonic). Archer-Hinds 1988: 118 identifies the *theoi* as gods, though he wonders if they could be the Forms; cf. Cornford 1956: 99–101, who insists that they must be the gods. The evidence against identifying the *theoi* here with the Forms (the "Intelligible Animal" that contains the classes of different kinds of animate beings) is that Plato does not call the Forms *theioi*. However, Plato does not talk about the Forms in any detail in this dialogue: once he identifies the intelligible paradigms, he moves onto the creation of the cosmos. In addition, although he does not explicitly describe the Forms as "divine" in this dialogue, he does say that humans should "think divine thoughts" (φρονεῖν ... θεῖα), which suggests that the *noêmata* of the gods, i.e., the Forms, are divine. Carone 2005: 71–2 offers an excellent reading of this passage.

[83] For references to *agalmata* in Plato, see *Charm.* 154c; *Protag.* 311c, 311e, 322a; *Meno* 97d; *Symp.* 215b, 216e, 222a; *Rep.* 517d; *Phaedrus* 230b, 251a, 252d; *Critias* 110b, 116d, 116e; *Phil.* 38d; *Laws* 738c, 931a, 931e, 956b. Aside from two passages, Plato uses *agalmata* in his corpus to refer to statues of the gods or men. In the two exceptional passages, Plato uses *agalma* (1) in metaphorical terms in reference to one's ancestors (*Laws* 931e); and (2) to refer to an image of a human that, up close, seems to be some sort of scarecrow (*Phil.* 38d). In these cases, *agalmata* are not copies of human or divine bodies. Note that Plato specifically uses *agalmata theôn* to refer to "statues of the gods" (*Prot.* 322a; *Symp.* 215b; we also find this phrase in *Epinomis* 983e).

that the Demiurge "fixed his gaze on the eternal" (πρὸς τὸ ἀίδιον ἔβλεπεν; 29a), i.e., the Forms, to create the cosmos. The cosmos, then, is a "sacred image (*agalma*) of the eternal Intelligible Animal (*to noêton zôon*) and the four classes of intelligible animals (*ta noêta zôa*, 31a) that it comprises. To be sure, Plato does not call the Form of Animal "divine" in this text. Still, as an "eternal Being" and as the paradigm for the divine cosmos, the Form of Animal must be divine. If we accept that the cosmos is a sacred image of the Form of Animal, then we can see the cosmos as a mobile statue that represents the divine Forms in a psychic and material form. Here, Plato draws on a common religious art form to show the cosmos in a new way. The universe is at once divine and also a sacred image of the higher divinities of the Forms.

Conclusion

In his description of the sanctuary for Demeter at Mount Pron (2.35–49), Pausanias details a strange sacrificial ritual of the people of Hermione. In the procession to the temple, men brought sacrificial cows to the open doors of the temple and then released them so that they could rush inside. When the cows had entered the temple, the people outside rapidly shut the doors. Then four old women inside the temple killed each cow in order. As Pausanias states: "A few statues of the women who have served Demeter as priestesses stand at the temple; when you go inside, you see seats where the old women wait for the cows to be driven in one by one, and also images, not all that old, of Athena and Demeter. But that which they worship more than everything else, I myself did not see (ἐγὼ μὲν οὐκ εἶδον), nor has any other man, be it a stranger or a person from Hermione. Only the old women know what sort of thing this is (μόναι δὲ ὁποῖόν τί ἐστιν αἱ γρᾶες ἴστωσαν)." As an outsider, Pausanias could not see or know what the women experienced. As readers of Plato, we are in a similar position as Pausanias: we stand outside the door (as it were) of his theological thinking. Like Pausanias, we can see the philosopher's upward "procession" to the realm of the Forms, and we can understand Plato's accounts of the activities and disciplines that the philosopher engages in. We can also view, following Plato's imagistic accounts, the philosophic soul contemplating the Forms. But we ultimately bump into closed doors. We cannot understand the philosopher's sacred way of seeing and knowing unless we contemplate the Forms ourselves.

If a reader accepts Plato's promises, she will become a philosopher herself and come to know the Forms. She will grasp the essences of the Forms, though she may not see the Form of the Good in a full way. However, she could not fully apprehend the divine aspects of the Forms. This goes beyond language. As we have seen, Plato uses mythic and analogical discourses to convey the theological aspects of his philosophy. These cannot be fully articulated in language. For this reason, Plato's discourse oscillates between the effable and the ineffable. He leads the reader to the edge of what can be known and articulated, and then points beyond it.

Plato's theological philosophy does not take on a systematic form. He addresses the divine aspects of the Forms in different ways. In each dialogue, Plato addresses a specific topic that determines the ideas that get covered. In addition, the drama in each dialogue occurs in a different social context, and this affects the way that he presents his theological philosophy. For example, the *Symposium* features a celebration of Agathon's victory in the tragic competition, and the dialogue takes place in the context of a drinking party. The text focuses on the power of eros and, for the most part, has a festive mood. The *Phaedo* takes us into an Athenian prison where Socrates awaits death. The mood in this text is darker. The interlocutors discuss death and the immortality of the soul. The dialogue in the *Phaedrus* takes place outside the city walls in a sacred spot that features votary gifts and an altar. The conversation focuses on love and rhetoric. This text has a pastoral and rather playful feeling. The discourse in the *Timaeus* occurs in an individual's house, and presents a full cosmology. This dialogue evokes a serious and sublime mood. Within these different parameters, Plato presents specific strands of his theological philosophy.

As I have shown, Plato gives a number of divinity-markers to the Forms. He calls the Forms "divine" (*theios*), and compares them to the gods or to the luminous realm of the gods. He also uses the poetic language of divine epiphany to convey the idea that the philosopher encounters divinity when he contemplates Beauty and the Good. In the *Symposium* and *Phaedrus*, Plato draws on the Eleusinian Mysteries – with their notion that the higher initiation features a revelation of the goddess – to indicate that the philosopher sees Beauty in terms of a divine epiphany. Finally, Plato uses the Orphic divinity-marker across a wider range of topics. In the *Phaedo*, he places the soul in the complex Orphic narrative that features a fall from divinity, punishment in the prison of the body, purification, initiation, and eternal life with the gods. Plato also refers to the Orphic notion of the body as the prison of the soul in this and other middle-period dialogues.

While Plato gives the soul a number of divinity-markers, his dialogues on Eros offer a special kind of divinity-marker. Using the Greek idea that Eros is a god, Plato confers the "Gods divinity-marker" on the mind's desire. He works with two different conceptions of the soul in the *Symposium* and *Phaedrus*: he treats Eros first as a daimon and then as a god. The mortal soul in the *Symposium* is not godlike but it has a "daimonic desire" for the divine realm of the Forms. In the *Phaedrus,* even the gods have eros for the Forms – their divine souls fly with the wings of desire up to the divine realm of reality. I identify this eros as a "divine desire" for the Forms. In Plato, then, the rational part of the soul has its own desire. Indeed, his "erotic mind" has aspects that go beyond mere intellection.

When the philosopher contemplates the Forms, he encounters divinity. In some cases, the philosopher responds to this divinity with religious wonder and reverence. In the *Phaedrus,* for example, the philosopher who recollects Beauty sees it standing on a holy pedestal and shrinks back in fear and awe. In this text, Plato presents both the epistemological and the affective aspects of philosophic contemplation. As I have argued, the philosopher confronts a Being much higher than himself when he contemplates the Forms. While he can attain knowledge of the essence of a Form, he cannot fully comprehend its divinity. His epistemic powers have their limits. He cannot grasp a divine Form in thought or in language. If we factor in the divinity of the Forms, we must reconsider Plato's ontology and epistemology.

In the *Timaeus,* Plato's philosophical theology achieves its fullest form and articulation. Plato weaves philosophy and theology together in almost every section in the dialogue. Indeed, he presents the cosmos as a divine animal designed by a hyperdivine maker. The cosmic soul runs the universe and keeps it moving by way of the rational circlings of its mind. The human soul is also divine: its *nous* operates in the same way as that of the cosmos (though it does not have the full perfection of the cosmic soul). The rational human soul begins its life in a star and sees "the nature of the all." Once the soul incarnates in mortal bodies, it encounters massive impediments. The soul must master its human body and work to recover its original rational abilities. It does this by practicing philosophy and astronomy. Studying the rotations in the heavens allows it to perfect the circlings of its own mind. The human soul studies the divine cosmos both physically and intellectually. Indeed, the cosmos manifests its divinity to the philosopher by way of the "visible gods" in the heaven. Here, Plato uses the traditional Greek notion of divine epiphany, in which a god could appear in a variety of bodies, including heavenly bodies. In fact, the star-gods show the divinity of the cosmos in their choral dances every single night.

The Demiurge creates the cosmos as a "moving image" of the eternal Form of Animal (the "Intelligible Animal"). To present this idea, Plato goes right down to the triangular atoms that serve as the building blocks of the material cosmos. He presents the *atopos* (strange, out-of-place) receptacle, which provides a *topos* or place for bodily particulars. He then shows how the atoms come together to make up bodies. Plato explains how humans take in the bodily realm through sensation, focusing in particular on the sensation of vision. Only mortal creatures can see the cosmos at the physical level, and only philosophers can see the cosmos as a divine phenomenon. Since the cosmos was designed to be seen and admired, the philosopher plays a key role in the perfection of the universe. At the same time, the divine human soul has its own personal mission: to make its way back to its native star in the heavens. The cosmos is both the object of philosophical study and a god to worship. This dialogue is Plato's fullest conception of his theological philosophy.

Bibliography

Adam, J. (1921) *The Republic of Plato*, 2 vols. (Cambridge).

Adluri, V. ed. (2013) *Philosophy and Salvation in Greek Religion* (Berlin).

Algra, K. (1995) *Concepts of Space in Greek Thought* (Leiden).

Anderson, G. (2018) *The Realness of Things Past: Ancient Greece and Ontological History* (Oxford).

Annas, J. (1981) *An Introduction to Plato's Republic* (Oxford).

  (1982) "Plato's Myths of Judgement," *Phronesis* 27: 199–43.

  (1993) *The Morality of Happiness* (Oxford).

  (1999) *Platonic Ethics, Old and New* (New York).

Archer-Hind, R. D., ed. and comm. (1988) *The Timaeus of Plato*, repr. (Salem, New Hampshire).

Armstrong, J. M. (2004) "After the Ascent: Plato on Becoming Like God," *Oxford Studies in Ancient Philosophy* 26: 171–83.

Arnott, W. G. (1996) *Alexis: The Fragments* (Cambridge).

Arrington, N. (2015) *Ashes, Images and Memories: The Presence of the War Dead in Fifth-Century Athens* (Oxford and New York).

Aurenche, O. (1974) *Les Groupes d'Alcibiade, de Léagoras, et de Teucros: Remarques sur la vie politique athénienne en 415 avant J.-C.* (Paris).

Bakhtin, M. (1981) *The Dialogic Imagination*, trans. C. Emerson and M. Holquist (Austin).

Baltes, M. (1997) "Is the Good in Plato's *Republic* beyond Being?" in M. Joyal, ed., *Studies in the Platonic Tradition* (Aldershot) 2–23.

Beerden, K. (2013) *Worlds Full of Signs: Ancient Greek Divination in Context* (Leiden).

Benitez, E. (1995) "The Good or the Demiurge: Causation and the Unity of Good in Plato," *Apeiron* 28: 113–40.

Benitez, R. (2016) "Plato and the Secularization of Greek Philosophy," in Eidinow, Kindt and Osborne, 301–16.

Bérard, C. (1985) "La lumière et le faisceau: images du rituel Éleusinien," *Recherches et documents du centre Thomas More* 48: 17–33.

Bernabé, A. (1995) "Una etymología platónica: σῶμα-σῆμα," *Philologus* 139: 204–37.

  (1997) "Platone e l'orfismo," in G. Sfameni Gasparro, ed., *Destino e salvezza: tra culti pagani e gnosi cristiana. Itinerari storico-religiosi sulle orme di Ugo Bianchi* (Cosenza) 37–97.

(2002) "La théogonie orphique du Papyrus de Derveni," *Kernos* 15: 91–129.

(2002a) "La toile de Pénélope: a-t-il existé un mythe orphique sur Dionysos y les Titans?" *Revue de l'Histoire des Religions* 219: 401–33.

(2004–5) *Poetae epici Graeci: Testimonia et Fragmenta*, vol. 2, fasc. 1, 2 (Munich).

(2007a) *Poetae epici Graeci: Testimonia et Fragmenta*, vol. 2, fasc. 3 (Berlin).

(2007b) "The Derveni Theogony: Many Questions and Some Answers," *Harvard Studies in Classical Philology* 103: 99–133.

(2007c) "L'âme après la mort: Modèles orphiques et transposition platonicienne," *Études platoniciennes* 4: 25–44.

(2008) "El mito órfico de Dioniso y los Titanes," in Bernabé and Casadesús 2008: 591–607.

(2009) "Orpheus and Eleusis," *Thracia* 18: 89–98.

(2009a) "Imago inferorum orphica," in G. Casadio and P. Johnston, eds., *Mystic Cults in Magna Graecia* (Austin) 95–130.

(2011) *Platon y el orphismo: Diálogos entre religion y filosofía* (Madrid).

(2016) "Aristotle and the Mysteries," in M. J. Martín-Velasco and M. J. García Blanco, eds., *Greek Philosophy and Mystery Cults* (Cambridge) 27–42.

Bernabé, A. and A. Jiménez San Cristóbal (2008) *Instructions for the Netherworld: The Orphic Gold Tablets* (Leiden).

Bernabé, A. and F. Casadesús, eds. (2008) *Orfeo y la tradición órfica: un reencuentro* (Madrid).

Berger, H. (1990) "The Politics of Inscription," in B. Dauenhauer, ed., *Textual Fidelity and Textual Disregard* (New York) 81–103.

Betegh, G. (2004) *The Derveni Papyrus: Cosmology, Theology and Interpretation* (Cambridge).

(2006) "Eschatology and Cosmology: Models and Problems," in Sassi 2006: 26–50.

(2006a) "Greek philosophy and religion," in M. L. Gill and P. Pellegrin, eds., *A Companion to Ancient Philosophy* (Malden, MA) 625–39.

(2010) "What Makes a Myth *Eikos*?" in Mohr and Sattler: 213–24.

(2014) "Pythagoreans, Orphism, and Greek Religion," in Huffman 2014: 149–66.

Betz, H. D. (2010) "'A Child of Earth I Am and of Starry Heaven': Concerning the Anthropology of the Orphic Gold Tablets," in Edmonds: 102–19.

Bianchi, U. (1965) "Initiation, mystères, gnose," in C. J. Bleeker, ed., *Initiation* (Leiden) 154–71.

(1974) "L'orphisme a existé," in *Mélanges d'histoire des religions offerts à Henri-Charles Puech* (Paris) 129–37.

(1976) *The Greek Mysteries* (Leiden).

(2004) "Mystéres d'Eleusis. Dionysisme. Orphisme," in J. Ries, A. Motte, and N. Spineto, eds., *Les civilisations méditerranéens et le sacré* (Turnhout) 255–82.

Bierl, A. (1991) *Dionysos und die griechische Tragödie. Politische und "metatheatralische" Aspekte im Text* (Munich).

(2013) "Maenadism as Self-Referential Chorality in Euripides' *Bacchae*," in R. Gagné and M. Hopman, eds., *Choral Mediations in Greek Tragedy* (Cambridge) 211–26.

Blondell, R. (2006) "Where Is Socrates on the 'Ladder of Love'?" in J. Lesher, D. Nails, and F. Sheffield, eds., *Plato's Symposium: Issues in Interpretation and Reception* (Cambridge, MA) 147–78.

Bluck, R. S. (1949) *Plato's Life and Thought* (London).

(1961) *Plato's Meno* (Cambridge).

Bobonich, C. (1991) "Persuasion, Compulsion and Freedom in Plato's *Laws*," *Classical Quarterly* n.s. 41: 365–88.

(2002) *Plato's Utopia Recast: His Later Ethics and Politics* (Oxford).

Bonnechere, P. (2011) "Divination," in Ogden: Chapter 9.

Bordt, M. (2006) *Platons Theologie* (Freiburg and Munich).

Bostock, D. (1986) *Plato's Phaedo* (Oxford).

Boyancé, P. (1947) "Le Religion de Platon," *Revue des Études Anciennes* 49: 178–92.

(1948) "Xénocrate et les Orphiques," *REA* 50: 218–31.

(1963) "Note sur la phroura platonicienne," *Revue de Philologie* 37: 7–11.

Bowie, A. (1993) *Aristophanes: Myth, Ritual, and Comedy* (Cambridge).

Bowden, H. (2003) "Oracles for Sale," in P. Derow and R. Parker, eds., *Herodotus and His World: Essays from a Conference in Memory of George Forrest* (Oxford) 256–74.

(2004) "Xenophon and the Scientific Study of Religion," in C. Tuplin and V. Azoulay, eds., *Xenophon and his World: Papers from a Conference Held in Liverpool in July 1999* (Wiesbaden) 229–46.

(2005) *Classical Athens and the Delphic Oracle: Divination and Democracy* (Cambridge).

(2010) *Mystery Cults of the Ancient World* (Cambridge).

Boyancé, P. (1937) *Les cultes des muses chez les philosophes grecs* (Paris).

(1948) "Xénocrate et les Orphiques," *REA* 50: 218–31.

(1966) "Dionysiaca: à propos d'une étude récente sur l'initiation dionysiaque," *REA* 68: 33–60.

Brague, R. (1999) *La sagesse du monde: Histoire de l'expérience; humaine de l'universe* (Paris).

Bravo. B. (2004) "Heroic Epiphanies: Narrative, Visual and Cultic Contexts," *Illinois Classical Studies* 29: 63–84.

Brecoulaki, H. (2015) "Greek Painting and the Challenge of *Mimêsis*," in Destrée and Murray: 218–36.

Breitenberger, B. (2007) *Aphrodite and Eros: The Development of Erotic Mythology in Early Greek Poetry and Cult* (New York).

Bremmer, J. (1983) *The Early Greek Concept of the Soul* (Princeton).

(1984) "Greek Maenadism Reconsidered," *Zeitschrift für Papyrologie und Epigraphik* 55: 267–86.

(1999) "Rationalization and Disenchantment in Ancient Greece: Max Weber among the Pythagoreans and Orphics?" in Buxton: 71–83.

(2002) *The Rise and Fall of the Afterlife* (London).

(2008) "Balaam, Mopsus and Melampus: Tales of Travelling Seers," in *Greek Religion and Culture, the Bible and the Ancient Near East* (Leiden) 133–51.

(2011) "The Place of Performance in Orphic Poetry (*OF* 1)," in de Herrero et al. 2011: 1–6.

(2014) *Initiation into the Mysteries of the Ancient World* (Berlin and Boston).

Brickhouse, T. and N. Smith (1990) "The Divine Sign Did Not Oppose Me: A Problem in Plato's *Apology*," *Canadian Journal of Philosophy* 16: 511–26.

(2014) "Socrates' Gods and the *Daimonion*," in Smith and Woodruff: 88–94.

Brill, S. (2009) "The Geography of Finitude: Myth and Earth in Plato's *Phaedo*," *International Philosophical Quarterly* 49: 5–23.

Brisson, L. (1974) *Le même et l'autre dans la structure ontologique du Timeé de Platon* (Paris).

(1982) *Platon, Les mots et les mythes: Comment et pourquoi Platon nomma le mythe?* (Paris).

(1985) "Les théogonies Orphique et le papyrus de Derveni: Notes critiques," *Revue de l'histoires des Religions* 202: 389–420.

(1992) *Platon: Timée/Critias* (Paris).

(1992a) "Le corps 'dionysiaque': l'anthropogonie décrite dans le *Commentaire sur le Phédon de Platon* (1.3–6), attribué à Olympiodore, est-elle orphique?," in *Sophies Maietores, Chercheurs de sagesse: Homage à Jean Pépin*, Collection des Études Augustiniennes, Série Antiquité 131 (Paris) 481–99.

(1995) *Orphée et l'Orphisme dans l'antiquité gréco-roman* (Aldershot).

(1997) "Plato's Theory of Sense-Perception in the *Timaeus*," *Boston Area Colloquium in Ancient Philosophy* 13: 147–74.

(1997a) "Perception sensible et raison dans le *Timée*," in Calvo and Brisson: 291–306.

Brisson, L. and F. W. Meyerstein (1995) *Inventing the Universe: Plato's Timaeus, the Big Bang, and the Problem of Scientific Knowledge* (Albany).

Broadie, S. (1991) *Ethics with Aristotle* (New York).

(1999) "Rational Theology," in Long 1999a: Chapter 10.

(2001) "Theodicy and Pseudo-History in the *Timaeus*," *Oxford Studies in Ancient Philosophy* 21: 1–28.

(2008) "Theological Sidelights from Plato's *Timaeus*," *Proceedings of the Aristotelian Society*, supplementary volume, 82: 1–17.

(2012) *Nature and Divinity in Plato's Timaeus* (Cambridge).

Bruit-Zaidman, L. and P. Schmitt-Pantel (1992) *Religion in the Greek City* (Cambridge).

Brumbaugh, R. S. 1989. *Platonic Studies of Greek Philosophy: Form, Arts, Gadgets, and Hemlock* (Albany).

Bryan, J. (2012) *Likeness and Likelihood in the Presocratics and Plato* (Cambridge).

Burkert, W. (1972) *Lore and Science in Ancient Pythagoreanism* (Cambridge, MA).

(1982) "Craft versus Sect: The Problem of Orphics and Pythagoreans," in B. Meyer and E. Sanders, eds., *Jewish and Christian Self-Definition*, vol. 3 (Philadelphia) 1–22.

(1983) *Homo Necans* (Berkeley).

(1985) *Greek Religion* (London).

(1987) *Ancient Mystery Cults* (Cambridge, MA).

(1993) "Bacchic *Teletai* in the Hellenistic Age," in Carpenter and Faraone: 259–75.

(1997) "From Epiphany to Cult Statue," in A. B. Lloyd, ed., *What Is a God? Studies in the Nature of Greek Divinity* (London) 15–34.

(1999) "The Logic of Cosmogony," in R. Buxton, ed., *From Myth to Reason? Studies in the Development of Greek Thought* (Oxford) 87–106.

Burnet, J. (1916) "The Socratic Doctrine of the Soul," *Proceedings of the British Academy* 7: 235–59.

(1928) *Platonism* (Berkeley).

Burnyeat, M. (1977) "Socratic Midwifery, Platonic Inspiration," *Bulletin of the Institute of Classical Studies* 24: 7–16.

(1979) "Conflicting Appearances," *Proceedings of the British Academy* 65: 69–111.

(1997) "The Impiety of Socrates," *Ancient Philosophy* 17: 1–12.

(2005) "ΕΙΚΩΣ ΜΥΘΟΣ," *Rhizai* 2: 143–65.

Büttner, S. (2011) "Inspiration and Inspired Poets in Plato's Dialogues," in Destrée and Herrmann: 111–29.

Bussanich, J. (2013) "Rebirth Eschatology in Plato and Plotinus," in Adluri: 243–88.

Buxton, R., ed. (1999) *From Myth to Reason: Studies in the Development of Greek Thought* (Oxford).

ed. (2000) *Oxford Readings in Greek Religion* (Oxford).

Calame, C. (1996) *L'Éros dans la Grèce antique* (Paris).

Calvo, T. and L. Brisson, eds. (1997) *Interpreting the Timaeus-Critias* (St. Augustin).

Camp J. (2004) *The Archaeology of Athens* (New Haven).

Cancik, H. (1990) "Epiphanie/Advent," in H. Cancik, B. Gladigow, and M. Laubscher, eds., *Handbuch religionswissenschaftlicher Grundbegriffe*, vol. 2 (Stuttgart) 290–6.

Carone, G. (1997) "The Ethical Function of Astronomy in Plato's *Timaeus*," in Calvo and Brisson: 341–50.

(2005) *Plato's Cosmology and its Ethical Dimensions* (Cambridge).

Carpenter, T. and C. Faraone, eds. (1993) *Masks of Dionysus* (Ithaca).

Carson, A. (1998) *Eros the Bittersweet* (Champaigne, IL).

Casadesús, F. (2000) "Nueva interpretatión del Crátilo platónico a partir de la aportaciones del *Papiro de Derveni*," *Emerita* 68: 53–71.

(2008) "Orfismo y pitagorismo," in Bernabé and Casadesús: 1053–78.

(2016) "The Transformation of the Initiation Language of Mystery Religions into Philosophical Terminology," in M. Martín-Velasco and Blanco: 1–26.

Cherniss. H. (1944) *Aristotle's Criticism of Plato and the Academy* (Baltimore).

Claus, D. (1981) *Toward the Soul* (New Haven).

Clinton, K. (1992) *Myth and Cult: The Iconography of the Eleusinian Mysteries* (Stockholm).

(1993) "The Sanctuary of Demeter and Kore at Eleusis," in N. Marinatos and R. Hägg, eds. *Greek Sanctuaries: New Approaches* (London) 110–24.

(2003) "Stages of Initiation in the Eleusinian and Samothracian Mysteries," in M. Cosmopoulos, ed.: 50–78.

(2004) "Epiphany in the Eleusinian Mysteries," *ICS* 29: 85–110.

Cole, S. (1980) "New Evidence for the Mysteries of Dionysus," *GRBS* 221: 223–38.

(1993) "Voices from Beyond the Grave: Dionysus and the Dead," in Carpenter and Faraone: 276–95.

(2003) "Landscapes of Dionysus and Elysian Fields," in Cosmopoulos, ed.: 193–217.

(2004) *Landscapes, Gender and Ritual Space: The Ancient Greek Experience* (Berkeley and Los Angeles).

(2007) "Finding Dionysus," in Ogden: 327–41.

(2008) Review of "Ritual Texts for the Afterlife. Orpheus and the Bacchic Gold Tablets," *Journal of Hellenic Studies* 128: 221.

Collard, C., M. Cropp, and K. Lee, eds. (1995) *Euripides: Selected Fragmentary Plays*, vol. 1 (Warminster).

Collobert, C. (2011) "Poetry as Flawed Reproduction: Possession and Mimesis," in Destrée and Hermann: 41–61.

Connor, R. (1988) "Seized by the Nymphs: Nympholepsy and Symbolic Expression in Classical Greece," *CA* 7: 155–89.

Cornford, F. (1912) *From Religion to Philosophy* (London).

(1956) *Plato's Cosmology*, repr. (London).

Cosmopoulos, M., ed. (2003) *Greek Mysteries: The Archaeology of Ancient Greek Secret Cults* (London).

Coxon, A. H. (2009) *The Fragments of Parmenides, Revised and Expanded Edition*, ed. R. McKirahan (Las Vegas).

Crapanzano, V. and V. Garrison, eds. (1977) *Case Studies in Spirit Possession* (New York).

Csapo, E. (1999–2000) "Later Euripidean Music," *Illinois Classical Studies* 24/5: 399–436.

(2003) "The Dolphins of Dionysus," in Csapo and Miller: 69–98.

(2004) "The Politics of the New Music," in Murray and Wilson: 207–48.

(2007) *The Origins of Theater in Ancient Greece and Beyond: From Ritual to Drama* (Cambridge).

(2008) "Star Choruses: Eleusis, Orphism, and New Musical Imagery and Dance," in M. Reverman and P. Wilson, eds., *Performance, Iconography and Reception: Studies in Honour of Oliver Taplin* (Oxford) 263–90.

(2016) "The 'Theology' of the Dionysia and Old Comedy," in Eidinow, Kindt, and Osborne: 117–52.

Csapo, E. and Miller, M., eds. (2003) *Poetry, Theory, Practice: The Social Life of Myth, Word and Image in Ancient Greece* (Oxford).

Curd, P. (2002) "The Presocratics as Philosophers," in Laks and Louguet: 115–38.

(2013) "The Divine and the Thinkable: Toward an Account of the Intelligible Cosmos," *Rhizomata* 1: 217–47.

Day, J. W. (2010) *Archaic Greek Epigram and Dedication: Representation and Reperformance* (Cambridge).

Denyer, N. (1985) "The Case against Divination: An Examination of Cicero's *De Divinatione*," *PCPS* 31: 1–10.

des Places, E. (1981) "Platon et la langue des mystères," *Études platoniciennes 1929–1979* (Leiden) 83–98.

Destrée, P. (2015) "Pleasure," in Destrée and Murray: 472–85.

Destrée, P. and G. Giannopoulou, eds. (2017) *Plato's Symposium: A Critical Guide* (Cambridge).

Destrée P. and F-G. Herrmann, eds. (2011) *Plato and the Poets*. Mnemosyne supplement vol. 328 (Leiden).

Destrée, P. and P. Murray, eds. (2015) *A Companion to Ancient Aesthetics* (Oxford).

Detienne, M. (1977) *The Gardens of Adonis. Spices in Greek Mythology*, trans. J. Lloyd (Princeton).

   (1989) *Dionysos at Large*, trans. A. Goldhammer (Cambridge, MA).

Detienne, M. and J.-P. Vernant, eds. (1989) *The Cuisines of Sacrifice in Ancient Greece*, trans. P. Wissing (Chicago).

Dicks, D. R. (1970) *Early Greek Astronomy to Aristotle* (Ithaca).

Dietrich, B. (1990) "Oracles and Divine Inspiration," *Kernos* 3: 157–74.

Dillery, J. (2005) "Chresmologues and *Manteis*: Independent Diviners and the Problem of Authority," in Johnston and Struck: 167–231.

Dillon, M. (1997) *Pilgrims and Pilgrimage in Ancient Greece* (London).

Dodds, E. R. (1951) *The Greeks and the Irrational* (Berkeley).

   (1959) *Plato: Gorgias* (Oxford).

Dougherty, C. and L. Kurke, eds. (1993) *Cultural Poetics in Archaic Greece* (Cambridge).

Dover, K. (1966) "Aristophanes' Speech in Plato's *Symposium*," *JHS* 1986: 41–50.

   (1970) "Excursus: The Herms and the Mysteries," in A. W. Gomme, A. Andrewes, and K. Dover, eds., *A Historical Commentary on Thucydides* (Oxford) 264–88.

   (1974) *Greek Popular Morality in the Time of Plato and Aristotle* (Oxford).

   (1975) "The Freedom of the Intellectual in Greek Society," *Talanta* 7: 24–54.

   (1978) *Greek Homosexuality* (London).

Dowden, K. (1980) "Grades in the Eleusinian Mysteries," *RHR* 197: 409–27.

Drozdek, A. (2007) *Greek Philosophers as Theologians: The Divine Arche* (Aldershot).

Ebert, T. (2002) "'Wenn ich einen schönen Mythos vortragen darf . . .' Zu Status, Herkunft und Funktion des Schlussmythos in Platons Phaidon," in M. Janka and C. Schäfer, eds., *Platon als Mythologe. Neue Interpretationen zu den Mythen in Platons Dialogen* (Darmstadt) 251–69.

Easterling, P. and J. Muir, eds. (1987) *Greek Religion and Society* (Cambridge).

Edmonds, R. (1999) "Tearing apart the Zagreus Myth: A Few Disparaging Remarks on Orphism and Original Sin," *CA* 18: 35–73.

   (2004) *Myths of the Underworld Journey. Plato, Aristophanes and the "Orphic" Gold Tablets* (Cambridge).

   ed. (2010) *The "Orphic" Gold Tablets and Greek Religion* (Cambridge).

   (2017) "Alcibiades the Profane: Images of the Mysteries," in Destrée and Giannopoulou: 194–215.

Eidinow, E. (2007) *Oracles, Curses, and Risk among the Ancient Greeks* (Oxford).

(2015) "Ancient Greek Religion: 'Embedded' ... and Embodied," in K. Vlassopoulos and C. Taylor, eds., *Communities and Networks in the Ancient Greek World* (Oxford) 54–79.

(2016) "Popular Theologies: The Gift of Divine Envy," in Eidinow, Kindt and Osborne: 205–32.

Eidinow, E., J. Kindt, and R. Osborne, eds. (2016) *Theologies of Ancient Greek Religion* (Cambridge).

Elsner, J. (2000) "Between Mimesis and Divine Power: Visuality in the Greco-Roman World," in R. Nelson, ed., *Visuality before and beyond the Renaissance: Seeing as Others Saw* (Cambridge) 45–69.

(2007) *Roman Eyes: Visuality and Subjectivity in Art and Text* (Princeton).

Evelyn-White, H., ed. (1914) *Hesiod, Homeric Hymns, Epic Cycle, Homerica* (Cambridge, MA).

Faraone, C. (2010) "Rushing and Falling into Milk: New Perspectives on the Orphic Gold Tablets from Thurii and Pelinna," in R. G. Edmonds, ed., *Further along the Path: Recent Studies in the Orphic Gold Leaves* (Cambridge) 304–24.

Ferber, R. (2005) "Ist die Idee des Guten nicht transzendent oder ist sie es doch? Nochmals Platons ΕΠΕΚΕΙΝΑ ΤΗΣ ΟΥΣΙΑΣ," in D. Barbaric, ed., *Platon über das Gute und die Gerechtigkeit* (Würzburg) 149–74.

Ferrari, G. R. F. (1986) *Listening to the Cicadas: A Study of Plato's Phaedrus* (Cambridge).

(1989) "Plato and Poetry," in G. Kennedy, ed., *The Cambridge History of Literary Criticism*, vol. 1 (Cambridge) 92–148.

(2008) "Socratic Irony as Pretence," *Oxford Studies in Ancient Philosophy* 34: 1–33.

(2016) "Platonic Love," in R. Kraut, ed., *The Cambridge Companion to Plato* (Cambridge) 248–76.

Festugière, A.-J. (1932) *L'Ideal Religieux Des Grecs Et L'Evangile* (Paris).

Fine, G. (2003) "Knowledge and Belief in Republic V–VII," in *Plato on Knowledge and Forms* (Oxford).

Flower, H. I. (2013) "Herodotus and Delphic Traditions about Croesus," in R. V. Munson, ed., *Oxford Readings in Classical Studies: Herodotus*, vol. 1: *Herodotus and the Narrative of the Past* (Oxford) 124–53.

Flower, M. (2008) *The Seer in Ancient Greece* (Berkeley).

Foley, H. (1977) *The Homeric Hymn to Demeter* (Princeton).

Fontenrose, J. (1959) *Python: A Study of Delphic Myth and Its Origins* (Berkeley).

(1978) *The Delphic Oracle: Its Responses and Operations* (Berkeley).

Ford, A. (1992) *Homer: The Poetry of the Past* (Ithaca).

(2011) "Dionysos' Many Names in Aristophanes' *Frogs*," in Schlesier: 343–55.

Frank, E. (1955) "Begriff und Bedeutung des Dämonischen," in *Knowledge, Will, and Belief* (Zürich and Stuttgart).

Frede, D. (1978) "The Final Proof of the Immortality of the Soul in Plato's *Phaedo* 102a–107a," *Phronesis* 23: 27–41.

(1985) "Rumpelstiltskin's Pleasures: True and False Pleasures in Plato's *Philebus*," *Phronesis* 30: 151–80.

(2005) *Platons Phaidon*, 2nd ed. (Darmstadt).

Furley, D. (1956) "The Early History of the Concept of Soul," *Bulletin of the Institute of Classical Studies* 3: 1–18.

(1989) *Cosmic Problems: Essays on Greek and Roman Philosophy* (Cambridge).

Furley, W. and J. Bremmer (2001) *Greek Hymns 1. The Texts in Translation* (Tübingen).

(2001a) *Greek Hymns II. Greek Texts and Commentary* (Tübingen).

Gadamer, H-G. (1980) "Plato and the Poets," in *Dialogue and Dialectic: Eight Hermeneutical Studies on Plato*, P. C. Smith, trans. (New Haven) 39–72.

Gagné, R. (2007) "Winds and Ancestors: The *Physika* of Orpheus," *HSCP* 103: 1–24.

Gaifman, M. (2016) "Theologies of Statues in Greek Art," in Eidinow, Kindt and Osborne: 249–80.

(2012) *Aniconism in Greek Antiquity* (Oxford).

Gallop, D., trans. and comm. (1975) *Plato Phaedo* (Oxford).

(1991) *Parmenides of Elea: Fragments, a Text and Translation* (Toronto).

Garland, R. (1992) *Introducing New Gods: The Politics of Athenian Religion* (Ithaca).

Gasparro, G. S. (2015) "Daimonic Power," in Eidinow, Kindt, and Osborne: 413–28.

Gentzler, J., ed. (1998) *Method in Ancient Philosophy* (Oxford).

Gernet, L. (1981) *The Anthropology of Ancient Greece*, trans. J. Hamilton and B. Nagy (Baltimore).

Gerson, L. P. (1990) *God and Greek Philosophy: Studies in the Early History of Natural Theology* (London).

Gertz, S. (2010) "Conversations Platonic and Neoplatonic: Intellect, Soul, and Nature," in J. Finamore and R. Berchman, eds., *Papers from the 6th Annual Conference of the International Society for Neoplatonic Studies* (Leiden) 73–87.

Ghiron-Bistagne, P., ed. (1989) *Transe et théâtre* (Montpellier).

Gill, C. and M. M. McCabe, eds. (1996) *Form and Argument in Late Plato* (Oxford).

Gill, M. L. and J. Lennox, eds. (1994) *Self Motion from Aristotle to Newton* (Princeton).

Goldschmidt, V. (1949) *La religion de Platon* (Paris).

Gonzalez, F. J. (2011) "The Hermeneutics of Madness: Poet and Philosopher in Plato's *Ion* and *Phaedrus*," in Destrée: 93–110.

Gould, J. (1987) "On Making Sense of Greek Religion," in Easterling and Muir: 1–35.

Gould, T. (1990) *The Ancient Quarrel between Poetry and Philosophy* (Princeton).

Graf, F. (1974) *Eleusis und die orphische Dichtung Athens in vorhellenistischer Zeit* (Berlin).

(1993) "Dionysian and Orphic Eschatology: New Texts and Old Questions," in Carpenter and Faraone: 239–58.

(1995) "Aphrodite," in K. van der Toorn, B. Becking, and P. W. van der Horst, eds., *Dictionary of Deities and Demons in the Bible* (Leiden) 118–25.

(2000) "Der Mysterienprozeß," in L. Burckhardt and J. von Ungern-Sternberg, eds., *Große Prozesse im Antiken Athen* (Munich) 114–27.

(2001) "Der Eigensinn der Götterbilder in antiken religiösen Diskursen," in G. Boehm, ed., *Homo Pictor* (Munich) 247–43.

(2004) "Trick or Treat? On Collective Epiphanies in Antiquity," *Illinois Classical Studies* 29: 111–30.

(2009) "Apollo, Possession, and Prophecy," in L. Athanassaki, R. Martin, and J. Miller, eds., *Apolline Politics and Poetics* (Athens) 587–605.

Graf, F. and S. I. Johnston (2007) *Ritual Texts for the Afterlife* (London and New York).

Graham, D. W. (2013) "The Theology of Nature in the Ionian Tradition," *Rhizomata* 1: 194–216.

Grand-Clément, A. (2015) "*Poikilia*," in Destrée and Murray: 406–21.

Griffith, M. (2002) "Slaves of Dionysos: Satyrs, Audience, and the Ends of the *Oresteia*," *Classical Antiquity* 21: 195–258.

Griswold, C. (1986) *Self-Knowledge in Plato's Phaedrus* (New Haven).

Gumbrecht, H. U. (2004) *The Production of Presence: What Meaning Cannot Convey* (Stanford).

Guthrie, W. K. C. (1952/1993) *Orpheus and Greek Religion*, repr. (London; Princeton).

(1962) *A History of Greek Philosophy*, vol. 1. *The Earlier Presocratics and the Pythagoreans* (Cambridge).

Hackforth, R. (1936) "Plato's Theism," in R. E. Allen, ed., *Studies in Plato's Metaphysics* (London) 439–47.

(1950) "Immortality in Plato's *Symposium*," *CR* 64: 43–5.

(1972) *Plato's Phaedo*, repr. (Cambridge).

Halliwell, S. (2000) "Plato and Painting," in K. Rutter and B. Sparkes, eds., *Word and Image in Ancient Greece* (Edinburgh) 99–116.

(2000a) "The Subjection of Muthos to Logos: Plato's Citations of the Poets," *Classical Quarterly* 50: 94–112.

(2002) *The Aesthetics of Mimesis: Ancient Texts and Modern Problems* (Princeton).

Halperin, D. (1985) "Platonic *Erôs* and What Men Call Love," *Ancient Philosophy* 5: 161–204.

(1986) "Plato and Erotic Reciprocity," *CA* 5: 60–80.

(1990) *One Hundred Years of Homosexuality* (New York).

(1992) "Plato and the Erotics of Narrativity," *OSAPh* supplementary volume: 93–129.

Hamilton, R. (1992) *Choes and Anthesteria: Athenian Iconography and Ritual* (Ann Arbor).

Hardie, A. (2004) "Muses and the Mysteries," in P. Murray and P. Wilson, eds. (Oxford) 11–37.

Harris, J. P. (2004) "*Technê* and *theia moira* in Plato's *Ion*," in R. Egan and M. Joyal, eds., *Daimonopylai: Essays in Classics and the Classical Tradition presented to Edmund G. Berry* (Winnipeg) 189–98.

Havelock, E. (1982) *Preface to Plato* (Cambridge, MA).

Heidegger, M. (1927/1962) *Being and Time*, trans. J. Maquerrie and E. Robinson (New York).

(1949/2008) "The End of Metaphysics," in D. F. Krell, ed., *Basic Writings* (New York) 9–110.

(1961/1973) *The End of Philosophy*, trans. J. Stambaugh (Chicago).

(1963/1973) "Kant's Thesis about Being," trans. T. Klein and W. Pohl, *Southwestern Journal of Philosophy* 4: 7–33.

(1957/2002) *Identity and Difference*, 2nd ed., trans. J. Stambaugh (Chicago).

(1967/1998) "Plato's Doctrine of Truth," trans. T. Sheehan, in W. McNeil, ed., *Pathmarks* (Cambridge) 155–82.

Henrichs, A. (1975) "Two Doxographical Notes: Democritus and Prodicus on Religion," *Harvard Studies in Classical Philology* 79: 93–103.

(1978) "Greek Maenadism from Olympias to Messalina," *Harvard Studies in Classical Philology* 82: 121–60.

(1990) "Between Country and City: Cultic Dimensions of Dionysos in Athens and Attica," in M. Griffith and D. J. Mastronarde, eds., *Cabinet of the Muses. Essays on Classical and Comparative Literature in Honor of Thomas G. Rosenmeyer* (Atlanta) 257–77.

(1993) "'He Has a God in Him': Human and Divine in the Modern Perception of Dionysus," in Carpenter and Faraone: 13–43.

(1995) "'Why Should I Dance?': Choral Self-Referentiality in Greek Tragedy," *Arion* 3: 56–111.

(2003) "Writing Religion: Inscribed Texts, Ritual Authority, and the Religious Discourse of the Polis," in H. Yunis, ed., *Written Texts and the Rise of Literate Culture in Ancient Greece* (Cambridge) 38–58.

(2008) "Dionysische Imaginationswelten: Wein, Tanz, Erotik," in R. Schlieser and A. Schwarzmeier, eds., *Dionysos. Verwandlung und Ekstase* (Berlin and Regensburg) 19–27.

(2010) "*Mystika, Orphika, Dionysiaka*. Esoterische Gruppenbildungen, Glaubensinhalte und Verhaltensweisen in der griechischen Religions," in T. Bierl and W. Braungart, eds., *Gewalt und Opfer: Dialog mit Walter Burkert* (Berlin) 87–114.

(2010a) "What Is a Greek God?" in J. Bremmer and A. Erskine, ed., *The Gods of Ancient Greece: Identities and Transformations* (Edinburgh) 19–39.

Herrero de Jáuregui, M. et al., eds. (2011) *Tracing Orpheus: Studies of Orphic Fragments. In honour of Alberto Bernabé* (Berlin and Boston).

Horky, P. S. (2006) "The Imprint of the Soul: Psychosomatic Affection in Plato, Gorgias, and the 'Orphic' Gold Tablets," *Mouseion: Journal of the Classical Association of Canada* 3: 383–98.

(2009) "Persian Cosmos and Greek Philosophy: Plato's Associates and the Zoroastrian *Magoi*," *Oxford Studies in Ancient Philosophy* 37: 47–103.

(2013) *Plato and Pythagoreanism* (Oxford).

(2013a) "Theophrastus on Platonic and 'Pythagorean' Imitation," *Classical Quarterly* 63: 686–712.

(2015) "Pseudo-Archytas' Protreptics? *On Wisdom* in Its Contexts," in D. Nails and H. Tarrant, eds., *Second Sailing: Alternative Perspectives on Plato* (Helsinki) 21–39.

(2016) "The Spectrum of Animal Rationality in Plutarch," *Apeiron* 50: 103–33.

(2018) "Speusippus and Xenocrates on the Pursuit and Ends of Philosophy," in H. Tarrant, D. A. Lane, D. Baltzly, and F. Renaud, eds., *Brill's Companion to the Reception of Plato in Antiquity* (Leiden) 29–45.

(2019) *Cosmos in the Ancient World* (Cambridge).

(forthcoming) "Pythagorean Immortality of the Soul?"

Hyland, D. (2008) *Plato and the Question of Beauty* (Bloomington, IN).

Ierodiakonou, K. (2005) "Plato's Theory of Colours in the *Timaeus*," *Rhizai* 2: 219–33.

Irwin, E. (1974) *Colour Terms in Greek Poetry* (Toronto).

Jaccottet, A.-F. (2003) *Choisir Dionysos. Les associations dionysiaques ou la face cachée du dionysisme*, 2 vols. (Kilchberg).

(2006) "Un dieu, plusieurs mystères? Les différents visages des mystères dionysiaques," in C. Bonnet et al., eds., *Religions orientales – culti misterici. Neue Perspektiven – nouvelles perspectives – prospettive nuove* (Stuttgart) 219–30.

Jackson, B. D. (1971) "The Prayers of Socrates," *Phronesis* 16: 14–37.

Jameson, M. (1993) "The Asexuality of Dionysus," in Carpenter and Faraone: 44–64.

(1999) "Theoxenia," in R. Hägg, ed., *Ancient Greek Hero Cult: Proceedings of the Fifth International Seminar on Ancient Greek Cult* (Stockholm) 35–56.

Janaway, C. (1995) *Images of Excellence: Plato's Critique of the Arts* (Oxford).

Janko, R. (1997) "The Physicist as Hierophant: Aristophanes, Socrates and the Authorship of the Derveni Papyrus," *Zeitschrift für Papyrologie und Epigraphik* 118: 61–94.

(2001) "The Derveni Papyrus ('Diagoros of Melos. Apopyrgizontes Logoi?'): A New Translation," *CPh* 96: 1–32.

(2002) "The Derveni Papyrus: An Interim Text," *ZPE* 141: 1–62.

(2008) "Reconstructing (again) the Opening of the Derveni Papyrus," *ZPE* 166: 37–51.

de Jáuregui, M. H. (2010) *Orphism and Christianity in Late Antiquity.* (Amsterdam).

Johansen, T. K. (2008) *Plato's Natural Philosophy: A Study of the Timaeus-Critias* (Cambridge).

Johnston, S. I. (1999) *Restless Dead: Encounters between the Living and the Dead in Ancient Greece* (Berkeley).

ed. (2005) *Religions of the Ancient World: A Guide* (Cambridge, MA).

(2008) *Ancient Greek Divination* (Malden, MA).

(2009) "'From Oracles, What Useful Words Have Ever Come to Mortals?' Delphic Apollo in the *Oresteia*," in L. Athanassaki, R. P. Martin, and J. F. Miller, eds., *Apolline Politics and Poetics* (Athens) 219–28.

Johnston, S. and P. Struck, eds. (2005) *Mantikê: Studies in Ancient Divination* (Leiden).

Jouanna, J. (2013) "The Typology and Aetiology of Madness in Ancient Greek Medical and Philosophical Writing," in W. Harris, ed., *Mental Disorders in the Classical World* (Leiden) 97–118.

Kahn, C. H. (1983) "Drama and Dialectic," in *Oxford Studies in Ancient Philosophy* 1: 75–121.

  (1996) *Plato and the Socratic Dialogue: The Philosophical Use of a Literary Form* (Cambridge).

Karfík, F. (2004) *Die Beseelung des Kosmos. Untersuchungen zur Kosmologie, Seelenlehre und Theologie in Platons Phaidon und Timaios* (Leipzig).

Keesling, C. (2012) "Syeris, Diakonos of the Priestess Lysimache on the Athenian Acropolis (IG 112 3464)," *Hesperia* 81: 467–505.

Kerenyi, K. (1980) *The Gods of the Greeks* (London).

Kern, O., ed. (1922/1963) *Orphicorum Fragmenta*, repr. (Berlin).

Keyt, D. (1969) "Plato's Paradox that the Immutable Is Unknowable," *Philosophical Quarterly* 19: 1–14.

Kindt, J. (2012) *Rethinking Greek Religion* (Cambridge).

  (2015) "Personal Religion: A Productive Category for the Study of Greek Religion?" *JHS* 135: 35–50.

  (2016) *Revisiting Delphi: Religion and Storytelling in Ancient Greece* (Cambridge).

Kingsley, P. (1995) *Ancient Philosophy, Mystery and Magic: Empedocles and the Pythagorean Tradition* (Oxford).

Kouremenos T., G. M. Parássoglou, and K. Tsantsanoglou, eds. (2006) *The Derveni Papyrus. Edited with Introduction and Commentary* (Florence).

Kowalzig, B. (2007) "'And Now All the World Shall Dance' (Eur. *Bacch.* 114): Dionysus' Choroi between Drama and Ritual," in E. Csapo and M. C. Miller, eds., *The Origins of Theater in Ancient Greece and Beyond: From Ritual to Drama* (Cambridge) 221–51.

Kraut, R. (1992) "Introduction to the Study of Plato," in R. Kraut, ed., *The Cambridge Companion to Plato* (Cambridge) 1–50.

  ed. (1997) *Plato's Republic: Critical Essays* (Lanham, MD).

Kurke, L. (1991) *The Traffic in Praise: Pindar and the Poetics of Social Economy* (Ithaca).

  (1993) "The Economy of Kudos," in Dougherty and Kurke: 131–63.

  (2012) "The Value of Chorality in Ancient Greece," in J. Papadoloupos and G. Urton, eds., *The Construction of Value in the Ancient World* (Los Angeles) 218–35.

Lada-Richards, I. (1999) *Initiating Dionysus: Ritual and Theatre in Aristophanes' Frogs* (Oxford).

Laks, A. (1997) "Between Religion and Philosophy: The Function of Allegory in the 'Derveni Papyrus,'" *Phronesis* 42: 121–42.

  (2001) "A propos de l'édition de l'Empédocle de Strasbourg," *Methexis* 14: 117–25.

(2002) "Reading the Readings: On the First Person Plurals in the Strasburg Empedocles," in V. Caston and D. W. Graham, eds., *Presocratic Philosophy* (Burlington) 127–37.

(2003) "Phénomènes et références: éléments pour une réflexion sur la rationalisation de l'irrationnel," *Methodos* 3: 9–33.

Laks, A. and G. Most, eds. (1997) *Studies on the Derveni Papyrus* (Oxford).

Laks, A. and C. Louguet, eds. (2002) *Qu'est-ce que la philosophie présocratique?* (Villeneuve d'Ascq).

Lear, G. (2007) "Permanent Beauty and Becoming Happy in Plato's *Symposium*," in J. Lesher and D. Nails, eds., *Plato's Symposium: Issues in Interpretation and Reception* (Cambridge, MA) 96–123.

Lear, J. (1998) "Inside and Outside the *Republic*," in *Open Minded: Working out the Logic of the Soul* (Cambridge, MA) 219–46.

Ledbetter, G. M. (2003) *Poetics before Plato* (Princeton).

Lee, E. N. (1976) "Reason and Rotation: Circular Movement as the Model of Mind (*Nous*) in Later Plato," in W. Werkmeister, ed., *Facets of Plato's Philosophy* (Assen), 70–102.

Lesher, J. (2008) "The Humanizing Knowledge in Presocratic Thought," in P. Curd and D. Graham, eds., *The Oxford Handbook of Presocratic Philosophy* (Oxford) 458–84.

Leutsch, E. von, and F. W. Schneidewin, eds. (1965) *Corpus Paroemiographorum Graecorum*, vol. 1 (Hildesheim).

Lewis, D. M. and R. Stroud (1979) "Athens Honors King Evagoras of Salamis," *Hesperia* 48: 180–93.

Liebert, R. S. (2010) "Apian Imagery and the Critique of Poetic Sweetness in Plato's *Republic*," *TAPA* 140: 97–115.

Lloyd, A. (1997) *What Is a God? Studies in the Nature of Greek Divinity* (London).

Lloyd, G. E. R. (1979) *Magic, Reason, and Experience: Studies in the Origins and Development of Early Greek Science* (Cambridge).

(1987) *The Revolutions of Wisdom: Studies in the Claims and Practice of Ancient Greek Science* (Cambridge).

Long, A. A. (1966) "Thinking and Sense-Perception in Empedocles: Mysticism or Materialism?" *CQ* 16: 256–76.

(1988) "Socrates in Hellenistic Philosophy," *CQ* 38: 150–71. Reprinted in Long 1996: 1–34.

(1992) "Finding Oneself in Greek Philosophy," *UIT Tijdschrift voor Filosofie* 2: 255–79.

(1996) *Stoic Studies* (Cambridge).

(1996a) "Parmenides on Thinking Being," *Proceedings of the Boston Area Colloquium on Ancient Philosophy* 12: 125–51.

(1998) "Plato's Apologies and Socrates in the *Theaetetus*," in Gentzler: chapter 5.

ed. (1999a) *The Cambridge Companion to Early Greek Philosophy* (Cambridge).

(1999b) "The Scope of Early Greek Philosophy," in Long 1999a, chapter 1.

(2000) "Platonic Ethics," *Oxford Studies in Ancient Philosophy* 19: 339–57.

(2001) "*Ancient Philosophy's Hardest Question: What to Make of Oneself?*" *Representations* 74: 19–36.

(2002) *Epictetus: A Stoic and Socratic Guide to Life* (Oxford).

(2015) *Greek Models of Mind and Self* (Cambridge, MA).

(forthcoming) "Politics and Divinity in Plato's *Republic*: The Form of the Good," *BICS* Supplement 141.

Lonsdale, S. (1993) *Dance and Ritual Play in Greek Religion* (Baltimore and London).

Lorenz, H. (2006) *The Brute Within: Appetitive Desire in Plato and Aristotle* (Oxford).

Luce, J. V. (1952) "Immortality in Plato's *Symposium*: A Reply," *CR* 66: 137–41.

Ludwig, P. W. (2008) "Eros in the *Republic*," in G. Ferrari, ed., *The Cambridge Companion to Plato's Republic* (Cambridge) 202–31.

MacDowell, D. M. (1962) *Andocides: On the Mysteries* (Oxford).

(1986) *Spartan Law* (Edinburgh).

Mansfeld, J. (1964) *Die Offenbarung des Parmenides und die Menschliche Welt* (Assen).

(1985) "Aristotle and Others on Thales, or the Beginnings of Natural Philosophy," *Mnemosyne* 38: 109–29.

(1990) *Studies in the Historiography of Greek Philosophy* (Assen).

(2013) "Detheologization: Aëtian Chapters and Their Peripatetic Background," *Rhizomata* 1: 330–62.

Martin, R. 1993. "The Seven Sages as Performers of Wisdom," in C. Dougherty and L Kurke, eds., *Cultural Poetics in Archaic Greece* (Cambridge) 108–28.

Martín-Velasco, M. and M. Blanco, eds. (2016) *Greek Philosophy and Mystery Cults* (Newcastle).

Masaracchia, A. (1998) "Orfeo e gli 'Orfici' in Platone," in A. Masaracchia, ed., *Orfeo e l'orphismo* (Rome) 173–203.

Maurizio, L. (1995) "Anthropology and Spirit Possession: A Reconsideration of the Pythia's Role at Delphi," *JHS* 115: 59–86.

(1997) "Delphic Oracles as Oral Performances: Authenticity and Historical Evidence," *CA* 16: 308–34.

(2001) "The Voice at the Centre of the World: The Pythia's Ambiguity and Authority," in A. Lardinois and L. McClure, eds., *Making Silence Speak: Women's Voices in Greek Literature and Society* (Princeton) 38–54.

McCoy, M. (2008) *Plato on the Rhetoric of Philosophers and Sophists* (Cambridge).

McKenzie, M. M. (1981) *Plato on Punishment* (Berkeley).

McPherran, M. (1991) "Socratic Reason and Socratic Revelation," *Journal of the History of Philosophy* 29: 345–73.

(1999) *The Religion of Socrates* (University Park, PA).

(2006a) "Platonic Religion," in H. Benson, ed., *A Companion to Plato* (Oxford) 244–59.

(2006b) "The Gods and Piety of Plato's *Republic*," in G. Santos, ed., *Blackwell Guide to Plato's Republic* (Oxford) 84–103.

Meijer, P. A. (1981) "Philosophers, Intellectuals and Religion in Hellas," in H. S. Versnel, ed., *Faith, Hope and Worship: Aspects of Religious Mentality in the Ancient World* (Leiden) 216–63.

Menn, S. (1995) *Plato on God as Nous* (Carbondale and Edwardsville).

Meyer, M. W., ed. (1987) *The Ancient Mysteries: A Sourcebook: Sacred Texts of the Mystery Religions of the Ancient Mediterranean World* (San Francisco).

Michelini, A., ed. (2003) *Plato as Author: The Rhetoric of Philosophy* (Leiden).

Mikalson, J. (1983) *Athenian Popular Religion* (Chapel Hill).

(2010a) *Ancient Greek Religion* (Chichester).

(2010b) *Greek Popular Religion in Greek Philosophy* (Oxford).

Miller, M. H. (1999) "Platonic Mimesis," in T. M. Falkner, N. Felson, and D. Konstan, eds., *Contextualizing Classics: Ideology, Performance, Dialogue* (Lanham, MD) 253–66.

Mohr, R. D. (1985) *The Platonic Cosmology* (Leiden).

(2006) *God and Forms in Plato* (Las Vegas).

Mohr, R. D. and B. M. Sattler, eds. (2010) *One Book, the Universe* (Las Vegas).

Moravcsik, J. and P. Temko, eds. (1982) *Plato on Beauty, Wisdom, and the Arts* (Totowa, NJ).

Morgan, C. (1989) "Divination and Society at Delphi and Didyma," *Hermathena* 147: 17–42.

(1990) *Athletes and Oracles: The Transformation of Olympia and Delphi in the Eighth Century* (Cambridge).

Morgan, K. (2000) *Myth and Philosophy from the Presocratics to Plato* (Cambridge).

(2010) "Inspiration, Recollection and *Mimesis* in Plato's *Phaedrus*," in A. Nightingale and D. Sedley, eds., *Ancient Models of Mind: Studies in Human and Divine Rationality* (Cambridge) 45–63.

(2010a) "The Voice of Authority: Divination and Plato's *Phaedo*," *CQ* 60: 63–81.

Morgan, M. L. (1990) "Plato and the Painters," Apeiron 23: 121–45.

(1990a) Platonic Piety (New Haven).

(2007) *Discovering Levinas* (Cambridge).

Morris, I. (1992) *Death Ritual and Social Structure in Classical Antiquity* (Cambridge).

Morrow, G. R. (1948) "Plato and the Law of Nature," in M. R. Konvitz and A. E. Murphy, eds., *Essays in Political Theory presented to George H. Sabine* (Ithaca) 17–44.

(1950/1965) "Necessity and Persuasion in Plato's *Timaeus*," *Philosophical Review* 59 (1950) repr. in Allen 1965: 421–37.

(1953) "Plato's Concept of Persuasion," *Philosophical Review* 62: 234–50.

(1960) *Plato's Cretan City: A Historical Interpretation of the Laws* (Princeton).

(1960a) "The Nocturnal Council in Plato's *Laws*," *Archiv für Geschichte der Philosophie* 42: 229–46.

Moss, J. (2007) "What Is Imitative Poetry and Why Is It Bad?" in G. Ferrari, ed., *The Cambridge Companion to Plato's Republic* (Cambridge) 415–44.

Most, G. W. (1997) "The Fire Next Time: Cosmology, Allegoresis, and Salvation in the Derveni Papyrus," *JHS* 117: 117–35.

(1998) "Mimesis," in E. Craig, ed., the *Routledge Encyclopedia of Philosophy*, vol. 6 (London) 381–2.

(1999) "Hesiod's Myth of the Five (or Four or Three) Races," *PCPS* 43: 104–27.

(2003) "Philosophy and Religion," in D. Sedley, ed., *The Cambridge Companion to Greek and Roman Philosophy* (Cambridge) 300–22.

ed. and trans. (2006) *Hesiod, Theogony, Works and Days, Testimonia* (Cambridge, MA).

Mourelatos, A. (1981) "Astronomy and Kinematics in Plato's Project of Rationalist Explanation," *Studies in the History and Philosophy of Science* 12: 1–21.

(2010) "The Epistemological Section (29b–d) of the Proem in Timaeus' Speech: M. F. Burnyeat on *Eikos Logos*, and Comparison with Xenophanes B34 and B35," in Mohr and Sattler: 225–47.

Mueller, I. (1992) "Mathematical Knowledge and Philosophical Truth," in R. Kraut, ed., *The Cambridge Companion to Plato* (Cambridge) 170–99.

(1998) "Platonism and the Study of Nature: *Phaedo* 95e ff.," in J. Gentzler, ed., *Method in Ancient Philosophy* (New York) 67–90.

Müller, J., ed. (2011) *Platon: Phaidon* (Berlin).

Murray, P. (1981) "Poetic Inspiration in Ancient Greece," *JHS* 101: 87–100.

(1990) "The Affair of the Mysteries: Democracy and the Drinking Group," in O. Murray, ed., *Sympotika: A Symposium on the Symposion* (Oxford) 149–61.

(1992) "Inspiration and Mimesis in Plato," in A. Barker and M. Warner, eds., *The Language of the Cave* (Edmonton) 27–46.

ed. (1996) *Plato on Poetry* (Cambridge).

(2003) "Plato and Greek Theatre," in E. Theodorakopoulos, ed., *Attitudes to Theatre from Plato to Milton* (Bari) 1–19.

(2004) "The Muses and Their Arts," in Murray and Wilson: 365–89.

Murray, P. and P. Wilson, eds. (2004) *Music and the Muses: The Culture of Mousikê in the Classical Athenian City* (Oxford).

Mylonas, G. (1961) *Eleusis and the Eleusinian Mysteries* (Princeton).

Mylonopolous, J., ed. (2010) *Divine Images and Human Imaginations in Ancient Greece and Rome* (Leiden).

Nadaff, R. A. (2002) *Exiling the Poets: The Production of Censorship in Plato's Republic* (Chicago).

Nails, D. (2002) *The People of Plato: A Prosopography of Plato and Other Socratics* (Indianapolis).

(2006) "Tragedy Off-Stage," in J. Lesher, D. Nails, and F. Sheffield, eds., *Plato's Symposium: Issues in Interpretation* (Cambridge, MA) 179–206.

Nails, D. and H. Tarrant, eds., 2015, *Second Sailing: Alternative Perspectives on Plato* (Helsinki).

Nancy, J. -L. (2001) "Le partage des voix," in *Platon: Ion* (Paris) 113–38.

Nehamas, A. (1975) "Plato on the Imperfection of the Sensible World," *American Philosophical Quarterly* 12: 105–17.

(1998) *The Art of Living: Socratic Reflections from Plato to Foucault* (Berkeley).

(1999) "Plato and the Mass Media," in *Virtues of Authenticity: Essays on Plato and Socrates* (Princeton) 279–99. •

(2007) "Beauty of Body, Nobility of Soul: The Pursuit of Love in Plato's *Symposium*," in D. Scott, ed., *Maieusis: Essays in Ancient Philosophy in Honour of Myles Burnyeat* (Oxford).

(2010) *Only a Promise of Beauty: The Place of Beauty in a World of Art* (Princeton).

Nehamas, A., and P. Woodruff, trans. (1997a) *Plato's Symposium* (Indianapolis). Trans. (1997b) *Plato's Phaedrus* (Indianapolis).

Neils, J. (1999) "Reconfiguring the Gods on the Parthenon Frieze," *Art Bulletin* 81: 6–20.

(2001) *The Parthenon Frieze* (Cambridge).

Neschker-Henschke, A. (1995) *Platonisme, politique et théorie du droit naturel* (Louvain).

Nightingale, A. (1993) "Writing/Reading a Sacred Text: A Literary Interpretation of Plato's *Laws*," *CPh* 88: 279–300.

(1995) *Genres in Dialogue: Plato and the Construct of Philosophy* (Cambridge).

(1999) "Plato's Lawcode in Context: Rule by Written Law in Athens and Magnesia," *CQ* 49: 100–22.

(2001) "Towards an Ecological Eschatology: Plato and Bakhtin on Other Worlds and Times," in B. Branham, ed., *Bakhtin and the Classics* (Evanston) 221–49.

(2004) *Spectacles of Truth: Theoria in Its Cultural Context* (Cambridge).

(2013) "The Orphaned Word: The *Pharmakon* of Forgetfulness in Plato's *Laws*," in A.-E. Peponi, ed., *The City Dancing: Performance and Culture in Plato's Laws* (Cambridge) 243–64.

(2015) "Sight and the Philosophy of Vision in Classical Greece: Democritus, Plato and Aristotle," in M. Squire, ed., *Sight and the Ancient Senses*, vol. 4 of *The Senses in Antiquity* (London) 54–67.

(2017) "The Mortal Soul and Immortal Happiness," in P. Destrée and Z. Giannapoulou, eds., *The Cambridge Critical Guide to Plato's Symposium* (Cambridge) 142–59.

(2017a) "Cave Myths and the Metaphorics of Light: Plato, Aristotle, Lucretius," *Arion* 24: 111–41.

(2018) "The Aesthetics of Vision in Plato's *Phaedo* and *Timaeus*," in E. Bakola, A. Kampakoglou, M. Tamiolaki, et al., eds., *Gaze, Vision, and Visuality in Ancient Greek Literature* (Berlin) 331–53.

(2018a) "Divine Epiphany and Pious Discourse in Plato's *Phaedrus*," *Arion* 26: 61–94.

(2020) "Plato's *Symposium*: Eros, Beauty, and Metaphysical Desire," in K. Seigneurie, ed., *A Companion to World Literature* (Hoboken) 1–11.

Nussbaum, M. (1979) "The Speech of Alcibiades: A Reading of Plato's *Symposium*," *Philosophy and Literature* 3: 131–72.

(1986) *The Fragility of Goodness: Luck and Ethics in Greek Tragedy and Philosophy* (Cambridge).

(1990) *Love's Knowledge: Essays on Philosophy and Literature* (New York).

Obbink, D. (1988) "The Origin of Greek Sacrifice: Theophrastus on Religion and Cultural History," in W. W. Fortenbaugh and R. W. Sharples, eds., *Theophrastean Studies* (New Brunswick) 272–95.

(1992) "'What All Men Believe – Must Be True': Common Conceptions and Consensio Omnium in Aristotle and Hellenistic Philosophy," *Oxford Studies in Ancient Philosophy* 10: 193–231.

(1997) "Cosmology as Initiation vs. the Critique of Orphic Mysteries," in Laks and Most: 39–55.

Ogden, D., ed. (2007) *A Companion to Greek Religion* (Oxford and Malden, MA).

O'Meara, D. (2017) *Cosmology and Politics in Plato's Later Works* (Cambridge).

Osborne, C. (1987) "The Repudiation of Representation and its Repercussions in Plato's *Republic*," *Proceedings of the Cambridge Philological Society* 33: 53–73.

(2000) "Rummaging in the Recycling Bins of Upper Egypt: A Discussion of A. Martin and O. Primavesi, *L'Empédocle de Strasbourg*," *Oxford Studies in Ancient Philosophy* 18: 329–56.

Osborne, R. (1988) *Archaic and Classical Greek Art* (Oxford).

(1994) "Looking on Greek Style. Does the Sculpted Girl Speak to Women Too?" in I. Morris, ed., *Classical Greece: Ancient History and Modern Archaeologies* (Cambridge) 81–96.

(1997) "The Ecstasy and the Tragedy: Varieties of Religious Experience in Art, Drama, and Society," in C. Pelling, ed., *Greek Tragedy and the Historian* (Oxford) 187–211.

Ostenfeld E. (1997) "The Role and Status of the Forms in the *Timaeus*: Paradigmatism Revisited?" in Calvo and Brisson: 167–78.

Otto, W. F. (1933) *Dionysos: Mythos und Kultus* (Frankfurt).

Owen, G. E. L. (1957) "A Proof in the *Peri Ideon*," *Journal of Hellenic Studies* 77: 103–11.

Pache, C. (2010) *A Moment's Ornament: The Poetics of Nympholepsy in Ancient Greece* (Oxford).

Padel, R. (1981) "Madness in Fifth-Century (BC) Athenian Tragedy," in P. Heelas and A. Lock, eds., *Indigenous Psychologies: The Anthropology of the Self* (London) 105–131.

Palmer, J. (1998) "Xenophon's Ouranian God in the Fourth Century," *Oxford Studies in Ancient Philosophy* 16: 1–34.

Parker, R. (1983) *Miasma: Pollution and Purification in Early Greek Religion* (Oxford).

(1985) "Greek States and Greek Oracles," in P. Cartledge, ed., *Crux: Essays in Greek History Presented to G. E. M. de Ste. Croix on His 75th Birthday* (London) 298–326.

(1995) "Early Orphism," in A. Powell, ed., *The Greek World* (London and New York).

(1996) *Athenian Religion: A History* (Oxford)

(2005) *Polytheism and Society at Athens* (Oxford).

(2011) *On Greek Religion* (Ithaca).

Pater, W. (1901) *Plato and Platonism* (London).

Peponi, A.-E. (2004) "Initiating the Viewer: Deixis and Perception in Alcman's Lyric Drama," *Arethusa* 37: 295–316.

(2012) *Frontiers of Pleasure: Models of Aesthetic Response in Archaic and Classical Greek Thought* (New York).

ed. (2013) *Performance and Culture in Plato's Laws* (Cambridge).

(2015) "Dance and Aesthetic Perception," in Destrée and Murray: 204–17.

Petridou, G. (2016) *Divine Epiphany in Greek Literature and Culture* (Oxford and New York).

Petrovic, A. and I. Petrovic (2016) *Inner Purity and Pollution in Greek Religion*, vol. 1: *Early Greek Religion* (Oxford).

Pfister, F. (1924) "Epiphanie," *RE* suppl. 4: 277–323.

Piano, V. (2011) "Ricostruendo il rotolo di Derveni. Per una revision papirologica di P. Derveni I–III," in *Papiri Filosofici. Miscellanea di Studi* 6 (Florence).

Piettre, R. (2001) "Images et perception de la présence divine en Grèce ancienne," *Mélanges de l'Ecole Française d'Athènes* 113: 211–24.

Pinto, R. (2017) "*Nous*, Motion and Teleology in Anaxagoras," *Oxford Studies in Ancient Philosophy* 52: 1–32.

Pirenne-Delforge, V. (1994) *L'Aphrodite greque* (Liège).

(1998) "Quand Eros a les honneurs d'un cult . . .," *Uranie* 8: 11–31.

Planinc, Z. (2003) *Plato through Homer: Poetry and Philosophy in the Cosmological Dialogues* (Columbia, MO).

Platt, V. (2011) *Facing the Gods: Epiphany and Representation in Graeco-Roman Art, Literature and Religion* (Cambridge).

Porter, J. (2010) *The Origins of Aesthetic Thought in Ancient Greece* (Cambridge).

(2016) *The Sublime in Antiquity* (Cambridge).

Powers, N. (2009) "The Natural Theology of Xenophon's Socrates," *Ancient Philosophy* 29: 249–66.

Price, A. (1990) *Love and Friendship in Plato and Aristotle* (Oxford).

Price, S. (1999) *Religions of the Ancient Greeks* (Cambridge).

Prier, R. (1989) *Thauma Idesthai: The Phenomenology of Sight and Appearance in Archaic Greek* (Tallahassee).

Primavesi, O. (2005) "Empedocles: Physical and Mythical Divinity," in P. Curd and D. W. Graham, eds., *The Oxford Handbook of Presocratic Philosophy* (Oxford) 250–83.

Purvis, A. (2004) *Singular Dedications: Founders and Innovators of Private Cults in Ancient Greece* (New York and London).

Reeve, C. D. C. (1989) *Socrates in the Apology* (Indianapolis).

(2014) "Socrates the Apollonian?" in N. Smith and P. Woodruff: 24–39.

Remes, P. (2014) "Plato: Interaction between the External Body and the Perceiver in *Timaeus*," in J. Silva and M. Yrjönsuuri, eds., *Active Perception in the History of Philosophy* (Cham, Switzerland) 9–18.

Reydams-Schils, G. (1997) "Plato's World Soul: Grasping Sensibles without Sense Perception," in Calvo and Brisson: 261–6.

(2011) "Myth and Poetry in the *Timaeus*," in Destrée and Herrmann: 349–60.

Ricoeur, P. (1981) "Mimesis and Representation," *Annals of Scholarship* 2: 15–32.

(2013) *Being, Essence, and Substance in Plato and Aristotle*, trans. D. Pellauer and J. Starkey (Cambridge).

Rijksbaron, A. (2011) "The Profanation of the Mysteries and the Mutilation of the Hermae: Two Variations on Two Themes," in J. Lallot et al., eds., *The Historical Present in Thucydides: Semantics and Narrative Function* (Leiden) 177–94.

Riedweg, C. (1987) *Mysterienterminologie bei Platon, Philon und Klemens von Alexandrien* (Berlin and New York).

(1998) "Initiation-Tod-Unterwelt," in F. Graf, ed., *Ansichten griechischer Rituale. Geburtstags-Symposium für Walter Burkert* (Stuttgart) 359–98.

(2002) "Poésie orphique et rituel initiatique. Éléments d'un 'discourse sacré' dans les lamelles d'or," *RHR* 219: 459–81.

(2005) *Pythagoras. His Life, Teaching, and Influence*, trans. S. Rendall (Ithaca).

(2010) "Initiation-Death-Underworld: Narrative and Ritual in the Gold Leaves," in Edmonds: 219–56.

Robertson, N. (2003) "Orphic Mysteries and Dionysiac Ritual," in Cosmopoulos: 218–40.

Robinson, T. M. (1970) *Plato's Psychology* (Toronto).

(2004) *Cosmos as Art Object: Studies in Plato's Timaeus and Other Dialogues* (Binghamton, NY).

(2008) "Presocratic Theology," in P. Curd and D. Graham, eds., *The Oxford Handbook of Ancient Philosophy* (Oxford) 485–500.

Rodriguez, F. B. (2016) "The Influence of Orphism in Plato's Psychology and Eschatology," in Martín-Velasco and Blanco: 102–21.

Roochnik, D. (1987) "The Erotics of Philosophical Discourse," *History of Philosophy Quarterly* 4: 117–29.

(1996) *Of Art and Wisdom: Plato's Understanding of Techne* (University Park, PA).

(2003) *Beautiful City: The Dialectical Character of Plato's Republic* (Ithaca).

Rosen, S. (1965) "The Role of Eros in Plato's *Republic*," *Review of Metaphysics* 18: 452–75.

(1988) *The Quarrel Between Philosophy and Poetry* (New York).

Rosenberger, V. (2001) *Griechische Orakel: eine Kulturgeschichte* (Darmstadt).

ed. (2013) *Divination in the Ancient World: Religious Options and the Individual* (Stuttgart).

Rosenzweig, R. (2004) *Worshipping Aphrodite: Art and Cult in Classical Athens* (Ann Arbor).

Ross, W. D. (1953) *Plato's Theory of Ideas*, 2nd ed. (Oxford).

Rowe, C. J., trans. and comm. (1986) *Plato: Phaedrus* (Warminster).

(1990) "Philosophy, Love and Madness," in C. Gill, ed., *The Person and the Human Mind* (Oxford) 227–46.

(1991) "Philosophy and Literature: The Arguments of Plato's *Phaedo*," *Boston Area Colloquium in Ancient Philosophy* 7: 159–81.

(1993) *Plato: Phaedo* (Cambridge).

(2007) "The Form of the Good and the Good in Plato's Republic," in D. Cairns, ed., *Pursuing the Good* (Edinburgh) 124–53.

(2013) "Socrates and His Gods: From the *Euthyphro* to the *Eudemian Ethics*," in V. Hart and M. Lane, eds., *Politeia in Greek and Roman Philosophy* (Cambridge) 329–48.

Rubel, A. (2000) *Stadt in Angst. Religion und Politik in Athen während des Peloponnesischen Krieges* (Darmstadt).

Runia, D. T. (1997) "Lucretius and Doxography," in K. A. Algra and M. H. Koenen, eds., *Lucretius and His Intellectual Background* (Amsterdam) 93–104.

Rutherford, I. (1998) "*Theoria* as Theatre: The Pilgrimage Theme in Greek Drama," in *Papers of the Leeds International Latin Seminar* 10: 131–56.

Rutherford, R. B. (1995) *The Art of Plato: Ten Essays in Platonic Interpretation* (Cambridge, MA).

(2004) *Platonic Legacies* (Albany).

Santamaría, M. (2012) "Orfeo y el orfismo. Actualización bibliográfica (2004–2012)," *'Ilu. Revista de Ciencias de las Religiones* 17: 211–52.

(2012a) "Critical Notes to the Orphic Poem of the Derveni Papyrus," *ZPE* 182: 55–76.

Santas, G. (1999) "The Form of the Good in Plato's *Republic*," in G. Fine, ed., *Plato 1. Metaphysics and Epistemology* (Oxford) 247–74.

Santayana, G. (1927) *Platonism and the Spiritual Life* (New York).

Sassi, M., ed. (2006) *The Construction of Philosophical Discourse in the Age of Presocratics* (Pisa).

(2013) "Where Epistemology and Religion Meet: What Do(es) the God(s) Look Like?" *Rhizomata* 1: 283–307.

(2015) "Perceiving Colors," in Destrée and Murray: 262–73.

(2016) "Parmenides and Empedocles on Krasis and Knowledge," *Apeiron* 49: 451–69.

(2018) *The Beginnings of Philosophy in Greece*, trans. M. Asuni (Princeton).

Sattler, B. (2013) "The Eleusinian Mysteries in Pre-Platonic Thought: Metaphor, Practice and Imagery for Plato's *Symposium*," in Adluri: 151–90.

Scalera McClintock, G. (1995) "L'antica natura titanica. Variazioni sul mito greco della colpa," *Filosofia e Teologia* 9: 307–25.

Scarpi, P. (2002) *Le religioni dei misteri*, 2 vols. (Milan).

Scarry, E. (1999) *On Beauty and Being Just* (Princeton).

Scheer, T. S. (2000) *Die Gottheit und ihr Bild. Untersuchungen zur Funktion griechischer Kultbilder in Religion und Politik* (Munich).

Scheffield, F. (2009) *Plato's Symposium: An Ethics of Desire* (Oxford).

(2017) "Erôs and the Pursuit of Form," in P. Destrée and Z. Giannopoulou: 125–41.

Schofield, M. (1987) "Coxon's Parmenides," *Phronesis* 32: 349–59.

Scodel, R. (2011) "Euripides, the Derveni Papyrus, and the Smoke of Many Writings," in A. Lardinois et al., eds., *Sacred Words: Orality, Literacy and Religion* (Leiden) 79–98.

Scott, D. (2011) "Plato, Poetry and Creativity," in Destrée and Herrmann: 131–54.

Scott, M. (2010) *Delphi and Olympia: The Spatial Politics of Panhellenism in the Archaic and Classical Periods* (Cambridge).

(2014) *Delphi: A History of the Center of the Ancient World* (Princeton).

Schlesier, R. (2011) *A Different God? Dionysos and Ancient Polytheism* (Berlin).

Seaford, R. (1981) "Dionysiac Drama and the Dionysiac Mysteries," *CQ* 31: 252–75.

(1986) "Immortality, Salvation, and the Elements," *HSCP* 90: 1–26.

(1994) *Reciprocity and Ritual: Homer and Tragedy in the Developing City-State* (Oxford).

Sedley, D. (1989) "Teleology and Myth in the *Phaedo*," *Boston Area Colloquium in Ancient Philosophy* 5: 359–83.

(1995) "The Dramatis Personae of Plato's *Phaedo*," in T. Smiley, ed., *Philosophical Dialogues: Plato, Hume, Wittgenstein* (Oxford) 3–26.

(1998) "The Etymologies in Plato's *Cratylus*," *CA* 118: 140–54.

(1999) "The Ideal of Godlikeness," in G. Fine ed., *Plato 2: Ethics, Politics, Religion, and the Soul* (Oxford) 309–28.

(1999a) "Parmenides and Melissus," in Long 1999a: 113–33.

(2008) *Creationism and Its Critics in Antiquity* (Berkeley).

(2008a) "Socrates' Place in the History of Teleology," *Elenchos* 29: 317–34.

(2009) "Three Kinds of Platonic Immortality," in D. Frede and B. Reis, eds., *Body and Soul in Ancient Philosophy* (Berlin) 145–62.

(2019) "Plato's Theology," in G. Fine, ed., *The Oxford Handbook of Plato*, 2nd ed. (Oxford) 627–44.

Shapiro, H. A. (1992) "Eros in Love: Pederasty and Pornography in Greece," in A. Richlin, ed., *Pornography and Representation in Greece and Rome* (Oxford) 53–72.

Sheffield, F. (2001) "Alcibiades' Speech: A Satyric Drama," *Greece and Rome* 48: 193–209.

(2006) *Plato's Symposium: The Ethics of Desire* (Oxford).

(2017) "Erôs and the Pursuit of Form," in P. Destrée and Z. Giannopoulou eds., *Plato's Symposium: A Critical Guide* (Cambridge) 125–41.

Shields, C. (2008) "Surpassing in Dignity and Power: The Metaphysics of Goodness in Plato's *Republic*," *Philosophical Inquiry* 30: 145–61.

Shorey, P. (1895) "The Idea of Good in Plato's *Republic*: A Study in the Logic of Speculative Ethics," *Studies in Classical Philology* 1: 188–239.

Silverman, A. (2003) *The Dialectic of Essence: A Study of Plato's Metaphysics* (Princeton).

Simms, R. (1990) "Myesis, Telete, and Mysteria," *GRBS* 31: 183–95.

Smith, N. and P. Woodruff, eds. (2000) *Reason and Religion in Socratic Philosophy* (Oxford).

Solmsen, F. (1942) *Plato's Theology* (Ithaca).

Sourvinou-Inwood (1981) "To Die and Enter the House of Hades: Homer, Before and After," in J. Whaley, ed., *Mirrors of Mortality* (London) 15–39.

(1988) "A Trauma in Flux: Death in the Eighth Century and After," in R. Hägg, ed., *The Greek Renaissance of the Eight Century B.C.* (Stockholm) 33–49.

(1995) *Reading Greek Death to the End of the Classical Period* (Oxford).

(2003) "Festivals and Mysteries: Aspects of the Eleusinian Cult," in Cosmopoulos: 25–49.

(2005) *Hylas, the Nymphs, Dionysus and Others: Myth, Ritual, Identity* (Stockholm).

Sourvinou-Inwood, C. and R. Parker, eds. (2011) *Athenian Myths and Festivals: Aglauros, Erechtheus, Panathenaia, Dionysia* (Oxford).

Stafford, E. (2013) "From the Gymnasium to the Wedding: Eros in Athenian Art and Cult," in E. Sanders and C. Thumiger et al., eds., *Eros in Ancient Greece* (Oxford) 175–208.

Steiner, D. T. (1996) "For Love of a Statue: A Reading of Plato's *Symposium* 215a–b," *Ramus* 25: 89–111.

(2001) *Images in Mind: Statues in Archaic and Classical Greek Literature and Thought* (Princeton).

(2014) "Greek and Roman Theories of Art," in C. Marconi, ed., *The Oxford Handbook of Greek and Roman Architecture* (Oxford) 21–40.

Strycker, E. (1970) "L'idée du Bien dans la Republique de Platon," *L'antiquité classique* 39: 450–67.

Taylor, A. E. (1926) *Plato, the Man and His Work* (London).

(1928) *A Commentary on Plato's Timaeus* (Oxford).

Thomas, R. (2003) "Prose Performance Texts: Epideixis and Written Publication in the Late Fifth and Early Fourth Centuries," in H. Yunis, ed., *Written Texts and the Rise of Literate Culture in Ancient Greece* (Cambridge) 189–212.

Thomas, R. (1989) *Oral Tradition and Written Record in Classical Athens* (Cambridge).

(1992) *Literacy and Orality in Ancient Greece* (Cambridge).

(1994) "Law and Lawgiver in the Athenian Democracy," in R. Osborne and S. Hornblower, eds., *Ritual, Finance, Politics* (Oxford) 119–34.

(1996) "Written in Stone? Liberty, Equality, Orality and the Codification of Law," in L. Foxhall and A. Lewis, eds., *Greek Law in Its Political Setting* (Oxford) 9–31.

Thomson, I. (2005) *Plato on Ontotheology: Technology and the Politics of Education* (Cambridge).

Tigerstedt, E. N. (1965) *The Legend of Sparta in Classical Antiquity*, vol. 1 (Stockholm).

(1970) "Furor Poeticus: Poetic Inspiration in Greek Literature before Democritus and Plato," *JHI* 31: 163–78.

Todd, S. (2014) "Revisiting the Herms and the Mysteries," in D. Cairns and R. Knox, eds., *Law, Rhetoric, and Comedy in Classical Athens* (Swansea) 87–102.

Tor, S. (2017) *Mortal and Divine in Early Greek Epistemology* (Cambridge).

Tortorelli Ghidini, M. (2006) *Figli della terra e del cielo stellato: Testi orfici con traduzione e commento* (Naples).

Trampedach, K. (2015) *Politische Mantik: Die Kommunikation über Götterzeichen und Orakel im klassischen Griechenland* (Heidelberg).

Trépanier, S. (2013) "Early Greek Theology: Gods as Nature and Natural Gods," in J. Bremmer and A. Erskine, eds., *The Gods of Ancient Greece: Identities and Transformations* (Edinburgh) 273–317.

Ustinova, Y. (2009) *Caves and the Ancient Greek Mind: Descending Underground in the Search for Ultimate Truth* (Oxford).

    (2017) *Divine Mania: Alteration of Consciousness in Ancient Greece* (London).

Van Camp, J. and P. Canart (1956) *Le Sens du Mot ΘΕΙΟΣ chez Platon* (Louvain).

Van Straten, F. T. (1981) "Gifts for the Gods," in H. S. Versnel: 65–151.

Verdenius, W. J. (1962) "Der Begriff der Mania in Platons *Phaidros*," *Archiv für Geschichte der Philosophie* 44: 132–50.

Versnel, H. S., ed. (1981) *Faith, Hope and Worship: Aspects of Religious Mentality in the Ancient World* (Leiden).

    (1987) "What Did Ancient Man See When He Saw a God? Some Reflections on Greco-Roman Epiphany," in D. Van der Plas, ed., *Effigies Dei: Essays on the History of Religions* (Leiden) 42–55.

    (2011) "*Heis Dionysus*! One Dionysus?" in Schlesier: 3–46.

Versnel, H. S., D. Frankfurter, and J. Hahn, eds. (2009) *Greek Religious Terminology: Telete & Orgia* (Leiden).

Vernant, J.-P. (1991) "Mortals and Immortals: The Body of the Divine," *Mortals and Immortals: Collected Essays*, ed. F. Zeitlin (Princeton) 27–49.

Vidal-Naquet, P. (1986) *Black Hunter: Forms of Thought and Forms of Society*, trans. A. Szegedy Maszak (Baltimore).

Vlastos, G. (1952) "Theology and Philosophy in Early Greek Thought," *PhQ* 2: 97–123.

    (1965) "Degrees of Reality in Plato," in R. Bambrough, ed., *New Essays on Plato and Aristotle* (London) 1–19.

    (1965–1966) "A Metaphysical Paradox," *Proceedings and Addresses of the American Philosophical Association* 39: 5–19.

    (1969) "Reasons and Causes in the *Phaedo*," *CR* 78: 291–325.

    ed. (1971) *The Philosophy of Socrates: A Collection of Critical Essays* (Garden City).

    (1973) *Platonic Studies* (Princeton).

    (1975) *Plato's Universe* (Seattle).

    (1980) "The Role of Observation in Plato's Conception of Astronomy," in J. Anton, ed., *Science and the Sciences in Plato* (New York) 1–31.

    (1981) *Platonic Studies*, 2nd ed. (Princeton).

    (1989) "Socratic Piety," *Proceedings of the Boston Area Colloquium in Ancient Philosophy* 5: 213–38.

(1991) *Socrates: Ironist and Moral Philosopher* (Ithaca).

(1993) *Studies in Greek Philosophy*, vol. 1: *The Presocratics*, ed. D. Graham (Princeton).

(1994) "Anamnesis in the *Meno*," in J. Day, ed., *Plato's Meno in Focus* (London) 88–111.

(2000) "Socratic Piety," in Smith and Woodruff: 55–73.

Werner, D. (2014) *Myth and Philosophy in Plato's Phaedrus* (Cambridge).

West, M. (1976) "Graeco-Oriental Orphism in the 3rd century BC," in D. Pippidi, ed., *Assimilation et résistance à la culture Gréco-romaine dans le monde ancient: Travaux du VIe Congrès International d'Études Classiques* (Paris) 221–6.

(1978) *Hesiod: Works and Days* (Oxford).

(1983) *Orphic Poems* (Oxford).

White, M. C. (2004) "Virtue in Plato's *Symposium*," *CQ* 54: 366–78.

Whitmarsh, T. (2015) *Battling the Gods: Atheism in Antiquity* (New York).

Wilson, P. (1999) "The Aulos in Athens," in S. Goldhill, ed., *Performance Culture in Athenian Democracy* (Cambridge) 58–94.

Winkler, J. J. (1990) *The Constraints of Desire: The Anthropology of Sex and Gender in Ancient Greece* (New York).

Winkler, J. J. and F. Zeitlin, eds. (1992) *Nothing to Do with Dionysus?* (Princeton).

Woodruff, P. (1998) "Plato on Mimesis," in M. Kelly, ed., *Encyclopedia of Aesthetics*, vol. 3 (New York) 521–3.

Yates, V. (2004) "The Titanic Origins of Humans: The Melian Nymphs and Zagreus," *GRBS* 44: 83–198.

Yunis, H. (2003) *Written Texts and the Rise of Literate Culture in Ancient Greece* (Cambridge).

Zeller, E. (1889) "Das Gute," in *Die Philosophie der Griechen in ihrer Geschichtlichen Entwicklung – Platon und die Alte Akademie*, vol. 2 (Leipzig) 707–18.

Index

Abravanel (Leon Ebreo), 9
Achilles, 76
Acropolis, 70, 71
Adonis, 179
Aeschylus
    Oreithuia, 176
Aether, 141, 155, 156–60
affections, 240
agalma. See statues
Alcestis, 76
Alcibiades, 107–8. *See also* Plato, *Symposium*,
    speech of Alcibiades
    mutilation of the Herms, 107
    profaning of the Eleusinian Mysteries, 107
al-Farabi, 9
al-Ghazali, 9
al-Kindi, 9
Anaxagoras, 125, 141, 157
Animal
    form of, 213, 217, 232, 247, 260
Aphrodite, 201
Apollo, 32, 149, 193
Apollodorus, 196
Aristophanes. *See also* Plato, *Symposium*, speech
    of Aristophanes
    Birds, 68
    Frogs, 115
    Wasps, 192
Aristotle, 6, 99, 154, 225
    Eudemian Ethics, 182
    On the Soul, 147
    Politics, 197–8
ascent, 156, 178, 188, 202, 251
    of the soul, 152
    to the Forms, 17, 29, 97, 103
Asclepius, 70
astronomy, 218, 238, 244, 250
atheism, 1
Athena, 69, 70, 72, 142
Athens, 90, 95, 107, 145, 159, 176, 182
atoms, 233, 236, 243

Augustine, 9
    Confessions, 48
aulos, 90, 196

Bacchic Mystery cult, 134, 139–40. *See also*
    Dionysian Mysteries
Bakhtin, Mikhail, 117
Beauty, 86–8, 164, 166
    as midwife, 83
    epiphany of the Form of, 96–101, 170,
        208–11
    Form of, 28, 31, 36, 55–6, 86, 103, 111,
        164
    sea of, 97, 98, 113
birthgiving, 83–4, 87, 103
body, 118–19, 153. *See also* World-Body
Boreas and Oreithuia, 169, 175–81

Castiglione, 9
chaos, 235
choreia. See dance
Christianity, 9, 64
Chronos, 231
Circle
    of the Different, 227, 228, 232
    of the Same, 227, 228, 229, 232,
        249
Clement of Alexandria, 9, 91
contemplation, 31, 63, 119, 151, 187, 189,
    214
Corybants, 196
cosmic body. *See* World-Body
cosmic soul. *See* World-Soul
cosmos, 161, 214–18, 252, 260
    motion of, 226, 253
Cybele, 196

d'Aragona, Tullia, 9
daimôn, 35, 66, 104–5, 231
Damascius, 8
dance, 3, 8, 197, 220, 255–9

death, 20, 22, 76, 82, 116, 128, 130–1, 135, 137, 144, 150, 154, 158, 179, 253
  practicing, 116, 144, 154
Delphi, 32, 192
Demeter, 19, 20, 89, 142, 204, 262
Demiurge, 213, 214–15, 223, 224–7, 230, 252, 255, 260
Derveni Papyrus, 140, 141–2, 144, 145–6, 157
desire. *See also* Eros
  metaphysical, 65, 85, 102–4, 171
dialectic, 47, 156, 218
Diogenes of Apollonia, 5, 45
Dionysian Mysteries, 157, 194–8
Dionysus, 20, 68, 137, 142, 143, 144, 149, 154, 191
Diotima, 19, 73. *See also* Plato, *Symposium*, speech of Diotima
divination, 3
divine cause, 252
divine inspiration, 170, 177
  erotic, 184, 200–3
  oracular, 192–4
  poetic, 198–9
  telestic, 194–8
divinity
  of the soul, 22
divinity-marker, 11
  Eleusinian Mysteries, 15–16, 18–19, 99–100, 205
  gods, 16–17
  of the soul, 22–3, 24, 116, 125
  Orphic Mysteries, 15, 20–1, 116, 133, 138–9
  poetic narratives of epiphany, 18, 88, 100, 206
  theios, 16, 49–55, 124, 132
  theorein, 16, 21–2
do ut des, 71
dualism
  of the Forms and particulars, 51
  of the soul and body, 9, 147

Eleusinian Mysteries, 18–19, 29, 31, 89–95, 145
  initiation, 19, 89, 109, 204
  light, 92, 95, 204
  purification, 95
Empedocles, 6, 45, 157
Enlightenment, 4, 7, 9
Ephialtes and Opus, 77
epiphany, 165, 203–6
  false, 111
  of gods, 3, 29–30, 33, 67–73
  of star-gods, 218, 244
  of the Forms, 31, 33
epopteia. *See* initiation
epoptês, 19, 31, 33, 89, 91, 100, 111
Eros, 66. *See also* desire
  as *daimôn*, 24, 35–6, 80, 86, 105–7

as god, 24, 36, 76, 184, 201–2
eschatology, 17, 159
Euripides
  Bacchae, 191
  Chrysippos, 157–8
  Electra, 257
  Erechtheus, 158
  Helen, 158–9
  Hippolytus, 191
  Orestes, 159
  Pirithous, 158, 257
  Suppliants, 158
exegesis, 221–4
eyes. *See* vision

festival, 3, 8, 69, 144, 145, 179, 210, 220, 256
  advent, 91
Ficino, 9
fire, 95, 157, 237, 239, 241, 243
Forms, the, 13, 46–8
  divinity of, 3, 14, 50, 58. *See* divinity-marker
  epiphany of, 4
  harmony of, 61
  ineffability of, 11
  terminology of, 13–14, 47–8
Frost, Robert, 2–3

gods, 11–12, 77, 81. *See also* star gods
  ancillary, 230–1, 238
  elemental, 3
  household, 3
  local, 3, 169
  Olympian, 3, 29, 77, 159
Good
  divinity of, 60, 63
  epiphany of the form of, 63
  form of, 56–63, 225
Gumbrecht, Hans Ulrich, 28

Hades, 21, 77, 115, 117–18, 121, 132, 137, 145, 146
  true vs. hellish, 128–9
harmonics, 227, 247
Heidegger, Martin, 9–10
Helios, 56
Hephaestus, 78
Hera, 231
Heraclitus, 45, 157
Hermias of Alexandria, 180
Herodotus, 71, 72, 136, 191, 195
Hesiod, 104, 198
hierophant, 19, 92, 108, 111, 204
Hippocratic corpus
  Sacred Disease, 191

Homer, 54, 104, 198
  Iliad, 18, 110, 207
  Odyssey, 69, 208, 257
Homeric Hymn, 18
  to Aphrodite, 165, 206, 207
  to Apollo, 32, 100, 218, 257
  to Demeter, 93–5, 165, 206, 207,
    244
  to Dionysus, 68, 100
Homeric scholia, 257

Iacchus. *See* Dionysus
Iamblichus, 8
ibn-Sina (Avicenna), 9
Ibycus, 186
Ilissus, 169, 175
immortality, 64–5, 81
  desire for, 76–85, 102–4
  of the soul, 114–16, 119–30, 172, 187
Ion of Chios, 136
Islam, 9

Jean-Luc Marion, 32
Judaism, 9

katharsis. *See purification*
Kore. *See* Persephone

Leopardi, Giacomo, 112–13
light, 57, 206–7, 239–40
Lucian, 193

madness, 170, 190–9. *See also* divine inspiration
mania. *See* madness
mathematics, 218, 238, 247, 253, 254
memory, 129, 180, 211
Mirandola, Pico de la, 9
molecules, 233, 236, 243
monotheism, 1
moon, 229
mortality
  of the soul, 74–6
motion, 247
  of the cosmos, 216
Mount Olympus, 17, 29, 77
Musaeus, 20, 140, 147
Muses, 149, 198
music, 195, 196, 197
mustês, 19, 31, 89, 91

Neoplatonism, 8
Night, 141
nympholepsy, 182–4
nymphs, 169

ocularcentrism, 21
offering, 12
Olympiodorus, 8, 149
Origen, 9
original humans, 65, 76–9
orpheotelists, 140, 144, 146
Orpheus, 20, 140, 149
Orphic Mysteries, 20, 137, 139–48. *See also*
  Derveni Papyrus
  anthropogony, 142–3
  bone plaques, 140
  doctrine of the afterlife, 133–5
  gold tablet, 22, 137, 138, 140, 143–4, 146
  initiation, 134, 137, 140–1, 144
  ritual enactment of death, 154–5
  story of the soul, 116, 138, 151
  theogony, 141–2
Ouranos, 142, 231

Pan, 71, 169
Parmenides, 6, 45
particulars, 46–7, 48–9, 97, 164, 234–6
Pausanias, 262
Pelopponesian War, 107
Persephone, 19, 20, 89, 137, 142, 143, 149, 204
pharmakon, 179
Philo, 9
Philolaus, 258
Phorcys, 231
piety, 184–6
Pindar, 148
Plato
  Apology, 116, 198
  Cratylus, 153
  Gorgias, 119
  Ion, 199
  Laws, 3, 75, 104–5, 154, 192, 195–6, 226–7
  Meno, 75
  Parmenides, 47
  Phaedo, 15, 17, 20, 22, 49, 50–1, 75, 173,
    213
  Phaedo, passim, 114
  Phaedrus, 18, 24, 52, 56, 75, 213
    Chariot of the Soul, 29, 36, 171–5, 188
  Philebus, 55
  Republic, 11–12, 16–17, 21–2, 52–3, 54, 55, 58–9,
    61, 75, 115, 147, 148–50, 170
    Allegory of the Cave, 17, 21, 48, 53, 60, 156
    Analogy of the Line, 59–60
    Analogy of the Sun-God, 58, 63
  Seventh Letter, 100
  Sophist, 17
  Symposium, 19, 24, 32–3, 35–6, 52, 65–7, 76,
    88, 200

Ladder of Love, 19, 29, 31–2, 48, 66, 87–8,
  96–9, 102–4, 156, 173
  speech of Alcibiades, 67, 108–12
  speech of Aristophanes, 65, 76–9
  speech of Diotima, 73–5, 79–88,
    105–6
Theaetetus, 250
Timaeus, 3, 29, 49, 75
plurality
  of the cosmos, 253
  of the Forms, 10
Poros and Penia, 106
prayer, 3, 8, 12, 69, 221, 222
presence-effect, 28, 86–8
Presocratic philosophy, 4–6, 7
Proclus, 8
purification, 15, 20, 138, 149, 150, 197
  of the soul, 117
  philosophical, 120
Pythagoras, 136
Pythagoreanism, 115, 135–7, 258
Pythia, 192–4

rationality, 7, 227, 238, 239
realm
  aethereal, 155, 160, 165
  divine, 130–1, 143
  intelligible, 57, 63, 228
  of the Forms, 51, 58, 60, 63, 106, 117, 123, 131–2,
    147, 152, 156
  physical, 57, 58, 60, 115, 117, 161, 227
  true earth, 161
receptacle, 222, 232, 233–4, 235–6
reincarnation, 20, 115, 119, 121, 135, 146, 173, 237,
    245, 250
reproduction. *See* birthgiving
Rhea, 142, 196, 231
Ricoeur, Paul, 10

Sacred Road, 90
sacrifice, 3, 8, 12
sanctuary
  of Asclepius, in Epidauros, 70
  of Demeter, at Eleusis, 91
  of Demeter, at Mount Pron, 262
  of the Mother at Agrai, at Eleusis,
    90
Selene, 149
Sicilian Expedition, 107
slavery, 89, 186
Sophocles, 176
soteriology, 20
soul, 120, 218–19. *See also* World-Soul,
    immortality
  Affinity Argument, 121, 123–30, 131

Cyclical Argument, 120, 121–2, 128–30
divinity of, 125, 127–8
immortality of, 231
imprisonment of, 20, 118, 153
incorporeality of, 119
motion of, 171–2, 187
preincarnate state, 122
punishment of, 116, 137, 138, 143
Recollection Argument, 121, 122–3, 151, 164,
    248
relation to body, 120, 248–50
relation to stars, 244–50
relation to the Forms, 120, 123–5,
    188–9
release of, 138, 150–1
tripartite, 170–1
wings of, 171, 172
star gods, 3, 29, 216, 229, 255
stars, 236, 255
state and religion, 1, 8
statues, 8, 108–10, 210–11,
    260–1
Stesichorus, 189
Stobaeus, 93
sun, 229, 236, 243

ta onta. See Forms, the terminology of
Telesterion, 90, 92, 204
temple
  of Poseidon and Cleito, 256
Thamus, 180
theologia, 4, 185
Theophrastus
  Characters, 30, 145
theoria. See visualization, ritualized
Thucydides, 30
time
  divine, 219, 254–5
  earthly, 219, 254
Titans, 20, 142, 154
to on. See Forms, the:terminology of
transcendence. *See* ascent
trial of Socrates, 108

utopia, 62

vegetarianism, 150
visible gods. *See* star-gods
vision, 109, 162, 216–17,
    238–41
  and blindness, 93
  of color, 241–3
  of the Form of Beauty, 166
visualization
  ritualized, 21, 69, 89

World-Body, 216, 227, 232–3, 236–7, 253
World-Soul, 215, 216, 225, 227–9, 232, 237, 247, 253

Xenocrates, 153
Xenophanes, 4, 45

Xenophon
   Memorabilia, 192
   Symposium, 192

Zeus, 20, 77, 142, 158, 231